The Forgotten Founders on Religion and Public Life

The
Forgotten Founders
on Religion and Public Life

edited by

Daniel L. Dreisbach, Mark David Hall,

and Jeffry H. Morrison

Foreword by

Mark A. Noll

University of Notre Dame Press

Notre Dame, Indiana

Manufactured in the United States of America

An earlier version of chapter 1 by Daniel L. Dreisbach was published as
"Founders Famous and Forgotten," *Intercollegiate Review* 42, no. 2 (2007): 3–12,
and is reprinted here by permission.

Chapter 10 was originally published in Robert H. Abzug, *Cosmos Crumbling: American
Reform and the Religious Imagination* (New York: Oxford University Press, 1994),
3–29, 233–37, and is reprinted here by permission of Oxford University Press, Inc.

Library of Congress Cataloging-in-Publication Data

The forgotten founders on religion and public life / edited by Daniel L. Dreisbach,
Mark David Hall, and Jeffry H. Morrison ; foreword by Mark A. Noll.
   p. cm.
  Includes bibliographical references and index.
  ISBN-13: 978-0-268-02602-8 (pbk. : alk. paper)
  ISBN-10: 0-268-02602-5 (pbk. : alk. paper)
   1. Founding Fathers of the United States—Views on religion.   2. Religion and
politics—United States—History—18th century.   3. United States—Religion—
To 1800.   4. Church and state—United States—History—18th century.
I. Dreisbach, Daniel L.   II. Hall, Mark David, 1966–   III. Morrison, Jeffry H., 1961–
  BR520.F67   2009
  322'.1097309033—dc22

                                    2009027582

To Linda and Ron, Dan and Priscilla, Dave and Cheryl,
Judi and Phil, and their families.

—D. L. D.

To my sister, Jillann Hall Rummel, and her family:
Erich, Nathan, Olivia, and Emily.

—M. D. H.

To my daughter, Ella Marie.

—J. H. M.

Contents

Foreword

MARK A. NOLL

The period of the American founding was filled with individuals of unusual interest as historical actors and unusual significance for the history of the United States. A recent burst of literary and televised attention has made John and Abigail Adams nearly as familiar to contemporary Americans as George Washington, Benjamin Franklin, or Thomas Jefferson. The roles of James Madison in crafting the Constitution and of Alexander Hamilton in putting the new nation on a sound financial footing continue to be studied, as do the actions of other larger-than-life figures from the Revolutionary era.

The same figures naturally attract attention with respect to issues of religion in public life, whether they be Washington praying (perhaps) at Valley Forge or delivering his Farewell Address on the importance of religion for a republic; Franklin calling the Constitutional Convention to prayer in imitation of fervent prayers during the War for Independence; Madison carefully parsing out the wording for the First Amendment of the Constitution; or Jefferson penning his famous opinion about "a wall of separation between church and state." What these major founders said about religion, did with religion, or ruled out of bounds for religion continues to engage the attention of historians and mold public opinion. Especially in the last quarter century, when religion has returned to political life with a vengeance, the views of the founders matter.

It is only a small step from the most popular or most studied founders to other founders. Their views on religion and politics were also influential, as revealed in winning historical detail in the finely crafted chapters that make up this book.

As set out clearly in the preface and in the first chapter by Daniel Dreisbach, it is artificial to limit "the founders" to a few individuals. Reasonable but historically distorting factors explain the overemphasis on relatively few founders and the underemphasis on a host of others who played key roles in hammering out the nation's original documents and guiding the new republic through its early years. Such reasons include self-promotion by founders, the availability of archival material to historians (especially letters and other private documents), and the brevity of certain founders' lives. The result, however, is a misunderstanding of the historical situation and, sometimes, mis-application in current debates over what "the founders" thought.

This book addresses the particular problems that result when the company of national founders is limited artificially. As the book's authors demonstrate convincingly, several of our founding leaders possessed a more orthodox Christian faith than did their more famous contemporaries (most of whom were deists of one kind or another). But lest anyone conclude, that by pointing to these more orthodox figures, the book is intended as a right-wing contribution to contemporary culture wars, it is important to note the complexity of what the authors achieve. By broadening the notion of "the founders," they draw in individuals who promoted a quite different kind of deism (Thomas Paine, author of the decisive piece of propaganda, *Common Sense*), or who adhered to a quirky individual religion (the Philadelphia physician Benjamin Rush), or who maintained a moderate Anglican position (the Virginia jurist and first U.S. Attorney General, Edmund Randolph). The historical payoff from studying a broad group of founders is to enrich rather than simplify our picture of what the founders "believed."

On questions of church-state relations, a similar complexity comes to the fore. Some of the founders discussed here wanted more space for religion in public life, but some did not. What they shared in common, however, was that their positions on sensitive church-state matters often differed considerably from those maintained by Jefferson and Madison, who in some recent jurisprudence have been read as representing the entire founding generation.

Individuals treated in the chapters include not only Abigail Adams, Patrick Henry, Oliver Ellsworth, Hamilton, Paine, Rush, and Randolph, but also several other influential early American leaders. John Jay of New York, for example, was a co-author (with Madison and Hamilton) of *The Federalist Papers*, the first Chief Justice of the Supreme Court, and an influential diplomat. Roger Sherman of Connecticut was the only American to sign the nation's four constituting documents (the Articles of Association, the Declaration of Independence, the Articles of Confederation, and the Constitution). Mercy Otis Warren was the nation's first female playwright and the author of one of the most notable histories of the American Revolution. John Adams's cousin, Samuel Adams, was both a firebrand leader of the Sons of Liberty in Boston and a careful negotiator in the Continental Congress. The thoughts of all these individuals on the role of religion in the new United States made a difference in their lifetimes. Now, with the publication of this outstanding collection, they and their opinions should make a difference in helping Americans in the twenty-first century understand the complex role of religion in our nation's first years.

Preface

Two weaknesses in much of the scholarship on the American founding inspired this collection of essays. First, there has long been a tendency to discount or ignore the role of religion in the American founding in general, and in the political thought of influential founders in particular. Second, much that has been written about the founders has emphasized the thoughts, words, and deeds of an elite fraternity of famous founders, ignoring a large company of now forgotten men and women who made salient, consequential contributions to the construction of the American republic and its institutions. In the course of their study, the editors have come to believe that religion played a vital role in the American founding project and that limiting the study of this period to the contributions of a select few famous figures impoverishes an understanding of the founding. This volume, which builds on the editors' prior collaborations, was conceived in order to redress these weaknesses in much of the existing scholarship.

Why is it that since the mid-twentieth century scholars have often discounted or ignored the role of faith in the founders' lives and political thought? It might reflect the inclination of many intellectuals to emphasize the strictly rational and avoid transcendent themes in their work. Some writers might be protecting their audiences from views on God and religion that offend twenty-first-century, secular sensibilities. George Washington, for example, warned that one who labors to subvert a public role for religion and morality cannot call himself a patriot,[1] yet this admonition from his Farewell Address is seldom mentioned in the scholarly literature. Such rhetoric, unexceptional in its time, is discordant with the secular ethos of our time. Other founders held views similarly out of step with secular academic and popular sentiments of the twentieth and twenty-first centuries, such as advocating state support for Protestant denominations and restricting the civil and religious rights of Catholics, Unitarians, atheists, and Jews.

Another explanation for the inattention given to the founders' faith has to do with a lack of familiarity with religion and religious themes—a form of "religious illiteracy"—among secular scholars.[2] Many Washington scholars, for example, have asserted that the Virginian rarely quoted or mentioned the Bible. Harvard historian Samuel Eliot Morison, winner of the Pulitzer and Bancroft Prizes, stated, "I have found no trace of Biblical phraseology" in Washington's letters.[3] That such an ill-informed statement could be made by a serious scholar is remarkable, indeed. Even a cursory review of Washington's papers reveals scores of quotations from and unmistakable allusions to the Bible. One finds in Washington's correspondence dozens of references to the ancient Hebrew blessing in which every man sits in safety under his own vine and fig tree (Micah 4:4; 1 Kings 4:25; Zechariah 3:10).[4] He was fond of the biblical description of an age when nations will convert "swords into plowshares" and "spears into pruninghooks" (Micah 4:3, Isaiah 2:4; Joel 3:10).[5] He incorporated Solomon's proverbs into the advice he dispensed.[6] In an April 1789 missive to Philadelphia's German Lutherans, Washington quoted Proverbs 14:34, which speaks of "that righteousness which exalteth a nation."[7] Again, a widespread biblical or religious "illiteracy" is one explanation for the failure of modern scholars to account adequately for the place of religion—specifically Christianity—in the lives of the American founders.

Limiting the focus to the perspectives of five or six elite founders is another unfortunate tendency exhibited by authors writing on the founders' views of Christianity, religious liberty, or church-state relations. These celebrated founders were among those most influenced by the Enlightenment and most likely to embrace church-state separation. It is true that founders like Thomas Jefferson and James Madison (those most likely to be discussed) were influential, but their religious views and their views on church-state relations are among the *least* representative of the founders. Other founders often covered in the leading scholarship include Benjamin Franklin, Thomas Paine, Ethan Allen, George Washington, and John Adams, all of whom were probably heterodox in their religious beliefs and who, with the exception of Washington and Adams, were ardent critics of the ecclesiastical establishments of their day.

A good example of this tendency is Edwin S. Gaustad's *Faith of Our Fathers*, which explores the founders' attitudes toward religion by carefully considering only the views of Jefferson, Madison, Franklin, Adams, and Washington.[8] More recently, Steven Waldman's *Founding Faith: Providence, Politics, and the Birth of Religious Freedom in America* also focuses on these "five main characters."[9] David L. Holmes's *The Religion of the Founding Fathers* dedicates individual chapters to the same five men, with an additional chapter on James Monroe.[10] In a revised edition, retitled *The Faiths of the Founding Fathers*, perhaps chastened by criticism of his narrow definition of the founders,[11] Holmes includes chapters on "Wives and Daughters" and "three orthodox Christians."[12] Popular author Brooke Allen, in *Moral Minority: Our Skeptical Founding Fathers*, likewise devotes chapters to Franklin, Washington, Adams, Jefferson, and Madison—although she includes a chapter on Alexander Hamilton as well.[13] A similar approach is taken by Frank Lambert, Richard Hughes, Steven J. Keillor, and many others.[14]

These authors typically concede that not all Americans in the founding era were as "enlightened" as these famous founders, but then they proceed to attribute the views of these select elites to the founding generation. More orthodox founders, and those who desired closer cooperation between religion and the polity, are largely ignored. These founders are occasionally discussed in books intended for popular religious audiences or in rare, specialized academic articles and monographs, but their views are regularly neglected in mainstream discourse on church-state issues.[15] The net result of this selective approach to history is the distortion of the founders' collective views on religion, religious liberty, and church-state relations.

If concerns about this distortion were merely of academic interest, it would still be necessary to address it simply to set the record straight. This distortion, however, is of more than academic interest because the founders' views carry significant weight in contemporary political and legal discourse. To provide one concrete example, United States Supreme Court justices have made it clear that "no provision of the Constitution is more closely tied to or given content by its generating history than the religious clause of the First Amendment. It is at once the refined product and the terse summation of that history."[16] Of the justices who have written at least one religion clause opinion, 76 percent have appealed to the founders or founding era history to shine light on the meaning of the religion clauses, and every one of the twenty-three justices who have authored more than four religion clause opinions have done so.[17] Yet, like the scholars mentioned above, justices have been selective in the founders to whom they have appealed. Collectively, when justices appeal to specific founders to cast light on the meaning of the religion clauses, 79 percent of their appeals have been to Jefferson or Madison, while only 21 percent of their appeals have been to one of thirty-one other founders.[18] This is particularly remarkable, given that Jefferson was not directly involved in writing or ratifying the First Amendment (he was serving as the American minister to France when the first federal Congress framed the amendment).

The proclivity of justices and students of the founding era to focus on a relatively limited company of famous founders when it comes to religion and church-state issues is understandable in some respects. Jefferson, Madison, Adams, Washington, Franklin, and Paine are among the more interesting founders. They are also among the most articulate and prolific writers of their generation. And few would deny that they were influential. It also makes sense to study these famous figures if one is interested in the seeds of modern separationism in America. One should be careful, however, not to generalize from their views to those of the founders as a whole.

This volume's predecessor, *The Founders on God and Government* (2004),[19] brought together respected scholars of history, political science, and law to write essays on prominent founders such as Washington, Adams, Jefferson, Madison, and Franklin, as well as a few lesser-known founders like John Witherspoon, James Wilson, George Mason, and the Catholic Carroll family of Maryland. In the current volume we broaden the discussion by offering essays on (in alphabetical order) Abigail Adams,

Samuel Adams, Oliver Ellsworth, Alexander Hamilton, Patrick Henry, John Jay, Thomas Paine, Edmund Randolph, Benjamin Rush, Roger Sherman, and Mercy Otis Warren. We are, again, delighted that eminent historians, political scientists, and law professors have agreed to write essays for this collection.

Most of the subjects of the essays in this volume are, indeed, "forgotten founders." True, the names of Abigail Adams, Samuel Adams, Alexander Hamilton, and Patrick Henry, unlike the subjects of some chapters in the book, are familiar to many Americans, but few can recount in meaningful detail their contributions to the American founding. If not their names, then certainly their roles in creating the American nation are now forgotten. As Daniel L. Dreisbach suggests in his chapter, the fact that many founders are now forgotten does not necessarily mean that they are unimportant. Indeed, he argues that factors other than a selected founder's actual contributions to the founding project may explain why he or she was remembered or forgotten by subsequent generations. One such factor, for example, is whether an important founder left a paper trail—public papers, a journal, or a memoir—documenting his or her salient contributions to the nation. Scholars of a later age must have a record with which to re-create and analyze the past.

Each of the founders profiled in this volume, we contend, contributed in important ways to the founding of the American republic. Their religious convictions as well as their approaches to religious liberty and church-state relations varied, but when we consider their perspectives, along with those of the founders examined in our earlier volume, a more complete picture of "the founders' views" begins to emerge. We recognize, of course, that "the founders" held a range of views on these matters, but as these essays suggest, there were areas of consensus. To be sure, an even more complete picture will require consideration of additional founders, which is something we hope to facilitate in future scholarship.

Our contributors come from a variety of disciplines, and we offered them the freedom to pursue their subjects according to the canons of their disciplines. We asked all the authors, however, to provide a brief biographical sketch of the profiled founder and, where possible, to identify the founder's religious beliefs and denominational commitments.

We also wanted each chapter to consider the scholarly treatment of the profiled founder, giving special attention to whether his or her understanding of religion and its public role has been adequately studied, to explore the relationship of the subject's religious beliefs to his or her political ideas and actions, and to discuss the founder's views of religious liberty and church-state relations. We should note that the contributors themselves hold a variety of religious beliefs (including unbelief) and significantly different views on how church and state should relate in America today. Whether or how the founders' views should inform contemporary questions of jurisprudence and politics is a matter we leave for another day.

Many of the chapters in this volume were presented at a conference entitled "Religion and the American Founding" held at George Fox University in the spring of 2007. We are grateful to the Council for Christian Colleges and Universities for a grant that supported the conference and the publication of this volume. We are also thankful to the Intercollegiate Studies Institute for sponsoring several of the speakers at this conference and at a debate engaging Derek H. Davis, Steven Green, Barry Alan Shain, and Mark David Hall on the question "Did America Have a Christian Founding?"

On a personal note, Daniel L. Dreisbach thanks American University for a sabbatical leave in the 2006–2007 academic year and its continuing support of his research, which made possible his contributions to this volume. He also thanks the faculty and fellows at the James Madison Program in American Ideals and Institutions in the Department of Politics at Princeton University, where he spent his sabbatical as the William E. Simon Visiting Fellow in Religion and Public Life. For their endless patience and good humor during the course of this and other projects, he thanks his wife, Joyce, and two daughters, Mollie Abigail and Moriah Esther. Mark David Hall, as always, is grateful for the love and encouragement provided by his family: Miriam, Joshua, Lydia, and Anna. He is thankful, as well, for the support of George Fox University and the Earhart Foundation. Research assistance from Janna McKee and Deanne Kastine and secretarial help from Vetta Berokoff contributed significantly to the success of this volume. He would also like to thank archivists at the Connecticut State Library, the Library of Congress, and Yale University for research assistance, and Vincent Phillip Muñoz for comments on his essay. Jeffry H. Morrison thanks his colleagues in the School of Government at Regent University for institutional support and his colleagues at the James Madison Memorial Fellowship Foundation, Washington, D.C.

Daniel L. Dreisbach
Mark David Hall
Jeffry H. Morrison

Notes

1. "Of all the dispositions and habits which lead to political prosperity, Religion and morality are indispensable supports. In vain would that man claim the tribute of Patriotism, who should labour to subvert these great Pillars of human happiness, these firmest props of the duties of Men and citizens." George Washington, "Farewell Address, 19 September 1796," in *The Writings of George Washington*, ed. John C. Fitzpatrick, 37 vols. (Washington, D.C.: Government Printing Office, 1931–1940), 35:229 (hereinafter WGW).

2. For a general discussion of "religious illiteracy," see Stephen Prothero, *Religious Literacy: What Every American Needs to Know — and Doesn't* (San Francisco: HarperOne, 2007).

3. Samuel Eliot Morison, *The Young Man Washington* (Cambridge, Mass.: Harvard University Press, 1932), 37. See also Paul F. Boller Jr., *George Washington and Religion* (Dallas: Southern Methodist University Press, 1963), 40: "There are astonishingly few references to the Bible in his letters and public statements"; Paul K. Longmore, *The Invention of George Washington* (Berkeley: University of California Press, 1988), 217: "He rarely alluded to or quoted the Scriptures"; "How the Bible Made America," *Newsweek*, Dec. 27, 1982, 47: "George Washington rarely referred to the Scriptures in his voluminous private letters."

4. See Daniel L. Dreisbach, "The 'Vine and Fig Tree' in George Washington's Letters: Reflections on a Biblical Motif in the Literature of the American Founding Era," *Anglican and Episcopal History* 76, no. 3 (Sep. 2007): 299–326.

5. See Washington, letter to Marquis de Chastellux, Apr. 25 [–May 1] 1788, in WGW, 29:485; Washington, letter to Doctor James Anderson, Dec. 24, 1795, in WGW, 34:407; Washington, letter to Marquis de Lafayette, Sep. 30, 1779, in WGW, 16:369–70; Washington, letter to the President of Congress, Dec. 20, 1776, in WGW, 6:402.

6. See, for examples, Circular to the [Northern] States, Jan. 31, 1782, in WGW, 23:478; Washington, letter to Howell Lewis, Nov. 3, 1793, in WGW, 33:148;

Washington, letter to William Vans Murray, Dec. 3, 1797, in WGW, 36:88; Washington, letter to George Washington Parke Custis, Mar. 19, 1798, in WGW, 36:187; Washington, letter to George Washington Parke Custis, Jun. 13, 1798, in WGW, 36:288.

7. Washington, letter to the German Lutherans of Philadelphia, Apr. 1789, in *The Papers of George Washington*, Presidential Series, ed. W. W. Abbot et al. (Charlottesville: University Press of Virginia, 1987), 2:180.

8. Edwin S. Gaustad, *Faith of Our Fathers: Religion and the New Nation* (San Francisco: Harper and Row, 1987).

9. Steven Waldman, *Founding Faith: Providence, Politics, and the Birth of Religious Freedom in America* (New York: Random House, 2008), xiii. Waldman has individual chapters on these five men, and he discusses a variety of other founders. However, he often generalizes from Franklin, Adams, Washington, Jefferson, and Madison to all founders, such as when he addresses the "Conservative Fallacy" that "most Founding Fathers were serious Christians" by remarking that "if we use the definition of *Christianity* offered by those who make this claim— conservative Christians—the Founders studied in this book were not Christians" (193). This claim may be true for his "five main characters," but it is highly debatable with respect to founders such as Samuel Adams, Fisher Ames, Isaac Backus, Elias Boudinot, Charles and Daniel Carroll, Samuel Davies, Timothy Dwight, Oliver Ellsworth, Patrick Henry, John Jay, John Leland, Henry Muhlenberg, Robert Treat Paine, Roger Sherman, Noah Webster, John Witherspoon, and many others who are mentioned (albeit often in passing) in his book.

10. David L. Holmes, *The Religion of the Founding Fathers* (Charlottesville, Va.: Ash Lawn-Highland; Ann Arbor, Mich.: Clements Library, 2003).

11. See, for example, Daniel L. Dreisbach, review of *The Religion of the Founding Fathers*, by David L. Holmes, *Virginia Magazine of History and Biography* 112, no. 2 (2004): 192–93.

12. David L. Holmes, *The Faiths of the Founding Fathers* (New York: Oxford University Press, 2006). The three orthodox Christians Holmes examines are Samuel Adams, Elias Boudinot, and John Jay.

13. Brooke Allen, *Moral Minority: Our Skeptical Founding Fathers* (Chicago: Ivan R. Dee, 2006).

14. See Frank Lambert, *The Founding Fathers and the Place of Religion in America* (Princeton, N.J.: Princeton University Press, 2003), 161, and generally 159–296. Lambert moves easily from the proposition that Franklin, Jefferson, Paine, Adams, Hamilton, Madison, and Jay "rejected the faith of their Puritan fathers" to the claim that the "significance of the Enlightenment and Deism for the birth of the American republic, and especially the relationship between church and state within it, can hardly be overstated." Leaving aside the fact that Paine was born an English Quaker and Hamilton was a bastard from the West Indies, thus making one wonder whose faith they rejected, Lambert's account of "the found-

ers" rests almost entirely on the writings of Jefferson, Madison, Adams, and Franklin. Although he mentions Jay, he gives no evidence that Jay rejected orthodox Christianity. See also Richard T. Hughes, *Myths America Lives By* (Urbana: University of Illinois Press, 2003), 50–57, who supports his claim that "most of the American founders embraced some form of Deism, not historically orthodox Christianity," with extensive quotations from Jefferson, two quotations from Paine, and one quotation each from Franklin, Madison, and John Adams; and Steven J. Keillor, *This Rebellious House: American History and the Truth of Christianity* (Downers Grove, Ill.: InterVarsity, 1996), 85, who supports his claim that "many of America's 'Founding Fathers' were not Christians in any orthodox sense" with references to Adams, Franklin, Paine, and Allen (and, by implication, Washington and Jefferson).

15. Books intended for popular Christian audiences that include discussions of orthodox founders (and that often attempt to make less-than-orthodox founders appear more orthodox) include John Eidsmoe, *Christianity and the Constitution: The Faith of Our Founding Fathers* (Grand Rapids: Baker Book House, 1987), and Tim LaHaye, *Faith of Our Founding Fathers* (Brentwood, Tenn.: Wolgemuth & Hyatt, 1987). Scholarly works on orthodox founders that give attention to their religious beliefs include M. E. Bradford, *Founding Fathers: Brief Lives of the Framers of the United States Constitution*, 2nd ed., rev. (Lawrence: University Press of Kansas, 1994); M. E. Bradford, "Religion and the Framers: The Biographical Evidence," *Benchmark* 4, no. 4 (1990): 349–58; Mark David Hall, *The Political and Legal Philosophy of James Wilson: 1742–1798* (Columbia: University of Missouri Press, 1997); Jeffry H. Morrison, *John Witherspoon and the Founding of the American Republic* (Notre Dame: University of Notre Dame Press, 2005); and John G. West Jr., *The Politics of Revelation and Reason: Religion and Civic Life in the New Nation* (Lawrence: University Press of Kansas, 1996). Barry Alan Shain's *The Myth of American Individualism: The Protestant Origins of American Political Thought* (Princeton, N.J.: Princeton University Press, 1994) considers a range of orthodox founders but does not explore their views of church-state relations in detail.

16. Associate Justice Wiley B. Rutledge, in *Everson v. Board of Education*, 330 U.S. 1, 33 (1947).

17. Mark David Hall, "Jeffersonian Walls and Madisonian Lines: The Supreme Court's Use of History in Religion Clause Cases," *Oregon Law Review* 85 (2006): 572.

18. Ibid., 569.

19. Daniel L. Dreisbach, Mark D. Hall, and Jeffry H. Morrison, eds., *The Founders on God and Government* (Lanham, Md.: Rowman and Littlefield, 2004).

CHAPTER 1

Famous Founders and Forgotten Founders

What's the Difference, and Does the Difference Matter?

DANIEL L. DREISBACH

Consider the political career of Roger Sherman (1721–1793) of Connecticut, a largely self-taught man, devout Calvinist, and lifelong public servant.[1] He was one of only two men who signed the three great expressions of American organic law: the Declaration of Independence, the Articles of Confederation, and the U.S. Constitution.[2] He was a delegate to the First and Second Continental Congresses (serving 1,543 days, longer than all but four men),[3] a signatory to the Declaration and Resolves (1774) and Articles of Association (1774), a member of the five-man committee that drafted the Declaration of Independence, and a member of the committee of thirteen that framed the Articles of Confederation. He was also a delegate to the federal Constitutional Convention of 1787 (delivering 138 speeches, more than all but three delegates), where he was a driving force behind the Great (Connecticut) Compromise. He was a member of the first U.S. House of Representatives (1789–1791) and, later, the U.S. Senate (1791–1793), where he played key roles in deliberations on the Bill of Rights (he proposed that amendments be added at the end of the Constitution rather than inserted piecemeal into the original text of the document, which James Madison had initially advocated), the elimination of accumulated state debts, and the creation of a national bank. If any man merited the mantle of "founding father," it was Roger Sherman. Yet few Americans recall, let alone mention, his name when enumerating the founding fathers, and even among those familiar with his name, most would be hard pressed to describe Sherman's role in the founding. Why is it that a man of such prodigious contributions to the new nation is today an all but forgotten figure? The same question could be asked about many other patriots—John Dickinson, Elbridge Gerry, John Jay, Richard Henry Lee, George Mason, Gouverneur Morris, Charles Pinckney, Benjamin Rush, John Rutledge, James Wilson, and John Witherspoon, just to name a few—who labored diligently to establish an independent American republic.

When asked to identify the "founding fathers," Americans typically respond (at least those capable of a response) with a short list of a half dozen or so notables who have achieved iconic status in the American imagination and collective memory. This is true of even serious students of American history. The small fraternity of "famous founders" typically includes (in no particular order) Benjamin Franklin, George Washington, John Adams, Thomas Jefferson, James Madison, and Alexander Hamilton. To this short list, individual historians occasionally add a favorite figure or two.[4]

There is, however, a much larger company of now "forgotten founders" who made salient contributions in thought, word, and deed to the construction of the American constitutional republic and its institutions. Unfortunately, many among the founding generation, whose contributions and sacrifices were consequential in the creation of a new nation, have slipped into unmerited obscurity, wrested from the elite fraternity of famous founders. Why are some individuals, whose well-documented contributions were valued by their peers and celebrated in their time, largely forgotten in our time? In short, why are a few founders "famous" and others now "forgotten"?

Framing the Framers: Who Are the Founding Fathers?

A preliminary question pertinent to this discussion is the following: What thoughts, words, and/or deeds qualify someone to be called a "founding father"? Historians have long debated this question.

A common but narrow construction of the term limits membership in the fraternity of founding fathers to the approximately one hundred and twenty men who signed the Declaration of Independence (1776), Articles of Confederation (drafted 1777, signed 1778, and ratified 1781), and/or U.S. Constitution (drafted and signed 1787 and ratified 1788).[5] Nothing like a verifiable presence at the creation confers on one a plausible claim to immortality as a founding father. This narrow definition, however, excludes Patrick Henry, Thomas Paine, John Jay, and John Marshall, among other prominent patriots. The term could be construed more broadly to include a generation or two of Americans from many walks of life who, in the last half of the eighteenth century and early nineteenth century, articulated the rights of colonists, secured independence from Great Britain, and established the new constitutional republic and its political institutions. Among them were citizen soldiers, elected representatives, polemicists, and clergymen. This definition of the founders includes members of the Stamp Act Congress; the Continental and Confederation Congresses; state legislative bodies of the period that debated and declared independence, drafted state constitutions and declarations of rights, deliberated the structure of a national union, and ratified the U.S. Constitution; the Constitutional Convention of 1787; and early federal Congresses under the U.S. Constitution (especially the First Congress, which framed the national Bill of Rights). This expansive definition includes a cast of thousands who played their patriotic part at the local, state, and/or national levels.

Although one speaks of the founders as a collective group, this is not to suggest that they all shared common perspectives, objectives, and values. The founders, to be sure, came from different backgrounds, and they had diverse views and interests (the extent of that diversity is a topic historians warmly debate). They did not agree on all political questions, but they held many views in common. Most were committed to republican government. They were united in the belief that a self-governing people must be a well-informed and virtuous people; thus, they encouraged education and religion, which they believed nurtured these qualities. Almost all believed that God was the author of the rights of men; and the rights God had granted to mankind, no man should take away. Most believed that man was a fallen creature and, therefore, should not be entrusted with unrestrained power over other human beings. Accordingly, they devised a government system defined by the separation of powers and checks and balances.

Why Are Some Founders Famous?

Before considering why some important founders are now forgotten, it is perhaps worth asking why the famous founders are famous. Do they share characteristics or experiences that explain their notoriety or separate them from lesser known founders? There is no single factor or set of factors that satisfactorily explains why certain founders are famous or forgotten. Rather, a variety of factors and circumstances is at play.

Today's lists of famous founders almost always include Franklin, Washington, Adams, Jefferson, Madison, and Hamilton. But has the fraternity of famous founders always been limited to this select group? The popularly accepted list of famous founders, one writer has recently argued, has not been static during the last two hundred years. The generation that lived through the War for American Independence venerated and celebrated military heroes above all,[6] men such as George Washington (always first), Nathanael Greene, Henry Knox, and even the Marquis de Lafayette (the French nobleman and war hero was warmly praised for his contributions to the founding when he made his grand tour of the states in the mid-1820s). Americans in the early nineteenth century placed the mantle of greatness on the "host of worthies," as Jefferson called them, who framed and signed the Declaration of Independence.[7] These men are depicted in John Trumbull's iconic twelve-by-eighteen-foot oil painting *Declaration of Independence* (commissioned in 1817), which now hangs in the Rotunda of the U.S. Capitol and is reproduced on the back of the two-dollar bill.[8] Later generations counted among the founding fathers the "assembly of demigods" (again, to use Jefferson's phrase) who crafted a new national Constitution in the summer of 1787.[9]

Those recognized today as famous founders have not always been assured a seat in this elite company. Merrill D. Peterson in *The Jefferson Image in the American Mind* and, more recently, Stephen F. Knott in *Alexander Hamilton and the Persistence of Myth* track the rise and fall of Jefferson's and Hamilton's respective standings in the public mind. "Alexander Hamilton's place at any period on the imaginary scale that charts American reputations is always a good index to Jefferson's," Peterson observed.[10] At different moments in history, for a variety of political reasons, Jefferson's reputation waxed as Hamilton's waned, and at other times the opposite was true.[11] Only a recent best-selling biography of John Adams by David McCullough, commentators have remarked with perhaps slight exaggeration, reinstated the irascible Bay Stater among the famous founders.[12] Thus, if the past is a reliable guide, future generations may celebrate selected founders for still other reasons—perhaps including women, whose contributions have been largely ignored in the standard histories, or honoring those who opposed slavery at a time when it was not popular to do so. Indeed, more than a few commentators have observed that Jefferson's reputation has waned in recent years in the wake of revived allegations of an illicit relation with his slave. All this suggests the fluid nature of membership in the exclusive fraternity of famous founders.

It may be that most individuals—and, by extension, the public mind—can reasonably retain only a short list of immediately recognizable and memorable founders. If this is true, then it is not surprising that only a half dozen or so figures are included in the widely accepted founders' "hall of fame." This, of course, does not answer the question why specific founders are selected for inclusion in that hall of fame and the rest are relegated to oblivion.

As a preliminary matter, it is worth noting that Benjamin Franklin was, at one point, the most famous American in the Western world, if not the most famous man in the world, celebrated widely as much for his scientific achievements as for his political contributions to the American cause. This was remarkable for a "colonial." And by the time independence from Great Britain was secured, George Washington was, perhaps, equally famous. Their celebrated status at home and abroad went far in securing their places in the pantheon of famous founders. Despite the vagaries of politics and fashion, Franklin and Washington, unlike all other founders, have never had their status as top-tier founders seriously questioned or challenged in the last two centuries, at least not in popular discourse.[13]

Fame is not easily manufactured. "The great whom the present recognizes," Robert G. McCloskey observed, "tend to be those who were thought of as great in their time. Tomorrow may enhance or diminish yesterday's reputation; it does not often create a wholly new one."[14] Every founder who has resided at one point or another in the upper echelon of founders was recognized in his day by his peers as worthy of fame; founders whose contemporaries—those who knew them personally—were reluctant to place the mantle of fame and greatness upon them have not risen above that initial, critical assessment in the public imagination.[15]

Students of the American founding know well that many founders—none more so than the elite famous ones—were extraordinarily attentive to their place in history. The notoriously vain John Adams frequently fretted about whether he would receive the recognition he rightly deserved.[16] In his final winter, Thomas Jefferson beseeched his Virginia neighbor James Madison to "take care of me when dead."[17] The founding generation was acutely aware that they had been present at the creation of something remarkable in human history. With an awareness of posterity's judgment, many recorded their recollections in contemporaneous journals and correspondence or later in memoirs. The famous founders, among others, recognized the value their papers and records were to history and went to great lengths to preserve them. Washington, for example, persuaded the Continental Congress to fund (at a time when many soldiers were going without proper pay, food, or clothing) a company of secretaries to compile and transcribe the general's extensive wartime records and correspondence. The team eventually produced twenty-eight volumes, which have proven a valuable trove for military historians.[18] Shortly before the colonists declared their independence, Adams tellingly announced to his wife, Abigail, that he intended to save all his letters to her and urged her to save her correspondence as well. He informed her that he had purchased "a Folio Book" to preserve his correspondence, which, presumably, would provide a record of "the great Events which are passed, and those greater which are rapidly advancing."[19] Both Jefferson and Madison were meticulous record keepers and assiduous correspondents (the former famously used a writing machine that made copies of his letters). Both men spent their twilight years, as did John Adams, defining and defending their political legacies. They wrote autobiographies, engaged in extensive correspondence about the dramatic political events many years before, and took steps to preserve important historical documents. It has long been whispered that Madison tailored his recollections and edited his notes of the Constitutional Convention to enhance his contributions to the project.[20] In retrospect, they were remarkably successful in defining how future generations would view them and their deeds.

Some of this behavior appears to be vain, petty jockeying for a preferred position in posterity. But was it? What did fame and the pursuit of fame mean to this generation of Americans? In his now classic essay, "Fame and the Founding Fathers," historian Douglass Adair argued that the founders' "obsessive desire for fame" was not merely a vain or vulgar quest for celebrity, popularity, or deification by their countrymen.[21] Rather, for this generation, steeped in the classical tradition, fame was akin to what we might call honor, virtue, and good reputation.[22] Indeed, there were, in this sense, few higher callings than the pursuit of fame. "The love of honest and well earned fame," James Wilson remarked, "is deeply rooted in honest and susceptible minds."[23] "The love of fame, [is] the ruling passion of the noblest minds," wrote Alexander Hamilton in the *Federalist Papers*.[24] As with the Romans, the founders thought fame meant placing duty to one's country above one's personal interests. Great men, despite the selfish impulses common to all men, earned true fame by curbing selfish appetites and wanton emotion and by performing acts of uncommon virtue and patriotism that promoted the commonwealth. "The love of fame," Hamilton reported, "would prompt a man to plan and undertake extensive and arduous enterprises for the public benefit."[25] Yes, fame is very much concerned with immortality, and, yes, "the greatest of the great generation" of founders became obsessively "concerned with posterity's judgment of their behavior." For the less noble among them, the love and pursuit of fame could be an idol, and unchecked ambition could be a dangerous vice. Yet as Adair observed, "the audience that men who desire Fame are incited to act before is the audience of the wise and the good in the future—that part of posterity that can discriminate between virtue and vice—that audience that can recognize egotism transmuted gloriously into public service." The noble passion for fame "can spur individuals to spend themselves to provide for the common defense, or to promote the general welfare, and even on occasion to establish justice in a world where justice is extremely rare." For the noble man, fame was a desirable incentive to pursue right principles and worthy objectives. The pursuit of fame, Adair continued, "thus transmuted the leaden desire for self-aggrandizement and personal reward into a golden concern for public service and the promotion of the commonwealth as the means to gain glory."[26] Fame, the founders were taught, was the spur that goaded men to live lives of honor, virtue, and personal sacrifice.

What, then, makes a founder famous? All the famous founders had strong, memorable, and (with the possible exception of Madison) colorful personalities. All came from and represented influential power centers in the new nation. None came from a small or isolated corner of the union. All, it goes without saying, made significant and enduring contributions to the national polity in the critical years between the formation of the Continental Congress and the establishment of the national government under the Constitution. All, except Franklin (who died in 1790), played a prominent role on the national political stage following implementation of the U.S. Constitution (indeed, four of the six famous founders became president). Throughout their adult lives, they were consistent and unceasing in their commitment to the American cause, rarely deviating to pursue ventures in other venues; in retirement they could reflect upon, as did George Washington in his Farewell Address (1796), "forty five years of my life dedicated to its [my country's] Service, with an upright zeal."[27] All were acutely aware of their place in history and took steps to ensure that their contributions would be remembered and to shape how their contributions would be remembered by future generations.

All of them also left a voluminous paper trail of public and private documents, providing historians with a record of their deeds and insights into their views and actions. Not only were they prolific writers, but also all were masters of the written word. Even Washington, often dismissed as an inferior wordsmith, could be surprisingly eloquent in both the spoken and the written word. Most left to posterity the enduring legacy of a monumental idea or institution that contemporaries and subsequent generations—accurately or inaccurately—identified with them individually and could be encapsulated in a phrase (for example, George Washington, "father of the country"; Thomas Jefferson, "author of the Declaration of Independence"; James Madison, "father of the Constitution and Bill of Rights"; Benjamin Franklin, "first American"; Alexander Hamilton, "architect of the nation's financial system").

These are the characteristics of the famous founders.

Why Are Some Founders Forgotten?

Many of these characteristics and achievements also describe selected forgotten founders. So what explains why some founders are famous and others not? Again, there is a variety of factors distinguishing the famous from the not-so-famous founders, and to some extent, each founder must be individually examined. A unique combination of factors and circumstances explains why some figures have not been duly recognized by history. That said, a number of factors are recurring features in the lives of founders now relegated to obscurity.

Age (or generational factors) and time of death may explain why some viable candidates for top-tier status are now largely forgotten. With the exception of Franklin, all the famous founders went on to distinguished careers in national politics under the U.S. Constitution, whereas some important forgotten founders, such as William Livingston (1723–1790), George Mason (1725–1792), John Hancock (1737–1793), Richard Henry Lee (1732–1794), and John Witherspoon (1723–1794), died in the early 1790s without playing a prominent role in the national government under the Constitution. These men, for the most part, were of a slightly older generation than the famous founders (with the exception of Franklin). For example, George Mason, born in 1725, was seven years older than his Northern Neck neighbor and lifelong friend George Washington (1732–1799). He was a decade older than John Adams

(1735–1826), eighteen years older than Thomas Jefferson (1743–1826), twenty-six years older than James Madison (1751–1836), and thirty or so years older than Alexander Hamilton (c. 1755–1804).

A failure or refusal to play a prominent role on the national political stage after the Constitution's implementation may have denied some otherwise worthy patriots seats in the founders' hall of fame. Their reasons for not taking to this stage are legion: death (as noted above), retirement from public life, a focus on state or local politics, or the pursuit of other ventures such as business or the law. In any case, their departure from the national political scene at the very moment when prominent compatriots were taking leading roles on the newly available national stage undoubtedly contributed to their disappearance from public memory. Fame has been especially elusive for those who channeled their energies into state and local politics following the bitter battles of the independence struggle, even though they were no less passionate about the cause of American liberty than their now more famous colleagues. Founders who tended to state and local concerns once the constitutional ratification debates were resolved include Samuel Adams of Massachusetts (lieutenant governor, 1789–1794; governor, 1794–1797); William Richardson Davie of North Carolina (state legislator, 1786–1798; governor, 1798–1799); John Hancock of Massachusetts (governor, 1780–1785, 1787–1793); Jared Ingersoll Jr. of Pennsylvania (state attorney general, 1791–1799; U.S. Attorney, 1800–1801); William Samuel Johnson of Connecticut (president of Columbia College, 1787–1800); John Lansing Jr. of New York (mayor of Albany, 1786–1790; state judge, 1790–1814); Luther Martin of Maryland (state attorney general, judge, and private lawyer); Thomas McKean of Delaware and Pennsylvania (Pennsylvania chief justice, 1777–1799; governor, 1799–1808); Thomas Mifflin of Pennsylvania (governor, 1790–1799); Robert Treat Paine of Massachusetts (state attorney general, 1777–1790; justice, 1790–1804); Edward Rutledge of South Carolina (state legislator, 1782–1798; governor, 1798–1800); and Robert Yates of New York (state judge, 1790–1798), just to name a few examples.

Fame has not smiled on founders of few words or those who left an insufficient paper trail to inform or interest historians. There must be enough of an extant record with which students of history can work.

A written record or historical narrative is vital for duly crediting a founder for his contributions and achievements. All the famous founders left enough words that, even two hundred years after their demise, archivists still labor to collect and transcribe their papers, filling many scores of published volumes.[28] Of particular value to historians are letters, journals, and diaries, which give an account of an individual's day-to-day activities, often provide a measure of a person's character, and open a window into his or her motivations and aspirations. A person's letters, Jefferson once remarked, "form the only full and genuine journal of his life."[29] ("Without Jefferson's letters," Gordon S. Wood asked, "what would we know of his mind?")[30]

The papers that were preserved and later archived and, still later, published reflected evolving private and public perceptions of whose contributions were consequential and, thus, whose papers were worthy of preservation for future generations. An individual founder's decision to keep a journal, write a memoir or autobiography, or preserve correspondence or other documents was an initial self-assessment of the importance of that founder's contribution to some event and indicated a desire to memorialize his or her role in history. Subsequent decisions made by family, acquaintances, or executors to preserve or discard such documents after an individual's death were, similarly, a pivotal assessment of whether or not the deceased's activities were noteworthy. Even before some had died, family members and others in society recognized the importance of preserving papers associated with particular founders. Unfortunately, the same generation failed to appreciate the value of other founders' papers, and thus many were lost to history.

Decisions of still later historians and archivists to preserve and publish a founder's papers reinforced earlier decisions regarding which founders were notable and which were not. Major papers publication projects sponsored by universities and historical societies and funded by private foundations and government initiatives, such as the National Historical Publications and Records Commission and the National Endowment for the Humanities, seemingly confirmed that the subjects of these projects were the truly consequential founders. A fresh review of history might well lead one to conclude that previously discounted or discarded papers of certain forgotten founders would be invaluable to a well-rounded understanding of the American founding. Regrettably, however, decisions and accompanying actions made at various points in the preceding two centuries have made it exceedingly difficult, if not impossible, to re-create the historical record. More important, the steps taken long ago to preserve or discard historical documents have shaped how subsequent scholars have assessed the thoughts, words, and deeds of the founders.

George Mason of Virginia and John Witherspoon of New Jersey are examples of founders whose reputations may have been diminished in subsequent historical accounts because of gaps in the relevant documentary records. Mason, the principal draftsman of the influential Virginia Declaration of Rights (1776) and among the most voluble members of the Constitutional Convention, is survived by a dearth of papers, which have been collected in a mere three volumes.[31] As his first major biographer observed in the late nineteenth century, "his life never having been written, his papers having been lost and scattered," it is, perhaps, no wonder that "justice has not been done to George Mason." Mason's biographers, unlike Washington's, Jefferson's, and Madison's, have not had their subject's extensive recollections and papers "before them" in which the subject's leading role in legislative deliberations "is chiefly dwelt on" and emphasized.[32]

Then there is the case of the Reverend Doctor John Witherspoon, a signer of the Declaration of Independence and Articles of Confederation and an active member of over a hundred and twenty committees in the Continental Congress. In Witherspoon's case, the problem concerns the papers that were lost or destroyed. Nine volumes of his collected works were published very early in the nineteenth century, but many of these papers pertained to his European career or his pursuits outside politics, and the published collection was out of print and exceedingly difficult to find for much of the last two centuries. More important, despite devoting two days per week in his later years to correspondence, only a handful of his many letters survive. The loss of so many primary documents giving insight into his political thought and actions at a critical time in the nation's history is due, among other reasons, to the sacking of the College of New Jersey's Nassau Hall and president's home following the Battle of Princeton and to Witherspoon's instructions shortly before his death to burn many of his papers.[33] Unlike Franklin, Adams, Jefferson, and Madison, neither Mason nor Witherspoon wrote an autobiography or left a journal or diary that might have given succeeding generations a revealing self-portrait of their characters, motives, and achievements and, perhaps, enhanced their standing in history. The paper trails left by a host of other founders are even more meager than those left by Mason and Witherspoon. History might well have been written differently had important figures such as Samuel Adams, Gerry, Henry, Jay, Randolph, Sherman, and Wilson left more papers, both public and private, for scrutiny by later generations.

Fame has often accompanied people, especially political leaders, who were eloquent in spoken and written word. The founders lived in an age in which political power and influence were often derived from and defined by oratorical prowess. (Contemporaneous biographical sketches of the founders frequently remarked on the subject's public speaking skills as if they were a measure of that figure's greatness.) Patrick Henry, for example, was greatly admired in his time, and he is remembered today, for his matchless gifts of oratory. James Madison, by contrast, had a weak voice and a diffident disposition, which seem for a time to have impeded justly deserved recognition and to have diminished his public standing. In short, individuals of great minds but weak elocution often are not duly appreciated in their own time. The founders' literal voices have long been silenced, and all that remains are their written words. It is ironic that, while masters of the *spoken* word may have garnered more power and acclaim in their own day, today the masters of the *written* word are more celebrated.

According to a well-worn axiom, history is written by the victors. The reputations of several important founders have been damaged, one suspects, because they were on the losing side of great debates or controversies, especially the bitter debates over the declaration of American independence and ratification of the proposed national constitution. Consider, for example, the Quaker John Dickinson of Delaware and Pennsylvania (serving both states as the elected chief executive), who championed the cause of American liberties in a series of brilliant "Letters from a Farmer in Pennsylvania" (1767–1768) and who was a delegate to the Stamp Act Congress, where he drafted the "Declaration of

Rights and Grievances" (October 1765); a member of the First and Second Continental Congresses, where he was the principal draftsman of the "Declaration of the Causes and Necessity of Taking Up Arms" (July 6, 1775); and one of Delaware's delegates to the Constitutional Convention of 1787. In 1776, however, he spoke eloquently against and refused to sign the Declaration of Independence because he thought it premature and intemperate, and his reputation and public career suffered for it, despite commendable subsequent service to the nation.

It has been said of George Mason that "his opposition to ratification of the federal Constitution—a document whose shape he helped mightily to craft—started his fall from the national memory."[34] The public standings of other vocal critics of the proposed Constitution were arguably diminished by their controversial stances in this most important national debate, despite the fact that some later became ardent admirers of the charter. Among the critics were Patrick Henry, Richard Henry Lee, Elbridge Gerry, Samuel Adams, Mercy Otis Warren, George Clinton, Luther Martin, and John Francis Mercer (Mercer was Mason's cousin). Other founders may have similarly fallen from public favor because of their advocacy of positions and causes that later proved unpopular.

The standing of some founders has risen and fallen with the vagaries of subsequent politics. As political parties emerged in the late eighteenth century and carved out well defined identities in the nineteenth century, partisans often appropriated selected founders as precursor spokesmen for or ideological models of their party perspectives or as avowed opponents of some partisan position. The Jacksonian Democrats of the 1820s and succeeding decades, for example, described themselves as inheritors of the Jeffersonian tradition and demonized Federalist Party stalwarts, such as Alexander Hamilton, John Adams (an especially inviting target because his son, John Quincy Adams, was Andrew Jackson's immediate foe), and John Marshall, for their opposition to Jeffersonian politics.[35] (The reputations of other prominent Federalists—such as Fisher Ames, John Jay, Rufus King, Gouverneur Morris, and C. C. Pinckney—may have similarly suffered in the wake of their party's demise and Republican ascendancy at the turn of the century.) Thus, Jefferson's reputation as a founder flourished, and Federalist founders' reputations floundered, as Jacksonianism ascended.

The Civil War and its aftermath prompted a reappraisal of Hamilton's staunch advocacy of a strong national government, and, in the North at least, Hamilton eclipsed the states-rights Jefferson as a "revered figure in the minds of most Americans."[36] According to Merrill D. Peterson, "Jefferson's reputation merely survived the War; Hamilton's was remade by it."[37] New Deal Democrats and their fellow travelers in the academy similarly appropriated Jefferson (as well as Jackson) as a defender of their policies, thus raising Jefferson's stature as a great founder among this constituency.[38] In summary, political partisans of succeeding generations have promoted or demoted selected founders in the public mind depending on whether a founder's views and associations advanced or impeded the goals of these latter-day partisans.

Another explanation focuses on certain founders' unappealing personal traits, quirks or eccentricities, or alleged moral failings. George Mason's truculent temperament and general aversion to public life almost certainly diminished his profile in the history of the founding era.[39] He was a most reluctant public figure. Mason seems to have been unconcerned about his place in the history books (he was not completely alone among the founders—mainly now forgotten founders—in this respect), having eschewed the limelight, declined to pursue high office (although reluctantly accepting public office when called), and taken few steps to preserve for posterity his papers and memoirs.

An abrasive, egotistical personality did little to enhance Thomas Paine's reputation, and pious Americans from his day to the present have reviled him for his heretical views on Christianity. John Adams described the radical pamphleteer as "the lying rascal," and Teddy Roosevelt denounced him as that "filthy little atheist."[40] And so the most influential polemicist of the age, renowned on both sides of the Atlantic, died in relative obscurity in 1809 without a eulogy from his former compatriots in the struggle for American independence.

Gouverneur Morris's well-earned reputation as a profligate rake and lecher may have diminished his standing among prudish nineteenth-century Americans. In a very different vein, Aaron Burr's widely publicized roguish, even "murderous," and allegedly treasonous conduct has kept him alive in the public memory, but it almost certainly has demoted him from the pedestal of a venerated founder.

There is the tragic case of James Wilson who died in ignominy in 1798 at age fifty-six, fleeing from creditors and debtors' prison for failed land speculation, and was buried in an obscure country graveyard in Edenton, North Carolina.[41] Today, Wilson is virtually unknown to students of American history, even though he was among the most trenchant thinkers and influential delegates at the Constitutional Convention (making more speeches than any other delegate, save Gouverneur Morris), where he was an ardent advocate of a democratic national government. He stamped an indelible mark on American legal theory through his influential law lectures and tenure on the U.S. Supreme Court.

Robert Morris, a signer of the Declaration of Independence, Articles of Confederation, and Constitution; a member of the first federal Congress; and the indispensable "financier of the Revolution"—a man who by any measure should be remembered as a founding father—similarly borrowed heavily and failed miserably in western land speculation. He languished for three and a half miserable years in a debtors' prison (February 1798 to August 1801), and his reputation has never recovered. Other lesser known founders—such as William Leigh Pierce of Georgia, Nathaniel Gorham of Massachusetts, Thomas Mifflin of Pennsylvania, John Rutledge of South Carolina, William Blount of North Carolina, and Luther Martin of Maryland—similarly found themselves financially embarrassed and disgraced in later years.

Few even moderately famous founders came from small (e.g., Delaware or Rhode Island) or far-flung (e.g., New Hampshire or Georgia) states. One must have come from or represented a major power center or constituency in the new nation, it would seem, to join the company of elite founders. Leading Baptists, for example, made interesting, substantive contributions to emerging American principles of religious liberty and related church-state issues; however, Baptist leaders and thinkers, such as the Reverend Isaac Backus of Massachusetts, are rarely mentioned in chronicles of the founding. Their constituencies and, perhaps, concerns were apparently too marginal to merit attention.

Finally, there seems to be an inclination among modern scholars to dismiss, discount, or ignore the views of pious founders whose ideas and actions were shaped by deeply held religious convictions. Trained in the rationalist traditions of the academy, some scholars are unfamiliar or uncomfortable with or closed to religiously informed arguments and rhetoric, and thus they dismiss or otherwise decline to engage founders whose worldview was profoundly religious. Founders steeped in the rationalist traditions of the Enlightenment are more familiar and accessible, and their exploits are advanced in modern scholarship. John Witherspoon's faith-based perspectives may have scared off more than one secular scholar; moreover, his clerical collar may have symbolically entangled church and state too excessively for modern sensibilities. Jeffry H. Morrison has noted that even in Witherspoon's day some citizens were uneasy with the idea of a clergyman-turned-politician and opined that "present-day Americans have become even more scrupulous about keeping church separate from state."[42] The profiles of Samuel Adams, Roger Sherman, Oliver Ellsworth, John Jay, Elias Boudinot, and Isaac Backus, among others, may have been similarly diminished by modern secular scholars on account of their profoundly religious identities and perspectives.

Does the Difference Matter?

Does the distinction in the public mind between famous founders and forgotten founders matter to us today? Yes, it matters for both symbolic and substantive reasons. An exclusive or even primary focus on a small fraternity of famous founders gives a limited, and thus potentially distorted, picture of the founders—their ideas, values, interests, aspirations, faith commitments, socioeconomic standings, etc. It slights, if not ignores, the services, sacrifices, and legacies of those forgotten founders who did much to birth a new nation.

Separating the famous from the now forgotten founders may erroneously convey the notion that the founders were a much more single-minded, monolithic fraternity than they really were. It obscures the founders' diverse backgrounds, interests, perspectives, and even biases, projecting an incomplete picture of this generation. Our understanding of the delicate balance of personalities, perspectives, and experiences so vital to the success of the founding generation is obfuscated when we train our sights on a select few famous founders and disregard the rest. As previously noted, for example, the most orthodox Christians among the founders (Samuel Adams, Elias Boudinot, Oliver Ellsworth, Patrick Henry, John Jay, Roger Sherman, and John Witherspoon) are rarely counted among the company of famous founders, despite their substantial contributions to the new nation, suggesting, perhaps, that the founders (and, more important, their ideas) were more heterodox than they really were. The contributions of traditional Christian thought to the American founding are, in large measure, diminished in the process. The unfortunate result is that we discount the views of a significant segment of the founding generation because they were not shared by a select few famous founders or we erroneously ascribe to an entire generation or a large company of forgotten founders the views of an elite few. The views of a handful of famous founders, in short, are not necessarily representative of all the founders.

These distortions, unfortunately, are sometimes translated into modern law and policy. Judicial interpretations of the First Amendment illustrate the potential problems. The U.S. Supreme Court's near exclusive reliance on the views of Thomas Jefferson and James Madison, two purported advocates of church-state separation, to divine the original understanding of the First Amendment, while ignoring the input of others who, in the deliberative process, championed an essential role for religion in public life, has promulgated an arguably distorted construction of the First Amendment. Mark David Hall has recently documented that, in its recourse to history, the U.S. Supreme Court has given inordinate attention to the words and deeds of Jefferson and Madison.[43] The focus on these two Virginians is odd, if not counter-historical, because Jefferson was, at most, indirectly involved in framing the First Amendment (he was serving as the American minister to France when the First Congress framed the amendment) and Madison suffered decisive defeats in his efforts to shape the content of the religion provisions. As Cushing Strout observed, "Madison did not carry the country along with Virginia's sweeping separation of churches from the state: indeed, the country in some degree carried him."[44]

At critical junctures in the First Congress's deliberations on the amendment, language was proposed by Samuel Livermore of New Hampshire and Fisher Ames of Massachusetts that arguably shaped the final text of the First Amendment. In an essay in this volume, William R. Casto presents evidence that U.S. Senator Oliver Ellsworth of Connecticut contributed to the final language of the First Amendment in a Conference Committee of the First Congress in September 1789. Legislative histories often gloss over these crucial contributions and insights of the now all but forgotten Livermore, Ames, and Ellsworth, suggesting instead that the First Amendment flowed fully formed from the pen of famous founder James Madison. Lost in these incomplete histories are the possible concerns and intentions behind Livermore's, Ames's, and Ellsworth's revisions that almost certainly influenced congressional colleagues, thus leaving their mark on the First Amendment.

The forgotten founders profiled and studied in this volume made valuable—perhaps even indispensable—contributions to articulating the colonists' constitutional claims against the British, crafting the declarations of rights and plans of civil government of their respective states and nation following independence, and establishing the institutions of republican government in the new nation. The American Revolution and political independence are difficult to imagine absent the inspiring and inciting voices of Samuel Adams, Patrick Henry, and Thomas Paine. They called Americans to the cause of liberty. Their words—Henry's "give me liberty or give me death" speech, for example—were on the lips of patriotic Americans.[45] Their rhetorical gifts were arguably unrivaled in the annals of American history. Moreover, in the fraternity of founders, Samuel Adams of Massachusetts and Patrick Henry of Virginia were among the most orthodox Christians. The immigrant Thomas Paine, by contrast, was among the most heterodox, openly contemptuous of the supernatural claims of the traditional Christian faith.

Samuel Adams, Benjamin Rush, and Roger Sherman were delegates at the Second Continental Congress and signed the first expression of American organic law—the Declaration of American Independence. Oliver Ellsworth, Alexander Hamilton, Patrick Henry, John Jay, and Edmund Randolph also served in the Continental and/or Confederation Congresses. Indeed, Jay served a term as president of the Continental Congress. Many of these patriots, especially Samuel Adams, Sherman, and Jay, were instrumental in forging a confederation of the former colonies following their assertion of independence. Sherman and Ellsworth, both of Connecticut, were devout Calvinists and active Congregation-alists. Rush of Pennsylvania was a serious Christian who advocated an expansive role for religion in public life, especially in education, but by his own admission, his religious views occasionally deviated from or-thodoxy.[46] Jay of New York, by all accounts, was a pious Anglican and actively engaged in a variety of religious ministries. Hamilton, a West Indian immigrant who settled in New York, gave evidence of Christian piety early and late in life, but religion apparently was less important to him in mid-life, when he was at the height of his power. Randolph of Virginia, a conventional Episcopalian, reflected the religious values of his class and culture.

Ellsworth, Sherman, Randolph, and Hamilton represented their states at the Philadelphia Convention of 1787, which framed the U.S. Constitution. Most of the founders profiled in this volume engaged in the debates on the Constitution's ratification. Indeed, Hamilton and Jay, together with famous founder James Madison, coauthored *The Federalist Papers*—the most trenchant defense of the proposed national char-ter. Patrick Henry, Mercy Otis Warren, and Samuel Adams offered inci-sive "anti-Federalist" critiques of the Constitution. Anti-Federalists, like Henry, framed and drove the debate on certain constitutional issues and features, and many of the strongest defenses of the Constitution were di-rect responses to anti-Federalist arguments. (Randolph initially refused to sign the final text but later endorsed the Constitution in the Virginia ratifying convention. Samuel Adams, too, was eventually persuaded to support the Constitution.)

Finally, Ellsworth, Sherman, Hamilton, Randolph, and Jay held in-fluential offices in the new national government under the ratified Con-stitution. Ellsworth and Sherman served in the first federal Congress; Hamilton was the first secretary of the treasury and Randolph the first attorney general and second secretary of state in President Washington's cabinet; and Jay was appointed the first chief justice of the U.S. Supreme Court. They helped define the principles, establish the institutions, and set the precedents of the nascent constitutional government of the United States.

These men and women were not on the sidelines; they were involved in every critical event in the political struggle to create a new nation.

And yet the figures profiled in this volume are, for the most part, "forgotten founders." The names Abigail Adams, Samuel Adams, Alexander Hamilton, and Patrick Henry, it is true, are familiar to many Americans, but few today can recall their significant contributions to the American founding. If not their names, then certainly their roles in establishing the American republic have faded from public memory. Instead, memories are drawn to the few famous founders. Giving inordinate attention to the short list of famous founders, unfortunately, leads us to overlook the substantial contributions in thought, word, and deed made by these and other forgotten founders.

The near exclusive focus on a select few virtually deified famous founders impoverishes our understanding of the American founding. It also departs from the canons of good scholarship. The demands of thorough, honest scholarship require scholars to give attention to the thoughts, words, and deeds of not only a few selected demigods but also an expansive company of men and women who contributed to the founding of the American republic.

Notes

1. An earlier, abbreviated version of this essay appeared in the *Intercollegiate Review* 42, no. 2 (2007): 3–12, and is reprinted here with permission.

2. The other was Robert Morris of Pennsylvania. Both men also served in the first federal Congress. In addition to these two men, four signed both the Declaration of Independence and the U.S. Constitution: Benjamin Franklin, James Wilson, George Clymer, and George Read. Elbridge Gerry and George Wythe, both signers of the Declaration of Independence, participated in the Constitutional Convention but, for different reasons, did not sign the U.S. Constitution. In addition to Sherman and Morris, fourteen men signed both the Declaration of Independence and the Articles of Confederation: Samuel Adams, Josiah Bartlett, William Ellery, Elbridge Gerry, John Hancock, Thomas Heyward Jr., Samuel Huntington, Francis Lightfoot Lee, Richard Henry Lee, Francis Lewis, Thomas McKean, John Penn, John Witherspoon, and Oliver Wolcott. In addition to Sherman and Morris, three men signed both the Articles of Confederation and the Constitution: Daniel Carroll, John Dickinson, and Gouverneur Morris. Gerry also signed the Articles and participated in the Constitutional Convention but declined to sign the Constitution.

3. John G. Rommel, *Connecticut's Yankee Patriot: Roger Sherman* (Hartford, Conn.: The American Revolution Bicentennial Commission of Connecticut, 1979), 28.

4. Joseph J. Ellis, for example, adds Abigail Adams and Aaron Burr to the usual six "most prominent political leaders in the early republic." Ellis, *Founding Brothers: The Revolutionary Generation* (New York: Alfred A. Knopf, 2005), 17.

5. See generally Richard D. Brown, "The Founding Fathers of 1776 and 1787: A Collective View," *William and Mary Quarterly* 3rd ser., 33 (1976): 465–80.

6. Ray Raphael, *Founding Myths: Stories that Hide Our Patriotic Past* (New York: New Press, 2004), 127.

7. Jefferson, letter to Roger C. Weightman, Jun. 24, 1826, in *Thomas Jefferson: Writings*, ed. Merrill D. Peterson (New York: Library of America, 1984), 1517.

8. See Clinton Rossiter, *1787: The Grand Convention* (New York: Macmillan, 1966), 317. In the early Republic, "it was generally considered a more noble achievement to have been a Signer of 1776 than a Framer of 1787. . . . The men of 1776 had shaken the earth while the men of 1787 had only helped to settle the dust."

9. Jefferson, letter to John Adams, Aug. 30, 1787, in *Thomas Jefferson: Writings*, 909.

10. Merrill D. Peterson, *The Jefferson Image in the American Mind* (New York: Oxford University Press, 1960), 222. See also Stephen F. Knott, *Alexander Hamilton and the Persistence of Myth* (Lawrence: University Press of Kansas, 2002).

11. This battle of interpretations, Joseph Ellis notes, is manifested in the "earliest histories of the period." In *History of the American Revolution* (1805), Mercy Otis Warren set forth the "pure republicanism" or Jeffersonian interpretation, whereas John Marshall articulated an alternative version friendlier to the Federalists in his expansive five-volume *The Life of George Washington* (1804–1807). Ellis, *Founding Brothers*, 13–14.

12. David McCullough, *John Adams* (New York: Simon & Schuster, 2001). See John Howe, review of *John Adams*, by David McCullough, *Journal of American History* 90 (Jun. 2003): 210: "Reviewers have properly celebrated McCullough's achievement in establishing Adams's place among the nation's principal founders."

13. Washington was the target of vituperative partisan attacks late in his presidency.

14. Robert Green McCloskey, introduction to *The Works of James Wilson*, ed. Robert Green McCloskey, 2 vols. (Cambridge, Mass.: Belknap Press of Harvard University Press, 1967), 1:47.

15. See David W. Maxey, "The Translation of James Wilson," *Supreme Court Historical Society 1990 Yearbook* (1990): 29.

16. Ellis, *Founding Brothers*, 212–27.

17. Jefferson, letter to Madison, Feb. 17, 1826, in *Thomas Jefferson: Writings*, 1515.

18. Joseph J. Ellis, *His Excellency George Washington* (New York: Alfred A. Knopf, 2004), 151–52.

19. John Adams, letter to Abigail Adams, Jun. 2, 1776, in *Adams Family Correspondence*, ed. L. H. Butterfield, 7 vols. (Cambridge, Mass.: Belknap Press of Harvard University Press, 1963), 2:3; John Adams, letter to Abigail Adams, May 17, 1776, in *Adams Family Correspondence*, 1:410.

20. With considerable discomfort, Madison scribbled transcripts and co-pious notes of proceedings in the Constitutional Convention that, not surprisingly, recorded his contributions in a favorable light and assured his place in history. This theme, along with Madison's alleged suppression of the so-called Pinckney Plan, are developed in Christopher Collier and James Lincoln Collier, *Decision in Philadelphia: The Constitutional Convention of 1787* (New York: Ballantine Books, 1986), 87–101, 109–11. But see the introduction to *Supplement to Max Farrand's The Records of the Federal Convention of 1787*, ed. James H. Hutson (New Haven, Conn.: Yale University Press, 1987), xx–xxv.

21. Douglass Adair, "Fame and the Founding Fathers," in *Fame and the Founding Fathers: Essays by Douglass Adair*, ed. Trevor Colbourn (New York: Norton and the Institute of Early American History and Culture, 1974), 7.

22. In this vein, a young John Adams declared in his diary (Mar. 14, 1759): "Reputation ought to be the perpetual subject of my Thoughts, and Aim of my Behaviour." *Diary and Autobiography of John Adams*, ed. L. H. Butterfield, 4 vols. (Cambridge, Mass.: Belknap Press of Harvard University Press, 1961), 1:78.

23. Wilson, *The Works of James Wilson*, 1:405.

24. Publius [Alexander Hamilton], *Federalist Paper*, no. 72. Cf. John Milton, *Lycidas*, lines 70–72: "Fame is the spur that the clear spirit doth raise / (That last infirmity of Noble mind) / To scorn delights, and live laborious dayes"; Samuel Johnson, *The Rambler* # 49 (Sep. 4, 1750): "the love of fame is to be regulated rather than extinguished; and that men should be taught not to be wholly careless about their memory, but to endeavour that they may be remembered chiefly for their virtues, since no other reputation will be able to transmit any pleasure beyond the grave"; William Hazlitt, "Lecture VIII: On the Living Poets," in *Lectures on the English Poets* (London, 1818), 286: "The love of fame, as it enters at times into his mind, is only another name for the love of excellence; or it is the ambition to attain the highest excellence, sanctioned by the highest authority—that of time."

25. Publius [Alexander Hamilton], *Federalist Paper*, no. 72.

26. Adair, "Fame and the Founding Fathers," 7, 11–12, 24. See also the chapter entitled "The Love of Fame, The Ruling Passion of the Noblest Minds," in *The Spur of Fame: Dialogues of John Adams and Benjamin Rush, 1805–1813*, ed. John A. Schutz and Douglass Adair (San Marino, Calif.: Huntington Library, 1966), 1–19.

27. George Washington, "Farewell Address, 19 September 1796," in *The Writings of George Washington*, ed. John C. Fitzpatrick, 37 vols. (Washington, D.C.: Government Printing Office, 1931–1940), 35:238.

28. The current George Washington papers project, once completed, is projected to contain approximately ninety volumes. The Adams family papers project is expected to include more than a hundred volumes. The Thomas Jefferson papers project is estimated to consist of seventy-five volumes. Both the James Madison and Benjamin Franklin papers projects are expected to contain approximately fifty volumes each. The papers of Alexander Hamilton, who died before his fiftieth birthday, were published in twenty-seven volumes. An additional five volumes are devoted to Hamilton's law practice.

29. Jefferson, letter to Robert Walsh, Apr. 5, 1823, as quoted in "A General View of the Work," *The Papers of Thomas Jefferson*, ed. Julian P. Boyd et al., 33 vols. to date (Princeton, N.J.: Princeton University Press, 1950–), 1:xi.

30. Gordon S. Wood, *Revolutionary Characters: What Made the Founders Different* (New York: Penguin Press, 2006), 246.

31. George Mason, *The Papers of George Mason, 1725–1792*, ed. Robert A. Rutland, 3 vols. (Chapel Hill: University of North Carolina Press, 1970).

32. Kate Mason Rowland, *The Life of George Mason, 1725–1792*, 2 vols. (New York, 1892), 1:272. See also Warren M. Billings, " 'That All Men Are Born Equally Free and Independent': Virginians and the Origins of the Bill of Rights," in *The Bill of Rights and the States: The Colonial and Revolutionary Origins of American Liberties*, ed. Patrick T. Conley and John P. Kaminski (Madison, Wisc.: Madison House, 1992), 337: "the disappearance of all but a modest remnant of his papers now confines him to relative obscurity, and he forever remains a shadowy figure whose qualities lie just beyond the reach of the biographer, the historian, or the curious citizen."

33. Jeffry H. Morrison, *John Witherspoon and the Founding of the American Republic* (Notre Dame, Ind.: University of Notre Dame Press, 2005), 14–15. The twenty-first century has witnessed at least two reprint editions of Witherspoon's works.

34. Billings, " 'That All Men Are Born Equally Free and Independent,' " 337. See also Robert A. Rutland, *George Mason: Reluctant Statesman* (Baton Rouge: Louisiana State University Press, 1961), 109: "By refusing to support the unamended Constitution, . . . Mason forfeited acclaim that history laid generously upon both his friends and his adversaries."

35. The Jeffersonian Republican and later Jacksonian charges were that the Federalists, especially Hamilton, were essentially aristocratic (elitist, Anglomaine, and even monarchist), autocratic (vesting excessive power in the executive), antidemocratic, anti-agrarian (and pro urban, manufacturing, and banking interests), and supportive of a strong central or national government. The Federalists, for their part, depicted Jefferson and his followers as Jacobins and

zealous advocates of states' rights, diffused governmental power, excessive democracy (mob rule), individualism, and church-state separation (and sometimes heterodoxy). They also emphasized the pro-slavery sentiments of many southern agrarian Republicans.

36. Knott, *Alexander Hamilton and the Persistence of Myth*, 47.

37. Peterson, *The Jefferson Image in the American Mind*, 222; see generally 209–11, 216–26.

38. See, for example, the works of Arthur M. Schlesinger Jr., especially *The Age of Jackson* (Boston: Little, Brown, 1945). For a more recent example, see Sean Wilentz, *The Rise of American Democracy: Jefferson to Lincoln* (New York: W. W. Norton, 2005).

39. See generally Brent Tarter, "George Mason and the Conservation of Liberty," *Virginia Magazine of History and Biography* 99 (1991): 282–85. See also Jeff Broadwater, *George Mason: Forgotten Founder* (Chapel Hill: University of North Carolina Press, 2006), viii–ix, outlining reasons for Mason's obscurity; Billings, "'That All Men Are Born Equally Free and Independent,'" 337–39:

> He was a forceful, curmudgeonly man. Patience was no virtue in him. He disdained colleagues for what he saw as their small accomplishments. Bored by legislative routines, he despised committee work. He shunned political office whenever possible, preferring instead to remain apart in the private world he created for himself at Gunston Hall, his estate, where he cultivated the ideal (much pursued at the time) of the disinterested, Romanlike citizen-patriot. And yet on those infrequent occasions when his sense of duty and his friends finally coaxed him into public service, he made his presence felt by the sheer weight of his mastery both of issues and of the written word.

40. Adams, letter to Benjamin Rush, Nov. 14, 1812, in *The Spur of Fame*, 252; Theodore Roosevelt, *Gouverneur Morris* (Boston: Houghton, Mifflin, 1898), 251.

41. See Maxey, "The Translation of James Wilson," 29–43.

42. Morrison, *John Witherspoon and the Founding of the American Republic*, 18.

43. Mark David Hall, "Jeffersonian Walls and Madisonian Lines: The Supreme Court's Use of History in Religion Clause Cases," *Oregon Law Review* 85 (2006): 563–614.

44. Cushing Strout, *The New Heavens and New Earth: Political Religion in America* (New York: Harper & Row, 1974), 97.

45. William Wirt, *Sketches of the Life and Character of Patrick Henry* (Philadelphia: James Webster, 1817), 120–23; William Wirt Henry, *Patrick Henry: Life, Correspondence and Speeches*, 3 vols. (New York, 1891), 1:262–66.

46. See Benjamin Rush, letter to John Adams, Apr. 5, 1808, in *Letters of Benjamin Rush*, ed. L. H. Butterfield, 2 vols. (Princeton, N.J.: American Philosophical Society; Princeton University Press, 1951), 2:963: "my creed . . . is a compound of the orthodoxy and heterodoxy of most of our Christian churches."

CHAPTER 2

The Way of Duty

Abigail Adams and Religion

EDITH B. GELLES

According to Adams family lore, when the Reverend William Smith preached the sermon at his daughter Abigail's marriage ceremony on October 25, 1764, he chose for his text Luke 7:33: "For John came, neither eating bread nor drinking wine, and Ye say 'He hath a Devil.'"[1] Even in the mid-eighteenth century's still puritanical New England, his topic lacked the felicity, comfort, or optimism that was generally associated with marriage, especially the marriage of his own daughter. Family members and biographers have puzzled over his sermon for two and a half centuries. Clearly, the good reverend was sending a message on that fall day in the parsonage at Weymouth, Massachusetts, when the bright-eyed nineteen-year-old Abigail Smith married John Adams of Braintree.

Born to Privilege, Raised in Piety

The reverend belonged to a prominent Boston family with ties to the mercantile communities that extended into South Carolina and the Caribbean. When the young Abigail visited Boston, she often stayed at the lavish Beacon Hill residence of Isaac Smith Sr., her father's brother, and his wife, Elizabeth. Another branch of the Smith family, typical in Puritan New England, attended Harvard and prepared for the clergy. The Reverend Zabdiel Smith, of neighboring Lunenburg, was William Smith's nephew. After graduating Harvard in 1734, William answered the call of the First Church of Weymouth, where he remained until his death in 1783, after a career marked by piety, intelligence, and compassion. But the reverend kept his hand in worldly enterprises as well. He speculated in land, purchasing several farms, and kept his business connections in Boston.[2]

The legacy of Elizabeth Smith, the reverend's wife and Abigail's mother, survived in her name: Quincy. She was born Elizabeth Norton Quincy, and her parents' distinguished past represented two different branches of Puritan pedigree, the religious elect of the Norton, Shepard, and Winthrop lines from her mother and the political elite of her father, John Quincy, the "Duke of Braintree." Elizabeth came of age in the privileged and religious household of the largest landholder in Braintree, who served for many years as a member of the local governing councils and particularly as an overseer of relations with the local Punkapog Indians. She was well-educated in the arts and skills appropriate to women of her era, which is to say she was prepared to run a large household and teach her own daughters the same, including reading, writing, account keeping, and some French.[3]

The Smith household, where Abigail was born on November 22, 1744 (O.S.), was permeated by its religious legacy, but it also valued worldly knowledge. She came of age with parents who cared about material prosperity as well as literature and politics. They were latter-day Puritans. The religious mandate of the early seventeenth century had become, by the early eighteenth century, a secular mandate as well. Further, Abigail grew up in a large extended family on both sides, among the Smiths and Quincys. As the second daughter, she was close to her older sister, Mary, and her younger sister, Elizabeth. William Jr., their younger brother, unlike his sisters, was destined to attend Harvard.[4]

Throughout her youth Abigail Smith, alongside her mother, Elizabeth, her sisters, and brother, sat through sermons many times each week not just because she was the daughter of the local minister, but also because, in that lackluster world of rural Massachusetts, a religious gathering provided entertainment and social life. It was school; it was theater; it was companionship. The religion that Abigail learned at home as well as sitting regularly through meetings at the First Church of Weymouth became rooted in her belief and behavior in ways that did not lead to reexamination in adulthood. The foundation of every experience, every joy and catastrophe in her life was rooted in her religious background. It was a legacy that she would, in turn, transmit to her own children.

An Unusual Marriage

Abigail was barely sixteen years old when she met John Adams,[5] who came to the parsonage at Weymouth as a companion to his friend Richard Cranch, who wooed Abigail's sister Mary. The attraction was not immediate, but some visits later, the observant young lawyer from Braintree did notice the bright, outspoken, and even impertinent younger woman. She showed a keen interest in the political discussions that took place among the men, and even more boldly, she contributed to those conversations. If at first he didn't approve, he soon became enamored of her. Three years later, in 1764, after a courtship marked by a combination of flirtation, sharpness of mind, affection, and humor, they were married. Those same qualities that had attracted them to each other, as well as their religious compatibility, remained alive to create a marriage that has become legendary. The legend, however, obscures the fact that theirs was less an ideal marriage than an ideal correspondence, for after their first decade of marriage, the circumstances of the American Revolution and its consequences kept them apart for effectively a quarter of a century.[6]

During their first decade of marriage, their lives followed a predictable pattern. They moved to the small "cottage," as Abigail called their farmhouse in Braintree, which John had inherited from his father and which served as their principal family home until their return from Europe. Their first child, a daughter also named Abigail, was born in 1765, after which Abigail gave birth to three sons who lived, John Quincy in 1767, Charles in 1770, and Thomas in 1772. A daughter, Susannah, died at the age of one in 1770; another child was stillborn in 1777. In the catastrophes of the deaths of her children—two adult children also predeceased her, Charles in 1800 and her daughter in 1813—religion was the source of solace and hope for Abigail.

After her marriage, Abigail anticipated that her life would repeat the same broad outlines of family life as her mother and grandmothers before her. That was not to be the case. Her marriage in 1764 coincided with the escalation of events that led to the rebellion and revolution. As internal taxation of the colonies by Great Britain and resistance on the part of the colonies grew in intensity, John Adams became more and more involved in the developing conflict. The Adamses' lives became increasingly politicized. Finally, with John's election as a delegate to the first Continental Congress at Philadelphia in 1774, he began to serve his nation in distant places.

For most of the next four years, John participated in the Congress at Philadelphia; then in 1778 Congress appointed him to join the American delegation in Paris. Hoping for another diplomatic post, he did not return home after the peace treaty was signed in 1783, so Abigail crossed the ocean to live with him in France and then England. Upon their return to the United States in 1788, she resided with him at the nation's capitals for two of the eight years that he was vice president, first in New York and then in Philadelphia. Finally, during his presidency, she lived sporadically at the capital cities. She resided in the newly built capital of Washington, D.C., for less than a year before John's defeat for a second term as president in 1800. For most of the years of his public service, then, the Adamses lived apart. They conducted their marriage through correspondence.

Abigail considered her separation from John Adams as her greatest sacrifice to the nation, just as John believed that living apart from his family was his great sacrifice. "I had it in my heart to disswade him from going and I know I could have prevaild," Abigail once wrote to her friend Mercy Otis Warren. "But our publick affairs at that time wore so gloomy an aspect that I thought if ever his assistance was wanted it must be at such a time. I therefore resignd myself to suffer much anxiety and many Melancholy hours for this year to come."[7] She could not have forecast at the beginning of the war that the years would stretch out as they did into decades. Nor did many of the revolutionaries anticipate a prolonged war when they began their rebellion.

Abigail lived with her children during the war years, liable to attack by the British when they occupied Boston, struggling to maintain her household as the breadwinner in John's absence, nursing her children and servants through a deadly dysentery epidemic and their later small pox inoculation, and, above all, suffering loneliness and fear for John's safety. Those years were tolerable because she saw them in providential terms, in religious terms. Just as she considered John's special talents necessary to the survival of the revolutionary endeavor, she understood that conditions of hardship and survival in her life were in the providence of God. Religion provided her with a way to understand the circumstances of her life.

Abigail's Faith

Abigail rarely accounted for herself as a Christian. She did not describe any crisis of belief, she rarely mentioned church attendance, and she seldom preached. Instead, religion became a subtle undercurrent in her recorded life—in the many hundreds of letters she wrote that have survived. She had learned her Bible well. She quoted easily from the Testaments. The result of all of those hours at church and all those hours of studying the Bible was a total command of Scriptures. As readily as any Puritan forebear, she found examples from the Bible to illustrate any point she wished to make. Different from them, she quoted literature as well. Her virtuosity, in fact, sometimes confounds modern readers who seek vainly for their sources. She undoubtedly composed some of her quotations herself, using a biblical cadence and diction. Abigail never lost the cast of mind that was implanted while she was growing up in a parsonage.

To say that Abigail was a "believer" is anachronistic. Belief was like the air she breathed; it surrounded her and was taken for granted as a truth that sustained life. She never doubted the underpinnings of Christian teaching. At the same time, she was not so fixed in a belief system that it did not alter as she aged. But she retained a moral scheme that she inherited from her Puritan past and that had been translated into values that governed her ideals and her behavior. She measured goodness not only from a set of rules but from people's capacity for virtue and generosity.

Abigail considered all of life providential; nothing occurred except by the will of God. "I [receive] pleasure and assurance from the source of inspration. That not a swallow falleth without notice," she wrote to John Quincy.[8] In times of crises—when her mother died, when children died, when her sisters passed on—she reverted to the Calvinism of her forebears. "Have pitty upon me, have pitty upon me o! thou my beloved for the Hand of God presseth me soar," she wrote to John after her mother died. "Yet will I be dumb and silent and not open my mouth because thou o Lord hast done it."[9] Some adversity she considered as punishment for human sinfulness. "Desire and sorrow were denounced upon our Sex as a punishment for the transgression of Eve," she wrote in a time of particular despair, when John had been gone for many years and her misfortunes had mounted. "I never wondered at the philosopher who thanked the Gods that he was created a Man rather than a woman."[10] In the worst of circumstances, she called up the Trinity for consolation. Following the death of her daughter in 1813, she wrote, "My own loss is not to be estimated by words and can only be alleviated by the consoling belief that my Dear Child is partaking of the Life and immortality brought to Light by him who endured the cross and is gone before to prepare a place for those who Love him and express his commandments."[11] Abigail poured her grief and her soul into her letters, and they became prayers that she could mail, perhaps to some relative, perhaps, she imagined, even to be read by God. Mostly, however, Abigail's religious language was laconic and casual; they were expressions of her personal providential code.

In the first letter written by Abigail that survives from her early married life, she wrote to a friend: "Your Diana [her youthful pen name] become a Mamma—can you credit it? Indeed it is a sober truth. Bless'd with a charming Girl whose pretty Smiles already delight my Heart."[12] When Abigail wrote "bless'd," she was not using a euphemism. To her, the birth of a child, a healthy, surviving child, was a blessing from God.

And just as birth was a blessing, illness was a mystery. To comfort her sister Mary, whose husband, Richard Cranch, became very ill in 1766, Abigail quoted: "Many are the afflictions of the righteous was a text which immediately occurred to my mind."[13] Such subtle religious references permeate Abigail's letters, manifesting her deep religious consciousness.

Not always were her comments either subtle or unconscious. Religion provided her with strength. When the streets of Boston were patrolled by British regulars in late 1773, and it was clear that a violent conflict was imminent, she wrote to her sister Mary that "such is the present Situation of affairs that I tremble when I think what may be the direfull consequences—and in this Town must the Scene of action lay. My Heart beats at every Whistle I hear, and I dare not openly express half my fears.—Eternal Reproach and Ignominy be the portion of all those who have been instrumental in bringing these fears upon me."[14] May they roast in Hell, she was saying of the British. About the same time, she lamented to John: "You cannot be, I know, nor do I wish to see you an Inactive Spectator, but if the sword be drawn, I bid adieu to all domestick felicity and look forward to that Country where there is neither wars nor rumors of War in a firm belief that thro the Mercy of its King we shall both rejoice there together."[15] While not giving an optimistic prognostication for the outcome of the conflict, should it occur, Abigail at least forecast a happy reunion with John in their afterlife.

Abigail's Legacy

While Abigail did not leave a testament of her religion, aside from a line here and there, in her vast correspondence, there is one likely place where it is possible to observe a condensed version of her belief system. That is in her teaching to her children and particularly in a few letters that she wrote to her eldest son, John Quincy, when he accompanied his father to France. In 1778, John was appointed by Congress to negotiate a treaty with France, and he took his eldest son, then not quite eleven years old, along for company. That trip was quickly terminated, but John was asked to return the next year to seek a further alliance. This time both John Quincy, twelve, and Charles, nine, went with him. It was a wrenching experience for Abigail, who wrote to a friend: "And now cannot you imagine me seated by my fire side Bereft of my better Half and added to that a Limb lopt of to heighten the anguish. In vain have I summoned philosiphy, its aid is vain. Come then Religion thy force can alone support the mind under the severest trials and hardest conflicts humane Nature is subject to."[16]

Abigail encouraged her children to travel abroad because she believed that they would receive an important education in Europe that they could not get at home. It meant, however, that they would be out of her purview; not only did she miss them, but she agonized about the possible corruption of their characters in dissolute Europe. As a result she chose to teach them in the best way she could from a distance: by correspondence. Several of her letters to John Quincy of this period survive that describe the religious ethos she felt compelled to teach her eldest son. The survival of those letters means that John Quincy saved them, and if he saved them, it was because they were valuable to him. They contained his mother's religious legacy to him. Central to her message was the Puritan concept of duty.

The historian Philip Greven has written that the Puritan concept of duty was fundamental to the child-rearing ethos of moderate Protestants, like the Adamses, in the late eighteenth century.[17] More generally, however, the concept of duty represented to Abigail Adams the method and the mechanism for living in this world. It was how she could comprehend the purpose of earthly existence. The concept of duty and its performance represented a formula for human conduct. It suggested a framework for behavior.

Duty implies obligations within both the family and the community at large, and ultimately to God. It implies subordination, deference, and respect. Duty further implies a "sense of connection and of relationships," ensuring that every relationship would be governed by rules and obedience. It also implies reciprocity. Duty symbolized the maintenance of position and place within the family, and in the social and cosmic order, by defining both the obligations of obedience and the limitations upon the exercise of authority and power.[18] Duty must be consciously learned in order to shape unconscious behavior. In a basic sense, duty is a stunning application of the Puritan understanding of human psychology. Abigail Adams consciously educated her children from earliest infancy to a sense of duty as her formula for how to live a virtuous life.

Therefore, when Abigail encouraged her eldest son to accompany his father to Europe in 1778, and again in 1779, it was because she believed it to be her duty to provide him with a unique educational opportunity.[19] After his departure in 1778, she wrote to him: "It is a very dificult task my dear son for a tender parent to bring their mind to part with a child of your years into a distant Land [but] You have arrived at years capable of improving under advantages you will be like to have if you do but properly attend to them." She praised him, but also pointed out his good fortune. "You are in possession of a natural good understanding and of spirits unbroken by adversity, and untamed with care." But she then reminded him that talent and his situation entailed obligations. "Improve your understanding for acquiring usefull knowledge and virtue, such as will render you an ornament to society, an Honour to your Country, and a Blessing to your parents."

Thus, with one grand pronouncement, Abigail organized John Quincy's obligations: to society at large, to his country, and to his parents. And in order to fulfill these worldly obligations, she cautioned, he must "adhere to those religious Sentiments and principals which were early instilled into your mind and remember that you are accountable to your Maker for all your words and actions." She concluded with words that, while they registered Abigail's deeply felt fears for her young son's future, sound harsh according to twenty-first-century sensibilities. She wrote, "I had much rather you should have found your Grave in the ocean you have crossd, or any untimely death crop you in your Infant years, rather than see you an immoral profligate or a Graceless child."[20] The message was harsh; to a child it would have been threatening. But Abigail's greatest fear was that she would fail in her duty as a mother to implant in her children her religious formula for the conduct of a good life. She needed to get her son's attention, to look him in the eye, figuratively, to impress him with the importance of her lesson. Her harsh words substituted for the expression and emphasis she could have conveyed in person. All of the difficulties she had experienced in the years since the outbreak of hostilities with England, a rupture that began in 1764, the year of her marriage, had been tolerable only because she understood life from within the religious framework that she now attempted to pass on to her eldest son.

It was never easy for Abigail to part with her children, even though she had insisted that they accompany their father on the second journey. Abigail wrote John Quincy, justifying her motive: "You however readily submitted to my advice, and I hope will never have occasion yourself, nor give me reason to Lament it." Then she persisted at length to outline the advantages of learning languages and of travel. "These are times in which a Genious would wish to live," she observed, citing Cicero and Mark Antony as models. She wanted her son to realize the significance of the Revolution for him, that his parents' sacrifices provided him with the opportunity and the obligation to continue the legacy of service.

The small ship that carried the Adamses to Europe suffered damage in a terrible storm off the Iberian coast. Instead of landing in France, they disembarked in Spain—barely—and traveled overland to Paris. Learning of the traumatic sea voyage, Abigail wrote, "You have seen how inadequate the aid of Man would have been, if the winds and seas had not been under the particular government of that Being who streached out the Heavens as a span, who holdeth the ocean in the hollow of his hand, and rideth upon the wings of the wind."[21] God had guided them through this harrowing voyage, she wrote, and "if you have a due sense of your preservation, your next consideration will be, for what purpose you are continued in Life?"

Abigail set herself up to answer her own question. Noting duties owed for privileges given, she provided a concise but forceful formula for his life: "every new Mercy you receive is a New Debt upon you, a new *obligation* to a diligent discharge of the various relations in which you stand connected; in the first place to your Great Preserver, in the next to Society in General, in particular to your Country, to your parents and to yourself." She then stated explicitly her understanding of acceptable human conduct: "The only sure and permanant foundation of virtue is Religion. Let this important truth be engraven upon your Heart, and that the foundation of Religion is Belief of the one only God, and a just sense of his attributes as a Being infinately wise, just, and good, to whom you *owe* the highest Reverence." That said, she explained to her young son that he must discharge his obligations by the "performance of certain duties which tend to the happiness and welfare of Society," expressed in one short sentence: " 'Thou shalt Love thy Neighbour as thyself.' "[22] She argued that it was his responsibility to repay his obligations by committing himself to public service.

"Justice, humanity and Benevolence are the duties you owe to society in general." But Abigail went further: "To your Country the same duties are incumbent upon you with the additional obligation of sacrificeing ease, pleasure, wealth and life itself for its defense and security." Abigail—operating from within a religiously prescribed social and familial tradition—was teaching civic responsibility before there was a republic. She was doing something else as well.

Unconsciously, perhaps, Abigail was justifying her own lack of normal family life for the past decade. She had sacrificed her own "ease, pleasure, wealth and [imminently, perhaps] life itself" for the defense and security of her country. Duty justified her existence just as it served as the motive for her sacrifices. She defined her political role as a woman in domestic terms. She characterized the sacrifices she made by the upheaval in her marriage, her household, and her management of family life as her personal contributions to the creation of her country.

She wasn't thinking about herself, however, as she continued: "To your parents you owe Love, reverence and obedience to all just and Equitable commands." Arriving at the end of her catalog, she concluded:

> To yourself—here indeed is a wide Field to expatiate upon. To become what you ought to be and, what a fond Mother wishes to see you, attend to some precepts and instructions from the pen of one who can have no motive but your welfare and happiness, and who wishes in this way to supply to you, the personal watchfulness and care which a seperation from you, deprives you of at a period of Life when habits are easiest acquired.

The letter went on to issue injunctions, analyses, and predictions, citing the dangers of self-deception, self-love, and passions. She called upon reason to control nature. "Virtue alone is happiness below," she stated, meaning on earth. Ironically, she concluded, "I will not over burden your mind at this time." In her extended finale, she promised to continue the subject of "Self-knowledge" at some later time and "give you my Sentiments upon your future conduct in life."[23]

Abigail's letters are replete with advice to her son: "Be dutifull my dear Son, be thoughtfull, be serious, do not gather the Thorns and the Thistles, but collect Such a Garland of flowers as will flourish in your native climate, and Bloom upon your Brows with an unfading verdure." She was anxious lest he would be as easily corrupted as educated. "This will rejoice the Heart and compensate for [my] continual anxiety."[24] She begged for reassurance. John Quincy wrote dutifully, describing his observations, his schools, his studies. Always he ended by sending his "duty" to his mother.

The powerful legacy of Puritan New England culture had survived into the late eighteenth century, governing values, attitudes, and behavior.[25] Abigail retained her belief in hierarchical relationships among family members, premised on duty owed reciprocally all along the line. These included social obligations that translated easily into civic obligations. The purpose of education involved more than individual gain, but obligations to the community. The religious basis of all these values retained primacy among people who read the Bible as the ultimate source of all human order and retained a providential understanding of human progress.

When the Reverend William Smith cited Luke at the marriage of his daughter, he chose a passage that described the sacrifices of John the Baptist, the martyr who came neither eating bread nor drinking wine. His mission was misread by his corrupt listeners, who indulged in material and worldly satisfaction. Sacrifice, like martyrdom, is not likely to deliver earthly rewards, but a moral life cannot be measured by standards of this world. This was the legacy that became the foundation of Abigail Adams's religion—and civic virtue.

Notes

1. Charles Francis Adams, *Letters of Mrs. Adams, The Wife of John Adams*, 2 vols. (Boston: C. C. Little and J. Brown, 1840), 1:xxxiii.

2. L. H. Butterfield et al., eds., *Adams Family Correspondence*, 7 vols. (Cambridge, Mass.: Belknap Press of Harvard University Press, 1962), 1:18. Cited hereafter as AFC.

3. Charles Francis Adams Jr., *Three Episodes of Massachusetts History: The Settlement of Boston Bay; The Antinomian Controversy; A Study of Church and Town Government*, 2 vols. (Boston: Houghton, Mifflin, 1893), 2:707–11.

4. For Abigail's early family life, see Edith B. Gelles, *Portia: The World of Abigail Adams* (Bloomington: Indiana University Press, 1992), and *Abigail Adams: A Writing Life* (New York: Routledge, 2002).

5. For John Adams's early life, see John Ferling, *John Adams: A Life* (Knoxville: University of Tennessee Press, 1992); Joseph Ellis, *Passionate Sage: The Character and Legacy of John Adams* (New York: W. W. Norton, 1993); David McCullough, *John Adams* (New York: Simon & Schuster, 2001).

6. For the Adamses' marriage, see Edith B. Gelles, *Abigail and John: Portrait of a Marriage* (New York: William Morrow, 2008).

7. AFC 2:150, Jan. 1777.

8. Adams Papers, microfilm edition, Reel 416, Jul. 1, 1813. Cited hereafter as AP. Cf. Matt. 10:29; Luke 12:6–7.

9. AFC 1:288, Oct. 1, 1775.

10. AFC 4:306, Apr. 10, 1782.

11. AP, Reel 416, July 1813. Cf. Heb. 12:2; John 14:2–3; Deut. 7:9.

12. AFC 1:51, post Jul. 14, 1765.

13. AFC 1:55, Oct. 6, 1766. Cf. Ps. 34:19.

14. AFC 1:89, Dec. 5, 1773.

15. AFC 1:172, Oct. 16, 1774. Cf. Matt. 24:6; Mark 13:7.

16. AFC 2:390, Feb. 15, 1778, to John Thaxter.

17. Philip Greven, *The Protestant Temperament: Patterns of Child-Rearing, Religious Experience, and the Self in Early America* (New York: Knopf, 1977).

18. Ibid., 178–79. Greven supplies the best explanation of the Puritan concept of duty and its application to child-rearing practices that I have found in contemporary literature. See also Joy Day Buel and Richard Buel Jr., *The Way of Duty: A Woman and Her Family in Revolutionary America* (New York: W. W. Norton, 1984).

19. John Adams's first mission to France in 1778 ended within a year, as Benjamin Franklin was appointed sole minister plenipotentiary. He returned home, only to sail again in June 1779 to participate in the negotiations of a French alliance. See Gelles, *Portia*, 136–39.

20. AFC 3:37, Jun. [10?], 1778.

21. AFC 3:310, Mar. 20, 1780. Cf. Isa. 40:22, 40:12; 2 Sam. 22:11; Pss. 18:10, 104:3.

22. AFC 3:311, Mar. 20, 1780, emphasis added. Cf. Lev. 19:18; Matt. 19:19; Mark 12:31. Benjamin Rush wrote in strikingly similar language to Abigail's:

"I beg leave to remark, that the only foundation for a useful education in a republic is to be laid in Religion." Also: "Religion teaches him, in all things to do to others what he would wish, in like circumstances, they should do to him." See Rush, "Of the Mode of Education Proper in a Republic," in *Essays: Literary, Moral and Philosophical* (Philadelphia, 1798), 8–9.

23. AFC 3:310–13, Mar. 20, 1780.

24. AFC 3:97–98, Sep. 29, 1778.

25. For continuity of religious themes in late-eighteenth-century America, see Ruth Bloch, "Religion and Ideological Change in the American Revolution," in Mark A. Noll, ed., *Religion and American Politics: From the Colonial Period to the 1980s* (New York: Oxford University Press, 1990), 44–61; also John P. Diggins, *The Lost Soul of American Politics: Virtue, Self-Interest, and the Foundations of Liberalism* (New York: Basic Books, 1984); Greven, *Protestant Temperament*; John M. Murrin, "Religion and Politics in America from the First Settlements to the Civil War," in Noll, ed., *Religion*, 19–43; Edmund S. Morgan, "The Puritan Ethic and the American Revolution," *William and Mary Quarterly*, 3rd ser., 24 (1967): 3–43. Morgan refers to a "set of values (and ideas) inherited from the age of Puritanism" (3).

CHAPTER 3

Samuel Adams

America's Puritan Revolutionary

GARY SCOTT SMITH

The "Indispensable Man"

Although scholars debate how important religion was to many of the nation's founders, they unanimously agree that Samuel Adams was one of the most devout. If George Washington is the "indispensable man" in winning the Revolutionary War and insuring that the new republic succeeded, Adams may lay claim to this title with regard to the colonies' decision to declare independence from England. He did much to publicize the colonists' grievances, defend their rights, and mobilize them to protest English policies. In so doing, this staunch Congregationalist continually argued that their cause was righteous. If Americans pursued their aims virtuously, God, who providentially directed history, would enable them to gain their independence. Adams continually exhorted patriots to maintain their religious fervor and lead godly lives. Inspired by his understanding of Scripture and strong faith in God, Adams worked to achieve three principal aims: attain American independence, protect people's constitutional liberties, and construct an upright society.[1] Fired by Puritan zeal and hatred of British rule, Adams used his political acumen and rhetorical skills to persuade many of his contemporaries to support independence.[2]

Samuel Adams was born on September 27, 1722, to Samuel and Mary Fifield Adams in Boston. His father owned a malt house and a wharf, and worked as a constable, tax assessor, selectman, justice of the peace, and representative to the Massachusetts Assembly. Samuel was educated at the Boston Latin School and at Harvard College, from which he graduated in 1740. During the 1740s and 1750s he earned a master of arts degree at Harvard, failed at a business enterprise, worked in the family brewery, wrote briefly for a newspaper, and served as a tax collector. Adams achieved little of note before age forty-two, but his life changed dramatically after the British decided to tax the colonies to raise revenue to fund their operations in North America. Upset by British intervention in American affairs, Adams organized Committees of Correspondence and helped lead the Boston Sons of Liberty. While serving as a member of the Massachusetts General Court from 1765 to 1774, he vigorously disputed British policies and agitated for independence primarily by writing legislative reports, publishing essays in the Boston *Gazette*, and organizing protests and boycotts. Adams served in the Continental Congress from 1774 to 1781, signed the Declaration of Independence, participated in the Massachusetts state constitutional conventions of 1779 and 1788, and was elected president of the Massachusetts state senate in 1781. He served as lieutenant governor of Massachusetts from 1789 to 1794 and as the state's governor from 1794 to 1797. The "helmsman of American independence" died in Boston on October 2, 1803, at the age of eighty-one.

In 1749 Adams married Elizabeth Checkley, the daughter of the pastor of Boston's New South Church. Elizabeth, a very devout Christian, died three weeks after giving birth to their sixth child in 1757. Her grieving husband declared that she had run "her Christian race with a remarkable steadiness and finished in triumph."[3] In 1764 Adams married Elizabeth Wells, the daughter of a Boston merchant, who also shared his strong Christian faith.

"Truly the Man of the Revolution"

His dogged determination and extraordinary political skills enabled Adams to play a pivotal role in the colonists' decision to sever their ties with England and declare independence. He spearheaded the creation of the Massachusetts Committee of Correspondence, which served as a model for other colonies, and led Boston's economic warfare against England in response to the Coercive Acts of 1774. Through his speeches and private conversations Adams helped persuade many other colonial representatives to promote joint objectives.[4]

More than any other American, biographer Benjamin Irvin argues, "Adams was responsible for making the Revolution happen."[5] "Would you believe," a British officer wrote in 1775, "that this immense continent, from New England to Georgia, is moved and directed by one man!—a man of ordinary birth and desperate fortune?" Adams, the officer complained, had used his "talent for factious intrigue" to foment revolution. John Adams declared that his cousin had been "born and tempered a wedge of steel to split" the lifeline "which tied North America to Great Britain."[6] Some New England Tories denounced Adams as the "grand Incendiary" who ignited the colonial conflagration, and labeled Boston's resistance "Adams' conspiracy."[7]

When Massachusetts royal governor Thomas Gage offered pardon to American rebels in 1775 if they laid down their arms, he excluded Samuel Adams and John Hancock because he deemed their offenses too villainous to be forgiven. Being excluded from Gage's Proclamation of Amnesty heightened Adams's renown. Adams was a devoted patriot, a skillful politician, and a keen student of human nature. Scholars describe him as "a pragmatic realist" who "pursued his political goals with an unflinching single-mindedness that impressed his allies and exasperated his foes."[8]

Adams also played an important role in the Revolutionary War, especially by helping to create a workable intercolonial government and to procure French money and troops. Moreover, as a member of the Continental Congress, he served on the Board of War (the major committee on army affairs), carefully studied military intelligence, and helped oversee strategic planning.[9] Thomas Jefferson maintained that Adams did more than any other member of Congress "in advising and directing our measures, in the Northern war especially."[10]

John Adams argued that his cousin had a very "thorough understanding of liberty . . . as well as the most habitual radical love of it."[11] Defending him in a letter to Englishman Richard Oswald, John declared: "You may have been taught to believe . . . that he eats little Children. But I assure you he is a Man of Humanity and Candor as well [as] Integrity."[12] Adams, prominent Pennsylvania loyalist Joseph Galloway maintained, "eats little, drinks little, sleeps little, thinks much, and is most decisive and indefatigable in the pursuit of his objects."[13] Even many of Adams's harshest detractors admitted that he was "remarkably upright" and not motivated by a desire for wealth or popularity.[14]

No one praised Adams more effusively than Jefferson, who labeled Adams "truly the *Man of the Revolution*."[15] "His principles, founded on the immovable basis of equal right & reason," the Virginian asserted in 1797, "have continued pure & unchanged."[16] While composing his first inaugural address, Jefferson wrote the Massachusetts statesman, "I often asked myself, is this exactly in the spirit of the patriarch of liberty, Samuel Adams? Is it as he would express it? Will he approve of it?"[17]

Adams has been called the last Puritan, a militant champion of democracy, the nation's first professional politician, the father of the American Revolution, the American Cato, and the nation's political parent.[18] He was one of America's senior statesmen in an era when age was highly respected.[19] When Adams was elected governor of Massachusetts, one pastor praised him as "venerable for his piety and unconquerable love of liberty."[20] After Adams's death in 1803, members of the House of Representatives wore crepe on their left arms for a month to express the nation's "gratitude and reverence" for the "undaunted and illustrious patriot."[21]

A Rabble-Rousing Demagogue or an Apostle of Liberty?

Since his death Adams has been lauded and lambasted, glorified and condemned, and often misunderstood. To renowned lecturer Edward Everett, he was "a New World reincarnation" of the Old Testament prophet

Samuel who was devoted to both Calvinist theology and republican principles. Adams would have been a reformer in any age in which power was abused, contended Boston journalist William Tudor.[22] Similarly, Adams's earliest biographers, most notably his grandson William V. Wells writing in 1865, depicted him as a knight in shining armor who rescued Americans from British tyranny and oppression. "Liberty as well as religion was his theme," Wells proclaimed. Led by Adams, Bostonians were "the champions of liberty for the world."[23]

Later scholars, by contrast, portrayed Adams as "a subversive, . . . a demagogue, [and] an advocate of mob violence."[24] Adams, Ralph Harlow argued, turned to politics to relieve "his troublesome mental problems." Adams had "the type of mind that made martyrs in the early days of the Christian Church, that sent heretics to the stake, or crusaders to the Holy Land, in the Middle Ages." His chief characteristics were "dogmatism, intensity of conviction, and 'exalted moral fervor.'"[25] Vernon Parrington labeled Adams a "professional agitator."[26] James Truslow Adams called him America's "greatest master in manipulating the masses," except perhaps for William Jennings Bryan.[27] To John C. Miller, Adams was a "pioneer in propaganda." The "'holy man' of Boston" was "a dour Calvinist" who continually complained "that New Englanders had lost their piety."[28] Clifford Shipton accused Adams of preaching "hate to a degree without rival."[29]

Since the 1960s, numerous scholars have helped rehabilitate Adams's reputation. William Appleman Williams contended that "as he was for his contemporaries," Adams had been "a troublemaker for American historians." Instead of identifying him "as the 'propagandist of the revolution,' a 'political radical,' 'the last Puritan,'" or "the most efficient agitator and organizer of mobs," Williams concluded, it was "both simpler and more accurate" to consider Adams a Calvinist who strove to create a "Christian corporate commonwealth."[30] Stewart Beach repudiated the common view that Adams was "a rabble-rousing demagogue."[31] Pauline Maier applauded Adams's work in guiding "Massachusetts through the decade before independence" and forging "a durable intercolonial union."[32] John K. Alexander praised Adams for exalting "virtue, liberty, a sense of duty, and education" and bringing "ordinary citizens into the political process."[33] To Ira Stoll, Adams "was the archetype of the religiously passionate American founder, the founder as biblical prophet, an apostle of liberty."[34]

While disagreeing about his motives and accomplishments, scholars concur that Adams's staunch religious commitments significantly shaped his political agenda and conduct. Among the founders, few were as pious as Samuel Adams. He attended church faithfully, read the Bible every day, observed the Sabbath scrupulously, and prayed diligently.[35] No Bostonian, Wells claimed, followed "the rigid faith of his pious ancestors" more closely than Adams.[36] Some Tories denounced Adams as a hypocrite who had "a religious Mask ready" for every occasion.[37] Most residents of Boston, however, considered Adams a sincere, "devout, old-fashioned Puritan." John Adams called him a "Man of . . . steadfast Integrity, . . . real as well as professed Piety, and a universal good Character."[38] Many scholars attribute the "intensity of his political passion . . . to his stern Puritan moralism."[39] Adams, writes Ira Stoll, "was the moral conscience of the American Revolution," never losing sight of its "political and religious goals, which for him were fundamentally intertwined."[40]

"A Religious Politician"

As a child, Adams's pious parents gave him extensive religious training and instilled Puritan values in him.[41] His father helped found the New South (Congregational) Church, and young Samuel worshipped regularly there. Samuel's father diligently instructed his children to be faithful to God and serve the community.[42] Adams's mother sang hymns to her son, insured that he read the Bible daily, and helped inject Puritan orthodoxy deeply into his thought and actions.[43]

Adams attended Harvard, where, in deference to his parents' wishes, he prepared for the ministry. Adams's education focused primarily on classical learning, logic, and natural philosophy. He learned Hebrew and studied with Edward Wigglesworth, a professor of divinity. Despite his parents' desires and his strong Christian commitment, Adams did not feel called to be a minister. He was most fascinated by the ancient Greek and Roman historians and English political philosophers, especially John Locke, who strongly influenced his views of liberty and republican government.[44] Inspired by their reading of Jean-Jacques Burlamaqui's *Principles of Natural Law* at Harvard, Adams and other key leaders of the American Revolution used reason to scrutinize nature to discern the laws God created.[45]

The First Great Awakening, which swept through New England from 1739 to 1741, deeply affected Adams's writings and actions. The books of Jonathan Edwards further strengthened Adams's commitment to Calvinism and conviction that God ruled the universe.[46] Adams, who signed many of his essays "a religious politician," became even more conservative, devout, and dedicated to Puritan principles as he aged.[47] His goal, Adams announced, was "to promote the *spiritual* kingdom of Jesus Christ."[48] In his will he declared his reliance "on the merits of Jesus Christ for the pardon of all my sins."[49]

Many founders, most notably George Washington, emphasized the role of God's providence in American history, especially with regard to the War for Independence. Few Americans were more convinced than Adams that God directed history or sought more diligently to be God's instrument. "I will endeavor by Gods Assistance, to act my little part well," Adams wrote to his wife in 1775, "and trust every thing which concerns me to his all-gracious Providence."[50] In September 1777, trying to inspire his fellow Congressmen, Adams declared that "numerous have been the manifestations of God's providence in sustaining us. In the gloomy period of adversity, we have had 'our cloud by day and pillar of fire by night.'" Writing to John Adams in 1780, he expressed gratitude for "the remarkeable Interposition of divine Providence in our favor." In a 1795 address to the Massachusetts legislature, Adams proclaimed, "Let the glory be given to Him who alone governs all events" and accomplished "his gracious designs."[51]

Adams's confidence in God's providence is also evident in his family relationships. He repeatedly assured his wife that he prayed for her health and safety every day. In December 1776, for example, he wrote to her: "I pray God to continue your Health and protect you in these perilous times from every kind of Evil."[52] Adams wrote similar letters to his daughter Hannah, often commending her "to the Care and Protection of the Almighty."[53] In 1780 he counseled Hannah to "Be equally attentive to every Relation into which all-wise Providence may lead you." He urged her to seek "most earnestly, the Favor of Him who made & supports you—who will supply you with whatever his infinite Wisdom sees best for you in this World, and above all, who has given us his Son to purchase for us the Reward of Eternal Life."[54] Adams exhorted her fiancé, Thomas Wells, to thank God for "the hourly Protection he afford us."[55]

Key Christian Convictions

Adams's Christian convictions are especially evident in his views of church-state relations, concerns about America's religious declension, rebuttal to Thomas Paine in 1802, and support of American independence. As did many other colonists, Adams supported an established church while resolutely defending "the free exercise of the rights of conscience" and vigorously opposing "any participation by the organized church in secular affairs."[56] Like many other revolutionary leaders, Adams denounced the attempt of some British Anglicans in the late 1760s and early 1770s to establish their church throughout the colonies. The joining of religious and civil power, he protested, had "been fatal to the Liberties of Mankind." "Ministerial Influence in America," he wrote, was "strong enough without the Aid of the Clergy." The Massachusetts Bay Colony strove to create a government that gave the clergy no formal authority.[57] Some were laboring "very zealously," he lamented, to establish a Protestant episcopate in America. This was especially alarming to those whose forebears had left their native country because of "the hardships they suffered, under such an establishment . . . in order peaceably to enjoy their privileges, civil and religious."[58]

At the same time, Adams argued (incorrectly) that "mutual toleration" of different denominations "is what all good and candid minds in all ages have ever practiced and both by precept and example, inculcated on mankind." Christians, he added, generally agreed "that this spirit of toleration in the fullest extent consistent with the being of civil society, 'is the chief . . . mark of the true church.' "[59] In November 1772 Boston adopted a declaration Adams penned, stating that each person had "a right peaceably and quietly to worship God according to the dictates of his conscience." "The eternal and immutable laws Of God and nature" clearly entitled all men to receive " 'just and true liberty, equal and impartial liberty' in matters spiritual and temporal."[60] In a proclamation as Massachusetts governor in the mid-1790s, Adams rejoiced that Americans enjoyed the "right of worshipping God according to His own Institutions and the honest dictates of our Consciences."[61]

Despite such rhetoric, as a member of the Massachusetts Constitutional Convention of 1780, Adams helped devise its provisions asserting that citizens had a "duty" to worship "the Supreme Being" and preserving the Congregational church as the state's established religion.[62] For him, religion's crucial role in maintaining the public morality societies need to function effectively justified this arrangement.

While Adams favored state support for Congregationalism and freedom of worship for all Protestants, he opposed toleration of Catholicism. In "The Rights of the Colonists as Christians" (1772) Adams insisted that "all christians except Papists" should be permitted to have their own worship services.[63] Locke, he noted, argued that sects that promulgated "Doctrines subversive of the Civil Government" should not be granted religious freedom. Catholics must be denied religious liberty because they taught that rulers their church excommunicated could be deposed and they considered the authority of the pope absolute.[64] Adams also opposed allowing Catholics "to hold public office" because they had divided loyalties; "either their allegiance to Rome was meaningless," which meant they were hypocrites, or they would side with the pope whenever his position clashed with the people they represented.[65] To Adams, Catholicism was not an alternative form of Christianity but rather the worship of *"graven images."* Thus for both political and religious reasons, he urged colonists to choose "sound Protestants" as their representatives and "avoid the danger of Popery."[66]

A "Christian Sparta"

Even more than most other founders, Adams was deeply concerned about American morality, and he frequently insisted that a republic could not succeed without upright citizens. Rectitude, he argued, would forever be "the Soul of a Republican Government."[67] "Virtue," he declared, "is our best Security. It is not possible that any State should long continue free" that did not supremely honor righteousness. Politicians who were "void of Virtuous Attachments in private life," he warned, would soon be "void of all Regard" for their country. It was crucial, therefore, that leaders have "*exemplary* Characters."[68] "Neither the wisest constitution nor the wisest laws," Adams maintained, "will secure the liberty and happiness of a people whose manners are universally corrupt."[69]

Adams was especially concerned about Boston's spiritual and moral health. He repeatedly chastised residents for forsaking the piety and simplicity of their Puritan forebears. Preoccupation with wealth and material possessions, he lamented, had caused many Bostonians to reject Christian faith and principles.[70] "My beloved Native town mortifies me greatly," he wrote a friend in 1778. He had hoped Boston "would afford examples of Industry, Frugality, Temperance and other publick Virtues." However, he complained, ambitious men were "confounding the Distinction between Virtue and Vice."[71]

Near the end of the war, Adams expressed his disgust at Boston's fashionable amusements, ostentatious displays of wealth, and gambling. Everywhere he saw extravagance and wastefulness. He protested that "the Example of Men of Religion, Influence & publick Station" threatened to counteract laws proposed to suppress "Idleness Dissipation & Extravagancy." "I once thought," he bemoaned, that Boston "would be the *Christian* Sparta. But Alas! Will men never be free! They will be free no longer than while they remain virtuous." People were "not worth saving" if they "lost their Virtue."[72] In various roles, including as the state's governor, Adams strove to elevate public morality. He led efforts in 1790 to stop the establishment of theaters in Boston, whose performances, he contended, promoted scandal and vice and "distracted audiences from their Christian responsibilities."[73]

To the end of his life, Adams accentuated the role religion played in creating moral citizens.[74] Despite the immorality and materialism he observed in Boston and the new nation, he never gave up hope that John Winthrop's city upon a hill could be built in America. To him, the ideal commonwealth blended "religious values and republican ideals." Adams continually urged Americans to emulate both the "charity and humility of his Puritan ancestors" and "the austerity and discipline of the Greek nation-states."[75]

These commitments prompted Adams to write to Thomas Paine in November 1802, after learning that Paine intended to publish another pamphlet attacking Christianity. Adams protested that, when he heard Paine had decided to defend "infidelity," he was "astonished" and "grieved that you had attempted a measure so injurious to the feelings and so repugnant to the true interest" of American citizens. "Do you think that your pen," Adams asked, "can unchristianize the mass of our citizens, or have you hopes of converting a few of them to assist you in so bad a cause?"[76] Adams expected instead that God would "erect a mighty empire in America" characterized by biblical morality and manners and zealous efforts to spread liberty and Christianity to the world.[77]

A Righteous Revolt

Although religion was not the principal reason for the American Revolution, it played a significant role in both encouraging Americans to seek independence and justifying their revolt. In the colonies politics and religion were inextricable. Much of the political literature of the 1760s and 1770s either was written by clergy or emphasized religious themes.[78]

Of all the founders, Adams arguably did the most to highlight the religious aspects of the colonial struggle for independence. During the crisis between the Continental Congress and the royal governor of Massachusetts, Adams called for days of fasting and prayer to "seek the Lord," helping give the American Revolution "the character of a moral and religious crusade."[79] Adams often employed religious rhetoric to describe colonial grievances and sometimes used biblical passages to criticize the monarchy. "What has been commonly called rebellion," he wrote in 1771, had often been a "glorious struggle" against "the lawless power of rebellious Kings and Princes." God appointed rulers to protect, but many of them instead enslaved their people. The Jews, Adams emphasized, exchanged the government God designed for them "for an absolute despotic monarchy." People must not obey the instructions of kings if doing so caused them to "sin against their own consciences." Clergy who called for "excessive" compliance with the government, he insisted, might be guilty of the sin of Ananias and Saphira—"*lying against the Holy Ghost!*"[80]

Americans' relationship with Britain, Adams argued, was adversely affecting their morality and inhibiting their calling to create a Christian society and spread the gospel to the world. Strongly influenced by the Puritan covenantal tradition and his understanding of history, Adams insisted that God blessed or punished nations and communities based on the moral conduct of their people. Because England had broken its contract with colonists by violating the agreements and laws it had stipulated and to which Americans had agreed, colonists had the right to form an independent government. As did many ministers, Adams also accused the British of thwarting America's mission to be light and salt to the world and of having a corrupting influence on colonists. The British, he protested, had tried to destroy Americans' "Sense of true Religion & Virtue." "The wise and just Ruler of the Universe" rewarded and punished nations, he added, "according to their general Character."[81] Thus if Americans wanted to receive God's blessing and fulfill the goal of their Puritan forebears to create a Christian commonwealth, they must cast off the chains of British oppression.[82]

Adams continually accused the British government of violating the rights of colonists as men and Christians, unjustly trying to enslave them, and pursuing devilish ends. The purpose of the Stamp Act, he alleged in 1768, was to inure people to see "themselves as the slaves of men; and the transition from thence to a subjection to Satan, is mighty easy."[83] "Have we not borne for these seven years past," Adams asked in 1771, "such *indignity* as no free people" ever suffered before?[84] Nevertheless, Adams had "an animating Confidence" that "the Supreme Disposer of Events" would not allow "a sensible, brave and virtuous People to be enslaved."[85] The "flagrant injustice and barbarity" of the Boston Port Bill, he claimed in 1774, was almost unmatched in human history. "But what else could have been expected from a parliament, too long under the . . . control of an administration" that had "totally lost" "all sense . . . of morality" and was instead "governed by passion, cruelty, and revenge"?[86]

Soon after dismissing the Massachusetts legislature in the spring of 1774, Governor Thomas Gage reportedly tried to bribe Adams to forsake his ideals. Adams responded that "no personal consideration shall induce me to abandon the righteous cause of my country."[87] He was "so fully satisfied in the Justice of our Cause," Adams wrote in October 1775, that he could "devoutly pray, that the righteous Disposer of all things would succeed our Enterprises."[88]

Although many members of the Continental Congress still wanted reconciliation with Britain in early 1776, Adams pushed for independence. George III, he protested, sought to gain complete control over the whole British empire.[89] When some advised compromising with Britain, Adams sharply replied that God "had already decided for liberty."[90] Doggedly opposing any concessions to Britain, he thundered, "I should advise persisting in our struggle for liberty, though it was revealed from heaven that . . . only one of a thousand [would] survive and retain his liberty. One such freeman" would "possess more virtue and enjoy more happiness than a thousand slaves."[91] In July 1776, Adams cynically noted that George III offered Americans a magnanimous pardon if they agreed to "be his abject Slaves."[92] Britain, he insisted, would "call wicked Men and Devils" to help subjugate America.[93] When tyrants gave people no other alternative than to rebel or be enslaved, then, as Locke had argued, insurgency was justified.[94]

Adams studied the Assyrians, Persians, Macedonians, and Romans to "discover the designs of Providence, and what measures we ought to pursue" in relation to Great Britain to "effectually co-operate with the Divine intentions." "From the [British] King . . . to the meanest freeman in the nation, all is corrupt," he lamented. England's princes, nobles, and members of Parliament all arrogated "the omnipotence of the Almighty." What advantages, he asked, were there to "being reconciled to such a government?" For more than twelve years, Americans had "labored by prayers, entreaties, non-importations, and every other peaceable mode of opposition" to prevent England from "enslaving us; but all to no purpose." "The King [had] despised and rejected them," and Parliament had "treated them with contempt." Even though their current situation might be "a judgment of God upon us for our sins," Americans would be much better off if they severed their relationship with England from which they received "little besides the contagion of vice and folly, not to say slavery and oppression."[95]

For all these reasons, Adams maintained, Americans had a righteous basis for revolt. In fact, he repeatedly warned, God would chastise the colonists if they submitted to tyranny. Like John Winthrop, he sometimes compared the colonists with the Israelites and argued that their behavior would bring God's blessings or curses.[96] "If Heaven punished Communities for their Vices," Adams declared, "how sore must be the Punishment of that Community who think the Rights of human Nature not worth struggling for and patiently submit to Tyranny." He prayed that New England would "never incur the Curse of Heaven for neglecting to defend her Liberties."[97] Adams was confident that God would protect those who conscientiously did their duty and someday give them "an ample Reward."[98]

Many clergy, Adams complained, were indifferent to America's "just & righteous Cause." Some were "Adulators of our Oppressors," while others were "extremely cautious" of publicly defending "the Rights of their Country" lest they offend "the little Gods on Earth." Adams urged colonists to assert and vindicate their "Rights as *Christians* as well as Men & Subjects."[99] He also denounced the argument that rulers could not be resisted because God used them "to punish Men for their Sins."[100]

Persuaded that Americans' quest for independence from Britain was biblically and morally justified, Adams repeatedly invoked God's aid to help them achieve this objective. Ending British oppression required a divine-human partnership. "May God afford" "abused" Americans, he declared, the necessary "Prudence, Strength & fortitude" to obtain "*their own* Liberties."[101] "God does the work," Adams argued, "but not without instruments"; no kingdom "was ever destroyed by a miracle which effectually excluded the agency of second causes. Even Herod . . . was devoured by vermin."[102] "May God give us Wisdom Fortitude Perseverance and every other virtue necessary" to maintain American independence, he wrote John Adams in September 1776.[103]

The "Smiles of Heaven"

Adams was confident that God would enable Americans, despite their immense military and economic obstacles, to prevail over England. "Righteous heaven," Adams assured a friend, would "graciously smile" on every courageous "and rational Attempt" to protect all God's "Gifts to man from the ravishing hand of lawless and brutal power."[104] "Our cause," Adams trumpeted in 1776, "is the Cause of God and Men, and virtuous Men by the Smiles of Heaven will bring it to a happy issue." If Americans depended upon God's blessing, He would "work Miracles if necessary to carry her thro this glorious Conflict and establish her feet upon a Rock."[105] Near the end of the war, Adams wrote his cousin John that America's cause was "righteous in the Sight of Heaven" and vital to humanity. "Our Creator has given us Understanding, Strength of Body and a Country full of Provisions. We must make a good Use of them, hoping that His blessing will crown our virtuous Struggle."[106]

Like Washington and many others, Adams credited American military victories to God, a conclusion easily reached given the numerical, tactical, and financial advantages the British enjoyed. Dozens of newspapers "invoked Divine Providence to explain revolutionary victories," and many ministers assured soldiers that God fought with them.[107] Perhaps no founder used more religious rhetoric during the war than Adams. After American successes in 1776, he urged patriots to "acknowledge the Goodness of the Supreme Being who . . . hath signally appeard for us."[108] "Gratitude is due to the God of Armies," Adams wrote to General Horatio Gates after his victory in Delaware in October 1777, because God had so favored "the Cause of America & of Mankind."[109] After the war ended, Adams declared, "we owe our unceasing gratitude to the Supreme Ruler of the universe, who safely carried us through our arduous struggle for freedom."[110]

In addition to marshalling religious arguments to justify American independence and trumpeting God's providential assistance of the patriots' cause, Adams contended that ultimate political sovereignty belonged to God and professed his desire to serve divine aims as a political leader. Government, he proclaimed, "is an ordinance of Heaven," which "the all-benevolent Creator" had designed to insure human happiness.[111] God had given people basic rights, he insisted, which governments must respect. Adams hoped that people everywhere would understand "their natural and just rights" and form systems of civil government to promote effectively "their Social Security and Happiness."[112] A legislature, he proclaimed, had "no Right to absolute arbitrary Power over the Lives and

Fortunes of the People." "Too high" even for angels, this prerogative belonged to "Deity alone."[113] A magistrate, he contended, needed "to be a Man of Religion and Piety" who understood both human nature and the organization and aims of government.[114] As governor, Adams hoped that his administration would "meet with the approbation of God, the Judge of all."[115] Adams, like King Solomon, frequently asked God, "the Fountain of all Wisdom," for wisdom to rule justly.[116]

To Adams, religion and political liberty were "intimately connected" and therefore always rose or fell together.[117] Both political and religious liberty, Adams maintained, were gifts of God that the state must insure and citizens must vigorously defend in order to establish an upright society. "In the state of nature," he asserted, "every man has a right to think and act" according to his own beliefs, which were subject only to the Creator's "laws and ordinances." The "bounteous Author of all things," Adams argued, had bequeathed both life and liberty to people. Liberty was God's "choicest gift" to humanity and was "guided by the laws of infinite wisdom."[118] "The Love of Liberty," Adams contended, "is interwoven in the soul of man" and could "never be totally extinguished." Because freedom was "the gift of God Almighty," no one had the right to "voluntarily become a slave."[119] Moreover, God had planted the love of freedom in everyone, so no matter how "irrational, ungenerous, and unsocial" individuals were, they could be "enlightened by Experience, Reflection, Education, and civil, and Political Institutions."[120] As governor, he appointed a day of fasting in 1795 for people to pray that Americans would continue to enjoy "the light of the Gospel and the rights of conscience . . . so that the name of GOD may be exalted and their own liberty and happiness secured."[121] Adams also asked that God's wisdom direct all their deliberations and enable Americans to "confirm and perpetuate" public liberty and protect citizens' "private and personal rights."[122]

Convinced that the American struggle for independence had global ramifications, Adams continually called for the spread of freedom throughout the world. He hoped that France, guided by "a spirit of wisdom and true religion" and relying on God's "Almighty Arm," would soon found a republic "on the just and equal rights of men."[123] Writing to Jefferson in 1801, Adams complained that "Tyrant Kings" tried "to exterminate those rights and liberties which the Gracious Creator has granted to Man."[124] Adams frequently asked God to end "all Tyranny and Usurpation" and to bring harmony and peace to the world. He entreated God to enable nations to create "wise systems of Civil Government, founded in the equal Rights of Men and calculated to establish their permanent Security and Welfare."[125] Adams beseeched "the Supreme Ruler of the World" to break "the rod of tyrants" into pieces, set the oppressed free, and end all wars on Earth.[126] For Adams, the expansion of democracy seemed to be a prerequisite for "a messianic age of world peace."[127]

Adams also continually urged his countrymen to protect liberty and promote equality in their new republic and to insure that future generations shared in these blessings. People usually defended the rights of others in order to safeguard their own freedom and equality, but they did not always act reasonably. Therefore, he argued, republican constitutions were necessary "to protect their fundamental rights." Adams demanded that "the just rights" of citizens be "defended by Constitutions founded upon equal rights."[128] The success of a government depended on fair elections.[129] The ideal biblical form of government, he contended, was a republic, which would thrive only if its citizens acted virtuously.[130] "The Constitution must be my rule," Adams proclaimed, "and the true interest of my Constituents, whose agent I am, my invariable object."[131] By having "the Christian Spirit of Piety, Benevolence," love of country, and "a sacred regard" for fundamental constitutional principles, Adams maintained, Americans could avoid God's "desolating Judgments."[132]

Adams frequently warned Americans that they would be happy only if they trusted in God and abided by His moral standards. Unlike the Romans, he claimed, Americans had no desire to dominate the world. Their "righteous" object was instead to procure "the Liberty of our Country and the Rights of human Nature." He urged citizens to acquire and model those moral habits and political traits that would enable succeeding generations to safeguard the nation Americans had purchased "with our Toils and Dangers."[133] He prayed that God would increase his countrymen's virtue and help them enjoy the liberties they had long highly prized.[134]

Adams insisted that education had a pivotal role to play in promoting human liberty, happiness, and morality. He repeatedly urged the state to educate all children to encourage rectitude; underscore their responsibilities to God, others, and society; and make them "better custodians of liberty."[135] Adams exhorted schools to teach "youth the fear and Love" of God and universal philanthropy, and as governor he extolled the value of education in all four of his state of the state messages.[136] Influenced by his arguments, Bostonians in 1789 took steps to provide free public education for both boys and girls.[137]

As governor, Adams went well beyond the civil religious rhetoric used by most founders and the nation's early presidents. Like many other leaders, he implored Americans to recognize their dependence upon God, fulfill their obligations to Him, and express their gratitude for His bountiful provisions.[138] However, he also repeatedly urged individuals to repent of their disobedience to God's laws, accept His "gracious and free pardon" through Jesus Christ, and work to spread Christianity and build God's kingdom throughout the world.[139]

While most founders and presidents rarely mentioned Jesus publicly, Adams frequently did. In a 1794 proclamation, he asked God "to cause the Religion of Jesus Christ . . . to spread far and wide, till the whole earth shall be filled with His glory."[140] The next year Adams prayed that all people might know and enjoy "the Peaceful and Glorious Reign of our Divine Redeemer."[141] In 1796 Adams beseeched God to "speedily" establish "the Kingdom of our Lord and Saviour Jesus Christ . . . everywhere" and inspire all people to submit to "the Prince of Peace."[142] Adams also expressed his hope that through the "sanctifying influence" of the Holy Spirit "our hearts and manners may be corrected, and we become a reformed and happy People."[143]

"The Father of the American Revolution"

Few of the founders made as great a financial and personal sacrifice as did Samuel Adams to help Americans win their independence and the fragile new republic to survive, and few of them cared as little about his legacy.[144] As Adams told his wife, "I have long ago learned to deny my self many of the sweetest Gratifications in Life for the Sake of my Country."[145] Speaking for many, the Boston *Independent Chronicle* declared that "the Father of the American Revolution" had been "the undeviating friend of civil and religious liberty."[146]

Near the end of his long life, Adams rejoiced in a letter to Jefferson that God seemed "to be rapidly changing the sentiments of Mankind in Europe and America. May Heaven grant that the principles of Liberty and virtue, truth and justice . . . pervade the whole Earth."[147] Adams expected the "Practice of the exalted Virtues of the Christian system" to introduce a "Golden Age" and fill the earth with "the Knowledge of the Lord." When this millennium began, Adams wrote his cousin John, "if there shall be any need of Civil Government, indulge me in the fancy that it will be in the republican form, or something *better*."[148] Throughout his long life Adams, inspired by his faith in God and confidence in republican principles, worked energetically and effectively to achieve and sustain American independence and advance God's kingdom on earth.

Notes

1. John K. Alexander, *Samuel Adams: America's Revolutionary Politician* (Lanham, Md.: Rowman and Littlefield, 2002), 223. The biography that most emphasizes Adams's strong faith is Ira Stoll, *Samuel Adams: A Life* (New York: Free Press, 2008).

2. Alexander Winston, "Firebrand of the Revolution," 1, http://www.americanheritage.com/articles/magazine/ah/1967/3. Cf. Mark Puls, *Samuel Adams: Father of the American Revolution* (New York: Palgrave Macmillan, 2006), 16–17, 234–37. Adams largely accepted the Puritans' view of covenant, the role of the civil magistrate, the creation of a godly commonwealth, the need for individual and corporate repentance and moral reform, resistance, revolution, and the political battle against the devil as developed in the writings of John Calvin and the ideology and practices of the Huguenots, the Marian exiles, and the English Puritans in the hundred years between 1560 and 1660. See Michael Walzer, *The Revolution of the Saints* (Cambridge, Mass.: Harvard University Press, 1965), esp. 3, 12, 18, 57–65, 78–81, 108–12, 167–71, 269–70, 300–302.

3. Quoted in William V. Wells, *The Life and Public Services of Samuel Adams*, 3 vols. (Boston: Little, Brown, 1865), 3:429.

4. Alexander, *Samuel Adams*, 155, 142.

5. Benjamin H. Irvin, *Samuel Adams: Son of Liberty, Father of Revolution* (New York: Oxford University Press, 2002), 164.

6. Ibid.

7. Winston, "Firebrand of the Revolution," 1.

8. John R. Galvin, *Three Men of Boston* (New York: Crowell, 1976), 292; Alexander, *Samuel Adams*, 142.

9. Alexander, *Samuel Adams*, 150; Stoll, *Samuel Adams*, 162–67, 190–92, 196–99.

10. Quoted in Alexander, *Samuel Adams*, 157.

11. Quoted in George Bancroft, *History of the United States, from the Discovery of the Continent*, 6 vols. (Port Washington, N.Y.: Kennikat, 1967), 3:157.

12. John Adams Diary, Nov. 17, 1782, http://www.masshist.org.

13. Quoted in Alexander, *Samuel Adams*, 142.

14. Ibid., 223.

15. Quoted in Irvin, *Samuel Adams*, 9.

16. Thomas Jefferson to James Sullivan, Feb. 9, 1797, Thomas Jefferson Papers, Library of Congress.

17. Jefferson to Adams, Mar. 29, 1801, Thomas Jefferson Papers.

18. Alexander, *Samuel Adams*, 222; Stewart Beach, *Samuel Adams: The Fateful Years, 1764–1776* (New York: Dodd, Mead, 1965), 14; Gary B. Nash, *The Unknown American Revolution* (New York: Viking, 2005), 97; Wells, *Life of Adams*, 3:447.

19. Pauline Maier, *The Old Revolutionaries: Political Lives in the Age of Samuel Adams* (New York: Vintage Books, 1980), 16–17.

20. The Reverend Perez Fobes, quoted in Wells, *Life of Adams*, 3:344.

21. Quoted in Irvin, *Samuel Adams*, 163.

22. Edward Everett, "The Battle of Lexington, April 19, 1835," in *Orations and Speeches*, 4 vols. (Boston: C. C. Little and J. Brown, 1850–68), 1:545; William Tudor, *Life of James Otis* (Boston: Wells and Lilly, 1823), 275–76. The first quotation is from Maier, *Old Revolutionaries*, 47, which called my attention to these other sources.

23. Wells, *Life of Adams*, 2:153.

24. Maier, *Old Revolutionaries*, 4. My literature review depends in part on Maier, *Old Revolutionaries*, 5–17.

25. Ralph Volney Harlow, *Samuel Adams: Promoter of the American Revolution: A Study in Psychology and Politics* (New York: H. Holt, 1923), 65, 187, 356.

26. Vernon Parrington, *The Colonial Mind, 1620–1800* (New York: Harcourt, Brace, 1927), 233.

27. James Truslow Adams, *The Epic of America* (Boston: Little, Brown, 1931), 81.

28. John C. Miller, *Sam Adams: Pioneer in Propaganda* (Stanford, Calif.: Stanford University Press, 1936), 87.

29. Clifford Shipton, "Samuel Adams," in *Sibley's Harvard Graduates: Biographical Sketches of Those Who Attended Harvard College*, vol. 10, 1736–40 (Boston: Massachusetts Historical Society, 1958), 420–65, esp. 434, 463.

30. William Appleman Williams, "Samuel Adams: Calvinist, Mercantilist, Revolutionary," *Studies on the Left* 1, no. 2 (Winter 1960): 47–48.

31. Beach, *Samuel Adams*, 9. Cf. Charles W. Akers, "Sam Adams—and Much More," *New England Quarterly* 47 (Mar. 1974): 120, 130.

32. Maier, *Old Revolutionaries*, 5.

33. Alexander, *Samuel Adams*, book jacket, ix.

34. Stoll, *Samuel Adams*, 8.

35. E.g., Miller, *Sam Adams*, 7, 84.

36. Wells, *Life of Adams*, 2:18.

37. Douglass Adair and John A. Schutz, *Peter Oliver's Origin and Progress of the American Revolution: A Tory View* (San Marino, Calif.: Huntington Library, 1961), 41.

38. Adams, *Diary*, Dec. 23, 1765.

39. E.g., Patricia U. Bonomi, *Under the Cope of Heaven: Religion, Society, and Politics in Colonial America*, updated ed. (New York: Oxford University Press, 2003), 104; Norman Cousins, ed., *"In God We Trust": The Religious Beliefs and Ideas of the American Founding Fathers* (New York: Harper, 1958), 344. Cf. Beach, *Samuel Adams*, 13–15.

40. Stoll, *Samuel Adams*, 9.

41. Cass Canfield, *Samuel Adams's Revolution, 1765–1776: With the Assistance of George Washington, Thomas Jefferson, Benjamin Franklin, John Adams, George III, and the People of Boston* (New York: Harper and Row, 1976), 3; Dennis Fradin, *Samuel Adams: The Father of American Independence* (New York: Clarion Books, 1998), 20; William M. Fowler Jr., *Samuel Adams: Radical Puritan* (New York: Longman, 1997), 4.

42. Fowler, *Samuel Adams*, 4.

43. David L. Holmes, *The Faiths of the Founding Fathers* (New York: Oxford University Press, 2006), 144; Wells, *Life of Adams*, 1:3; Beach, *Samuel Adams*, 16.

44. Irvin, *Samuel Adams*, 21, 23; Beach, *Samuel Adams*, 19; Alexander, *Samuel Adams*, 3; Wells, *Life of Samuel Adams*, 1:6.

45. Frank Lambert, *The Founding Fathers and the Place of Religion in America* (Princeton, N.J.: Princeton University Press, 2003), 167.

46. Williams, "Samuel Adams," 49–50; Stoll, *Samuel Adams*, 21.

47. E.g., Galvin, *Three Men of Boston*, 301; Irvin, *Samuel Adams*, 148.

48. Samuel Adams and Thomas Cushing, letter to Rev. G—— W——, Nov. 11, 1765, in *The Writings of Samuel Adams*, ed. Harry Alonzo Cushing, 4 vols. (New York: G. P. Putnam's Sons, 1904–08), 1:33 (hereinafter *Writings*).

49. "Last Will and Testament of Samuel Adams," in Wells, *Life of Adams*, 3:379.

50. Adams, letter to Elizabeth Adams, Nov. 7, 1775, in *Writings*, 3:240. Cf. Adams, letter to Elizabeth Adams, Jun. 28, 1775, in *Writings*, 3:220; Adams, letter to Elizabeth Adams, Nov. 24, 1780, in *Writings*, 4:226–27.

51. Wells, *Life of Adams*, 2:493; Adams, letter to John Adams, Dec. 17, 1780, in *Writings* 4:232; Samuel Adams, "Address to the Legislature in 1795 . . ." in Wells, *Life of Adams*, 3:347.

52. Adams, letter to Elizabeth Adams, Dec. 26, 1776, in *Writings*, 3:334. Cf. Adams, letter to Elizabeth Adams, Mar. 10, 1776, in *Writings*, 3:270; Adams, letter to Elizabeth Adams, Dec. 9, 1776, in *Writings*, 3:326.

53. Adams, letter to Hannah Adams, Sep. 8, 1778, in *Writings*, 4:57.

54. Adams, letter to Hannah Adams, Aug. 17, 1780, in *Writings*, 4:201.

55. Adams, letter to Thomas Wells, Nov. 22, 1780, in *Writings*, 4:225.

56. Williams, "Samuel Adams," 49.

57. Adams, letter to Arthur Lee, Sep. 27, 1771, in *Writings*, 2:236.

58. See *Writings*, 1:149. On this issue, see Carl Bridenbaugh, *Mitre and Sceptre: Transatlantic Faiths, Ideas, Personalities, and Politics, 1689–1775* (New York: Oxford University Press, 1962), esp. 91–99, 215–17, 238–41, 246–47, 267–68, 288–89, 316, 322; and Arthur L. Cross, *The Anglican Episcopate and the American Colonies* (Hamden, Conn.: Archon Books, 1964 [1902]), esp. 161–94, 215–25.

59. "The Rights of the Colonists: A List of Violations of Rights and a Letter of Correspondence, adopted by Town of Boston," Nov. 20, 1772, *Writings*, 2:352.

60. Ibid.

61. Samuel Adams, Proclamation, Oct. 6, 1796, *Writings*, 4:394.

62. See Holmes, *Founding Fathers*, 148.

63. "The Rights of the Colonists," 355.

64. Ibid., 353.

65. Williams, "Samuel Adams," 49.

66. *Boston Gazette*, Apr. 11, 1768, in *Writings*, 1:205. See also *Boston Gazette*, Apr. 4, 1768, in *Writings*, 1:202; *Boston Gazette*, Apr. 18, 1768, in *Writings*, 1:208; *Boston Gazette*, Nov. 25, 1771, in *Writings*, 2:279–81; and Adams, letter to James Warren, Oct. 3, 1775, in *Warren-Adams Letters, Being Chiefly a Correspondence among John Adams, Samuel Adams, and James Warren*, 1917–25, 2 vols. (New York: AMS Press, 1972), 1:125.

67. Adams, letter to James Warren, Jan. 16, 1777, in *Warren-Adams Letters*, 1:286.

68. Adams, letter to James Warren, Nov. 4, 1775, in *Warren-Adams Letters*, 1:171–72.

69. Quoted in Wells, *Life of Adams*, 1:22. Cf. Adams, letter to Samuel Cooper, 1778, in *Writings*, 4:108; Adams, letter to John Scollay, Apr. 30, 1776, in *Writings*, 3:286; Adams, letter to James Warren, Nov. 23, 1778, in *Warren-Adams Letters*, 2:67.

70. Irvin, *Samuel Adams*, 33.

71. Adams, letter to James Warren, Nov. 9, 1778, in *Warren-Adams Letters*, 2:66.

72. Adams, letter to John Scollay, Dec. 30, 1780, in *Writings*, 4:236–38. Cf. Adams, letter to Elizabeth Adams, Sep. 28, 1778, in *Writings*, 4:65; Adams, letter to William Cooper, Sep. 30, 1778, in *Writings*, 4:67.

73. Irvin, *Samuel Adams*, 149–50.

74. Alexander, *Samuel Adams*, 216.

75. Irvin, *Samuel Adams*, 148. Cf. Stoll, *Samuel Adams*, 60–61.

76. Adams, letter to Thomas Paine, Nov. 30, 1802, in *Writings*, 4:412.

77. Boston *Gazette*, Aug. 24, 1772, quoted in Miller, *Sam Adams*, 311. See also Miller, *Sam Adams*, 359.

78. Kevin Phillips, *The Cousins' Wars: Religion, Politics, and the Triumph of Anglo-America* (New York: Basic Books, 1999), 95. Cf. Gordon S. Wood, *Creation of the American Republic, 1776–1787* (New York: W. W. Norton, 1969), 8.

79. Miller, *Sam Adams*, 84.

80. Boston *Gazette*, Nov. 11, 1771, in *Writings*, 2:268–73.

81. Adams, letter to John Scollay, Apr. 30, 1776, in *Writings*, 3:286.

82. Williams, "Samuel Adams," 50. Cf. Wood, *The Creation of the American Republic*, 91–124; Alan Heimert, *Religion and the American Mind, from the Great Awakening to the Revolution* (Cambridge, Mass.: Harvard University Press, 1966), chaps. 8 and 9; Alice M. Baldwin, *The New England Clergy and the American Revolution* (New York: F. Ungar, 1958).

83. Boston *Gazette*, Apr. 11, 1768, in *Writings*, 1:203.

84. Boston *Gazette*, Dec. 2, 1771, in *Writings*, 2:283. Cf. Boston *Gazette*, Oct. 5, 1772, in *Writings*, 2:336.

85. Committee of Correspondence for the Town of Boston, Sep. 21, 1773, quoted in Bancroft, *History of the United States*, 3:444.

86. Adams, letter to Arthur Lee, May 18, 1774, in *Writings*, 3:117.

87. As reported by Hannah Adams and quoted in Alexander, *Samuel Adams*, 136.

88. Adams, letter to Elizabeth Adams, Oct. 20, 1775, in *Writings*, 3:228. Cf. Adams, letter to James Warren, Sep. 17, 1777, in *Warren-Adams Letters*, 1:369.

89. Alexander, *Samuel Adams*, 153.

90. Winston, "Firebrand of the Revolution," 6.

91. Quoted in ibid.

92. Adams, letter to Samuel Cooper, July 20, 1776, in *Writings*, 3:302.

93. Adams, letter to James Warren, Dec. 12, 1776, in *Warren-Adams Letters*, 1:281.

94. Alexander, *Samuel Adams*, 223.

95. Samuel Adams, "People in General," in Wells, *Life of Adams*, 2:369–74. Cf. Adams, letter to James Warren, Oct. 20, 1778, in *Warren-Adams Letters*, 2:58.

96. See Stoll, *Samuel Adams*, 89–90. For examples, see Adams, letter to Benjamin Franklin, June 29, 1771, in *Writings* 2:180, 184; Adams, letter to Arthur Lee, Nov. 3, 1772, in *Writings*, 2:345.

97. Adams, letter to Elizabeth Adams, Dec. 19, 1779, in *Writings*, 3:328–29.

98. Adams, letter to Elizabeth Adams, Jan. 29, 1777, in *Writings*, 3:349.

99. Adams, letter to Elbridge Gerry, Nov. 14, 1772, in *Writings*, 2:349.

100. Adams, letter to James Warren, Oct. 20, 1778, in *Warren-Adams Letters*, 2:58.

101. Adams, letter to Arthur Lee, Sep. 27, 1771, in *Writings*, 2:231.

102. "To the People in General," 375 ff. Cf. Adams, letter to Arthur Lee, Oct. 31, 1771, in *Writings*, 2:267.

103. Adams, letter to John Adams, Sep. 16, 1776, in *Writings*, 3:313.

104. Adams, letter to James Warren, Mar. 31, 1774, in *Warren-Adams Letters*, 1:25.

105. Adams, letter to James Warren, Dec. 12, 1776, in *Warren-Adams Letters*, 1:280–81.

106. Adams, letter to John Adams, Dec. 17, 1780, in *Writings*, 4:231.

107. J. C. D. Clark, *The Language of Liberty, 1660–1832: Political Discourse and Social Dynamics in the Anglo-American World* (New York: Cambridge University Press, 1994), 119.

108. Adams, letter to James Warren, Apr. 16, 1776, in *Warren-Adams Letters*, 1:224.

109. Adams, letter to Horatio Gates, Oct. (?) 1777, in *Writings*, 3:414. Cf. Adams, letter to Warren, Oct. 29, 1777, in *Warren-Adams Letters*, 1:377.

110. Adams, inaugural speech, June 3, 1794 in Wells, *Life of Adams*, 3:345.

111. Boston *Gazette*, Dec. 19, 1768, in *Writings*, 1:269.

112. Adams, Proclamation, Oct. 6, 1796, in *Writings*, 4:395.

113. *The Voters and Proceedings of the Freeholders . . . of the Town of Boston . . .* (Boston, 1772), 7.

114. Adams, letter to James Warren, Oct. 29, 1777, in *Warren-Adams Letters*, 1:377.

115. Samuel Adams, "To the Legislature of Massachusetts," May 31, 1796, in *Writings*, 4:393.

116. Samuel Adams, "To the Legislature of Massachusetts," Jun. 3, 1795, in *Writings*, 4:376. Cf. Adams, "To the Legislature of Massachusetts," Jan. 17, 1794, in *Writings*, 4:354.

117. Boston *Gazette*, Oct. 5, 1772, in *Writings*, 2:336. Cf. Adams, letter to William Checkley, in *Writings*, 2:381.

118. Wells, *Life of Adams*, 1:19–20.

119. Adams, *The Rights of Colonists*, 419. Cf. Adams, letter to John Adams, Oct. 4, 1790, in *Writings*, 4:342.

120. Adams, letter to John Adams, Nov, 25, 1790, in *Writings*, 4:349.

121. Adams, Proclamation, Mar. 5, 1795, in Wells, *Life of Adams*, 3:347.

122. Adams, "To the Legislature of Massachusetts," May 31, 1796, in *Writings*, 4:393.

123. Samuel Adams, Proclamation, Feb. 19, 1794, in *Writings*, 4:362.

124. Adams, letter to Thomas Jefferson, Nov. 18, 1801, in *Writings*, 4:411.

125. Samuel Adams, Proclamation, Oct. 14, 1795, in *Writings*, 4:385.

126. Samuel Adams, Proclamation, Mar. 20, 1797, in *Writings*, 4:407. Cf. Adams, Proclamation, Oct. 6, 1796, in *Writings*, 4:395.

127. Stoll, *Samuel Adams*, 226. See Adams, letter to Richard Henry Lee, Apr. 14, 1785, in *Writings*, 4:314–15.

128. Adams, Proclamation, March 5, 1795, in Wells, *Life of Adams*, 3:347. Although Adams saw a strong federal government as a danger to liberty, he did vote in the Massachusetts convention to ratify the Constitution.

129. Samuel Adams, "To the Legislature of Massachusetts," Jan. 27, 1797, in *Writings*, 4:400.

130. Alexander, *Samuel Adams*, 222–23.

131. Samuel Adams "To the Legislature of Massachusetts," Jan. 17, 1794, in *Writings*, 4:354.

132. Adams, Proclamation, Mar. 20, 1797, in *Writings*, 4:406.

133. Adams, letter to Alexander McDougall, May 13, 1782, in *Writings*, 4:272.

134. Adams, letter to Elizabeth Adams, Dec. 19, 1779, in *Writings*, 3:329.

135. Alexander, *Samuel Adams*, 193–94. E.g., Adams, "To the Legislature of Massachusetts," Jan. 27, 1797, in *Writings*, 4:401.

136. Adams, letter to John Adams, Oct. 4, 1790, in *Writings*, 4:343.

137. Alexander, *Samuel Adams*, 193–94.

138. E.g., Adams, Proclamation, Oct. 14, 1795, in *Writings*, 4:383.

139. Adams, Proclamation, Feb. 19, 1794, in *Writings*, 4:361.

140. Ibid., 4:362.

141. Adams, Proclamation, Oct. 14, 1795, in *Writings*, 4:385.

142. Adams, Proclamation, Mar. 20, 1797, in *Writings*, 4:407.

143. Adams, Proclamation, Oct. 6, 1796, in *Writings*, 4:395.

144. Compared with many other founders, he left little correspondence. Moreover, he often commanded those to whom he wrote letters to "Burn this," and he consigned "nearly all of his correspondence files to the flames." See Galvin, *Three Men of Boston*, 293. Cf. Puls, *Samuel Adams*, 230; Irvin, *Samuel Adams*, 9.

145. Adams, letter to Elizabeth Adams, Jul. 30, 1775, in *Writings*, 3:221.

146. Quoted in Alexander, *Samuel Adams*, 221.

147. Adams, letter to Thomas Jefferson, Apr. 24, 1801, in *Writings*, 4:410.

148. Adams, letter to John Adams, Oct. 4, 1790, in *Writings*, 4:343. Cf. Adams, letter to John Adams, Nov. 25, 1790, in *Writings*, 4:348.

CHAPTER 4

Oliver Ellsworth's Calvinist Vision of Church and State in the Early Republic

W I L L I A M   R.   C A S T O

Oliver Ellsworth (1745–1807) is, unfortunately, an obscure person to most twenty-first-century Americans—even to historians. But he was well-regarded in late-eighteenth-century America and played an influential role in creating our federal republic. James Madison wrote that he "always regarded [Ellsworth's] talents of a high order, and [believed] they were generally so regarded." In the Senate, Ellsworth, who was the de facto majority leader until 1796, exerted so much influence that Aaron Burr joked, "If Ellsworth had happened to spell the name of the Deity with two d's, it would have taken the Senate three weeks to expunge the superfluous letter." Ellsworth played a particularly influential role in framing the Bill of Rights' religion clauses. He was the Senate floor leader for the amendments and the Senate chairman for the Bill of Rights Committee of Conference. His understanding of the religion clauses is particularly interesting because few, if any, founders had a more comprehensive or deeper understanding of the role of religion in public affairs.[1]

Ellsworth was a thoroughgoing Calvinist. As a boy he studied under Joseph Bellamy, one of New England's leading theologians. After graduation from the College of New Jersey (now

Princeton University), he entered postgraduate studies with another leading theologian, John Smalley. Although Ellsworth became a lawyer and a highly successful judge and politician, he continued his theological studies for the rest of his life. Toward the end of his life, he helped write *A Summary of Christian Doctrine and Practice*, which restated Connecticut's orthodox Calvinism. Shortly after Ellsworth's retirement as chief justice of the United States Supreme Court, a young Daniel Webster noted with respect that Ellsworth was "as eminent for piety as for talents" and that piety made him an "ornament" of the profession.[2]

Ellsworth was a child of the Great Awakening that swept through America in the early 1740s and was a powerful source of political turmoil in Connecticut. The Awakening was sparked in 1740 by George Whitfield's electrifying revival tour. Almost immediately itinerant preachers began holding revival meetings throughout New England. These revivalists, who were called New Lights, rejected the halfway covenant, which had loosened the rules for church membership. Instead, the revivalists insisted that every individual must personally experience his or her election to salvation in order to be admitted to the Lord's Supper and to enjoy other privileges of adult membership in the church. This challenge upset most members of the Standing Order, who described themselves as Old Lights. For a period of ten or fifteen years, the Old Lights conducted a campaign of religious harassment of the New Lights. Eventually, however, the New Lights achieved political dominance. First, the New Lights formed a political alliance with the Anglicans, who were always in the minority. Later, the New Lights and the Old Lights reached an accommodation.[3]

During the Revolutionary War, Ellsworth progressed from obscure but important administrative assignments to become one of the state's most important young political leaders. By 1780, at age thirty-five, he was state's attorney for Hartford County and a member of the upper house of the state legislature and the Council of Safety. He also served six years in the Continental Congress.[4]

After the war, Ellsworth was appointed by the General Assembly to the Connecticut Superior Court, the state's highest judicial court, and served until 1789. During this service he also represented Connecticut at the Constitutional Convention in Philadelphia and played a significant role in crafting the Constitution. In the Convention's plenary sessions, he helped shape the Constitution on comparatively minor points like enlarging Congress's authority to define crimes and the election of senators by state legislatures rather than popular vote. More significantly, he was a member of the five-person Committee of Detail, which wrote the working draft of the document finally adopted by the Convention.[5]

Ellsworth also played a significant role in brokering some of the Convention's most important compromises. He was a leading proponent of the compromise on the importation of slaves, and he was similarly involved in resolving the dispute over whether states would be represented in Congress on an equal footing or proportionally by population. As a small-state delegate, he was dead set against proportional representation, but he was also a skilled politician who understood the value of compromise. He participated in shaping the Grand Compromise that gave the big states control of the House but provided for equal state representation in the Senate. He was the delegate who formally moved the adoption of this compromise and subsequently was selected as the only small-state delegate on the Committee of Detail. In later years, James Madison recollected that, "from the day when every doubt of the right of the smaller states to an equal vote in the senate was quieted . . . Ellsworth became one of [the general government's] strongest pillars."[6]

After ratification, Ellsworth was Connecticut's unanimous choice to represent the state in the new federal Senate. For seven years, he was the de facto majority leader for the Federalists in the Senate, and during that time he worked on more committees than any other senator. Today, he is best known for his preeminent role in drafting the Judiciary Act of 1789.[7] He also played a significant role in drafting the Bill of Rights (discussed below). Ellsworth served as chief justice of the United States Supreme Court from 1796 to 1799 and envoy to France in 1799–1800. Retiring from the national stage for health reasons, he died in Windsor, Connecticut, in 1807.

Religious Liberty and Church-State Relations

Americans have never reached a consensus on all aspects of the proper relationship between government and religion. Virtually everyone agrees with the general propositions that government should not prevent people from freely exercising their religion and that government should not establish a religion. At the same time virtually everyone agrees that government should impede or prevent some forms of admittedly religious conduct and that some forms of government support for religion are appropriate. The question is where to draw the lines. Many Americans are accommodationists who are inclined to permit governments to promote religion, but others are separationists who believe in a much stricter separation of church and state.

In the first Congress, James Madison is generally viewed as the champion of separationism. In addition to being a separationist, he was a significant progenitor of the Bill of Rights, and he was the House chairman of the Committee of Conference on the Bill of Rights. Therefore we may reasonably believe that his separationism influenced the drafting of the First Amendment's religion clauses. In terms of leadership in the creation of the Bill of Rights, Ellsworth was Madison's analog in the Senate, but unlike Madison, Ellsworth clearly was an accommodationist. Although much has been written on Madison's views on the proper relationship between church and state, Ellsworth's views present unexplored territory.[8]

Ellsworth's views on church and state were deeply influenced by the fact that throughout the eighteenth century his home state of Connecticut was governed by Congregationalists, for Congregationalists. At the beginning of the century, the General Assembly formally recognized the colony's de facto Congregationalist establishment by enacting the Saybrook Platform, which included a Confession of Faith based upon the Westminster Confession. The Platform also established a kind of presbyterian system of church governance in which county consociations dominated by the ministers were given authority to resolve local church disputes and to license ministers. This superstructure of church governance was a deviation from the traditional congregationalism of the Cambridge Platform that left the resolution of disputes and licensing of ministers exclusively to individual congregations. The General Assembly also expressly and formally established Congregationalism by providing that "all the Churches within this government that are, and shall be thus united in doctrine, worship and discipline, be, and for the future shall be, owned and acknowledged, established by law."[9]

As part of this formal establishment, every person in the state was required to attend the established Congregationalist churches and to pay a tax that was dedicated to their ministers' salaries and other religious purposes. As the century progressed, Connecticut passed a series of exemption or toleration acts to allow Baptists, Anglicans, and Quakers to attend churches of their own persuasion and to have their taxes paid to their own ministers. Connecticut's exemption acts, however, applied only to individuals who could prove that they actually attended a dissenting church of one of the three specified denominations. Thus the general requirement of church attendance was maintained, and all Congregationalists and many dissenters who lacked a dissenting church in their town continued to be taxed for the support of the established church. The basic system of taxation, tilted in favor of the Congregationalists, continued throughout the century and into the next.[10]

The last quarter of the century witnessed significant expansions of toleration for dissenters. In 1770 the legislature extended religious toleration to all persons "professing the Christian protestant religion, who soberly and conscientiously dissent from the . . . established [religion]." Then in 1784, Ellsworth's close friends and political allies, Roger Sherman and Richard Law, edited a complete revision of the laws of Connecticut that eliminated the Saybrook Platform. Their revision was approved by the legislature, which included Ellsworth in the upper house. Under the Saybrook Platform, Connecticut Congregationalists had had a presbyterian form of church governance, and many Congregationalists in Connecticut called themselves presbyterians for this reason. The elimination of the Saybrook Platform officially permitted individual churches to revert to the pure congregationalism of the Cambridge Platform.[11]

Although these changes were noteworthy advances in religious toleration, Connecticut's late-eighteenth-century Standing Order had a narrow concept of the separation of church and state. For example, Zephaniah Swift, a deist who converted to Anglicanism and one of Ellsworth's friends and political allies, celebrated these changes as "a complete renunciation of the doctrine, that an ecclesiastical establishment is necessary to the support of civil government."[12] This insular or perhaps wishful thinking ignores the fact that toleration was extended only to those "professing the Christian protestant religion." Roman Catholics need not have applied. Moreover, the state continued to tax its citizens for the specific support of the Protestant religion, and the Congregationalist churches retained their place of preference.

Connecticut also used criminal law to punish certain types of public religious dissent. Blasphemy was a crime at common law and by statute regardless of the blasphemer's religion, and the blasphemy statute was drafted with a specific eye to protecting two of the central tenets of Calvinism. Individuals were forbidden to deny either the Holy Trinity or God's "Government of the World." The latter provision affirmed the doctrine of Providence, and the former was directed toward Unitarianism. Another statute required all persons to attend some public worship even if against their conscience. In 1793, Jesse Root, who was a judge on the Superior Court and who had taught Ellsworth the practice of law, explained that this provision did not violate a person's freedom of conscience because "no man can plead as an excuse, for not worshiping his Maker, in some way or other, that it is against his conscience." Two years later, however, Zephaniah Swift claimed that the mandatory public worship law had fallen into desuetude.[13]

Connecticut law also required all persons to comply with days of public fasting and thanksgiving proclaimed by the governor. Because the governor was always Congregationalist, these days were proclaimed according to Congregationalist wishes. Moreover, during the first four years of the statute, feasts frequently were proclaimed on Episcopalian fast days and fasts on Episcopalian feast days. This practice was not stopped until a Congregationalist governor was elected who happened to be a friend of the state's Episcopalian bishop.[14]

In addition to prohibiting blasphemy, Connecticut law criminalized the espousal of atheism or polytheism "by writing, printing, teaching, or advisedly speaking." The people were further forbidden to "deny the Christian Religion to be true." More specifically, Unitarians and others were forbidden to deny the Holy Trinity and to deny "the Holy Scripture of the Old and New-Testament to be of Divine Authority." Although the statute was technically limited to Christians and individuals educated in Christianity, the limitation was irrelevant because virtually everyone in the state was a Christian. Moreover, parents and masters were required by law to have children memorize "some short orthodox catechism without books, so as to be able to answer to the Questions that shall be propounded to them out of such Catechism, by their Parents, Masters, or Ministers." In practice, this requirement was implemented by having schoolmasters "catechise the children weekly, and have them read daily in the Bible." Because the state was so uniformly Christian, Latitudinarians like Zephaniah Swift believed that these laws verged on being superfluous. Nevertheless, even Swift agreed that "to punish the open, public, and explicit denial of the popular religion of a country, is a necessary measure to preserve the tranquility of government."[15]

The Baptist Petition Movement

The most pervasive manipulation of state laws in favor of the predominant Congregationalists was found in Connecticut's tax system. Notwithstanding the Congregationalists' steadily increasing tolerance of different strands of Protestantism, dissenters—particularly Baptists—remained quite dissatisfied with the state's fiscal support of religion. This dissatisfaction resulted in the Baptist Petition Movement at the beginning of the first decade of the nineteenth century: the Baptists petitioned the Connecticut General Assembly to bring about a complete disestablishment of religion. The movement is significant contemporaneous evidence of the extent of Connecticut's remaining establishment of religion and also provides valuable insight into Ellsworth's understanding of the propriety of state support for religion.[16]

The Baptists presented their initial petition to the General Assembly in 1802. The following year they lodged a second petition reiterating their basic complaint but including a more detailed account of specific grievances. Their fundamental complaint was that the existing laws of Connecticut constituted "the Presbyterian denomination an established religion." In addition to objecting generally to laws establishing a particular mode of worship, the Baptists objected to all laws that compelled the payment of a tax to support religion or that in any way subordinated one Christian sect to another. All their specific complaints about Connecticut's religious establishment fell under these latter two heads.[17]

The Baptists' principal objection was that Connecticut's laws, especially the tax laws, gave the Congregationalists a favored position. This advantage was fostered by an act allowing a majority of qualified voters in any locality to select ministers and to establish taxes for their support. Because the Congregationalists were predominant, only Congregationalist ministers were settled under the act. Quite aside from this de facto position of power, the state's superficially neutral laws created a de jure presumption that everyone was a member of the Standing Order societies with officially settled ministers. Therefore all who did not file a qualifying certificate continued to be taxed for the benefit of the local Congregationalist society. These taxpayers included, in addition to actual members of the established societies, (1) those who chose to attend no religious services; (2) sincere dissenters who were unable to "continue ordinarily, to attend the Worship and Ministry" in a dissenting congregation; (3) nonresident dissenting landowners; and (4) "widows, strangers, persons newly come of age, and all [others] who do not legally dissent." Baptists thought that the requirement that dissenters pay taxes for the support of their dissenting church was particularly officious and pernicious. Baptist "ministers cannot consistently with such their principles receive monies for their support, which have been collected by force of law, and especially from persons who never agreed to pay the same."[18]

Although the Baptists failed in their initial efforts to disestablish Congregationalism in Connecticut, their petitions stimulated a good deal of debate. In addition to petitioning the state legislature, the Connecticut Baptists sought assistance from President Thomas Jefferson. In reply, Jefferson offered moral support and coined his famous phrase "a wall of separation between church and state." Needless to say, the Standing Order clergy were not sympathetic. In a subsequent election sermon, Asahel Hooker talked about the "deluge of tears and blood" caused by the "modern philosophers" who disestablished religion in France. Similarly, the Connecticut legislature offered no support and instead appointed a Select Committee chaired by Ellsworth to consider the Baptists' initial, general petition.[19]

The appointment of Ellsworth was a shrewd choice. Even among non-Congregationalists, he was one of the most respected men in the state and a key member of the state's political power structure. In addition, he had a serious interest in religion and was quite traditional in his views on the proper relationship between church and state. At the Select Committee's first meeting, he reaffirmed his support of Connecticut's establishment when he reportedly threw the Baptist petition under the table, put his foot on it, and declared, "This is where it belongs."[20]

A key to understanding his overdetermined reaction to the Baptist petition is found in God's promise to His people in Isaiah 49:23 that "kings shall be thy nursing fathers." This passage probably is the origin of Connecticut Congregationalists' habit of using the word "king" as a generic word for ruler. Connecticut Congregationalists frequently described the Righteous Ruler as a "nursing father," and the metaphor was part of Ellsworth's worldview. The upper house of the Connecticut legislature was commonly referred to as "the Fathers," and Ellsworth described his 1780 election to that chamber as giving him a "seat with the Fathers." This paternalistic view of government is also found in a section of Ellsworth's *Summary of Christian Doctrine*, which treats society as a family headed by a king. This paternalism turned the Baptists' Petition into an insulting complaint by children about their fathers' stewardship of the family—a violation of the children's filial duties.[21]

Consistent with this paternal metaphor, the Righteous Rulers had obligations to their family. In particular, the Standing Order ministers preached that "the ruler ought to be a nursing father to a religion, which is calculated to root out iniquity, and make men good citizens." The notion of a nursing father being neutral in religious matters was described as "absurd" and "the greatest quackery." To the contrary, a Righteous Ruler had a positive duty to foster the Christian religion as a counter to man's natural depravity. Although the church was a beneficiary of this duty, Connecticut's clergy also stressed the secular objects of the duty. One of Ellsworth's former ministers explained, "religion and its institutions are the best aid of government, by strengthening the ruler's hand, and making the subject faithful in his place, and obedient to the general laws." The traditionalist clergy recognized the general importance of separating church and state. In particular, they objected to European-type establishments built on "laws prescribing faith, binding the conscience, and distinguishing by civil privilege the several classes of religion, or magistrates usurping the throne of the creator, and claiming the prerogatives of the supreme head of the church." Nevertheless, they obviously were not separationists in the modern understanding of the term. As one minister frankly stated, "A sweet and harmonious union of church and state to promote the general good, must meet the full approbation of heaven."[22]

After a deliberation of less than a week, Ellsworth's committee issued a report that basically restated the traditionalist position. The report, which was published in the state's leading newspaper under Ellsworth's sole signature, began with the axiom that "the primary objects of government are the peace, order and prosperity of society." Because good morals are essential to the promotion of these objects, "institutions for the promotion of good morals, are therefore objects of legislative provision and support: and among these, in the opinion of the committee, religious institutions are eminently useful and important." Connecticut Federalists had advanced the same argument in a mid-1790s dispute over the proper use of the proceeds from the sale of the state's Western Reserve. Although this argument for the state support of religion frequently was made by New England Congregationalists, the argument was not unique to them.[23]

To clarify his reference to "the promotion of good morals," Ellsworth emphasized that he was not talking about "speculative opinions in the theology and mere rites and modes of worship." Like the Standing Order ministers, he was opposed to European-type establishments. Instead he endorsed state support of religious institutions because they are "wisely calculated to direct men to the performance of all the duties arising from their connection with each other, and to prevent or repress those evils which flow from unrestrained passion."[24]

In addition to supporting the general idea of the state's providing financial support to religion, Ellsworth squarely addressed the Baptists' central objection. He stated and restated that "every member of society should, in some way, contribute to the support of religious institutions." He concluded his report with a clever lawyer's analogy comparing religious institutions to courts of justice and schools. All three institutions serve valuable secular functions. Therefore, no "individual [should be] allowed to refuse his contribution, because he has no children to be instructed, no injuries to be redressed, or because he conscientiously believes those institutions useless."[25]

This secular idea of comparing religious institutions to courts and schools was not original. Noah Webster had suggested the same analogy about ten years earlier. Webster served on Ellsworth's Committee, and he probably had a hand in drafting the Committee Report that appeared under Ellsworth's signature. Nevertheless, Webster probably was not the principal drafter. A preliminary draft by Webster reached the same conclusion as the final report but was significantly different in the presentation of supporting reasons.[26]

The General Assembly adopted Ellsworth's report by a large majority and dismissed the petition. The next year the more detailed petition was lodged, and another committee was appointed. The second committee dismissed the more detailed petition on the basis of Ellsworth's original report, and for many years afterwards Ellsworth's report was cited as the definitive defense of Connecticut's religious establishment.[27]

Freedom of Conscience

Although Ellsworth was a staunch supporter of Connecticut's preferential support of particular Protestant sects, he was equally adamant in defending freedom of conscience in matters of religion. Fifteen years before his 1802 report, and a year before he wrote the Establishment Clause, he vigorously defended the proposed federal Constitution's provision forbidding religious test oaths in one of his "Landholder" essays. In this essay, he wrote forcefully against the idea of a religious test as a prerequisite to holding public office. By religious tests, he meant any "act to be done, or profession to be made, relating to religions (such as partaking of the sacrament according to certain rites and forms, and declaring one's belief of certain doctrines)." His argument was based upon a shrewd combination of historical fact, human nature, and political theory.[28]

Ellsworth's central proposition was the following: "In our country every man has a right to worship God in that way which is most agreeable to his conscience." He explicitly based this fundamental freedom on the cruel lessons of English history. Before the Protestant Reformation, "tyrannical kings, popes, and prelates [enforced] systems of religious error [i.e., Catholicism] by severe persecuting laws." After the Reformation, religious persecution was continued by the Church of England, then by the Puritans under Cromwell, and finally once more by the Church of England upon Charles II's restoration. Ellsworth concluded his history lesson by reminding his readers, "The pretense for [the post-Restoration persecution] was to exclude the baptists; but the real design was to exclude the protestant dissenters."[29]

Ellsworth's brief excursion into the pages of history was more than a simple scholarly flourish to edify the reader. He was a pragmatic advocate, not a scholar. His lesson was aimed at the heart, not the mind. He did not have to remind his readers that the "protestant dissenters" who were the real targets of the post-Restoration persecution were the direct ancestors and coreligionists of Connecticut's Congregationalists. Just four years earlier, Joseph Huntington, in the course of an election sermon, had reminded Connecticut that the "hateful persecution . . . of our progenitors, many and great, for their religion and strict piety, impelled them to forsake their native land." Nor did Ellsworth have to mention the Old Light outrages of the 1740s. By invoking past persecutions directed at New England–style Calvinists, he evoked in his readers a personal sense of empathy with the victims of religious persecution.[30]

Ellsworth continued on his empathic tack when he moved from history to demography. He advanced an argument similar to one later made by James Madison in Virginia: "if [a national religious oath] were in favour of either congregationalists, presbyterians, episcopalians, baptists, or quakers, it would incapacitate more than three-fourths of the American citizens for any publick office; and thus degrade them from the rank of freemen." Like the history lesson, this general analysis was a veiled invitation to consider the issue in a personal context. For example, his distinction between Congregationalists and Presbyterians probably is a reference to the modified Presbyterianism of the Saybrook Platform. Both New Lights and Old Lights had used the Platform to mount vicious attacks on each other. This sensitive issue of church governance finally had been resolved by deleting the Platform from the 1784 revision of the state's laws, and most in Connecticut were glad to put the issue behind them. Perhaps of even greater significance, little imagination was necessary to deduce that a detailed national oath was unlikely to embody Connecticut Congregationalism.[31]

Ellsworth's argument against a detailed national test oath was cogent and compelling. He then turned to what he considered "the least exceptional" type of religious oath, one "requiring all persons appointed to office to declare, at the time of their admission, their belief in the being of God, and in the divine authority of the scriptures." Here was no strawman. The state's then-existing statutory crimes against religion were directed primarily at individuals who denied God and the Scriptures, and there was support in Connecticut for a general, Christian test oath. Furthermore, Ellsworth explicitly recognized a self-evident policy consideration favoring a general oath: "One who believes these great truths, will not be so likely to violate his obligations to his country, as one who disbelieves them; we may have greater confidence in his integrity."[32]

Ellsworth began his attack on this "least exceptional" form of oath by presenting a pragmatic analysis resonating with Calvinism. The "declaration of such a belief is no security at all. For . . . an unprincipled man, who believes neither the word nor the being of God and [is] governed merely by *selfish motives* [easily will] dissemble." This insight was not original. Joseph Bellamy and others had previously made the same argument. The argument's real power comes from an unspoken assumption shared by Ellsworth and his Calvinist readers. There are, in fact, many unprincipled men who are ruled by selfishness. The reference to "selfish motives" is an invocation of the Calvinist doctrine that man, by his very nature, is depraved and ruled by self-love.[33]

For empirical proof of the danger posed by selfish manipulators, Ellsworth pointed to England, where "the most abandoned characters partake of the sacrament, in order to qualify themselves for public employments." Indeed, he argued that the English system actually had a negative impact on religion. By mixing civil and religious matters, "the clergy are obliged . . . to . . . prostitute the most sacred office of religion, for it is a civil right . . . to receive the sacrament." In view of selfish men's propensity to dissemble, religious oaths serve only to "exclude . . . honest men, men of principle, who will rather suffer an injury, than act contrary to the dictates of their conscience."[34]

In referring to honest men of principle who might refuse to swear on oath, Ellsworth did not mean individuals who were not Christians. In the next sentence, he clarified this potentially radical idea by noting that he was referring to honest men of principle who nevertheless "are sincere friends of religion." Perhaps he had in mind Quakers. About a year later when he drafted the Judiciary Act, he included a provision allowing Quakers to affirm rather than swear an oath in judicial proceedings. Senator Maclay argued that the provision was too narrow because "all persons conscientiously scrupulous of taking an Oath, should [be permitted to] take the affirmation." Over Ellsworth's objection, the Senate agreed to expand the provision.[35]

Ellsworth's arguments about selfish men and the English system were, however, secondary to his principal objection to religious test oaths. In the penultimate paragraph of his essay, he stated "the true principle" by which this question ought to be decided: "The business of civil government is to protect the citizen in his rights, to defend the community from hostile powers, and to promote the general welfare. Civil government has no business to meddle with the private opinions of the people." To justify this restriction of government to secular matters, he stated what he evidently regarded as a truism: "I am accountable not to man, but to God, for the religious opinions which I embrace, and the manner in which I worship the supreme being." These arguments virtually duplicated passages from John Locke's *Letter Concerning Toleration.*[36]

Ellsworth's ideas about freedom of conscience were by no means original. Protestants had long celebrated religious liberty, a theme often reflected in Connecticut election sermons.[37] Moreover, Ellsworth seems to have been particularly influenced by Locke's *Letter on Toleration.* He owned a copy of the book, and he borrowed some of Locke's imagery for his own arguments. Locke frequently used the phrase "fire and sword" to describe religious persecution, while Ellsworth used the phrase "her bloody axe and flaming hand." A particularly significant aspect of Ellsworth's espousal of Locke's analysis is the brevity of the presentation. Although Ellsworth urged this analysis as the central argument of the entire essay, he limited his presentation to a single brief and conclusory paragraph. A reasonable inference is that he knew that his readers already accepted this "true principle" as a matter of course.[38]

Locke's analysis would have been particularly appealing to pragmatic individuals like Ellsworth who earned their political spurs in a state where political power was divided among three competing religious corps of New Lights, Old Lights, and Episcopalians. During and after the Great Awakening, first the Old Lights and later the New Lights used the state's civil power to intervene in religious matters. Although the New Lights eventually gained control of the civil government, they never gained predominant control, which necessitated coalition building with Episcopalians. Later the Revolutionary War encouraged a stable working relationship between the Old and New Lights. Among all the rebelling colonies, Connecticut stands out as the most politically stable state during the Rebellion. Clearly the erstwhile warring religious factions were able to set aside their traditional hostility. This Congregationalist coalition probably took a number of years to accomplish and was symbolized by the deletion of the Saybrook Platform from the 1784 revision of the state's acts. Given this prior history, Ellsworth could state with confidence that civil government had no business meddling in religious affairs.

Although Ellsworth was a firm advocate of freedom of conscience in religious matters, he saw no conflict between this freedom and Connecticut's limited establishment of religion. He clearly approved of the state's financial support of Protestantism in general and Congregationalism in particular, and throughout his political life he consistently endorsed a limited civil power to intervene in religious affairs. A hundred years before Ellsworth wrote his essay defending freedom of conscience, John Locke had argued that civil authority might properly intervene in matters where secular and religious concerns coincide. Ellsworth agreed in the final paragraph of his essay against religious test oaths. The state, he wrote, "has a right to prohibit and punish gross immoralities and impieties; because the open practice of these is of evil example and detriment." Therefore, he "heartily approve[d] of our laws against drunkenness, profane swearing, blasphemy, and professed atheism." Again, Ellsworth was doing little more than reciting Locke and the then-current understanding of religious freedom embodied by Connecticut's laws. His subsequent defense of Connecticut's official support of Christianity was founded upon an identical analysis.[39]

The First Amendment's Religion Clauses

Ellsworth was to play the leading role in the Senate's consideration of the Bill of Rights, but he was not particularly enthusiastic about the task. During the ratification process, he had actively opposed requests that a declaration of substantive rights be added to the Constitution. In part his opposition stemmed from pragmatic political concerns. He believed that in talking of amendments, the Anti-Federalists' "design is to procrastinate, and by this carry their own measures." Other Connecticut Federalists also believed that the issue of constitutional amendments was being raised in part simply to stall the proposed Constitution's ratification. Therefore Connecticut's ratification convention rejected all proposed amendments because the convention "deemed it too dangerous to hazard Delays under a tottering Constitution" based upon the Articles of Confederation.[40]

Although Ellsworth was dubious about the need or efficacy of a declaration of substantive rights, he did not ignore the political reality of amending the Constitution. When the constitutional amendments proposed by the House of Representatives were presented to the Senate, he paid careful attention to them. The Senate debated the House proposals for a week, and numerous ad hoc amendments were considered. At the conclusion of these debates, there was some confusion regarding the net effect of the various motions that had been approved or rejected. Throughout the debate, Ellsworth kept careful track of the ebb and flow of motions, and at the end he was able to resolve the confusion by proposing a single, omnibus amendment keyed to the original House proposals. His consolidated motion passed by the required two-thirds majority. In effect Ellsworth was the Senate floor leader for the Bill of Rights, and his fellow senators formally recognized his leadership when they selected him to chair the Committee of Conference that worked out the differences between the House and Senate versions of the Bill of Rights.[41] As chairman, Ellsworth personally wrote the committee report that established the final wording of the Constitution's Establishment Clause. Although there is no surviving record of what Ellsworth actually said during the Senate's consideration of the Bill of Rights, his understanding of the First Amendment's religion clauses is fairly easy to deduce from his writings before and after the First Amendment was drafted.

The Bill of Rights originated in the House of Representatives, and the House's proposed amendments included two significant articles that dealt with religion. The third article read: "Congress shall make no laws establishing Religion, or prohibiting to free exercise thereof, nor shall the rights of conscience be infringed." The fourteenth article read: "No State shall infringe the right of trial by Jury in criminal cases, nor the *rights of conscience*, nor the freedom of speech, or of the press" (emphasis added). After the House approved a number of amendments, they were submitted to the Senate.[42]

When the Senate took up the House's third article respecting the absence of congressional power over religious matters, some of the senators evidently believed that the House's prohibitions were too broad. Rather than use general terms, someone moved to replace the House's language with a simple and more specific prohibition against establishing "One Religious Sect or Society in preference to others." This motion, however, failed to pass. Next a motion was made to strike the entire third article, but it too failed. Then a substitute article was proposed that would have forbidden Congress to "make any law, infringing the rights of conscience, or establishing any Religious Sect or Society." Again the motion failed. A fourth motion was made that would have retained the House language except that the general prohibition against "establishing Religion" would have been replaced by more specific language against "establishing any particular denomination of religion in preference to another." After this motion was defeated, someone—perhaps in exasperation—called the question in the House's original proposal, but that too was rejected.[43]

Careful grammarians have teased a number of meanings out of these various motions, but the bottom line is that the Senate rejected each and every one of them. Obviously many—probably a majority—of the senators believed that the House language was too broad, but no one was able to devise an acceptable alternative approach. The senators were, however, able to reach an agreement on the House proposal that "the rights of conscience [shall not] be infringed." The Senate agreed to strike all reference to "the rights of conscience."[44]

After reaching an impasse on the House's third proposed article, the Senate considered the rest of the articles in sequence and also considered a number of matters not covered by the House proposals. During this process, the House's fourteenth article protecting rights of conscience from state action was rejected. Finally, on the last day of debate, the senators returned to the House's third article and agreed to change it to read that "Congress shall make no law establishing articles of faith or a mode of worship, or prohibiting the free exercise of religion." This change was incorporated into Ellsworth's consolidated motion that passed the Senate and was sent back to the House.[45]

In sending these and other proposed changes to the House, the Senate was, in effect, formally opening negotiations between the two chambers on the final wording of the Bill of Rights. The House agreed to many of the Senate's changes but stood firm on the original wording of the third and fourteenth articles on religion. In response, the Senate voted to recede from or give up on its proposed version of the third article's establishment and free exercise clauses but to "insist on all the others." Disagreements like this are inevitable in any legislative body having two co-equal chambers. The same problem routinely arose in Great Britain when the House of Commons and the House of Lords disagreed on proposed legislation. The British solution to this kind of disagreement was to convene a Committee of Conference in which representatives or managers from each chamber would confer with each other and work out a compromise that would be recommended to their respective chamber. Not surprisingly, this same procedure was used by Congress, and a Committee of Conference was formed to resolve the differences between the House and Senate versions of the Bill of Rights. The Senate appointed three managers, with Ellsworth as chairman, to confer with three managers from the House, who were led by Madison.[46]

The differences between the House and the Senate were quickly resolved, and Ellsworth personally penned the Conference Committee report embodying the House and Senate managers' agreement. Notwithstanding the Senate's prior recession from its proposed establishment and free exercise clauses, the Committee of Conference recommended changing the establishment clause to read: "Congress shall make no law *respecting an establishment of Religion*, or prohibiting the free exercise thereof." The Committee also agreed to the Senate's insistence on striking the House's proposed fourteenth article forbidding infringements of rights of conscience by the states. The Senate's version of the Bill of Rights as modified by the Conference report was immediately approved by both chambers. Ten of the twelve proposals were subsequently ratified by the states, and they became the first ten amendments to the Constitution.[47]

Free Exercise and the Rights of Conscience

Ellsworth's Committee of Conference Report followed the general philosophy of church and state that he consistently advocated before and after the Bill of Rights was framed. Consistent with his firm belief in freedom of religion, his report recommended that "Congress shall make no law . . . prohibiting the free exercise [of Religion]." Although this recommendation technically deleted the House's additional language guaranteeing "rights of conscience" against congressional infringement, Ellsworth undoubtedly viewed the deletion as simply a matter of style and not substantive. In the eighteenth century, rights of conscience and freedom of religion were synonymous terms. The leading example of equating rights of conscience with freedom of religion is John Locke's influential *Letter Concerning Toleration*, which he wrote in terms of freedom of conscience.[48]

The same rights-of-conscience phraseology was commonly used in Connecticut to refer to freedom of religion. Connecticut's Toleration Act was called "An Act for securing the Rights of Conscience," and Connecticut writers and ministers routinely wrote and spoke in terms of rights of conscience when they meant freedom of religion. Those who vigorously opposed the preferences that Connecticut conferred upon Congregationalism used the same phraseology. Two years after the Bill of Rights was framed, John Leland, a leading Baptist theoretician and minister, strenuously attacked Connecticut's preferential laws in a pamphlet entitled *The Right of Conscience Inalienable*. Similarly, both petitions in the Baptist Petition movement began their criticism of Connecticut's laws by invoking "the rights of conscience." Finally, when Ellsworth himself wrote about religious freedom, he used the term "rights of conscience." Therefore the deletion of "rights of conscience" from the Bill of Rights should not be viewed as a decision to narrow the scope of rights under the Constitution. Instead, Ellsworth almost certainly viewed the deletion as a matter of style.[49]

A detailed account of what Ellsworth may have understood the free exercise of religion to mean is difficult to reconstruct. To be sure, there was a consensus among Connecticut's Standing Order that the state had no business in interfering with the personal religious beliefs of its citizens. Nevertheless, in one of his "Landholder" essays, Ellsworth had written, "while I assert the rights of religious liberty, I would not deny that the civil power has a right, in some cases, to interfere in matters of religion." Ellsworth's touchstone was whether the civil power was being exercised to accomplish secular goals. Thus he had no objection to the punishment of "gross . . . impieties . . . profane swearing, blasphemy, and professed atheism" because "the open practice of these is of evil example and detriment." In his time, this position was neither anomalous nor even extreme. It was virtually a restatement of Connecticut's criminal laws related to religion. Moreover, John Locke and Connecticut religious liberals like Zephaniah Swift agreed.[50]

Ellsworth's attitudes on freedom of religion and state support for religion also provide an explanation of the Conference Committee's rejection of the House's fourteenth article forbidding the states to "infringe . . . the rights of conscience." Ellsworth certainly approved of the general principles embodied by the rights of conscience. Similarly, the House may have passed the fourteenth article as an expression of general principle without taking into account the article's potential for a national intrusion into local relations between church and state. Although there probably was general agreement within the Congress regarding the general principle, specific applications of the principle might be subject to dispute. The problem was that general phrases like "establishment of religion" and "rights of conscience" are ambiguous and subject to dramatically diverse interpretations. We are painfully aware of this problem today, and the founding generation was no less sophisticated. While the House of Representatives was pondering the prohibition of religious establishments and the guaranty of rights of conscience, Peter Silvester of New York specifically expressed an apprehension that these concepts were "liable to a construction different from what had been made by the committee." Indeed, Silvester "feared it might be thought to have a tendency to abolish religion altogether."[51]

Silvester's concerns were essentially general and theoretical, but Connecticut's representatives fully understood how a constitutional provision for religious rights might affect their state's religious establishment. Benjamin Huntington stated Connecticut's objection in the clearest possible terms. These "words," he said, "might be taken in such latitude as to be extremely hurtful to the cause of religion." He specifically noted that the "ministers of their congregations to the Eastward [by which he meant New England in general and Connecticut in particular] were maintained by the contributions [i.e., taxes] of those who belonged to their society; the expense of building meeting houses was contributed in the same manner." He went on to raise the specific fear that the religion clauses might empower "a Federal Court" to interfere with Connecticut's approach to supporting religion.[52]

The proposed amendment prohibiting the states from interfering with individuals' rights of conscience clearly presented problems for Connecticut's establishment. When the Baptists later vigorously attacked Connecticut's system of taxation, they did so on the express basis that the system infringed their rights of conscience.[53] Congregationalists like Ellsworth sincerely believed that the tax structure did not infringe rights of conscience. When the Baptists subsequently petitioned the Connecticut legislature, the legislature preempted the problem of an erroneous understanding of "rights of conscience" by appointing a committee of right-thinking Congregationalists who put a proper spin on the issue. But Connecticut's Standing Order did not control the national government. Therefore, the creation of federal rights of conscience that might be enforced against Connecticut in a national forum was quite unacceptable.

Given the firm basis for opposing the creation of ambiguous federal rights regulating state establishments, the decision of the Committee of

Conference to strike this proposed right from the Bill of Rights is entirely understandable. Obviously Ellsworth, who chaired the managers from the Senate, was a firm defender of Connecticut's establishment. In addition, his friend Roger Sherman was one of the House managers and would have been equally firm on this issue.

An Establishment of Religion

Ellsworth's recommendation that "Congress shall make no law respecting an establishment of Religion" requires a more complicated explanation. There is no doubt that he believed a government should provide direct financial assistance to Protestant churches, even to the extent of preferring one Protestant denomination over all others. Therefore, his role as the father of the Constitution's Establishment Clause seems at first glance peculiar. In fact, however, the most plausible explanation of his role in drafting the Clause is that he simply did not care whether the Bill of Rights included an establishment clause.

Ellsworth's indifference to the Establishment Clause was multilayered. In the first place, Calvinist political psychology provided little support for the adoption of a Bill of Rights. In the words of a Standing Order minister, written laws "exist only on paper and ink." What counts is the presence of righteous rulers who will provide good government. This reasoning had led Ellsworth and other Connecticut Congregationalists to dismiss the need for a Bill of Rights during the ratification process.[54]

In addition to this Calvinist inclination to view declarations of rights as mere "paper and ink," some aspects of the Bill of Rights seemed doubly superfluous. After the Constitutional Convention in Philadelphia, Ellsworth and Roger Sherman had penned a joint letter explaining that the powers "vested in Congress . . . extend only to matters respecting the common interests of the Union." Among other things, Sherman believed that matters of religion were basically of local interest and therefore essentially beyond the national government's powers. In the House of Representative debates on the Establishment Clause, Sherman flatly stated that "the amendment [was] altogether unnecessary, inasmuch as congress had no authority whatever delegated to them by the constitution, to make religious establishments."[55]

Ellsworth was of much the same mind. When he thought of religious establishments, he thought of the imposition of a single type of Protestantism upon an entire nation similar to the establishment of the Church of England. In view of the pluralism of American Protestantism, such an establishment was a practical impossibility. As he had explained in one of his "Landholder" letters, to establish any one type of Protestantism would be to the detriment of "more than three-fourths of the American citizens." Like Sherman, he believed that matters of religion were essentially of local rather than national concern. As he had noted during the Constitutional Convention, the federal government "could only embrace objects of a general nature. He turned his eyes therefore for the preservation of his rights to the State Govts." Similarly, during the ratification process, he flatly denied that Congress had the "power to prohibit . . . liberty of conscience." His practical understanding that religion is primarily a local matter is evident in a letter that he and William Samuel Johnson, his fellow Connecticut senator, wrote to their governor about six months after the Bill of Rights was framed. In response to an enquiry from Governor Huntington as to whether President Washington would proclaim a "General Fast" later in the Spring, Ellsworth and Johnson stated that "except on great National Occasions the appt of both Fasts & Thanksgivings should be left to the particular states." Because Ellsworth thought that matters of religion generally should be left to the states, his approval of government support for religion was not implicated by the Establishment Clause, which applied only to the federal government.[56]

Consistent with this view, Ellsworth approved a federal entanglement with religion in a few instances involving a clear federal interest. He obviously thought that the president could declare national days of Fasts and Thanksgivings "on great National Occasions." Similarly, he was the Senate chairman of a joint committee that recommended the appointment of House and Senate chaplains, and he presumably voted for the provision of chaplains to the armed forces. A 1795 treaty providing the Oneida Indians with money to rebuild a church destroyed by the

British (the Oneida were allied with the Americans during the Revolutionary War) fits this same pattern. The paucity of these ad hoc entanglements with religion suggests that the early Congresses agreed with Ellsworth's idea that religion was generally a matter for the states rather than the national government.[57]

In addition to viewing the Establishment Clause as relatively unimportant and even superfluous, Ellsworth almost certainly would have limited the Clause's impact to forbidding federal establishments similar to Great Britain's establishment of the Church of England. This narrow view of religious establishments was the orthodox Standing Order doctrine espoused by leading Connecticut Congregationalists. Ellsworth's friend, Timothy Dwight, who sometimes was called the "Pope of Connecticut," recognized that some believed that the state had an "ecclesiastical establishment." He explained, however, that the critics (undoubtedly the Baptists) were in error because the "phrase . . . denoted *the establishment of a national or state church, or the establishment of exclusive privileges in the possession of one class of christians.*" Ellsworth's subsequent legislative report on the Baptist Petitions indicates that he subscribed to Dwight's particular view of religious establishments. Under this narrow view of religious establishments, the Establishment Clause in the Bill of Rights was virtually nugatory.[58]

Although Ellsworth held a narrow view of improper religious establishments, others had a far broader view. In fact, the concept of improper religious establishments was ambiguous in the late eighteenth century. In 1761, Ezra Stiles, later Ellsworth's friend and president of Yale College, had described Connecticut's relationship between church and state as one of the British colonies' "provincial establishments." In the same decade, separationists in Connecticut already were attacking the colony's system as an improper establishment. Indeed, during the years before and after Ellsworth penned the Establishment Clause, there actually was a general agreement that Connecticut's laws created an establishment of religion. The dispute was over whether the establishment was proper or improper. Timothy Dwight denied that Connecticut had an establishment like the Church of England, which obviously was improper. In the same paragraph, however, Dwight conceded that Connecticut had a religious establishment, which he called "*the legal establishment of the public worship of God in this state.*"[59]

Ellsworth was a sophisticated lawyer who had drafted countless contracts, statutes, resolutions, and other documents, and his experience had made him well-versed in the problems of ambiguity. "Perhaps no two men," he once wrote, "will express the same sentiment in the same matter, and by the same words; neither do they connect precisely the same ideas with the same words. From hence arises an ambiguity in all languages, with which the most perspicuous and precise writers are in a degree chargeable."[60] When an ambiguous rights-of-conscience clause directly applicable to the states was proposed, the clause's ambiguity led him to oppose it. But he had no qualms about drafting a similarly ambiguous Establishment Clause applicable to the federal government, because he viewed the federal government's role in religious matters to be relatively unimportant.

Presumably, Ellsworth intended the Establishment Clause to have a comparatively narrow meaning, but given his knowledge that the clause was ambiguous, he could not safely predict such an outcome. James Madison, who chaired the Committee of Conference managers from the House was, ironically, in a similar predicament. Unlike Ellsworth, Madison had an expansive understanding of improper religious establishments, but like Ellsworth, he undoubtedly was familiar with the contrary view.[61] In other words, both men were capable politicians, knowledgeable in the law, who consciously embraced ambiguity in framing the Establishment Clause.

Ellsworth and Madison were sophisticated men who represented opposing points of view on the proper relationship between church and state, and they can be viewed as ideal types for the clash of ideas within the First Congress—indeed within the nation—that gave birth to the Establishment Clause. When competent negotiators and drafters consciously agree to ambiguous language in an important document, the usual explanation is that in order to reach general agreement they have tacitly postponed the resolution of the issue to a later date and, perhaps, to a different forum. Madison had specific reservations about clearly defining the scope of religious liberties in the Constitution because he feared that such a "public definition" would be unduly narrow. When the Committee of Conference agreed to an Establishment Clause that the managers knew to be ambiguous, they must have understood that the ambiguity would have to be resolved at a later date.[62]

Some have proposed a different interpretation of the drafting of the Establishment Clause. Because the final language of the Committee of Conference differs from both the House and the Senate proposals, the Clause frequently has been viewed as a compromise hammered out in the Committee of Conference.[63] Under the compromise thesis, Madison's personal beliefs and position of leadership in the House suited him as the natural advocate of separationism. For the same reasons, Ellsworth would have been the natural advocate for accommodating the direct state support of religion.

Consistent with the compromise thesis, some scholars have argued that the House and Senate managers added the word "respecting" to the Establishment Clause in order to forbid Congress from making a "law respecting [a state] establishment of religion"—in other words, to protect existing state establishments.[64] As historical analysis, this ingeniously subtle reading is implausible. One wonders who on the Committee of Conference would have pushed a states' rights position. Ellsworth and Sherman clearly were protective of state establishments, but they considered matters of religion to be of local interest and therefore beyond the power of the national government. Surely Madison did not waste any bargaining chips in order to protect existing state establishments. In addition, we will see that there was a serious parliamentary impediment to a substantive compromise by the Committee of Conference on the Establishment Clause.

If the Establishment Clause actually was the result of a compromise between the House and Senate managers, Ellsworth was seriously disadvantaged in his negotiations with Madison. At the same time that the Senate agreed to a Committee of Conference, the Senate formally receded from its proposed Establishment Clause and thereby officially accepted the House version. As a matter of technical parliamentary procedure, this Senate action deprived the Committee of Conference of authority to change the Clause. The English parliamentary rules for conferences between the Lords and the Commons were quite formal and drew a technical distinction between ordinary conferences and "free" conferences. In the former, the managers were limited to a formal reading of the reasons for their chamber's disagreement, whereas in free conferences the managers were permitted to engage in a free discussion of their disagreement. Under the English practice, a Committee of Conference was not allowed to change the provisions upon which both the Commons and the Lords had agreed. Therefore the Senate's recession on the Establishment Clause barred the Committee of Conference from changing the meaning of the Clause.[65]

Ellsworth fully understood the concept of a Committee of Conference and the basis of the Committee in English parliamentary practice. In the bicameral Connecticut General Assembly, he had sat on many Committees of Conference. Similarly, in presiding over the Senate, both Vice President Adams and Vice President Jefferson recognized English parliamentary practice as valid precedent. Jefferson explained that the English parliamentary practice was the preferred basis for congressional practice because it "is the model which we have all studied, while we are little acquainted with the modifications of it in our several States." Ellsworth himself was wont to rely upon arcane parliamentary rules. When the Senate in its second session was debating the status of unfinished business from the first session, Senator Maclay noted in his diary that Ellsworth "had much parliamentary stuff."[66]

More importantly, less than five months before the Committee of Conference on the Bill of Rights was convened, Ellsworth had chaired the committee that drafted the Congress's rule on Committees of Conference. This rule from Ellsworth's committee was clearly based on the well-established parliamentary practice and demonstrated a detailed knowledge of the practice by providing that in all conferences the managers "shall . . . confer freely." In other words, the rule allowed the managers to discuss their differences and therefore, taking into account the English parliamentary distinction, provided for free conferences rather than conferences that were not free. Under the rule, the House and Senate managers' discussions were limited to the "amendment to a bill agreed to in one House and dissented to in the other." This provision evidently followed the parliamentary practice that limited Committees of Conference to specific matters over which the two houses actually had disagreed. The effect of this technical limitation was to deprive the Bill of Rights Committee of Conference of the power to change the meaning of the House's version of the Establishment Clause. Seven years later, Vice President Jefferson explained, "It is unparlimentary to strike out, at a conference, anything in a bill which hath been agreed and passed by both Houses." Therefore a variance from the House's version would have been subject to a point of order by any member of the House or Senate. To be sure, the Committee changed the precise wording of the Establishment Clause, but the most plausible explanation of the change is that the Committee viewed it merely as a matter of style and not of substance—in which the Senate managers deferred to James Madison. This explanation resolves the apparent departure from parliamentary practice and would have been a powerful rebuttal to a point of order.[67]

In addition to this arcane parliamentary complication, the Senate recession had serious practical implications for the Senate managers chaired by Ellsworth. The recession was a substantive institutional decision to accept the House's position. Furthermore, the Senate receded on only one point and disagreed with the House on sixteen other issues.[68] Therefore, at the very least, Ellsworth's brief instructed him to concentrate his negotiations on the latter sixteen points.

In addition to receiving no institutional support on the Establishment Clause issue, Ellsworth was personally inclined to view the matter as unimportant. In contrast, we may infer that he was quite interested in scotching the House provision guaranteeing rights of conscience in the states, and we know that the Senate managers were adamantly opposed to other House proposals relating to the federal judiciary.[69] The Senate managers were not appointed until the late afternoon or early evening of September 21, and they apparently concluded their deliberations two days later. Given this press of time, Ellsworth surely would have concentrated on the issues that he believed were really important.

Although the precise language of the Establishment Clause was obviously changed, the most plausible explanation is that the change was viewed merely as a matter of style in which the Senate managers deferred to Madison. In addition to being a powerful rebuttal to a parliamentary point of order, this explanation comports with the Senate's prior recession from its more narrow establishment language. The House language formally accepted by the Senate provided that "Congress shall make no law establishing religion." The Committee changed this language to read: "Congress shall make no law respecting an establishment of religion." A careful grammarian might find substantive distinctions between these two sentences,[70] but to suggest that the change was intended to record a significant substantive compromise is not convincing. If Ellsworth and Madison, in fact, worked out a substantive change to the House's proposal, it is incredible that they did not draft language that more clearly indicated the change.

When considered in the historical context of the Conference Committee's formation and deliberations, the common assumption that the language of the Establishment Clause is the result of a compromise within the Committee is implausible. There was, in fact, no disagreement between the House and the Senate because the Senate specifically agreed to the House's language. The Conference Committee technically lacked jurisdiction to alter the House's proposal, the Senate managers lacked institutional support to negotiate a compromise, and Ellsworth, their leader, not only thought the matter was unimportant but had much more important differences to discuss.

Concluding Thoughts on an Originalist Construction of the First Amendment

Today—some two centuries after the Constitution and its Bill of Rights became effective—many are inclined to seek the Constitution's meaning by exploring the founders' original intent.[71] This has been particularly true with respect to the First Amendment's religion clauses.[72] Whether this quest for original intent is appropriate is beyond the scope of this essay. Nevertheless, one conclusion should be clear: justices and scholars who wish to understand the founders' views on religious liberty and church-state relations should not limit themselves to particular founders whose views happen to support a particular twenty-first-century political agenda. As the present essay demonstrates, James Madison and Oliver Ellsworth—both critical framers of the First Amendment—had significantly different views regarding the proper relationship between church and state. Given this clear disparity, no one should pretend that either man's carefully thought-out views represent those of the entire founding generation.

Notes

1. See James Madison, letter to Joseph Wood, Feb. 27, 1836, in *Letters and Other Writings of James Madison* (Philadelphia: Lippincott, 1867), 4:427–28; William G. Brown, *The Life of Oliver Ellsworth* (New York: Macmillan, 1905), 225, quoting Burr; Ronald J. Lettieri, *Connecticut's Young Man of the Revolution: Oliver Ellsworth* (Hartford, Conn.: American Revolution Bicentennial Commission of Connecticut, 1978); William R. Casto, *Oliver Ellsworth and the Creation of the Federal Republic* (New York: Second Circuit Committee on History and Commemorative Events, 1997). The present essay is drawn in significant part from this last book.

2. See William R. Casto, "Oliver Ellsworth's Calvinism: A Biographical Essay on Religion and Political Psychology in the Early Republic," *Journal of Church and State* 36 (1994): 508; Missionary Society of Connecticut, *A Summary of Christian Doctrine and Practice: Designed Especially for the Use of the People in the New Settlements of the United States of America* (Hartford, Conn.: Hudson & Goodwin, 1804). Daniel Webster, letter to Thomas A. Merrill, Jan. 4, 1803, in *Papers of Daniel Webster, Legal Papers*, eds. A. Konefsky and A. King (Hanover, N.H.: University Press of New England, 1983), 1:19–20.

3. William G. McLoughlin, *New England Dissent, 1630–1833: The Baptists and the Separation of Church and State*, 2 vols. (Cambridge, Mass.: Harvard University Press, 1971), vol. 1, chaps. 18–20; Oscar Zeichner, *Connecticut's Years of Controversy, 1750–1776* (Chapel Hill: University of North Carolina Press, 1949); Richard L. Bushman, *From Puritan to Yankee: Character and the Social Order in Connecticut, 1690–1765* (Cambridge, Mass.: Harvard University Press, 1967), chaps. 12–14.

4. Lettieri, *Connecticut's Young Man*, chaps. 2–3.

5. Max Farrand, ed., *Records of the Federal Convention* (New Haven, Conn.: Yale University Press, 1966), 1:466, 2:97, 316.

6. Lettieri, *Connecticut's Young Man*, chap. 5.

7. Ibid.; *Records of the Federal Convention*, 4:88–89; *The Documentary History of the Ratification of the Constitution*, ed. Merrill Jensen et al., 22 vols. (Madison: State Historical Society of Wisconsin, 1976–2008), 3:553 (judicial review); Rufus King, letter to Jeremiah Wadsworth, Dec. 23, 1787, in Jensen et al., *Documentary History*, 15:70–71.

8. According to Mark David Hall, when Supreme Court justices have appealed to specific founders to shine light on the First Amendment's religion clauses, they have appealed to Madison 189 times, Jefferson 112 times, but Ells-

worth only 3 times. Mark David Hall, "Jeffersonian Walls and Madisonian Lines: The Supreme Court's Use of History in Religion Clause Cases," *Oregon Law Review* 85 (2006): 568.

9. McLoughlin, *New England Dissent*, 1:264; *The Public Records of the Colony of Connecticut, 1636–1776* (Hartford, Conn.: Brown & Parson, 1850), 5:87 (hereinafter *Connecticut Colonial Records*). See generally Williston Walker, *The Creeds and Platforms of Congregationalism* (New York: Scribner, 1893); Paul R. Lucas, *Valley of Discord: Church and Society along the Connecticut River, 1636–1725* (Hanover, N.H.: University Press of New England, 1976).

10. See McLoughlin, *New England Dissent*, vol. 1, chap. 15; vol. 2, chaps. 47–50.

11. "An Act in Addition to a Law of this Colony Entitled an Act for the Due Observation and Keeping the Sabbath or Lord's Day, and for Preventing and Punishing Disorders and Prophaneness on the Same," in *Connecticut Colonial Records*, 13:360. For the elimination of the Saybrook Platform, see Bushman, *From Puritan to Yankee*, 219; McLoughlin, *New England Dissent*, 2:923–24.

12. Zephaniah Swift, *A System of Laws of the State of Connecticut* (Winham, Conn.: printed by John Byrene for the author, 1796), 1:42.

13. Swift, *System*, 2:321, 325, 347; "An Act for the Punishment of Divers Capital and Other Felonies," in *Acts and Laws of the State of Connecticut in America* (New London, Conn.: Timothy Green, 1784), 67 (hereinafter *Connecticut Acts*); "An Act for the Due Observation of the Sabbath or Lord's-Day," in *Connecticut Acts*, 213; discussed in Jesse Root, "Introduction," *Root's Reports* (Conn., 1793), xxii, and Swift, *System of Laws*, 2:325.

14. "An Act to Enforce the Observances of Days of Public Fasting and Thanksgiving," in *The Public Records of the State of Connecticut* (Hartford, Conn.: State of Connecticut, 1948), 7:313 (hereinafter *Connecticut State Records*); Richard Purcell, *Connecticut in Transition, 1775–1818* (Washington, D.C.: American Historical Association, 1918), 55–56, 90; M. Louise Greene, *The Development of Religious Liberty in Connecticut* (Boston: Houghton, Mifflin, 1905), 378.

15. "An Act for the Punishment of Divers Capital and Other Felonies," in *Connecticut Acts*, 67; Abel Flint, Secretary of the Connecticut Missionary Society, to the London Missionary Society, May 14, 1804, in *United Church of Christ Connecticut Conference* (Hartford); Swift, *System of Laws*, 2:322–23.

16. See McLoughlin, *New England Dissent*, vol. 2, chap. 50.

17. "The Baptists' Petition," in *Connecticut State Records*, vol. 2, appendix D; 11:369–71; "The 1803 Petition," in *Connecticut State Records*, 11:374–80.

18. See McLoughlin, *New England Dissent*, vol. 2, chap. 50; "The Baptist Petition" and "The 1803 Petition."

19. Asahel Hooker, *The Moral Tendency of Man's Accountableness to God* (Hartford, Conn.: Hudson & Goodwin, 1805), 33–35; Danbury Baptists Association, letter to Thomas Jefferson, Oct. 1801, quoted and discussed in McLoughlin, *New*

England Dissent, 2:1004–5; Thomas Jefferson, letter to Nehemiah Dodge, Jan. 1, 1802, in *Thomas Jefferson: Writings*, ed. Merrill Peterson (New York: Library of America, 1984), 510; Daniel L. Dreisbach, *Thomas Jefferson and the Wall of Separation between Church and State* (New York: New York University Press, 2002).

20. Ellen D. Larned, *History of Windham County, Connecticut* (Worcester, Mass.: Ellen D. Larned, 1880), 296.

21. See, e.g., Joseph Bellamy, "An Election Sermon" in *The Works of Joseph Bellamy* (Boston: Doctrinal Tracts and Book Society, 1853), quoted in text accompanying note 18 in chap. 3; Charles Backus, *A Sermon Preached Before His Excellency Samuel Huntington* (Hartford, Conn.: Hudson & Goodwin, 1793), 22. For the upper house, see Oliver Ellsworth, letter to Abigail Ellsworth, May 30, 1780, quoted in *Letters of Delegates to Congress, 1774–1789*, ed. Paul Smith (Washington: Library of Congress, 1988), 15:216 n.2; Josiah Whitney, *The Essential Requisites to Form the Good Rulers' Character* (Hartford, Conn.: Elisha Babcock, 1788), 29–30; Ammi R. Robbins, *The Empires and Dominions of This World* (Hartford, Conn.: Hudson & Goodwin, 1789), 26, 30, 32–33; Missionary Society of Connecticut, *Christian Doctrine*, chap. 20, par. 9. For the son's filial duties, see Missionary Society of Connecticut, *Christian Doctrine*, par. 5, 7.

22. Backus, *A Sermon*, 22; Timothy Stone, *A Sermon Preached Before His Excellency Samuel Huntington* (Hartford, Conn.: Hudson & Goodwin, 1792), 23; Benjamin Trumbull, *The Dignity of Man, Especially as Displayed in Civil Government* (Hartford, Conn.: Hudson & Goodwin, 1801), 23; Cyprian Strong, *The Kingdom Is the Lord's* (Hartford, Conn.: Hudson & Goodwin, 1799), 17–18, 40; Timothy Dwight, *Virtuous Rulers a National Blessing* (Hartford, Conn.: Hudson & Goodwin, 1795), 18; Zebulon Ely, *The Wisdom and Duty of Magistrates* (Hartford, Conn.: Hudson & Goodwin, 1804), 34. See also Asahel Hooker's defense of "a union of religion with civil government, as has always existed in this State" in A. Hooker, *The Moral Tendency of Man's Accountableness to God* (Hartford, Conn.: Hudson & Goodwin, 1805), 24.

23. "Report of the Committee to Whom Was Referred the Petition of Simeon Brown and Others, Complaining of Certain Existing Laws Respecting the Support of the Gospel," 1802, reprinted in *Connecticut State Records*, 2:371–74. James Beaseley, "Emerging Republicanism and the Standing Order: The Appropriation Act Controversy in Connecticut, 1793 to 1795," *William and Mary Quarterly*, 3rd ser., 29 (1972): 595, 609; Linda K. Kerber, *Federalists in Dissent: Imagery and Ideology in Jeffersonian America* (Ithaca, N.Y.: Cornell University Press, 1970), 208–12. Kerber uses many Calvinist examples and a few non-Calvinist ones. See generally, McLoughlin, *New England Dissent*, vol. 2, chap. 50.

24. "Ellsworth's Report," *Connecticut State Records*, 2:373.

25. Ibid., 2:371, 373–74.

26. Noah Webster, *A Collection of Essays and Fugitiv Writings* (Worcester, Mass.: Thomas & Andrews, 1791), 345; John Devotion, *The Duty and Interest of a*

People to Sanctify the Lord of Hosts (Hartford, Conn.: Eben Watson, 1777), 31; Noah Webster, "Draft Report," 1802, Noah Webster Papers, Manuscripts and Archives, New York Public Library.

27. McLoughlin, *New England Dissent*, 2:989–94.

28. U.S. Constitution, art. 6; Oliver Ellsworth, "Landholder VII," in Jensen et al., *Documentary History*, 14:448–52.

29. Ibid.

30. Joseph Huntington, *God Ruling the Nations for the Most Glorious End* (Hartford, Conn.: Hudson & Goodwin, 1784), 13; Benjamin Trumbull, *A Complete History of Connecticut Civil and Ecclesiastical* (Hartford, Conn.: Hudson & Goodwin, 1797), 128. Trumbull discusses Old Light "outrages."

31. Oliver Ellsworth, "Landholder VII," in Jensen et al., *Documentary History*, 14:450; Jonathan Elliot, ed., *The Debates in the Several State Conventions, on the Adoption of the Federal Constitution, as Recommended by the General Convention at Philadelphia in 1787*, 2nd ed. (Philadelphia: J. B. Lippincott, 1876), 3:330 (James Madison); Bushman, *From Puritan to Yankee*, 211–12, 215–19.

32. For the "strawman," compare William Williams, letter to the Printer, Feb. 2, 1788, in Jensen et al., *Documentary History*, 3:588–90, with Oliver Ellsworth, "Landholder VII," in Jensen et al., *Documentary History*, 14:450. For Connecticut support for a general Christian test oath, see Williams, letter to the Printer, Feb. 2, 1788; Samuel Parsons, letter to William Cushing, Jan. 11, 1788, in Jensen et al., *Documentary History*, 3:573; "A New Test," *New Haven Gazette*, Jan. 31, 1788, in Jensen et al., *Documentary History*, 3:588; "Elihu," *American Mercury*, Feb. 18, 1788, in Jensen et al., *Documentary History*, 3:590–92.

33. Oliver Ellsworth, "Landholder VII," in Jensen et al., *Documentary History*, 14:451; Joseph Bellamy, letter to a friend, circa 1766, in *Bellamy's Works*, 1:xxxi–xxxiii; William Paley, *The Principles of Moral and Political Philosophy* (Dublin, 1785); *The Works of and Life of William Paley*, ed. Alexander Chalmers (London: F. C. and J. Rivington, 1819), 2:36; Inventory of Oliver Ellsworth's Estate, 7 ("Payley's Moral Philosophy"), Archives, Connecticut State Library, Hartford.

34. Oliver Ellsworth, "Landholder VII," in Jensen et al., *Documentary History*, 14:451. See generally, Norman Sykes, *Church and State in England in the Eighteenth Century* (Hamden, Conn.: Archon Books, 1962).

35. Oliver Ellsworth, "Landholder VII," in Jensen et al., *Documentary History*, 14:451; "A Bill to Establish the Judicial Courts of the United States," sec. 9, in *Documentary History of the First Federal Congress of the United States, March 4, 1789–March 3, 1791*, eds. Linda Grant De Pauw, Charlene Bangs Bickford, and Helen E. Veit, 17 vols. (Baltimore: Johns Hopkins University Press, 1972–2004), 5:1176; *The Diary of William Maclay*, ed. Kenneth R. Bowling and Helen E. Veit (Baltimore: Johns Hopkins University Press, 1988), 88–89.

36. Oliver Ellsworth, "Landholder VII," in Jensen et al., *Documentary History*, 14:451; John Locke, *Letter Concerning Toleration*, trans. W. Popple (1789), in

98 | William R. Casto

The Second Treatise of Civil Government and a Letter Concerning Toleration, ed. J. W. Gough (Oxford: B. Blackwell, 1946), 122, 134, 152–54.

37. See, for instance, Andrew Murphy, *Conscience and Community: Revisiting Toleration and Religious Dissent in Early Modern England and America* (University Park, Pa.: Pennsylvania State University Press, 2001).

38. Compare Oliver Ellsworth, "Landholder VII," in Jensen et al., *Documentary History*, 14:451, with Locke, *Letter Concerning Toleration*, 124–25, 134, 146–47. See "Inventory of Ellsworth's Estate," 6, Archives, Connecticut State Library, Hartford.

39. John Locke, *Letter Concerning Toleration*, 150–59; Oliver Ellsworth, "Landholder VII," in Jensen et al., *Documentary History*, 14:451. On punishing atheism, see Locke, *Letter Concerning Toleration*, 156; Locke, *A Vindication of the Reasonableness of Christianity* (1696), in *The Works of John Locke* (London: Thomas Tegg, 1823), 7:161; Nathan Strong, *A Sermon Delivered in the Presence of His Excellency Samuel Huntington* (Hartford, Conn.: Hudson & Goodwin, 1796), 20–21.

40. Oliver Ellsworth, "Landholder IX," in Jensen et al., *Documentary History*, 15:192; Samuel Huntington, letter to Samuel Johnston, Sep. 23, 1788, in Jensen et al. *Documentary History*, 3:362–63 (microfiche supp.). See also Rufus King, letter to Jeremiah Wadsworth, Dec. 13, 1787, excerpted in *Supplement to Max Farrand's The Records of the Federal Convention of 1787*, ed. James Hutson (New Haven, Conn.: Yale University Press, 1987), 290.

41. De Pauw et al., *History of the First Federal Congress*, 4:43–45.

42. Ibid., 4:36, 39.

43. Ibid., 1:151.

44. Leonard W. Levy, *The Establishment Clause: Religion and the First Amendment* (New York: Macmillan, 1986), 81–82; Rodney K. Smith, *Public Prayer and the Constitution* (Wilmington, Del.: Scholarly Resources, 1987), 87–89; *Senate Legislative Journal* in De Pauw et al., *History of the First Federal Congress*, 1:182.

45. De Pauw et al., *History of the First Federal Congress*, 1:158, 166; 4:43–45.

46. Ibid., 1:181–82.

47. Ibid., 4:47–48; emphasis indicates change.

48. Locke, *Letter Concerning Toleration*, 141, 153.

49. *Connecticut Acts*, 21–22; Elisha Williams, *The Essential Rights and Liberties of Protestants* (Boston: Kneeland & Green, 1744), 7–8, 42–45; Joseph Huntington, *God Ruling the Nations for the Most Glorious End* (Hartford, Conn.: Hudson & Goodwin, 1784), 13; Levi Hart, *The Description of a Good Character Attempted and Applied to the Subject of Jurisprudence and Civil Government* (Hartford, Conn.: Hudson & Goodwin, 1786), 23; John Leland, *The Rights of Conscience Inalienable, and Therefore Religious Opinions not Cognizable by Law; or, The High-flying Church-man Stripped of His Legal Rule, Appears a Yaho* (1791), in *The Writings of the Late Elder John Leland*, ed. L. F. Greene (New York: G. W. Wood, 1845), 177–92; *Connecticut State Records*, 2:369–74.

50. Oliver Ellsworth, "Landholder VII," in Jensen et al., Documentary History, 14:451; Oliver Ellsworth, "Landholder VI," in Jensen et al., Documentary History, 14:401 n.46.

51. Thomas J. Curry, The First Freedoms: Church and State in America to the Passage of the First Amendment (New York: Oxford University Press, 1987), 204–6; De Pauw et al., History of the First Federal Congress, 11:1260; see also 2:1257.

52. De Pauw et al., History of the First Federal Congress, 11:1261–62.

53. Leland, Rights of Conscience Inalienable; John Leland, A Stroke at the Branch, Containing Remarks on Times and Things (Harford, Conn.: Elisha Babcock, 1801), 23–24; "The Baptist Petitions," Connecticut State Records, 10:369, 374.

54. Moses Mather, Sermon, Preached in the Audience of the General Assembly (New London, Conn.: Timothy Green, 1781), 9 nn.11–12.

55. Oliver Ellsworth and Roger Sherman, letter to Samuel Huntington, Sep. 26, 1787, in Jensen et al., Documentary History, 3:351–53; De Pauw et al., History of the First Federal Congress, 2:1261.

56. Oliver Ellsworth, "Landholder VII," in Jensen et al., Documentary History, 14:450; Oliver Ellsworth, "Landholder VI," in Jensen, Documentary History, 401; William Samuel Johnson and Oliver Ellsworth, letter to Samuel Huntington, Mar. 18, 1790, in William Samuel Johnson Papers, Connecticut Historical Society, Hartford.

57. Senate Legislative Journal in De Pauw et al., History of the First Federal Congress, 1:12, 16; Act of March 3, 1791, chap. 28, sec. 2, I Stat. 350; A Treaty between the United States and the Oneida, Tuscarora, and Stockbridge Indians, Dwelling in the Country of the Oneidas, Art. IV, 7 Stat. 47, 48 (1795).

58. Timothy Dwight, Travels in New-England and New York, ed. Barbara Miller Soloman, (Cambridge, Mass.: Harvard University Press, 1969 [1822]), 4:283. See also Isaac Lewis, The Political Advantage of Godliness (Hartford, Conn.: Hudson & Goodwin, 1797), 27. Dwight's Travels was published posthumously based on essays and notes written between 1798 and 1814.

59. Curry, First Freedoms, 178–84, 209–17; Ezra Stiles, A Discourse on the Christian Union (Boston: Edes and Gill, 1761), 80–83; Ebenezer Frothringham, A Key to Unlock the Door (1767), discussed in McLoughlin, New England Dissent, vol. 1, chap. 22; Timothy Dwight, Travels, 4:283.

60. Oliver Ellsworth, "Landholder V," in Jensen et al., Documentary History, 14:335.

61. See William G. McLoughlin, "The Role of Religion in the Revolution," in Essays on the American Revolution, ed. Stephen G. Kurtz and James H. Hutson (New York: W. W. Norton, 1973), 219–22.

62. James Madison, letter to Thomas Jefferson, Oct. 17, 1788, in Madison Papers, 2:297. For a somewhat different analyses reaching similar conclusions, see Cushing Strout, The New Heavens and New Earth: Political Religion in America (New York: Harper & Row, 1974), 93–98.

63. See, e.g., Chester James Antieau, Arthur T. Downey, and Edward C. Roberts, *Freedom from Federal Establishment* (Milwaukee: Bruce, 1964), 130–31, 140–42; Michael J. Malbin, *Religion and Politics: the Intentions of the Authors of the First Amendment* (Washington, D.C.: American Enterprise Institute, 1978), 13–15; Robert L. Cord, *Separation of Church and State: Historical Fact and Current Fiction* (New York: Lambeth Press, 1982), 8–9; Levy, *Establishment Clause*, 83; Smith, *Public Prayer and the Constitution*, 90–96. See also Philip Kurland, "The Origins of the Religion Clauses of the Constitution," *William and Mary Law Review* 27 (1986): 855–56; Douglas Laycock, "'Nonpreferential' Aide to Religion: A False Claim about Original Intent," *William & Mary Law Review* 27 (1986): 879–81, 904.

64. Levy, *Establishment Clause*, 95.

65. John Hatsell, *Precedents of Proceedings in the House of Commons*, 2nd ed. (reprint, South Hackensack, N.J.: Rothman, 1971 [1818]), 4:48–55; 35 (discussing sixteenth-century precedent).

66. Thomas Jefferson, *Manual of Parliamentary Practice* (1796), H. R. Doc. No. 277, 98th Cong., 2nd less., at 113 n.a. (1985); *The Diary of William Maclay*, 189.

67. *Senate Legislative Journal* in De Pauw et al., *History of the First Federal Congress*, 1:12, 16; Jefferson, *Manual of Parliamentary Practice*, sec. xlv; Hatsell, *Precedents of Proceedings*, 4:35.

68. *Senate Legislative Journal*, in De Pauw et al., *History of the First Federal Congress*, 1:16, 181–82.

69. James Madison, letter to Edmund Pendleton, Sep. 23, 1789, in *The Papers of James Madison* (Charlottesville: University Press of Virginia, 1979), 12:418–20.

70. On the Conference Report's use of the article "an" and the participle "respecting," compare Levy, *Establishment Clause*, 94–96, with Smith, *Public Prayer and the Constitution*, 92–93.

71. On Congress's constitutional authority to limit the federal courts' jurisdiction, see William R. Casto, "The First Congress's Understanding of Its Authority over the Federal Courts' Jurisdiction," *Boston College Law Review* 26 (1985): 1101. On the concurrent foreign affairs powers, see William R. Casto, *Foreign Affairs and the Constitution in the Age of Fighting Sail* (Columbia: University of South Carolina Press, 2006), chaps. 5 and 10.

72. See generally Hall, "Jeffersonian Walls and Madisonian Lines," 563–614.

CHAPTER 5

Alexander Hamilton, Theistic Rationalist

GREGG L. FRAZER

The study of Alexander Hamilton's religion presents a daunting, but interesting, challenge to the historian. Most biographers discuss the early religious influences on Hamilton and his apparent piety during his youth, then mention his religion briefly or not at all until the final years of his life. Hamilton is generally considered to be a religious enigma during the prime of his life, when he had a significant impact upon the American political scene. There are two reasons for this difficulty. First, as Douglass Adair astutely observes, Hamilton appears to have gone through different religious stages. Adair identifies four stages in Hamilton's religious life: (1) a conventionally religious youth, (2) religious indifference while in power, (3) opportunistic religiosity while in political opposition, and (4) Christian faith in retirement.[1] The second reason for why biographers have difficulty addressing Hamilton's religion is that his religious beliefs and practices do not fit neatly into either of the two generally accepted categories for the period: deism and Christianity. In the prime of his life, Alexander Hamilton appears to have been neither a deist nor a Christian, but a theistic rationalist.

A Brief Biography

Alexander Hamilton was born on the island of Nevis in the British West Indies in either 1755 or 1757 (depending on the evidence one accepts) to unwed parents whose relationship lasted nearly fifteen years and who presented themselves as James and Rachel Hamilton.[2] He was left an orphan in 1768, after James abandoned the family and Rachel died. Aided by prominent sponsors, Hamilton entered King's College in 1773 because his first choice, the College of New Jersey at Princeton, would not grant him special status. He gained notoriety by publishing patriot pamphlets in 1774 and 1775, and was appointed an artillery captain in 1776. Following distinction in combat engagements, Hamilton's meteoric rise continued with his appointment as General Washington's aide-de-camp in 1777. He married Elizabeth Schuyler in 1780, and she eventually bore eight children. In 1781, he led a critical assault in the decisive battle at Yorktown. After the war, Hamilton's political reputation grew as a result of his writings, and he was named a delegate to the Continental Congress. In successive years, he opened a law office and founded the Bank of New York. In 1786, Hamilton drafted the resolution calling for what would become known as the Constitutional Convention.[3]

After service as a delegate to the convention, Hamilton led the fight for ratification of the new Constitution in New York. Toward that end, Hamilton proposed writing a series of essays designed to explain and support the Constitution, which became known as *The Federalist Papers.* Although he enlisted James Madison and John Jay to help him, Hamilton wrote about fifty-five of the eighty-five essays. Hamilton was appointed the first secretary of the treasury in the new government. As such, he saw himself as President Washington's prime minister and became the primary initiator of the administration's program. In what was perhaps at once his greatest and most controversial achievement, Hamilton established American credit and a sound financial footing for the fledgling nation. After his stint as secretary of the treasury, he remained a powerful player behind the scenes in domestic politics (as the recognized leader of the Federalist Party) and in American foreign policy. Largely due to Hamilton's efforts and influence, Aaron Burr was defeated in the presidential election of 1800 and in the New York gubernatorial election of 1804.

Burr accused Hamilton of sullying his character, famously challenged him to a duel, and, in July 1804, fatally wounded him.

Biographers and Hamilton's Religion

Scholarly treatment of Hamilton's religion has been sketchy at best. Standard accounts leap from his childhood to the waning years of his life. Typically, there is coverage of the influence of Presbyterian minister Hugh Knox on the youthful Hamilton and mention of the teenage Hamilton's newspaper account of a hurricane—then little or nothing until a brief reference to his use of religion for political purposes and discussion of his renewed interest in religion in his last few years of life.

Most scholars mention Hugh Knox's influence on Hamilton as a boy, but they differ as to the substance and persistence of that influence.[4] Another part of Hamilton's youth that is consistently mentioned by scholars is the testimony of his college roommate, Robert Troup, concerning Hamilton's religious practice while at King's College. Troup recalls that Hamilton attended church regularly and was "on his knees both morning and night offering up fervent prayers."[5] Troup's story is recounted in one form or another by several biographers.[6] For most scholars, a great gap in the treatment of Hamilton's religion immediately follows the account of his collegiate religiosity.[7] Only John Miller suggests that Hamilton's religious beliefs had any significant effect on his thinking or view of government during the postwar years and during the period in which he exercised power and profound influence.[8]

Religion becomes important to nearly all of Hamilton's biographers in their coverage of the last ten years of his life. Some deal with his criticism of the atheism of the French Revolution, some touch on his comments concerning religion and morality in his draft of Washington's Farewell Address, and all but a few discuss his renewed interest in Christianity in the last two years of life. Most of them mention something of Hamilton's use of religion for partisan political purposes in the late 1790s and early 1800s. In particular, almost all note his controversial 1802 proposal to create a Christian Constitutional Society.[9] In fact, that is the only reference to religion in Henry Cabot Lodge's well-known biography of Hamilton.[10] The general consensus is that Hamilton returned to the piety of his youth during the final two years of his life and after the death of his eldest son, Philip.

Categorizing Hamilton's Religion

Scholars have difficulty dealing with Hamilton's religious beliefs because they do not fit conveniently into the two accepted categories: deism and Christianity. A kind of false dichotomy has been created by scholars studying the religion of the American founders. Damage has been done to the actual beliefs of key founders because of attempts to fit, if you will, square peg beliefs into round belief systems. In his recent massive biography, Ron Chernow struggles to place Hamilton within the accepted categories.[11] Forrest McDonald simply writes of Hamilton's "blend of skepticism and faith."[12]

There is a better way to approach Hamilton's religious beliefs; it requires a recognition that it is difficult to place him in either the deist or the Christian camp because he was not a deist or a Christian (at least for most of his life). Instead, I contend that Alexander Hamilton was a theistic rationalist during the period in which he had significant impact on America.[13] A study of Hamilton offers us a unique opportunity because he became a Christian at the end of his life. In the words and actions of this one man at different stages of his life, then, we can see some of the difference between Christianity and theistic rationalism.

Theistic rationalism was a hybrid belief system mixing elements of natural religion, Protestant Christianity, and rationalism—with rationalism as the controlling element. Rationalism here refers to the philosophical view that regards reason as the chief source and test of knowledge. Theistic rationalists believed that these three elements would generally complement one another, but when conflict between them could not be resolved or ignored, reason must play the decisive role. Adherents of theistic rationalism, who were raised in a loosely Christian environment but educated in Enlightenment rationalism, were willing to define God in whatever way their reason dictated and to jettison Christian beliefs that did not conform, in their minds, to reason. While an emphasis on reason had long been accepted practice in Christianity, Christians saw reason as a supplement to revelation and a support for faith. The theistic rationalists made reason the ultimate standard and considered revelation to be a supplement to reason. If there was a discrepancy between reason and supposed revelation, they considered the "revelation" to be flawed or illegitimate. Reason determined what counted as valid revelation.

Theistic rationalists believed in a powerful, rational, and benevolent creator God who established laws by which the universe functions. Their God was a unitary personal God who was present and who actively intervened in human affairs. Consequently, they believed in the efficacy of prayer. For them, the key factor in serving God was living a good and moral life. In their view, promotion of morality was central to the value of religion, and the morality engendered by religion was indispensable to a free society. Because virtually all religions promote morality, they held that many, if not all, religious traditions or systems are valid and lead to the same God. Theistic rationalists looked forward to a personal afterlife in which the wicked will be temporarily punished and the good will experience happiness forever. Although they believed that God primarily reveals Himself through nature, theistic rationalists believed that some written revelation was legitimate revelation from God. Although they were convinced that reason and revelation generally agree with each other, theistic rationalists believed that revelation was designed to complement reason.

Natural religion was a system of thought centered on the belief that reliable information about God and about what He wills is best discovered and understood by examining the evidence of nature and the laws of nature that He established. While the two were not synonymous, the primary expression of natural religion in the eighteenth century was deism. Eighteenth-century American deism was, at once, a belief system on its own and a critique of Christianity. The critical elements of deist belief were the effective absence of God and the denial of any written revelation from God.[14] These two elements clearly divided the deists and theistic rationalists. Deism was as much a critique of Christianity as a religion of its own, however. Deists rejected virtually all of the fundamentals of Christianity and condemned it for intolerance, persecution, a faulty depiction of the deity, and promoting an illogical and irrational supernatural worldview. Most deists were also extremely critical of Jesus. He was criticized by them for being petty, for exalting humility and meekness to virtues, and for not being original in his ethics.[15] Deists wanted nothing to do with Christianity or its central figure. While theistic rationalists shared some ideas with deists, they had a much greater regard for Christianity and for Jesus than did most deists.

For the purposes of this study, Christianity as a belief system will be defined by the standards of eighteenth-century American Christians. It refers, then, to a set of beliefs officially espoused by all of the major Christian sects in eighteenth-century America. Those who held these beliefs were considered to be Christians, and those who did not were considered to be "infidels." The fundamentals of Christianity were common knowledge to contemporaries of the period. Despite disputes over church polity and sacramental issues, which resulted in a number of sects, the period saw remarkable unanimity regarding central doctrines. According to the creeds, confessions, catechisms, and articles of faith of the major denominations in America during the period, all of them shared common belief in the following: the Trinity, the deity of Jesus, a God active in human affairs, original sin, the Virgin birth, the atoning work of Christ in satisfaction for man's sins, the bodily resurrection of Jesus, eternal punishment for sin, justification by faith, and the authority of the Scriptures.[16] The fact that the Catholic Church, though separated from the Protestant churches, also embraced all of these fundamental doctrines is further evidence of the consensus concerning the substance of Christianity. Theistic rationalists shared some beliefs with Christians, but only those that seemed to them to be reasonable.

Hamilton's Theistic Rationalism

Hamilton, like theistic rationalists in general, shared certain beliefs with both Christians and deists. For example, Hamilton believed in a benevolent creator God. He asserted that "the Supreme Being gave existence to man, together with the means of preserving and beautifying that existence." Further, this creator "has established laws to regulate the actions of His creatures" and "this is what is called the law of nature,"[17] according to Hamilton. All of the key founders[18] shared with Christians and deists a belief in a creator God who is the author of nature; Hamilton was no exception.

Hamilton's view of the afterlife was also consistent with both Christianity and deism, but most of his references reflected Christian terminology. He indicated belief in "the immortality of the soul" and referred to "endless bliss," going to "a peacefull Shore," "eternal bliss," and to "lay[ing] up a treasure in Heaven." He expressed confidence that his son had, upon death, "safely reached the haven of eternal repose and felicity." Occasionally, he used language more common to deists: "a future state of rewards and punishments." Early in his career, Hamilton stressed that God "will be the final judge, of the universe"[19]—a belief held by both Christians and deists. More poignant were Hamilton's references to the afterlife when he was facing the immediate prospect of his own death. In a letter to his wife written a week before the duel, Hamilton expressed hope in "a happy immortality" and "the sweet hope of meeting you in a better world." In his will, written two days before the duel, Hamilton wrote of God's possible "call . . . to the eternal world."[20] Throughout his life, Hamilton believed in an eternal afterlife.

Turning to the beliefs that Hamilton as a theistic rationalist shared with Christianity, one must for the moment set aside his expressions of faith as he faced death. In contrast to the deists, Hamilton believed in an active and intervening, all-wise God. He often used the term "Providence," common to Christians, when referring to God's intervention. Until the latter part of his life, most of Hamilton's references to Providence were on a large scale. As a youth and a young man, Hamilton expressed belief in a "superintending" God "who rules the world" and in a God who actively controls the elements of nature. Late in life, he suggested that the nation could and should "trust in Heaven."[21] In the latter portion of his life, he extended the work of Providence to individual lives: "Arraign not the dispensations of Providence, they must be founded in wisdom and goodness; and when they do not suit us, it must be because there is some fault in ourselves which deserves chastisement; or because there is a kind intent, to correct in us some vice or failing, of which, perhaps, we may not be conscious; or because the general plan requires that we should suffer partial ill. In this situation it is our duty to cultivate resignation, and even humility."[22] On receipt of condolences on the death of his son, Hamilton responded that "[it] was the will of heaven."[23] Though he always believed in a present and active God, expressions of belief in God's intervention in individual lives were confined to the period in which he actively sought a relationship with God.

Related to his belief in a present God was Hamilton's belief in the efficacy of prayer. Prayer is arguably meaningless if God is not present to hear it or if He does not intervene in affairs of this world. As a young man, Hamilton reported praying, and that God heard his prayer. Hamilton's college roommate, Robert Troup, reported being "often powerfully moved by the fervor and eloquence of his prayers."[24] The next recorded instance of Hamilton's involvement with prayer was the wisecrack he allegedly made in response to Franklin's suggestion that the sessions of the Constitutional Convention be opened with prayer. The same source that recounted an apocryphal version of the event reported that Hamilton supposedly said they were competent to conduct their business and had no need to call in "foreign aid." Given the unreliable source and Madison's report that Franklin's "proposition was received & treated with the respect due to it,"[25] it is likely that this story is merely one of a number of attempts to besmirch Hamilton's character. In Hamilton's later years, his son reported that Hamilton "now" engaged in "the habit of daily prayer,"[26] so it is likely that his prayer life was minimal during his years in power. The fact that he thought he could get by without divine help during the height of his personal power does not change the fact that he believed in prayer and that God was there if he felt he needed Him. As will be seen below, Hamilton returned to active prayer when he later felt that he did, indeed, need God's help.

There were aspects of Hamilton's religious life that were not consistent with Christianity or deism. As previously mentioned, Hamilton was "conventionally religious" in the early part of his life. He was, however, not affiliated with any church or denomination, and as Adair notes, "there is little evidence to show any great depth or intensity of religious feeling." Nonetheless, he was sponsored by men who would not have "backed a youth who showed signs of religious heterodoxy." The testimony of his college roommate would lead one to believe that Hamilton was a sincere Christian.[27] There is reason to question Troup's assessment, however.

Adair characterizes the years 1777 to 1792 as a period of "religious indifference" on the part of Hamilton. He observes that "there is nothing in Hamilton's published letters during this era of fantastic personal success to indicate that he was emotionally or intellectually concerned with God, the Church, or any religious problems whatsoever."[28] While in the military, Hamilton wrote to a general to recommend a particular minister as a military chaplain. In the letter, Hamilton said: "He is just what I should like for a military parson, except that he does not whore or drink." He said approvingly of the minister that "he will not insist upon your going to heaven whether you will or not." It was also during this period that Hamilton was accused of making two wisecracks about God. The first concerned Franklin's prayer motion. The second was Hamilton's reputed remark when asked by old friend Dr. John Rodgers why God was not recognized in the Constitution. Hamilton supposedly cavalierly replied, "We forgot it." Finally, during this period, Hamilton carried on an adulterous affair with Maria Reynolds, a married woman, "for a considerable time" and wrote a less-than-humble public confession of it.[29]

During the "third stage" of his religious life—when he was out of power but still actively involved in politics—Hamilton used religion to advance his own causes in a way that would not be sanctioned by Christianity or deism. When a biographer says that "Hamilton . . . toward the end, confused Federalism with Christianity," he means that Hamilton did so intentionally and for his own purposes. Adair puts it more clearly when he says that Hamilton "attempted to enlist God in the Federalist party to buttress that party's temporal power."[30] Using religion for political purposes was nothing new for Hamilton; he did so as early as 1774. In this "third stage" of life, however, Hamilton primarily used religion in his attempts to thwart Jefferson's presidential ambitions. As early as 1792, he was concerned about Jefferson's "ardent desire" to be president. With Washington's decision not to seek reelection in 1796, Hamilton declared, "All personal and partial considerations must be discarded, and every thing must give way to the great object of excluding Jefferson."[31] In his 1796 Phocion essays, Hamilton linked Jefferson with the atheism of the French Revolution. He then wrote essays emphasizing the threat to society of atheism's attack on Christianity, culminating in his claim that a "league has at length been cemented between the apostles and disciples of irreligion and of anarchy."[32] By implication, Hamilton used religion to convince the masses that Jefferson was an anarchist. He may even have embedded an attack on Jefferson in his draft of Washington's Farewell Address. Washington retained much of Hamilton's draft of what became the Farewell Address, and the section on religion and morality is almost completely by Hamilton.

Given what else Hamilton was writing in 1796, one wonders if he had Jefferson in mind when he wrote, "In vain does that man claim the praise of patriotism who labours to subvert or undermine these great pillars of human happiness [religion and morality]." Or again when he wrote, "concede as much as may be asked to the effect of refined education in minds of a peculiar structure—can we believe—can we in prudence suppose that national morality can be maintained in exclusion of religious principles?" Or finally: "Who that is a prudent & sincere friend to them can look with indifference on the ravages which are making in the foundation of the Fabric? Religion?"[33]

Hamilton's use of religion for political purposes and his efforts to prevent a Jefferson presidency did not end with Jefferson's loss in 1796. In a letter to William Loughton Smith in 1797, Hamilton suggested mobilizing "the Religious Ideas" of Americans against France and called them "a valuable resource." According to Hamilton, "this is an advantage which we shall be very unskilful, if we do not improve to the utmost." He went on to argue that "a day of humiliation and prayer besides being very proper would be extremely useful." In recommending "a day of fasting, humiliation and prayer" to three other Federalists over the next year, Hamilton emphasized that it would be "politically useful," "very expedient" on political grounds, politically "proper," and "useful." He wrote, "The Government will be very unwise, if it does not make the most of the religious prepossessions of our people—opposing the honest enthusiasm of Religious Opinion to the phrenzy of Political fanaticism" and, in another case, that "[we] must oppose to political fanaticism religious zeal."[34]

In a series of 1798 articles entitled *The Stand*, Hamilton again fulminated against the irreligion of France and made sure to link Jefferson to it. The first three essays—particularly the third—denounced the irreligious and anti-religious features of the French Revolution and resultant

French government. Having verbally blasted the French for their specifically anti-Christian deeds in the first three essays, Hamilton used the last three to associate Jefferson with the irreligious, anti-Christian French. In the fifth essay, he referred to "the political leader of the adherents to France" in America—and then, in case anyone wondered to whom he referred, included a footnote identifying him as Jefferson. While he did not name anyone in the sixth essay, he referred to "the partisans and tools of France" in America; given the essay published three days earlier, there was little doubt as to whom he referred. In the seventh and final essay, all of the gloves were off. Speaking of France, he questioned "the true character of their faction in this country, at least of its leaders" and charged that they were more attached to France than to the United States. He called "the high priest of this sect" [Jefferson] an "inventor of . . . subterfuge" and of "a systematic design to excuse France at all events . . . to prepare the way for implicit submission to her will." If that were not enough, Hamilton said of Jefferson, "To be the pro-consul of a despotic Directory over the United States . . . can alone be the criminal, the ignoble aim of so seditious, so prostitute a character." Having essentially accused Jefferson of treason, it was easy to call him and the other Republicans "subaltern mercenaries" and "our Jacobins." Just in case anyone was still unclear as to how to vote, Hamilton asserted that "France places absolute dependence on this party in every event, and counts upon their devotion to her" and that "the true source of the evils" perpetrated on Americans by France was "the unnatural league of a portion of our citizens with the oppressors of their country."[35]

Hamilton wrote another article in 1799 designed to arouse the American people against the French and, by extension, their Republican allies.[36] He again tapped into the "valuable resource" of religious ideas and sensibilities. Concerned that Jefferson would be elected president in 1800, Hamilton devised a scheme by which to deny Jefferson New York's electoral votes. His letter to Governor John Jay proposing the plan stressed the importance of preventing "an *Atheist* in Religion" from ascending to the presidency.[37] Hamilton's assessment is ironic because, as Adair points out, Hamilton's preferred candidate (Pinckney) held religious views similar to those of Jefferson.[38]

After the Federalists' devastating loss in 1800, Hamilton continued to work for the party and against Jefferson's Republicans—and he continued to use religion for those political purposes. The most prominent of such efforts was his proposal for the establishment of "The Christian Constitutional Society." While those seeking evidence of a Christian America extol this proposal, Adair describes it as a "familiar" effort to use religion to strengthen the Federalists at the expense of the "devilish Jeffersonians." Hamilton proposed it in the context of the Federalists' need for a plan to cultivate "popular favour" and win over public opinion in order to reinvigorate the party. Miller explains the motive: "Religion was an emotional force which Jefferson, a suspected Deist, had signally failed to exploit."[39] The three stated goals of the Society were designed to benefit the Federalist Party. The first was "diffusion of information"—apparently from what follows, Federalist information. The second goal was "the use of all lawful means in concert to promote the election of fit men." In the context of a plan for reinvigorating the Federalist Party, "fit men" of course means Federalists. The third goal was "the promoting of institutions of a charitable & useful nature in the management of Federalists."[40] Clearly, the primary purpose here was not the institutions themselves, but that Federalists would get credit for them and gain "popular favour." Chernow sums it up thusly: "By signing up God against Thomas Jefferson, Hamilton hoped to make a more potent political appeal. . . . Hamilton was not honoring religion but exploiting it for political ends."[41]

The Influence of Deism on Hamilton

Hamilton's religious life and beliefs showed the influence of deism. Hamilton's vision of God emphasized the same deistic triad of attributes as did other theistic rationalists: power, wisdom, and goodness. He alternately spoke of God as "Omnipotence," "the Almighty," "Supreme Intelligence," "rational," and "benefactor." He maintained that whatever God does "must be founded in wisdom and goodness." Other than "the Almighty," Hamilton did not use Christian or biblical terms for God. As Chernow notes, Hamilton "never talked about Christ and took refuge in vague references to 'providence' or 'heaven.'" Hamilton's God was "beneficent" and the personification of "Infinite Wisdom."[42] He shared that understanding with deists.

Hamilton also shared with deists an emphasis on the connection between God and nature. His dynamic report of a hurricane as a young man stressed God's expression of himself in nature. He suggested that God and nature were one when he wrote, "That which, in a calm unruffled temper, we call a natural cause, seemed then like the correction of the Deity." In the view Hamilton expressed here, emotional response points to God, while rationality points to nature. He also stressed God's role as the author of natural law in an attack on an opponent's similarity to Thomas Hobbes.[43] John Miller argues that Hamilton believed that "God and Nature" had established political orders, the sacredness of property, and the economic foundations of the United States.[44]

One of the best known of Hamilton's statements emphasized God's role in shaping human nature: "The sacred rights of mankind are not to be rummaged for among old parchments or musty records. They are written, as with a sunbeam, in the whole volume of human nature, by the hand of the Divinity itself, and can never be erased or obscured by mortal power."[45] According to his son, Hamilton's spiritual growth in the latter stage of his life was stimulated by contemplation of the God of nature: "His religious feelings grew with his growing intimacy with the marvellous works of nature, all pointing in their processes and their results to a great pervading, ever active Cause." His son also reported Hamilton's study of "Paley's Evidences,"[46] which was an attempt to prove the existence and attributes of God primarily from the evidence of nature.

Hamilton also stressed the element of deism that was a fundamental tenet of theistic rationalism: the centrality of morality to religion and religion's benign influence on the morality of society. Like many of the theistic rationalists, Hamilton rarely mentioned religion without mentioning morality.[47] For them, the two went hand in hand. In his draft of the Farewell Address, Hamilton said that "Religion and Morality are essential props" of "political happiness" and "great pillars of human happiness," and he connected "moral and religious obligation" in judicial oaths before adding, "Nor ought we to flatter ourselves that morality can be separated from religion." He then asked, "Can we in prudence suppose that national morality can be maintained in exclusion of religious principles? Does it not require the aid of a generally received and divinely authoritative Religion?" He concluded the religious section by asking, "Can it be that Providence has not connected the permanent felicity of a nation with its virtue?"[48]

In other writings, Hamilton displayed particular concern about the influence of French atheism and argued that "the moral decay of the United States" would follow "the loss of religious principle" and abandonment of "the simple faith of the early patriots."[49] Among other evils, Hamilton believed that irreligion was "subversive of social order."[50] Hamilton vehemently opposed the idea that "religious opinion of any sort is unnecessary to society," and he identified religion as one of the "venerable pillars that support the edifice of civilized society." He further argued that morality cannot be separated from religion and that those who love liberty know that "morality must fall with religion." While several of these statements were generated in criticism of the French and used for political purposes, there is no reason to believe that they did not represent Hamilton's sincere perspective, and they were consistent with what he said in other circumstances. Religion *was* under attack in France, and it was the appropriate time for observers to comment on the relationship between "religion, morality, and society,"[51] which were, for theistic rationalists, certainly connected. On at least one occasion, the death of Washington, Hamilton indicated belief that a life of morality and virtue would secure a place in heaven. Of Washington he said, "If virtue can secure happiness in another world, he is happy. In this the seal is now put upon *his* glory."[52] As was noted above, theistic rationalists believed that man's duty to God was to be a good man and good citizen.

There was another way in which Hamilton's beliefs corresponded with those of the deists: he opposed particularist religion and supported toleration—even equality—of religions. As previously noted, Hamilton was never formally affiliated with any particular church or denomination. His wife, Eliza, was "a staunch member" of the Dutch Reformed church and was "assiduous in the practices of piety." Adair notes, however, that "Hamilton's marriage to her . . . did not lead him to join her church after the fashion of so many indifferent husbands with devout wives." When he was seeking a wife, he told a friend, "As to religion a moderate stock will satisfy me. She must believe in God and hate a saint." Hamilton was looking for a match for himself: "moderate" where religion was concerned; that is, one who believed in God but was not too enthusiastic. Ironically, Eliza's nickname was "the Saint." According to his nephew, Hamilton had a "simple faith, quite unemotional in this respect."[53] Chernow likewise notes that Hamilton "did not belong formally to a denomination, even though Eliza rented a pew at Trinity Church. He showed no interest in liturgy, sectarian doctrine, or public prayer."[54] Like his fellow theistic rationalists, Hamilton felt that belief in God was important and beneficial, but that one should not be too specific or enthusiastic about religion.

The most important of Chernow's observations is Hamilton's lack of interest in sectarian doctrine. Theistic rationalists disdained sectarian doctrines or "dogmas," as they called them. Exhortation to morality was the value and purpose of religion; doctrines were ultimately irrelevant and only served to cause conflict. According to Hamilton, bigotry (which in the eighteenth century meant exclusive devotion to a particular sect) was dangerous. "There is a bigotry in politics, as well as in religions, equally pernicious in both." He publicly decried New England's bigotry. He warned that Europe had lost thousands due to religious bigotry and that bigotry in religion was an unwise policy. "While some kingdoms were impoverishing and depopulating themselves, by their severities to the non-conformists, their wiser neighbors were reaping the fruits of their folly, and augmenting their own numbers, industry and wealth, by receiving with open arms the persecuted fugitives." Hamilton, then, saw the matter as a policy issue and ignored—or pretended not to know—the fact that people could be completely devoted to a particular sect because they believe its specific doctrines to be true. This was the common view of theistic rationalists. Hamilton also used terminology often used by theistic rationalists to describe doctrines when he called them mere "speculative notions of religion."[55] Hamilton stressed the idea that religion is a matter of individual conscience. He said of the typical Protestant Englishman, for example: "The privilege of worshipping the deity in the manner his conscience dictates . . . is one of the dearest he enjoys." He likewise said of Roman Catholics, "Why should we wound the tender conscience of any and why present oaths to those who are known to be good citizens?"[56] That was the issue for theistic rationalists—did a religion produce good citizens? If so, it fulfilled its primary purpose and any barriers to its practice should be removed.

Along with the other theistic rationalists and some Christians, Hamilton opposed establishment of religion. Of course, it was an easy and natural thing for theistic rationalists to encourage and promote freedom of religion, because they had no vested interest in any particular denomination or sect. It is difficult for those who believe in the importance of fundamental doctrines and in a specific road to Heaven (for example, the Puritans in seventeenth-century New England) to allow "false" religions to be practiced within their sphere of authority. The theistic rationalists, however, held to no particular creed but the "essentials" to which "all good men" could agree. In a sense, they could *afford* to grant religious liberty in a way that those with exclusive beliefs could not. For his part, Hamilton gave a detailed explanation of the difference between establishment of religion and religious toleration and warned of the dangers of established religion. In doing so, he argued that "civil and religious liberty always go together, if the foundation of the one be sapped, the other will fall of course." He went so far as to suggest "what is far more precious than mere religious toleration—a perfect equality of religious privileges."[57] The theistic rationalism of the key founders, including Hamilton, may go a long way toward explaining America's exaltation of religious liberty. As long as a religion promoted morality—and all of the religions with which they were familiar did—there was no reason to restrict religious practice.

Hamilton's Conversion

The close of Hamilton's life, the fourth of Adair's "stages," illuminates the difference between one adhering to theistic rationalism and one devoted to orthodox Christianity. Hamilton's basis of confidence and his entire attitude and language were transformed by his conversion to Christianity at the end of his life.

Hamilton's religious awakening began with his fall from political power. His son reported that in 1801, "withdrawn for a time from politics, [Hamilton] sought and found relief . . . in the duties of religion." He began to study the Bible and other theological works and to engage in daily prayer. His fall from political power started Hamilton's religious quest, but it was personal tragedy that "crystallized the change."[58] Hamilton's eldest son, Philip, was killed in a duel, and Hamilton's eldest daughter lost her sanity in grief over his death. Hamilton turned to a more personal, less generic God for solace and comfort.

With his change of perspective, Hamilton's attitude showed signs of change as well. Despite his career-long bitter rivalry with Jefferson, he used his influence to try to keep Federalist newspapers from printing the Jefferson-Hemings scandal as exposed by James Callender.[59] He gained an appreciation for and began "to cultivate resignation, and even humility"[60] before God and men—in stark contrast to the arrogance for which he was known in public life and which he clearly exhibited in his response to the Maria Reynolds affair. Finally, the formerly ambitious and ruthless politician determined "to expose my own life to any extent rather than subject my self to the guilt of taking the life of another"— that is, rather than fire at Aaron Burr in their duel.[61] In the end, Hamilton apparently found something more important than reason to guide his actions. His second, Nathaniel Pendleton, tried to convince him to fire at Burr, but Hamilton replied that his decision was "the effect of a *religious scruple*, and does not admit of reasoning. It is useless to say more on the subject, as my purpose is definitely fixed."[62]

But what religious scruple had Hamilton found? Close friend Oliver Wolcott told his wife that "Genl Hamilton has *of late* expressed his conviction of the truths of the Christian Religion."[63] Wolcott distinguished Hamilton's newfound belief in Christianity from his previous religious position. Hamilton's son reported that during this period Hamilton told a boyhood friend, "I have examined carefully the evidence of the Christian religion; and, if I was sitting as a juror upon its authenticity, I should unhesitatingly give my verdict in its favor." He said of Christianity to another person: "I have studied it, and I can prove its truth as clearly as any proposition ever submitted to the mind of man."[64]

Hamilton's words and actions in the final week of his life are particularly revealing. He led his family in the Episcopal family worship service on the Sunday before he died. In the two letters written to his wife in the final days before the duel, Hamilton confessed that he was a Christian, twice spoke of his humility before God, asked that God's will be done, and placed his hope for the next life on "redeeming grace and divine mercy" rather than on confidence in any works he had done.[65] Here is the language of a Christian: reliance upon "redeeming grace" from God. Hamilton was no longer a theistic rationalist using generic religious language and counting on his own morality.

Hamilton, of course, would have need to rely on that grace and mercy, as he was mortally wounded by Burr. On his deathbed, he requested that Bishop Benjamin Moore administer communion to him. Moore, wanting to "avoid every appearance of precipitancy in performing one of the most solemn offices of our religion" to one who had never joined the church or publicly declared faith in Christ, refused to "comply with his desire."[66] Hamilton then sent for Dr. John Mason for the same purpose, but Mason refused because it was against church policy to administer communion privately "to any person under any circumstances." Mason assured Hamilton that communion was only a sign and that "the absence of the sign does not exclude from the mercies signified."[67] Mason then shared the Gospel with Hamilton and reported Hamilton's response. Mason wrote:

> In the sight of God all men are on a level, as *all have sinned, and come short of his glory;* and that they must apply to him for pardon and life, *as sinners,* whose only refuge is in his *grace reigning by righteousness through our Lord Jesus Christ.* "I perceive it to be so," said he; "I am a sinner: I look to his mercy." I then adverted to "the infinite merit of the Redeemer," as the *propitiation for sin,* the sole ground of our acceptance with God; the sole channel of his favour to us; and cited the following passages of scripture: ——"*There is no other name given under heaven among men, whereby we must be saved, but the name of Jesus. He is able to save them to the uttermost who come unto God by him, seeing he ever liveth to make intercession for them. The blood of Jesus Christ cleanseth from all sin.*" . . . He assented, with strong emotion, to these representations.[68]

Mason went on to discuss the grace "which brings salvation," and Hamilton interrupted him to affirm that "it is *rich* grace." Then, according to Mason, "the General . . . looking up towards heaven, said, with emphasis, 'I have a tender reliance on the mercy of the Almighty, through the merits of the Lord Jesus Christ.'"[69] In identifying himself as a "sinner," emphasizing "grace," and appealing specifically to "the Lord Jesus Christ," Hamilton illustrated the difference in language between a theistic rationalist and a Christian. It is also instructive to note that Mason more than once mentioned that Hamilton displayed religious emotion—which also separates the Christian Hamilton from his former theistic rationalism.

Because Mason would not perform the desired service, Hamilton called for Moore to return. He did, and discussed with Hamilton the subject of communion. Moore then asked Hamilton the standard questions preceding Episcopal communion, including: "Do you sincerely repent of your sins past? Have you a lively faith in God's mercy through Christ, with a thankful remembrance of the death of Christ?" Moore reported that Hamilton "lifted up his hands and said, 'With the utmost sincerity of heart I can answer those questions in the affirmative.'" Being convinced of Hamilton's sincerity, Moore administered communion to Hamilton, who received it with "great devotion." Moore saw him again the next morning and reported that "with his last faultering words, he expressed a strong confidence in the mercy of God through the intercession of the Redeemer."[70] There is no reason to disbelieve these accounts of Hamilton's death. Indeed, as Chernow concludes, "It is not certain that Hamilton was as eloquent on his deathbed as his friends later attested, but their accounts corroborate one another and are remarkably consistent."[71]

Hamilton's deathbed confession is discussed at length here to highlight some of the differences between theistic rationalism and Christianity. In Christianity, the central issue is the person and work of Christ. It is His work as redeemer and God's grace to the undeserving that is key, rather than good works or virtuous and moral living. Hamilton, who as a theistic rationalist avoided mentioning Jesus in his writings, could not help but focus on Him when he embraced Christianity. While Alexander Hamilton apparently became a Christian in his waning days, his life and beliefs did not evince Christian faith during the time in which he made such an impact on the American political scene.

Notes

1. Douglass Adair, *Fame and the Founding Fathers*, ed. Trevor Colbourn (New York: W. W. Norton, 1974), 145–49.

2. The best source for the dispute over the date and circumstances of Hamilton's birth is Ron Chernow, *Alexander Hamilton* (New York: Penguin, 2004), 15–17.

3. "Address of the Annapolis Convention," in *Alexander Hamilton: Writings*, ed. Joanne B. Freeman (New York: Literary Classics of the United States, 2001), 142–45.

4. See John C. Miller, *Alexander Hamilton and the Growth of the Nation* (New York: Harper & Row, 1959), 6, 46; Chernow, *Hamilton*, 35; James Thomas Flexner, *The Young Hamilton: A Biography* (Boston: Little, Brown, 1978), 46, 47, 59; Forrest McDonald, *Alexander Hamilton: A Biography* (New York: W. W. Norton, 1979), 10.

5. Miller, *Hamilton*, 8.

6. Ibid.; Flexner, *Young Hamilton*, 63; Chernow, *Hamilton*, 53; Broadus Mitchell, *Alexander Hamilton: A Concise Biography* (New York: Oxford University Press, 1976), 24.

7. Mitchell, *Hamilton*, 24; Claude G. Bowers, *Jefferson and Hamilton: The Struggle for Democracy in America* (Boston: Houghton Mifflin, 1966), 40; John Lamberton Harper, *American Machiavelli: Alexander Hamilton and the Origins of U.S. Foreign Policy* (New York: Cambridge University Press, 2001), 14; McDonald, *Hamilton*, 16, 54–56, 71; Chernow, *Hamilton*, 127, 132.

8. Miller, *Hamilton*, 14, 121, 285.

9. See, for example, Richard Brookhiser, *Alexander Hamilton, American* (New York: Simon & Schuster, 1999), 203.

10. Henry Cabot Lodge, *Alexander Hamilton* (New York: A. S. Barnes, 1946), 264–65.

11. Chernow, *Hamilton*, 205.

12. McDonald, *Hamilton*, 71.

13. Some scholars today distinguish between "providential" and "non-providential" deism, with the former term often used in order to make certain founders fit within the category of deist. As a concept, theistic rationalism differs from providential deism in at least two ways. First, theistic rationalists believed in intervention by a personal God; while "providence," as understood by those deists who used the term, was a representation of the natural order. Second, neither type of deism includes other beliefs of the theistic rationalists, such as acceptance of some written revelation, the efficacy of prayer, and a high opinion of Jesus.

14. See Kerry S. Walters, *The American Deists* (Lawrence: University Press of Kansas, 1992), 41; Harold R. Hutcheson, ed., *Lord Herbert of Cherbury's De Reli-*

gione Laici (New Haven, Conn.: Yale University Press, 1944), 55; E. Graham Waring, ed., *Deism and Natural Religion: A Source Book* (New York: Frederick Ungar, 1967), x; and especially Peter Gay, *Deism: An Anthology* (Princeton, N.J.: D. Van Nostrand, 1968), 11–12, 42, 167–68, 176.

15. Walters, *American Deists*, 26–33; John Leland, *A View of the Principal Deistical Writers* (London: W. Richardson and S. Clark, 1764), 2:360; Elihu Palmer, *Principles of Nature*, as quoted in Kerry S. Walters, *Elihu Palmer's "Principles of Nature"* (Wolfeboro, N.H.: Longwood Academic, 1990), 35, 114–15, 231–32.

16. The major denominations and the relevant creeds or confessions were: Congregational and Presbyterian (Westminster Confession); Baptist (Philadelphia Confession); Anglican and Episcopalian (Apostles' Creed, Nicene Creed, Athanasius's Creed, 39 Articles); Lutheran and Reformed (Augsburg Confession); and Catholic (Council of Trent). While Catholics disagreed with Protestants about the sufficiency of faith for justification, they agreed that justification required faith.

17. "The Farmer Refuted" (1775) in *The Republic of Reason: The Personal Philosophies of the Founding Fathers*, ed. Norman Cousins (San Francisco: Harper & Row, 1988), 332–33.

18. The "key founders" to which I refer are Hamilton, John Adams, Thomas Jefferson, Benjamin Franklin, George Washington, James Madison, Gouverneur Morris, and James Wilson. They are arguably the most responsible for the content and application of the founding documents: the Declaration of Independence and the Constitution.

19. "The Stand" (Mar. 10, 1798) in *The Works of Alexander Hamilton*, ed. Henry Cabot Lodge (New York: Knickerbocker Press, 1904), 6:275, as quoted in George Adams Boyd, *Elias Boudinot: Patriot and Statesman* (Princeton, N.J.: Princeton University Press, 1952), 23–24; *The Royal Danish-American Gazette*, Oct. 3, 1772, in *Republic of Reason*, 330, 331; Hamilton, letter to Benjamin Rush, Mar. 29, 1802, in *Writings*, 987; "Fragment on the French Revolution" (c. 1796), in *Alexander Hamilton and the Founding of the Nation*, ed. Richard B. Morris (New York: Dial Press, 1957), 422; "The Farmer Refuted," in *Republic of Reason*, 332.

20. Hamilton, letter to Elizabeth Hamilton, Jul. 4, 1804, in *Writings*, 1019; "Last Will and Testament" (Jul. 9, 1804) in *Republic of Reason*, 342.

21. Miller, *Hamilton*, 285; "The Farmer Refuted" and *The Royal Danish-American Gazette* in *Republic of Reason*, 332–33, 331; "The Stand" (Apr. 19, 1798), in *Works*, 6:310.

22. Hamilton, letter to unknown friend, Apr. 12, 1804, in *Works*, 10:456.

23. Hamilton letter to Benjamin Rush, Mar. 29, 1802, in *Writings*, 987.

24. *Royal Danish-American Gazette* in *Republic of Reason*, 331; Robert Troup, "Narrative," *William and Mary Quarterly*, 3rd ser., 4 (1947): 212–25, as quoted in Flexner, *Young Hamilton*, 63.

25. William Steele, letter to Jonathan D. Steele, Sep. 1825, in *The Records of the Federal Convention of 1787*, ed. Max Farrand (New Haven, Conn.: Yale University Press, 1966), 3:472; James Madison, letter to Thomas S. Grimke, Jan. 6, 1834, in *Records*, 3:531.

26. John C. Hamilton, *History of the Republic of the United States of America, as Traced in the Writings of Alexander Hamilton* (Philadelphia: J. B. Lippincott, 1864), 7:790.

27. Adair, *Fame and the Founding Fathers*, 144, 146.

28. Ibid., 146–47.

29. Hamilton, letter to General Anthony Wayne, Jul. 6, 1780, in *The Basic Ideas of Alexander Hamilton*, ed. Richard B. Morris (New York: Pocket Books, 1956), 39–40; John Rodgers, as quoted in Isaac A. Cornelison, *The Relationship of Religion to the Civil Government, in the United States of America: A State Without a Church, but Not Without a Religion* (New York, G. P. Putnam's Sons, 1895), in Adair, *Fame and the Founding Fathers*, 147n8; *Basic Ideas*, 427–32.

30. Mitchell, *Hamilton*, 105; Adair, *Fame and the Founding Fathers*, 148.

31. "A Full Vindication of the Measures of Congress, &c.," Dec. 15, 1774, in *The Papers of Alexander Hamilton*, ed. Harold C. Syrett (New York: Columbia University Press, 1961–1987), 1:69; Hamilton, letter to Colonel Edward Carrington, May 26, 1792, in *Basic Ideas*, 395; Hamilton, letter to an unknown person, 1796, in *Basic Ideas*, 397.

32. Chernow, *Hamilton*, 659; "Fragment," in *Founding of the Nation*, 422.

33. Hamilton, letter to George Washington, Jul. 30, 1796, in *Writings*, 862–63.

34. Hamilton, letter to William Loughton Smith, Apr. 10, 1797, in *Writings*, 879; Hamilton, letter to Timothy Pickering, Mar. 22, 1797, in *Basic Ideas*, 326; Hamilton, letter to James McHenry, Jan. 27–Feb. 11, 1798, and letter to Theodore Sedgwick, Mar. 1–15, 1798, and letter to Timothy Pickering, Mar. 17, 1798, in *Papers*, 21:345, 362–63, 365.

35. "The Stand," nos. 1–3, Mar. 30–Apr. 7, 1798, in *Papers*, 21:386, 391, 402–5; "The Stand," no. 5, Apr. 16, 1798, in *Papers*, 21:421; "The Stand," no. 6, Apr. 19, 1798, in *Papers*, 21:435; "The Stand," no. 7, Apr. 21, 1798, in *Papers*, 21:441, 442, 444n, 447.

36. "The War in Europe" (1799) in *Works*, 6:330–32.

37. Hamilton, letter to John Jay, May 7, 1800, in *Writings*, 924; Miller, *Hamilton*, 514; Mitchell, *Hamilton*, 344.

38. Adair, *Fame and the Founding Fathers*, 152n18.

39. Ibid., 157; Miller, *Hamilton*, 552.

40. Hamilton, letter to James Bayard, Apr. 1802, in *Writings*, 988–90 ("*fit men*," Hamilton's emphasis; "*in the management of Federalists*," emphasis mine).

41. Chernow, *Hamilton*, 659.

42. See, for example, *Royal-Danish American Gazette*, Oct. 3, 1772, and "The Farmer Refuted," in *Republic of Reason*, 330–32; Hamilton, letter to an unknown friend, Apr. 12, 1804, in *Works*, 10:456; Chernow, *Hamilton*, 659; Miller, *Hamilton*, 14.

43. *Royal-Danish American Gazette*, Oct. 3, 1772, in *Republic of Reason*, 330–31; "The Farmer Refuted," in *Republic of Reason*, 332–33.

44. Miller, *Hamilton*, 14, 121, 285.

45. "The Farmer Refuted," in *Works*, 1:113.

46. John C. Hamilton, *History of the Republic*, 7:790.

47. See, for example, "Memorandum on the French Revolution," in *Writings*, 834–35; "The Stand," nos. 2–3, in *Papers*, 21:391, 404–5; "Fragment," in *Founding of the Nation*, 422–23.

48. Hamilton, letter to George Washington, Jul. 30, 1796, in *Writings*, 862–64.

49. Allan McLane Hamilton, *The Intimate Life of Alexander Hamilton* (New York: Charles Scribner's Sons, 1910), 334.

50. John C. Hamilton, *History of the Republic*, 7:790.

51. "The Stand," no. 3, in *Writings*, 402, 404, 405; "Fragment," in *Founding of the Nation*, 422, 423.

52. Hamilton, letter to Tobias Lear, Jan. 2, 1800, in *Basic Ideas*, 394.

53. Adair, *Fame and the Founding Fathers*, 144, 148; Hamilton letter to John Laurens, Dec. 1779, in *Basic Ideas*, 40; Allan McLane Hamilton, *Intimate Life*, 334.

54. Chernow, *Hamilton*, 659–60.

55. "Second Letter from Phocion," Apr. 1784, in *Papers*, 3:553; "Remarks on the Quebec Bill: Part Two," Jun. 22, 1775, in *Papers*, 1:175; "Second Letter," in *Papers*, 3:554.

56. "Remarks" in *Papers*, 1:173, as quoted in Miller, *Hamilton*, 104.

57. "Remarks," in *Papers*, 1:171–72; "Full Vindication," in *Papers*, 1:68; "Report on the Subject of Manufactures," Dec. 5, 1791, in *Writings*, 662.

58. John C. Hamilton, *History of the Republic*, 7:499, 790; Adair, *Fame and the Founding Fathers*, 155.

59. Adair, *Fame and the Founding Fathers*, 157.

60. Hamilton, letter to an unknown friend, Apr. 12, 1804, in *Works*, 10:456.

61. Hamilton, letter to Elizabeth Hamilton, Jul. 10, 1804, in *Writings*, 1023; "Personal Notes," 1804, in *Republic of Reason*, 339–41.

62. As quoted in John C. Hamilton, *History of the Republic*, 7:826.

63. Oliver Wolcott, letter to his wife, Jul. 12, 1804, in Allan McLane Hamilton, *Intimate Life*, 406 (emphasis mine).

64. As quoted in John C. Hamilton, *History of the Republic*, 7:790.

65. John C. Hamilton, *History of the Republic*, 823, cited in Adair, *Fame and the Founding Fathers*, 158; Hamilton, letters to Elizabeth Hamilton, Jul. 4 and 10, 1804, in *Writings*, 1019, 1023.

66. Bishop Benjamin Moore, letter to the editor of the *Evening Post*, Jul. 12, 1804, in *A Collection of the Facts and Documents, Relative to the Death of Major-General Alexander Hamilton*, ed. William Coleman (Boston: Houghton, Mifflin, 1904), 50.

67. Dr. John Mason, letter to the editor of the *Evening Post*, Jul. 18, 1804, in *A Collection*, 54.

68. Ibid., 54–55.

69. Ibid., 55.

70. Moore, letter to the *Evening Post*, in *A Collection*, 51–52.

71. Chernow, *Hamilton*, 706.

CHAPTER 6

Patrick Henry, Religious Liberty, and the Search for Civic Virtue

THOMAS E. BUCKLEY, S.J.

The Virginia Statute for Religious Freedom ranks among the foremost documents in the history of American liberties. In sweeping terms it placed the rights of conscience—the freedom to believe and to worship without pressure or coercion of any kind—beyond the reach of the state. Thomas Jefferson was so proud of his composition that he ordered its title inscribed on his tombstone. In his old age, James Madison congratulated himself for guiding its passage through the Virginia legislature.[1] And generations of historians, political scientists, and jurists have recognized the crucial role the statute played in expanding religious liberty in the new republic and laying the foundation for the First Amendment's religion clause and its subsequent interpretation by the Supreme Court. Too often minimized or misunderstood, however, has been the larger context in which the statute won approval and the roles that others, particularly Patrick Henry, played in the long struggle for religious freedom in the Old Dominion. In fact, historians, political scientists, and journalists writing about the Virginia contests sometimes place Henry among the opponents of religious liberty because of his support for a general assessment proposal in 1784. But by making that moment indicative of Henry's entire career, they miss his role as a leader in the struggle for conscience rights. He is, indeed, a forgotten founder of religious liberty.

Context is crucial. Before any legislature would approve a measure as capacious in its language and implications as the Statute for Religious Freedom, a transformation needed to be worked in the way in which Virginians, especially the politically powerful elites who shaped public opinion, thought about the role of religion in society and the relationship between church and state. The value they placed on religion found expression, practically from the earliest days of the colony, in a formal religious establishment. They conceived of their society in organic terms. Just as all belonged to a single political entity—the English colony of Virginia governed from Williamsburg—so all should be members of the Church of England. Church and civil government on the local level were thoroughly entwined. The relationship between church and state was mutually beneficial and necessary. The church supported the state by its prayers in public worship and by teaching the Christian gospel, the moral law, and the obligations of good citizens. The government supported the church by favorable laws, public taxes, and benevolent oversight. Church and state worked together in friendly partnership for the well-being of the whole society. Of course the authorities recognized the existence of religious "dissenters"—Quakers, Presbyterians, and Baptists. But in Virginia, as in England, they were a tiny minority of the total population, the exception rather than the rule, whose presence necessitated at most a grudging, limited toleration. On the eve of the Revolution, the overwhelming majority of the men who governed the Old Dominion in the Williamsburg legislature and sat on the county courts and church vestries envisioned no change in that situation.[2]

But drastic changes were coming in both church and state and the relationship between them. The political and religious revolutions began at the same time, with events in the mid-1760s that ushered in a decade of controversy over the toleration of religious "dissenters." Then in 1776 the revolutionary convention's approval of the sixteenth article of the new state's Declaration of Rights recognized the rights of conscience. Those two moments are crucial to the church-state drama. In them we can identify Henry's leadership in the evolution of religious liberty. Moreover, the two are intrinsically connected. Henry's role in the formulation of the Declaration of Rights can only be understood and appreciated in light of his multiple interventions on behalf of dissenters in the years preceding it. Finally, in January 1786, the passage of Jefferson's Statute was the culmination of the third act in the unfolding drama.

In the Service of Religious Liberty

Let us first consider what Henry did, and then attempt to assess his motivation. It must be admitted that Virginia's first governor is a difficult subject. From the perspective of historians he possessed one egregious fault: he did not save his mail. Today we know much more about some of the other founding fathers because they saved theirs. Jefferson, for example, was such a meticulous pack rat that he acquired and improved a polygraph machine that produced a copy as he wrote a letter. He, Madison, John Adams, George Washington, and people of that ilk lived their lives with one eye cast self-consciously toward their future reputations. Not Henry. His paper trail is scanty. Fortunately, his son-in-law and first biographer, William Wirt, canvassed his relatives and associates for their memories a few years after Henry's death.[3] These sources can be augmented and sometimes corrected by legislative records, newspaper reports, and his contemporaries' correspondence.

Appropriately, if somewhat ironically, church-state politics first brought Henry into the limelight. Throughout the colonial era, a system of tithes or taxes, paid in tobacco, supported the Anglican clergy. In 1763 a legal case involving the back payment of these taxes—the so-called Parson's Cause—gave the young, self-educated lawyer an opportunity to display his oratorical skill. The case arose because of a 1755 Virginia law designed to alleviate the financial distress caused by a tremendous increase in the value of tobacco. It permitted the colonists to pay their tithes either in tobacco or in money at the rate of two pence per pound, although the actual value of tobacco was more than twice that amount. When a group of clergymen, which included the Reverend Patrick Henry, uncle of the young lawyer, vigorously protested, London sided with them and disallowed the act.[4] Then in 1758 the assembly passed a second Two Penny Act, which the British government also annulled.

When the Reverend James Maury sued the tithe collectors in Hanover County Court for back payment of his salary, Henry represented the defendants. The trial created a sensation in the colony. Because the British government had vetoed the law, the only issue at stake was the damages Maury might collect. In his lengthy address to a packed courtroom, Henry attacked the parson and the established clergy generally as "enemies of the community" who deserved to be "severely punished," and he charged that King George II had behaved tyrannically in disallowing a just law passed by the Virginia assembly and signed by the governor. At this some in the crowd murmured "treason," but the jury, which included at least several New Light dissenters from the established church, accepted Henry's characterization of Maury and awarded the furious clergyman one penny in damages.[5]

The Parson's Cause propelled Henry into the colonial assembly, where he quickly seized center stage with inflammatory resolutions against the Stamp Act in 1765. The movement toward Revolution had begun. In the legislature, Henry encountered the religious, legal, and financial penalties dissenters suffered. Quaker pacifists, for example, sought relief from the militia laws, and in 1767 Henry served on the committee that drafted a bill that partly assuaged their concerns. Encouraged perhaps by the Quaker success, two years later the Mennonites requested similar exemptions from military service and war-related taxes. But this time the assembly rejected the petition.[6]

This shift in the legislature may have resulted from a growing concern over the expanding presence of dissenters in the colony. In the 1730s, the authorities had welcomed the settlement of Scotch-Irish Presbyterians in the great Valley of Virginia, where they provided a buffer against the Indians. They were only grudgingly tolerant of the development of a new center of Presbyterianism in Hanover County, the result of the preaching of Samuel Davies and others in the 1740s.[7] The arrival of the Separate Baptists in the late 1760s posed an entirely new threat.

As early as 1725, some General (Arminian or Six-Principle) Baptists could be found in the lower Tidewater region of the colony. Two years later they organized Virginia's first Baptist church in Isle of Wight County and ordained Richard Jones as their minister. The Baptists multiplied slowly on the South Side of the James River, spread into neighboring North Carolina, formed the Kehukee Association, and eventually became Regular (Calvinist) Baptists. Other Regular Baptists migrated into Virginia from Maryland and established churches in the Northern Neck.[8] They were called "Regular" to differentiate them from the "irregular" Separate Baptists, who originated in New England during the Great Awakening and then expanded into the South, especially North Carolina and Virginia, after the middle of the eighteenth century. The Separate Baptists' itinerant preachers formed New Light communities of enthusiastic evangelicals, and by the late 1760s their lively preaching attracted numerous converts. On the eve of the Revolution, their association included some thirty-four churches spread around the Tidewater and Piedmont. Anglican minister Jonathan Boucher complained bitterly about these "swarms of separatists."[9]

So did the Anglican gentry who held power in the House of Burgesses and the county courts. The English Toleration Act of 1689 permitted Protestant dissenters to worship at their own services. Although some magistrates thought the English law did not apply to the colonies, most authorities in Virginia interpreted that act to approve a limited number of licensed meetinghouses for dissenting preachers who would apply for permits to preach. Quakers, Presbyterians, and Regular Baptists conformed to this interpretation of the law. The Separates refused—hence they were "irregular." They rejected such limitations on their ministry. Their mandate came from God, and such divine authority superseded any human law.[10]

By 1770 their preachers were petitioning the assembly for relief from laws that required them to train for military duty and limited their preaching to specific meetinghouses. The legislature refused their petitions, and some clergymen experienced the penalties of noncompliance.[11] The harassment occurred on the local level. When magistrates like Edmund Pendleton, a justice of the peace in Caroline County, enforced the licensing laws, Baptist ministers suffered fines, whippings, and incarceration. During this era, the Baptists found a major ally in Patrick Henry, who volunteered his services in the courtroom and the assembly. In 1769 he sat on a committee of burgesses to prepare a law "exempting his Majesty's Protestant Dissenters from the Penalties of certain Laws."[12] That bill went nowhere, but when the Baptists came forward in 1772, petitioning the assembly for relief, he took up their cause in Williamsburg and elsewhere.[13] In response to multiple Baptist petitions that year, the Committee on Religion, of which Henry was a member, drew up a bill that would have definitively extended the English Act of Toleration to Virginia.[14]

Among the fragments of Henry's writing that we possess, there are notes for a lengthy speech in support of "a general toleration" that he probably gave at this time. In it he insisted that the law would give Virginia "a virtuous clergy" who would be free "to reprehend vice." That was, from the beginning, the major sociopolitical role he saw for religion. His chief argument, however, was shrewdly calculated to appeal to the colony's economic elite who sat in the legislature. For their benefit, he stressed Virginia's future prosperity, which he tied to encouraging European immigration. Two years before, Henry had made his first trip to Philadelphia and New York. Now, on the floor of the House of Burgesses, he enthusiastically endorsed the practical advantages of the religious freedom he had observed in Pennsylvania: "A Dutch, Irish, or Scotch emigrant finds there his religion, his priest, his language, his manners, and everything, but that poverty and oppression he left at home." Virginia should encourage a growing immigrant population, including artisans who would manufacture the products people needed and enhance the colony's prosperity. "A general toleration of Religion," he wrote, "appears to me the best means of peopling our country. . . . The free exercise of religion hath stocked the Northern part of the continent with inhabitants." That policy would do the same for Virginia, drawing in European Calvinists, Lutherans, and Quakers in search of complete religious freedom.[15] Madison would incorporate these arguments in his famous *Memorial and Remonstrance* a dozen or so years later. But despite Henry's pleas, the colonial assembly killed the bill.[16]

During the next few years, controversy over religious toleration and the status and rights of dissenters repeatedly roiled the assembly, the College of William and Mary, meetings of Baptist and Presbyterian leaders, and the press. While conservative forces resisted change in the colonial legislature, Henry remained active on the county level. As Robert Semple, an early historian of Virginia Baptists, wrote, Henry "only needed to be informed of their oppression, when, without hesitation, he stepped forward to their relief. . . . Baptists found in [him] an unwavering friend."[17] Judge Spencer Roane, who married one of Henry's daughters, later recalled his father-in-law's description of the contests in the Caroline County Court, in which he defended "several Baptist Preachers" after Pendleton had slapped them in the county jail. To secure their release, Henry paid their fines out of his own pocket.[18] He also encouraged civil disobedience. One of the irritating disabilities imposed on dissenting ministers was the inability to witness marriages. To be valid in Virginia, a marriage had to be performed by an Anglican clergyman using the ritual in the *Book of Common Prayer*. According to Semple, Henry proposed that Baptist preachers perform marriages anyway and argued that this would be "the most certain method" to reform the law. A scrupulous Semple questioned "*whether this was not doing evil that good might come*," but he wrote his history after that liberty had been won.[19]

The exigencies of wartime mobilization finally broke the dike of opposition to religious toleration. In August 1775 the Virginia Baptist Association petitioned the Revolutionary Convention to permit Baptist preachers to minister to Baptist soldiers. Henry drafted the resolution that the Convention approved to instruct the commanders of the Virginia regiments "to permit dissenting Clergymen to celebrate divine Worship and to preach . . . or exhort" the soldiers.[20] A guarantee of religious liberty was overdue when the Convention met in Williamsburg in May 1776 to recommend that the Continental Congress declare the colonies' independence from Great Britain and to draw up a state constitution and a Declaration of Rights. Edmund Pendleton chaired the session, and the committee that drafted the Declaration included George Mason, Edmund Randolph, and Patrick Henry. Mason had the principal role in the composition, and the drafts of the articles are in his handwriting. But as Pendleton and Randolph attest, he did not act alone.[21]

The sixteenth article offered a ringing affirmation of the rights of conscience. As originally published in the *Virginia Gazette*, it included the following words: "That religion or the duty which we owe to our Creator, and the manner of discharging it, can be directed only by reason and conviction, not by force or violence, and therefore all men should enjoy the fullest toleration in the exercise of religion, according to the dictates of conscience." When that article was debated on the floor of the convention, Madison maneuvered to have the toleration phrase amended to read that "all men are equally entitled to the free exercise of religion."[22]

What role did Henry play? We know that he was vitally concerned with the "portrait of Government" that the convention would approve because he wrote John Adams of his anxieties that it be done properly.[23] While the issue of who wrote what in the Declaration remains contested ground for historians, when Randolph composed his *History of Virginia* in the 1780s, he credited Henry with proposing what became the fifteenth and sixteenth articles in the Declaration.[24] That Henry first urged the inclusion of an article on religious liberty is not inconsistent with the premise that Mason composed the actual draft. In fact, given Henry's outspoken advocacy of religious liberty for dissenters from the outset of his political career and the leadership role he held in the assembly, it would have been completely out of character for him to be silent. After all, the sixteenth article more than achieved the promise of the toleration act of 1772, which he had so vigorously supported.

On the floor of the Convention Henry offered another of Madison's amendments to that article. After the statement on free exercise, he urged this addition: "and therefore that no man or class of men ought on account of religion to be invested with peculiar emoluments or privileges; nor subjected to any penalties or disabilities." At that point in the debate someone asked whether Henry's amendment was "a prelude to an attack on the Established Church." Henry denied that objective. He probably thought the language in the amendment would guarantee a fundamental equality to all the churches, providing, in effect, a level playing field. Madison, on the other hand, envisioned something else. Had the amendment passed, it would have justified ending immediately the tax system that supported the established church and its clergy and seizing all church property. But neither Henry nor the majority in the Convention desired so radical a course of action.[25] The next fall the new state legislature did in fact begin the slow process that would eventually after many years end in disestablishment, but Henry was not there. In June, after approving Virginia's first constitution, the Convention had elected Patrick Henry as the state's first governor.

Religious Pluralism and Civic Virtue

The dissenters must have been delighted. By this point in his career Henry had earned a solid record of support for their rights of conscience. He was so supportive, in fact, that some of his political confreres in the revolutionary convention actually thought he was a dissenter himself, perhaps a Presbyterian. Randolph wrote of his "partiality for the dissenters from the Established church. He often listened to them," sympathized with "their sufferings," and brought their issues into the political arena.[26]

How had this happened? What motivated this man? To understand Henry's views on religion and the situation of the dissenters, we must appreciate the religious influences that marked his formative years, and especially the unusual combination of establishment churchman and dissenter that distinguished his own family. The values of both would resonate throughout his life. Consider the environment in which he grew up as a boy in the 1740s and lived as a young man coming to adulthood in the 1750s. Baptized in the Church of England as an infant, he was named for his uncle, the rector of St. Paul's parish in Hanover County and therefore the religious leader of the local community. John Henry, Patrick's father, was a vestryman for the parish. By the 1740s, however, Hanover County was becoming more religiously pluralistic. The most important dissenting clergyman in the Old Dominion was Presbyterian Samuel Davies, who, after obtaining a license to preach, planted himself in Hanover County and proceeded to siphon off members of the established church. His converts included Patrick's mother, Sarah Henry, and his grandfather Isaac Winston.

Young Patrick found himself driving his mother and sisters in the carriage to Sunday services at Davies's meetinghouse and sitting in the congregation spellbound by the preacher's sermons. Historians have stressed the impact the Presbyterian evangelist made on the impressionable boy and speculated on the influence of Davies's rhetoric on

Henry's oratorical style.[27] Edmund Randolph, his contemporary, thought that contact with the "sufferings" of religious dissenters "unlocked" for Henry "the human heart," and his political rhetoric contained the same "bold licenses" that marked evangelical preaching.[28]

But what did young Patrick observe and learn at home? What did it mean for him to grow up in a household in which his parents, who by all accounts loved and cared for one another, attended religious services in opposing churches? How did these tolerant domestic arrangements of his formative years affect his later outlook on religion and religious liberty? Rhys Isaac has emphasized the threat the Evangelical movement posed not only to the established church but also to the whole hierarchical, gentry-dominated society of Virginia. Other historians have highlighted the patriarchal qualities of that society before the Revolution. Yet in the Henry family, where the husband's adherence to the Church of England was sealed even by ties of blood, the wife elected an alternative service and took her children with her.

Patrick Henry never joined his mother's church but remained a member of the Church of England, which became the Protestant Episcopal Church after the Revolution. At his death, his relatives and friends testified to Henry's personal religious convictions.[29] But his family background gave him a practical experience of religious tolerance and a respect for different faiths that few politicians of his generation understood, much less shared at the outset of the Revolution. He was, as Roane noted, above all a "plain, practical man . . . emphatically one of the people."[30] In matters of both church and state, his policies and politics were based on a profound understanding of human nature rather than any philosophical premises or theoretical presuppositions.

That practical streak also informed his concern for civic virtue in the nascent republic. During the Revolution, Virginia's leadership focused attention on fighting and winning the war. In a conciliatory move, the autumn assembly of 1776 eliminated the taxes on dissenters for support of the established church and suspended them for church members. Then, in 1779, the legislature entertained two contrasting proposals. One essentially copied a South Carolina statute that would tax everyone for the religious group of their choice. The alternative was Jefferson's Statute, which he had drawn up in his role as one of the revisers of Virginia's legal system. Both prospective laws were tabled.[31] The times were too uncertain as the British army invaded Virginia and forced Jefferson, Henry's successor as governor, out of his home at Monticello and over the Blue Ridge Mountains. That invasion ended at Yorktown with the British surrender.

After the peace treaty, the Old Dominion could again consider domestic policy. A central tenet of this generation maintained that the success or failure of the republican experiment depended ultimately on the virtue of the people and the leaders they selected. The subject of virtue occurs repeatedly in the founders' correspondence. As early as May 1776, when the revolutionary Convention met to draft a plan of government, Henry became outspoken on the issue. Carter Braxton, one of Virginia's delegates to the Continental Congress meeting in Philadelphia, had published an "address" to the Williamsburg meeting "on the Subject of Government in general, and recommending a particular Form to their Consideration."

Braxton favored the British system and distrusted democracy. In making his case against a democratic form of government, he distinguished between private and public virtue. Democracy, which he equated with a republic, was unworkable, because it depended upon the "*public virtue*" of the citizens—that is, a concern for "the public good independent of private interest." According to Braxton, if citizens wished to be truly virtuous in public life, they must abandon the pursuit of wealth, ambition, popularity, and every other self-interested motive. But most people would find this impossible. Therefore Braxton concluded that a democratic government was not feasible. In private life, on the other hand, the cultivation of private virtue produced human "happiness and dignity." So self-interest, which rejects public virtue, placed private virtue within the realm of human possibility.[32]

Henry rejected Braxton's premise outright. Writing to Adams, he criticized the pamphlet as a "silly Thing" and "an Affront and Disgrace" to Virginia. Virtue was indivisible, and he found Braxton's "Distinction" between private and public virtue to be "weak shallow [and] evasive."[33] That same month, according to Randolph, Henry proposed in committee what became the fifteenth article of the Declaration of Rights. Unlike the other articles that outlined the principles, purposes, and structures of government and enumerated the rights that citizens retain, the fifteenth article imposed an obligation on Virginians and linked virtue to the success of the republican experiment. It stated: "That no free Government or the Blessing of Liberty can be preserved to any People but by a firm adherence to Justice, Moderation, Temperance, Frugality, and Virtue and by frequent recurrence to fundamental Principles."[34] The Convention designated its new republic as the Commonwealth of Virginia, a political society established to maintain the common weal—the common good—of the people who comprised it. To promote the virtue vitally needed in this new form of government, Henry saw the value of religion. For eighteenth-century republicans, virtue meant allowing the common good to set the standard for individual behavior.[35] Success or failure would depend, in the ultimate analysis, on the virtue of both the people and those who governed them.

This concern was uppermost in the mind of George Mason when the war finally ended in 1783. By this time Henry had completed a successful stint as wartime governor and resumed his place in the legislature as its preeminent leader. Mason turned to him as the one man above all others who could guide Virginia into a new era. "Justice and Virtue," Mason wrote, "are the vital Principles of republican Government." Henry agreed, and like most Virginians he linked virtue with religion and morality. In that triumvirate, if one declined, the other two suffered. Mason worried about "a Depravity of Manners and Morals," and in America many thoughtful people related such corruption to the body blows organized religion had suffered during the war.[36]

Some linked the decline in virtue and religion to the growing influence of deism, a theological perspective that denied divine revelation and traditional Christian doctrines such as the divinity of Christ. Henry was among those concerned. Apart from his treasured Bible, his favorite theological works were two important refutations of the deist position: *The Analogy of Religion: Natural and Revealed* by Anglican Bishop Joseph Butler of Durham and *The Rise and Progress of Religion in the Soul* by Philip Doddridge, a preeminent dissenting clergyman in England. Henry had also read with enthusiastic approval a small book by Soame Jenyns, a member of the British House of Commons and no friend to Henry's politics or the American cause. In 1776 Jenyns published a *View of the Internal*

Evidence of the Christian Religion, a vigorously antirationalist defense of Christianity. The sphere of reason is narrowly restricted, Jenyns argued. Only the superior doctrines and ethics of the New Testament, which "must derive its origin from God," can produce morality and a virtuous life. Henry was so impressed by Jenyn's work that he paid to have the volume reprinted and distributed several hundred copies wherever he thought they would do the most good.[37] One wonders if he gave a copy to Jefferson.

The Assessment for "Teachers of the Christian Religion"

Apart from challenges from deism, organized religion faced practical problems in post-Revolutionary Virginia. The General Assembly no longer financially supported what was now called the Protestant Episcopal Church. Half of its clergy had died, resigned, or retired. Many church buildings were in disrepair or ruins. Adding insult to injury, the church was still legally tied to the government and so unable to manage its own affairs without legislative approval. The former dissenters also labored under legal disabilities—residues of the old establishment—and deeply resented the privileged place they mistakenly imagined the former establishment still possessed. In the past, religion had always looked to civil government for support. Nothing had come of the assessment idea in 1779, but in 1783 and 1784 that proposal was revived, and Henry placed himself at the head of a campaign to get a law enacted. According to its terms, each person would be able to designate a religious group to receive the tax, and it could be used to support both clergy and church buildings.

That law might well have passed, but first James Madison maneuvered Henry out of the assembly and back into the governor's seat. Then, with Madison's support, the legislature passed another measure that Henry had sponsored, a bill incorporating the Protestant Episcopal Church. At the same time, the assembly offered to incorporate any other religious societies that wished it. But incorporation doomed the assessment. The growing ranks of evangelical Christians, mainly Baptists, Presbyterians, and the newly formed Methodists, read the incorporation act as legislative favoritism for the Episcopalians. Fearing that the assessment proposal was really intended to revive the former established church's preeminent position, they fought it with a vigorous petition campaign that effectively killed the issue in the next legislative session. At that juncture, Madison brought forward Jefferson's Statute for Religious Freedom, and the assembly passed it by a wide margin. In retrospect, that proved one of the great defining moments in the history of religious liberty.[38]

What can we make of Henry's role in this? Too often historians have skipped over his prewar leadership in the struggles to expand religious toleration and focused on his assessment proposal. Thus he is portrayed as a religious conservative whose gaze was fixed on a world that had passed away. In contrast, Jefferson, with Madison as his close confederate, wins plaudits for a modern vision of religious freedom enunciated in the Virginia Statute. The reality is more complex. The contest was not restricted to religious freedom. It also concerned the value one placed on religion in society. A year or so earlier, while serving in France as American minister, Jefferson expressed his position in his *Notes on Virginia*: "It does me no injury for my neighbour to say there are twenty gods, or no god. It neither picks my pocket nor breaks my leg."[39] Belief and conduct were totally unrelated, and religion was utterly private.[40]

Henry disagreed. He struggled with the tension between two values: freedom of conscience and the public importance of religion. During the Parson's Cause, he had insisted that the established clergy's principal function was to promote civic responsibility. Later, in the colonial assembly, he argued that the duty of the ministry was to "censure vice."[41] Few of his generation would disagree. Though they argued about the best method of forming a virtuous society, many Virginians shared Henry's concerns. And his assessment proposal received strong support in the Old Dominion and elsewhere. From Philadelphia, Richard Henry Lee, presiding over the government under the Articles of Confederation, urged its passage. At Mount Vernon, George Washington endorsed an assessment. In Massachusetts a few years earlier, John Adams had helped enact a state constitution that provided for the financial support of "public Protestant teachers of piety, morality and religion." The other New England states, with the exception of Rhode Island, had followed suit. In

Virginia Henry's bill was designed to provide "for teachers of the Christian religion." From the perspective of Adams, Henry, and others, the clergy were educators, teaching the religiously based moral values and virtues essential in a healthy society.[42] Evangelicals would not disagree with that perspective, and for the next century and a half in Virginia and elsewhere, they would utilize the schools, first private and then public, to achieve their objectives in education.

Henry's Views on Virtue and Religion

Henry lost the assessment fight, but his convictions about the connection between virtue and religion remained and even deepened in the last decades of his life. In the 1790s he wrote an old friend, Archibald Blair, that only "virtue, morality, and religion" would protect America.[43] Before his death in 1799, Henry devoted time and effort to preparing his will and final testament. After disposing of his property, Henry concluded, "This is all the inheritance I can give to my dear family. The religion of Christ can give them one which will make them rich indeed." Together with this will, Henry's executors found a small envelope. It contained a copy of the Stamp Act resolves that had begun the movement for American Independence. In itself this was surprising. On the back of the resolves, Henry inscribed his last testament to the American people. Speaking of the successful Revolution, which the Stamp Act resolves had initiated, he wrote, "Whether [Independence] will prove a blessing or a curse will depend upon the use our people make of the blessings which a gracious God hath bestowed on us. . . . Righteousness alone can exalt them as a nation. Reader!" he concluded, "whoever thou art, remember this; and in thy sphere practice virtue thyself, and encourage it in others."[44]

For Patrick Henry, as for so many of the founders, liberty was purposeful. What some consider liberty today—the freedom to do whatever one wishes—Henry and the Revolutionary generation regarded as license. True liberty meant possessing sufficient control over oneself to choose the virtuous course of action, to do what one ought to do, to live and act in "rationally or religiously responsible ways."[45] Like most of his contemporaries, including evangelical Christians, Henry valued organized religion and saw the churches as essential props for civic virtue in the new republic. Despite the rejection of his assessment proposal, his perspective on the importance of religion in a republican society would become the dominant ethos in Virginia and the nation.

Notes

1. James Madison, letter to George Mason, in *Letters and Other Writings of James Madison*, ed. William Cabell Rives and Philip R. Fendall (Philadelphia: J. B. Lippincott, 1865), 3:525.

2. For a classic statement from this perspective, see Edmund Pendleton (?), "An Address to the Anabaptists Imprisoned in Caroline County," Aug. 8, 1771, *The Virginia Gazette*, Feb. 20, 1772. The best study of the colonial church is John K. Nelson, *A Blessed Company: Parishes, Parsons, and Parishioners in Anglican Virginia, 1690–1776* (Chapel Hill: University of North Carolina Press, 2001).

3. These are in the William Wirt papers at the Library of Congress, Washington, D.C. (hereinafter LC), and some of them have been reproduced in the appendices of George Morgan, *Patrick Henry* (Philadelphia: J. B. Lippincott, 1929). See also Moses Coit Tyler, *Patrick Henry* (Boston: Houghton, Mifflin, 1887), 69. For Wirt's efforts at historical accuracy, see David A. McCantis, "The Authenticity of William Wirt's Version of Patrick Henry's 'Liberty or Death' Speech," *Virginia Magazine of History and Biography* 87 (Oct. 1979): 387–402 (hereinafter VMHB).

Unfortunately Wirt depended heavily on Thomas Jefferson for his recollections, not knowing of his hatred for Henry. See, for example, Wirt, letter to Jefferson, Jul. 23, 1805, Thomas Jefferson Papers, University of Virginia (hereinafter UVA), Main Series 3, (microfilm, Roll 5). Soon after the Revolution, Jefferson averred that Henry was a coward and called him "all tongue without either head or heart" (Jefferson, letter to George Rogers Clark, Nov. 26, 1782, in *The Papers of Thomas Jefferson*, ed. Julian P. Boyd [Princeton, N.J.: Princeton University Press, 1950–], 6:205). Jefferson thought that Henry had instigated the assembly's investigation into his performance as governor when the British invaded Virginia in 1781. Although Jefferson was exonerated, he never quite got over the perceived insult (Jefferson, letter to Clark, 6:85, 144). For this incident and Henry's conduct in it, see Edmund Randolph, *History of Virginia*, ed. Arthur H. Shaffer (Charlottesville: University Press of Virginia, 1970), 296; Robert Douthat Meade, *Patrick Henry* (Philadelphia: J. B. Lippincott, 1957–1969), 1:245–50; and Dumas Malone, *Jefferson and His Time*, 6 vols. (Boston: Little, Brown, 1948–1981),

1:355–69. When pressed by Wirt for a factual basis for the charge of cowardice against Henry, Jefferson later admitted that he knew none (Jefferson, letter to Wirt, Sep. 26, 1816, Jefferson Papers, UVA, Main Series 3 (microfilm, Roll 7). For a detailed analysis of Jefferson's assault on Henry's life and character, see James M. Elson, ed., *Patrick Henry and Thomas Jefferson* (Brookneal, Va.: Patrick Henry Memorial Foundation, 1997).

4. The Clergy of Virginia, letter to the Bishop of London, Feb. 25, 1754, in *Virginia*, vol. 1 of *Historical Collections Relating to the American Colonial Church*, ed. William Stevens Perry (Hartford, Conn.: Church Press Company, 1870), 440–46.

5. James Maury, letter to John Camm, Dec. 12, 1763, in *Memoirs of a Huguenot Family: Translated and Compiled from the Original Autobiography of the Rev. James Fontaine*, ed. Ann Maury (New York: G. P. Putnam and Sons, 1872), 420, 422–23 (first quotation at 423); [James Maury], "Narrative of the Determination of a Suit between the Minister of Fredericsville Pltf, and the Collectors of said Parish Debt, for Arrears of Salary, detained in Consequence of what is vulgarly called the 2 penny Act, in Hanover Court, in the Months of Novr and Decr 1763," Jonathan Boucher Papers, Box 2, Folder 1, Earl Gregg Swem Library, the College of William and Mary in Virginia; William Robinson, letter to the Bishop of London, Aug. 17, 1764, in *Historical Collections*, 1:489–501 (second and third quotations at 497). A full account of the Parson's Cause may be found in Meade, *Patrick Henry*, 1:114–38.

6. *Journal of the House of Burgesses, 1766–1769*, ed. John Pendleton Kennedy (Richmond: Colonial Press, 1906), Mar. 28, 31, 1767 and Nov. 14, 17, 1769, 101, 104, 256, 267 (hereinafter JHBV). For the militia law affecting Quakers, see William Waller Hening, ed., *The Statutes at Large: Being a Collection of All the Laws of Virginia, From the First Session of the Legislature, in the Year 1619* (Richmond, Va.: J. and G. Cochran, 1823), 8:242–43.

7. Ernest Trice Thompson, *Presbyterians in the South*, 3 vols. (Richmond, Va.: John Knox, 1963), 1:43–46, 54–59; William Henry Foote, *Sketches of Virginia: Historical and Biographical, First Series* (Richmond: John Knox, 1966 [1850]), 98–221; Wesley M. Gewehr, *The Great Awakening in Virginia, 1740–1790* (Gloucester, Mass: Peter Smith, 1965 [1930]).

8. For early histories of Baptists in Virginia, see William Fristoe, *A Concise History of the Ketocton Baptist Association* (Staunton: William Gilman Lyford, 1808), 5–11; Lemuel Burkitt and Jesse Read, *A Concise History of the Kehukee Baptist Association, From Its Original Rise to the Present Time* (Halifax: A. Hodge, 1803), 28–40; and David Benedict, *A General History of the Baptist Denomination in America, and Other Parts of the World*, 2 vols. (Boston: Printed by Lincoln & Edmands, 1813), 2:23–36. The standard modern study for Virginia Baptists is Reuben Edward Alley, *A History of Baptists in Virginia* (Richmond: Virginia Baptist General Board, 1973). For the earliest Baptist history, see Morgan Edwards, "A History of the Baptists in the Province of Virginia," *Virginia Baptist Register* 39 (2000): 1940–81.

9. Benedict, *History of the Baptist Denomination*, 2:53–58; Jonathan Boucher, *A View of the Causes and Consequences of the American Revolution: In Thirteen Discourses, Preached in North America between the Years 1768 and 1775* (New York: Russell & Russell, 1967 [1797]), 100.

10. "An Act for Exempting Their Majesties' Protestant Subjects Dissenting from the Church of England from the Penalties of Certain Laws," 1 William and Mary, c. 18 (1689), in *English Historical Documents*, vol. 8: 1660–1714, ed. Andrew Browning (New York: Oxford University Press, 1955–1967), 400–403. For its effect on dissenters in England, see Robert E. Rodes Jr., *Law and Modernization in the Church of England: Charles II to the Welfare State* (Notre Dame, Ind.: University of Notre Dame Press, 1991), 80–93. For the confusion over its application in Virginia, see Foote, *Sketches of Virginia*, 174–200. Rhys Isaac provided the classic analysis of the contest between Separate Baptists and the Virginia authorities in "Evangelical Revolt: The Nature of the Baptists' Challenge to the Traditional Order in Virginia, 1765–1775," *William and Mary Quarterly*, 3rd ser., 31 (1974): 345–68.

11. JHBV, 1770–1773, May 26, Jun. 1, 1770, 20, 40. For Baptist persecution, see Lewis Peyton Little, *Imprisoned Preachers and Religious Liberty in Virginia* (Lynchburg, Va.: J. P. Bell, 1938).

12. JHBV, 1766–1769, May 11, Nov. 11, 1769, 205, 252.

13. Robert B. Semple, *A History of the Rise and Progress of the Baptists in Virginia*, rev. ed. (Richmond: Pitt and Dickinson, 1894), 41; Foote, *Sketches of Virginia*, 317–18. For these Baptist petitions, see JHBV, Feb. 23, Mar. 14, 1772, 185–86, 188, 245.

14. JHBV, 1770–1773, Feb. 27, 1772, 194, 197.

15. William Wirt Henry, *Patrick Henry: Life, Correspondence, and Speeches* (New York: Charles Scribner's Sons, 1891), 1:112–16.

16. JHBV, Feb. 27, Mar. 17, 1772, 194, 197, 249; *Virginia Gazette*, Mar. 26, 1772.

17. Semple, *Rise and Progress of the Baptists* 41.

18. "Statement of Spencer Roane," in Morgan, *Patrick Henry*, 440.

19. Semple, *Rise and Progress of the Baptists*, 87. The marriage law was finally changed in 1784; see Thomas E. Buckley, S.J., *Church and State in Revolutionary Virginia, 1776–1787* (Charlottesville: University Press of Virginia, 1977), 111.

20. Religious Petitions, 1774–1802, Presented to the General Assembly of Virginia, Aug. 16, 1775 (Miscellaneous), microfilm, Library of Virginia, Richmond; William J. Van Screeven, Robert L. Scribner, and Brent Tarter, eds., *Revolutionary Virginia: The Road to Independence* (Charlottesville: University Press of Virginia, 1977), Aug. 14, 16, 1775, 3:441–42, 450–51. For Henry's role, see 3:453n3.

21. Mays, *Letters of Pendleton*, 1:180. For this Declaration, see Daniel L. Dreisbach, "George Mason's Pursuit of Religious Liberty in Revolutionary Virginia," *VMHB* 108 (2000): 5–44.

22. Buckley, *Church and State*, 17–18.

23. Henry, letter to John Adams, May 20, 1776, in *Paper of John Adams*, ed. Robert J. Taylor, Gregg L. Lint, and Celeste Walker (Cambridge, Mass.: Harvard University Press, 1979), 4:201.

24. Randolph, *History of Virginia*, 254.

25. For this Declaration, see Buckley, *Church and State*, 17–21.

26. Randolph, *History of Virginia*, 179.

27. The best treatment of Davies's oratorical style is George William Pilcher, *Samuel Davies: Apostle of Dissent in Colonial Virginia* (Knoxville: University of Tennessee Press, 1971), 54–85. For his impact on Henry, see, for example, Meade, *Patrick Henry*, 1:71–74.

28. Randolph, *History of Virginia*, 179.

29. See Isaac, "Evangelical Revolt"; for the testimony of his widow and children to Henry's religious character, see Francis L. Hawks, *Contributions to the Ecclesiastical History of the United States of America* (New York, 1836), 1:100–101. His modern biographers acknowledge that, though he apparently never served as a vestryman, Henry remained until his death a member of what became at the Revolution the Episcopal Church. See, for example, Meade, *Patrick Henry*, 1:70, 138; George F. Willison, *Patrick Henry and His World* (Garden City, N.Y.: Doubleday, 1969), 314, 383; and Henry Mayer, *A Son of Thunder: Patrick Henry and the American Republic* (New York: Franklin Watts, 1986), 165. Mayer is probably most accurate in recognizing that, for much of his life, Henry was "a latitudinarian" who most valued religion's "ethical principles" for the benefits they offered the new republic. But in later life, as he himself testified, the Bible became much more important to Henry's own personal religious life, and it might be fairly stated that he died a devout Christian.

30. "Statement of Roane," in Morgan, *Patrick Henry*, 444.

31. For these legislative sessions and their work, see Buckley, *Church and State*, 21–62.

32. [Carter Braxton], "An Address to the Convention of the Colony and Ancient Dominion of Virginia; on the Subject of Government in General, and Recommending a Particular Form to Their Consideration" (Philadelphia: John Dunlap, 1776), 7, 15.

33. Henry, letter to Adams, *Papers of Adams*, 4:201.

34. Van Screeven, et al., *Revolutionary Virginia*, 7:450; Randolph, *History of Virginia*, 254.

35. See Barry Alan Shain, *The Myth of American Individualism: The Protestant Origins of American Political Thought* (Princeton, N.J.: Princeton University Press, 1994), 122.

36. Robert A. Rutland, ed., *The Papers of George Mason, 1725–1792* (Chapel Hill: University of North Carolina Press, 1970), 2:769–74; Gordon Wood, *The Creation of the American Republic, 1776–1787* (Chapel Hill: University of North Carolina Press, 1969), 65–70, 117–18, 427–28.

37. Soame Jenyns, *View of the Internal Evidence of the Christian Religion* (London: J. Dodsley, 1776), 50, 98–99 (quotation), 109–13, 175–79; "Statement of Samuel Meredith," in Morgan, *Patrick Henry*, 423; "Ed Winston's Memoir of Patrick Henry," [undated folder] in Patrick Henry Papers, 1776–1818, LC. For Butler, see David Brown, "Butler and Deism," in *Joseph Butler's Moral and Religious Thought: Tercentenary Essays*, ed. Christopher Cunliffe (Oxford: Clarendon Press, 1992), 1–35. For Doddridge, see Malcolm Deacon, *Philip Doddridge of Northampton* (Northampton: Northamptonshire Libraries, 1980), and the essays in G. F. Nuttall, *Philip Doddridge, 1702–51: His Contribution to English Religion* (London: Independent Press, 1951).

38. For this history, see Buckley, *Church and State*, 74–165.

39. Thomas Jefferson, *Notes on the State of Virginia*, ed. William Peden (Chapel Hill: University of North Carolina Press for the Institute of Early American History and Culture, 1955), 159.

40. This was, of course, only one side of Jefferson. He was fully capable of harnessing religion to political goals when it suited his purposes. See, for example, Thomas E. Buckley, S.J., "The Religious Rhetoric of Thomas Jefferson," in *The Founders on God and Government*, ed. Daniel L. Dreisbach, Mark D. Hall, and Jeffry H. Morrison (Lanham, Md.: Rowman and Littlefield, 2004), 53–82.

41. [Maury], "Narrative of a Suit"; Maury, letter to Camm, in Maury, *Memoirs of a Huguenot Family*, 423; Henry, *Patrick Henry*, 1:112.

42. South Carolina and Maryland seriously considered establishing a religious tax system but never carried it into law. The extraordinary religious pluralism in the mid-Atlantic states made such proposals impractical there, and it would ultimately doom the New England system.

43. "Statement of Spencer Roane," in Morgan, *Patrick Henry*, 452; Patrick Henry, letter to Archibald Blair, Jan. 8, 1799, in Tyler, *Patrick Henry*, 409–10.

44. Henry, *Patrick Henry*, 1:81–82.

45. Shain, *Myth of American Individualism*, 201.

CHAPTER 7

John Jay and the "Great Plan of Providence"

JONATHAN DEN HARTOG

In 1809, the Congregationalist minister and author Jedidiah Morse wrote the retired statesman John Jay to ask for advice about writing a history of the American Revolution. Jay responded that "a proper history of the United States . . . would be singular, or unlike all others." Jay believed such a history would be exceptional because "it would develop the great plan of Providence, for causing [North America] to be gradually filled with civilized and Christian people and nations." The American republic was significant to Jay because God had willed both its existence and its character as a Christian nation. Jay's pointing to the Christian character of the nation suggested that he saw a close tie between orthodox Christianity and the politics of the new nation. Before he closed his letter, he reiterated his opinion that "the historian, in the course of the work, is never to lose sight of that great plan."[1] Jay's injunctions point contemporary historians to how he viewed the American experiment.

Throughout his life, John Jay interpreted both personal events and national developments through a lens of Providence—a usage that undoubtedly grew out of his family's Huguenot Calvinist background. The contexts of Jay's repeated references to Providence make clear that he meant it in an orthodox Christian sense—that the Christian God had not only intervened in the world in the person of Christ but also continued to be active (often through secondary causes) to fulfill His own purposes.[2] Jay's belief in Providence also called him to active service, as a response to the divine will. Jay's Providence was thus more than a personal belief; it had important national consequences. An orthodox Protestant perspective shaped Jay's public activities by giving transcendent significance to temporal political affairs, and those activities influenced the development of the new nation.

How Jay interpreted the world providentially and sought to bring Protestant Christianity to bear on the new republic evolved over time. This chapter organizes that growth into three periods: republican, federalist, and voluntarist. The republican period comprehended the Revolution through the ratification of the Constitution. At that time, Jay was most concerned with the nation's survival and organization, and his religious language focused on those goals. Jay's federalist period covered the years when he was connected to the Federalist party—primarily the 1790s. In the final decade of the eighteenth century, Jay saw the republic being undermined by wrong doctrine ("infidelity") and immorality. He thus worked for a more robust place for Christianity in the public sphere. After Jay retired from public life in 1801, he followed a voluntarist course, supporting voluntary societies. His final activities centered on efforts in the private sphere as the only hope for the nation. In each of these stages, Jay bent his efforts to preserve the nation he believed had come about by the "great plan of Providence."

Biography

As a member of the founding generation, John Jay's credentials sparkle. Born in 1745 into a New York merchant family of Huguenot ancestry, Jay received an early education colored by both Anglican teaching and Huguenot piety. He studied at King's College (later Columbia) under the American Samuel Johnson. Graduating from King's in 1764, Jay embarked on his legal studies and was soon admitted to the New York bar.

In 1774, Jay married Sarah Livingston. They would have a happy and harmonious marriage until Sarah's death in 1801.

As troubles with Britain increased in the 1770s, Jay supported the interests of the American colonists. The citizens of New York City selected him as a delegate to the First Continental Congress. Although he was one of the youngest members, he soon became heavily involved, even drafting the Congress's *Address to the People of Great Britain*. In the Second Continental Congress, Jay was loath to make the final break from Great Britain, and so he cooperated with John Dickinson to draft the Olive Branch Petition. Nevertheless, when independence was declared, Jay fully supported it.

During the War for Independence, Jay performed a number of services for the new nation. He worked in the New York Provincial Congress to ensure the state's commitment to independence. Hoping to continue the rule of law, which was so important to him as a lawyer, Jay helped draft the state's first constitution and then served as the first chief justice of the state's Supreme Court. Called back to the Continental Congress, Jay was elected its president, where he struggled to keep the government functioning. Congress then appointed Jay as minister to Spain. Because he was able to make little headway in Spain, he welcomed orders to relocate to Paris, where he, John Adams, and Benjamin Franklin were to negotiate the final peace with Great Britain. Resisting pressure from the French minister Vergennes, the Americans made their own peace— one that proved advantageous in securing both the nation's independence and its territory all the way to the Mississippi River.

Returning to America, Jay confronted problems in the new nation. New York elected him to the Confederation Congress, and Congress soon made him its secretary for foreign affairs, a position he held from 1784 to 1790. During this time, Jay experienced the weakness of the Confederation government firsthand. In his dealings with other nations, he had to struggle to defend American rights—even those already recognized by treaty.

Having witnessed the weakness of the government, Jay's support for the Federalist cause was no surprise. He was not named to the Constitutional Convention—the New York assembly wanted a small delegation to limit Alexander Hamilton's influence. Still, Jay approved of the proposed Constitution and then actively worked to ensure ratification. He contributed multiple pieces to the public debate over the document, writing several of the *Federalist Papers*—he drafted numbers 2 through 5 and 64—and an independent plea for the Constitution, *An Address to the People of the State of New York*. In the New York ratifying convention, Jay was a critical Federalist voice. His character, reputation, sincerity, and reasoned arguments counted for much—indeed probably even more than Hamilton's oratorical fireworks.[3] Jay thus played a significant role in the critical state of New York, which was not predisposed to accept the Constitution.

President George Washington gave Jay his choice of positions in the new government, and Jay chose to be the first chief justice of the Supreme Court. Jay hoped that a confident and competent court would encourage American support for the new Constitution. He viewed the law as the bulwark protecting liberty from anarchy. As chief justice, Jay used the power of the court to defend the federal government's standing from the states and the interests of America against foreigners who brought suit against the nation. Jay also used his public charges to grand juries to instruct citizens in their republican duties.[4]

When war with England threatened in 1794, Washington asked Jay to serve as a special envoy to the Court of St. James. Jay agreed, relinquished his chief justiceship, and sailed for England. The Jay Treaty ensured peace, although it failed to address some of the major American grievances, such as the neutrality rights of American shipping. Even so, many historians agree that Jay had negotiated the best deal possible, given the circumstances.[5] Before sailing for home, Jay was able to interact with a number of prominent Englishmen, including Edmund Burke and William Wilberforce—two men who would shape Jay's approach to society in the coming years. In America, Jay's Treaty served as a lightning rod for the emerging political parties. Whereas Federalists supported both Jay and the treaty, Democratic-Republicans burned Jay in effigy and decried him as a dupe of England.

Despite such criticisms, Jay was elected New York's governor in 1795, and he served in that position for six years. After almost thirty years of unbroken service to his country, Jay desired retirement and embarked on building a country home in Bedford, New York. That retirement would not be entirely happy. His wife died before the house was fully finished. A daughter died in 1818, and he even endured the deaths of several grandchildren. In the midst of such personal struggles, Jay expressed a deep, confident, articulate faith. Such faith led to Jay's involvement in a number of benevolent organizations, support for his denomination, and finally the presidency of the American Bible Society (ABS). As president, he worked to make the ABS the archetype of voluntary societies in the new republic.

Jay remained active in retirement, keeping up a busy correspondence. By the 1820s, though, his health began to deteriorate. He suffered a stroke in 1825, which proved a hindrance to further activity. With the words "The Lord is better than we deserve" on his lips, he died in April 1829.[6]

Jay and the Scholars

Given Jay's accomplishments, one might suspect that his reputation would have benefited from the outpouring of scholarship relating to the founding generation. Such has not been the case. Jay himself contributed to this lack of understanding by requesting his sons to cull and burn many of his letters after his death.[7] Many of Jay's other letters were separated into multiple holdings, making it difficult for scholars to access his papers. Jay's son William, his first biographer, did his father's reputation no favors when he produced a long and meandering "life and letters" biography after Jay's death.[8] Most modern scholars have been forced to rely on Frank Monaghan's 1935 biography of Jay. Monaghan, although mentioning Jay's religious and charitable works at the end of his life, paid little attention to Jay's religious beliefs. Walter Stahr, Jay's most recent biographer, has sought to ensconce Jay in the front rank of founders. While noting that Jay's religiosity may have contributed to the lack of attention paid him, Stahr offers little analysis of Jay's religion. It shows up only intermittently in Stahr's narrative.[9]

Similarly, two other attempts to connect Jay's religion and his politics have left much unsaid and unanalyzed. Patricia Bonomi offered some initial thoughts, suggesting that Jay was orthodox and that to some extent his beliefs did influence his politics. Unfortunately, her description was short, barely touched on events after the outbreak of the Revolution, and was not built on any archival work. Recently, David Holmes profiled Jay in *The Faiths of the Founding Fathers*. Holmes treated Jay—along with Samuel Adams and Elias Boudinot—as one of three orthodox Christians. Holmes makes a good assessment of Jay's faith, but more could be said. Holmes does little beyond describing Jay's beliefs, and he makes no attempt to connect those beliefs to Jay's political activities.[10] Greater attention to both Jay's beliefs and his politics is needed.

Jay's Faith

Jay's orthodoxy and piety were inculcated from an early age. His father, Peter, raised his children in a context of piety that blended Huguenot seriousness with the family's newly adopted Anglicanism. As a boy, John was educated by the Rev. Peter Stouppe, under whose tutelage he learned piety in a Huguenot-American setting. While attending King's College in New York City, he regularly participated in services at Trinity Church at a time when fellow students were exploring other, less savory aspects of the city. Jay's attachment to Trinity Church would last many years, and he would be active in both the church and the emerging Episcopal denomination.[11]

In public, Jay defended an orthodox Christianity. Responding to a minister who had sent him a refutation of Tom Paine's *Age of Reason*, Jay confessed, "I have long been of opinion, that the evidence of the truth of Christianity, requires only to be carefully examined to produce conviction in candid minds." Jay believed there were good—even rational—reasons to defend orthodox Christian belief. When confronted with the unbelief of the era, he scornfully rejected it. The *Age of Reason*, he said, "never appeared to me to have been written from a disinterested love of truth, or of mankind."[12] Similarly, during his peace mission in France, Jay was confronted by atheists who challenged his belief in Christ, prompting him to respond "that I did [believe], and that I thanked God that I did." Such religious challenges usually met with "a cold reception."[13] Jay's public words and deeds thus suggested a strong attachment to a traditional Protestantism.

Additionally, Jay's orthodoxy appeared in his familial relations. He instructed his children in faith. When he learned that his eldest son, Peter Augustus, read his Bible daily and had learned some hymns, Jay encouraged him. "The Bible is the best of all Books, for it is the word of God, and teaches us the way to be happy in this world and in the next. Continue therefore to read it, and to regulate your Life by its precepts." In multiple letters he encouraged his other children to prepare their souls, not only for this world, but also for the one to come. Similarly, he told his daughters that "Virtue and Religion must be the corner Stones" of their lives. A belief in a future state motivated Jay's life, and he urged his children to adopt a similar belief.[14] Such a belief in heavenly rewards also helped Jay when confronted with death. When Jay's wife died, his immediate response was to take the family into the other room, read I Corinthians 15 on Christian resurrection, and lead them in prayers. Similarly, after the death of his daughter Sarah Louisa, Jay remarked, "The removal of my excellent daughter from the house of her earthly, to the house of her Heavenly Father, leaves me nothing to regret or lament on her account. . . . This temporary separation will terminate in a perpetual reunion."[15] Faith provided Jay a language for grief and a reason not to despair.

Jay's religious beliefs flourished during his time in retirement. After 1801, as partisan politics took up less of his time, religious reflection took up more. He weekly attended worship services at a local church—first a Presbyterian congregation and then an Episcopalian congregation he helped form. Jay's daily schedule also reflected a regularity of religious practice. William, who lived with his father's habits for many years, described his conduct as precise and ordered: "Every morning immediately before breakfast, the family, including the domestics, were summoned to prayers and the call was repeated precisely at nine at night, when he read to them a chapter in the Bible, and concluded with prayer."[16] Guests also commented on these practices and attitudes. A. H. Stevens remarked that he had long remembered his time spent at Bedford, witnessing the Jays "uniting in thanksgiving, confession, and prayer."[17] Timothy Dwight observed that Jay spent his time in a "profound attention to those immense objects which ought ever supremely to engage the thoughts, wishes, and labors of an immortal being."[18]

More than just a feeling, Jay's faith engaged his intellect. As the years passed, William reported, "The Scriptures were pre-eminently his study, and were the subjects of his daily and careful perusal."[19] The result was a collection of spiritual meditations on various topics, which strengthened his opposition to those "infidels" whose unbelief would weaken the American republic. In one study, he compiled a list of verses from the book of Revelation that pointed to the divinity of Christ, an exercise in opposition to Unitarian beliefs. In another, he wrestled with the creation account of Genesis 1, which placed the creation of light on the first day of creation but the creation of the sun and moon on the fourth day. After considering different possibilities, Jay concluded that the lights were two different types: the first spiritual, the second physical. These considerations led Jay to anticipate the coming of the New Heavens and the New Earth. Finally, Jay wrestled with the problem of Jacob and Esau, especially God's election of Jacob as argued by the Apostle Paul in Romans 9. Jay attempted to resolve the conundrum by setting the problem in a dialogue between the main characters—a debate that went on for thirty-nine manuscript pages. Jay concluded, "The Scriptures give us to understand that the works of neither of them had any Influence on the Election of Jacob, or the Rejection of Esau, but it strongly intimates that Regard was had to the Faith of Jacob and the Infidelity of Esau."[20] He thus solved the problem in a way that preserved a Reformed reading of the passage while allowing room for the human action he had so long stressed. Jay valued this production so highly that he gave the original to his son Peter but demanded that Peter give a copy to each of the other Jay children.

His biblical investigations also appeared in his correspondence. For instance, in an 1813 letter he asked Jedidiah Morse a question about an obscure passage in 1 Corinthians that mentioned baptism for the dead. Jay gave an extended exposition of what he believed it to mean and asked Morse if he could add to his understanding.[21] Jay also expressed some interest in prophecy. As early as 1797 he wrote to Benjamin Rush, after Rush had recommended a book on prophecy to him, that the "subject naturally excites attention." Even while reflecting on the possibilities of judgment, Jay rejoiced "that every scourge of every kind by which nations are punished or corrected, is under the control of a wise and benevolent

Sovereign."[22] As time progressed, Jay grew increasingly concerned with the place of evangelism in prophecy, as he stressed "the bringing in of the Gentiles" (Romans 11:25).[23] Such discussions show Jay actively engaged in religious and theological discussions.

Jay's piety led him to support specifically Christian voluntary societies, especially the ABS. He had actively participated in his local Westchester County Bible Society and had become a vice president of the ABS at its formation. After the death of Elias Boudinot, the managers of the ABS asked Jay to assume the presidency. As part of his duties, Jay offered addresses at the society's annual meetings. In these messages, Jay insisted that Christians faced an imperative to be involved in evangelical outreach. In such activity, Jay hoped for Christian unity—for Christians of multiple denominations to work together. He decried continued denominationalism and pressed the point that, "as *real* Christians are made so by Him without which we 'can do nothing,' it is equally certain that He receives them into His family, and that in his family mutual love and uninterrupted concord never cease to prevail."[24] Such a vision of varied groups uniting together for a common cause also fit nicely with Jay's political federalism. Just as a united country was necessary for national greatness, so Christian unity was necessary for the great work of the Gospel.

From these statements, it is clear that a number of elements helped define the contours of Jay's belief. First, it reflected the mixture of Reformed Huguenot beliefs and attitudes with Anglican ideals—the product of the Jay family's religious history over the past several generations. Second, it posited a high place for human reason, especially as Jay had imbibed it from Samuel Johnson at King's. Jay was definitely influenced by the "rational enlightenment," from which came his value for order in the world, order in society, and order in relationships.[25] Third, Jay's religious beliefs grew and were expressed more strongly over time, particularly in retirement.

Throughout his life, though, Jay kept returning to the religious themes of Providence and Duty. For Jay, God was no deistic clockmaker but was instead actively engaged in the world, directing the courses of both individuals and nations. Holmes rightly observes about Jay: "He did use Deistic designations for God, such as 'Providence.' . . . But most of his language was that commonly used in the orthodox Protestant circles of his time: 'Saviour,' 'King of Heaven,' 'Author and Giver of the Gospel,' 'Lord of the Sabbath,' 'Almighty God,' 'Lord of Hosts,' 'Almighty and benevolent Being,' 'Master,' and 'Captain of our Salvation.'"[26] Because Jay used such orthodox language, his use of terms such as "Providence" should not be seen as endorsing the more rationalist view of God. Rather, when Jay used it, he meant the traditional, Calvinist view of God as actively working in the world—usually through secondary causes—to bring about His purposes. Although he believed in Providence, Jay also believed that human beings had a concomitant duty to respond actively to the conditions Providence created. For Jay, then, faith without works truly was dead.

Religion and Politics in Theory and Practice

Although Jay was involved in political matters for many years, he never expressed his political theory in extended essays, such as John Adams's *Defence of the Constitutions of the United States of America* or *Discourses on Davila*. Instead, his political ideas were expressed more intermittently. They appear in his polemical writings, where he argued for the benefit of a specific policy or political decision. Many of his letters also evince significant reflection on political matters. Unfortunately, even these are at times elliptical, and the press of business often kept him from elaborating on his principles. It is therefore proper to consider Jay's political thought about religion and politics and his political actions together, for as a practical politician Jay's theory was most clearly seen by the actions he took and the words he used.

Jay as Republican

Jay's work in the 1770s and 1780s reflected a republican approach to Christianity's place in the new nation, one that was very prevalent in the founding generation. Here his concerns were largely structural and formal. Protestant Christianity supported the fight for independence. It engendered republican virtue and undergirded the morality necessary for republican institutions to survive. It also set a standard of right by which the new nation could be judged. When the nation under the Articles of Confederation began to fall short of that standard, religious language could be used to call for a stronger and—to Jay's sense—more just government. Providence thus encouraged both independence and the ratification of the new Constitution. Jay's reflection on Christianity's role in American politics at this early period is present but less emotionally engaged than it would be later.

Early in the Revolution, Jay's view of religion's role in politics was a decidedly narrow one—particularist and Protestant. Jay's commitment to Protestantism—not a generalized Christianity or broadly defined religion—suggests both that Jay took his Protestantism seriously and that he had deeply imbibed British imperial attitudes that connected Protestantism and English liberties.[27] At the first Continental Congress in 1774, he was unsure of the legitimacy of a clergyman opening sessions in prayer because he might offend other denominations. Others finally convinced him to accept an Anglican clergyman.[28] Even more dramatically, in the New York Provincial Congress he attempted to shape the state's constitution to exclude Roman Catholics from the political process. He proposed that members of "the church of Rome" be excluded from citizenship until they would forswear the authority of "pope, priest, or foreign authority," as well as "the dangerous and damnable doctrine, that the pope, or any other earthly authority, have power to absolve men from sins or their obligation to the state of New York."[29] Although this measure was rejected, Jay did succeed in requiring that for naturalization immigrants would "renounce all subjection to all and every foreign king, prince, potentate and state, in all matters, ecclesiastical as well as civil."[30] On a personal level, Jay's hostility probably had its roots in the persecution his Huguenot ancestors had suffered at the hands of Catholic France. On a political level, Jay's strategy also had a logic to it: if Catholics were opposed to liberty, were ruled authoritatively by foreign powers, and were hoping to enslave Protestant Americans, they could not be good republicans. Nor could they participate in the Protestant republic Jay hoped would be formed. Although this Protestant nationalism was now disconnected from England, it still carried a great deal of weight in Jay's thinking. Ironically, the logic behind the New York Provincial Congress proposal calling for discrimination against Catholics enabled him to overcome his scruples against other Protestant denominations. In subsequent years, Jay would thus be much more cooperative with other Protestant groups than his 1774 objections suggest.

Because Providence favored the American cause, Jay could display a guarded optimism in "An Address of the Convention of the Representatives of the State of New York to Their Constituents." Jay used the pamphlet, published in December 1776 during the darkest days of the British army's advance into New Jersey, to strengthen New Yorkers' flagging morale by highlighting his belief in the providential character of the contest.[31] Jay pictured the Americans as having received their lands and their freedoms "under the auspices and direction of divine Providence." They were thus called to defend their "inheritance" against a king who had declared them out of his protection and waged war on them. The king's armies had "no regard for religion or virtue" and had even desecrated churches. The outcome of this struggle would have a huge impact, because "the freedom and happiness, or the slavery and misery, of the present and future generation of Americans is to be determined." On an even higher level, only a free people could advance God's kingdom on earth, since "the Almighty will not suffer slavery and the gospel to go hand in hand."[32] On both political and spiritual levels, Jay cast the struggle in monumental terms, with an impact to be felt for generations to come.

Given such stakes, Jay's recommendations are striking. Rather than focusing on practical steps to be taken, Jay issued a call for a reformation of morals, because vices had always brought people into slavery. In that light, the war for independence might have a purifying effect, "to punish the guilt of this country, and bring us back to a sense of duty to our Creator." Jay envisioned a communal guilt and hence the possibility of communal repentance and communal blessing. Jay expanded on this thought when he exhorted: "The King of Heaven is not like the King of Britain, implacable. If his assistance be sincerely implored, it will surely be obtained. If we turn from our sins, he will turn from his anger. . . . Let us do our duty and victory will be our reward." Jay here viewed repentance on a state and even national level as both possible and necessary. A merciful God would surely help a nation that implored His favor—especially when their cause was just. Duty in this case meant both spiritual and practical response. In the face of an advancing British army, Jay demanded, "Let universal charity, public spirit and private virtue, be inculcated, encouraged, and practiced. Unite in preparing for a vigorous defence of your country, as if all depended on your own exertions. And when you have done these things, then rely upon the good providence of Almighty God for success; in full confidence that without his blessing, all our efforts will inevitably fail." In a pattern Jay would often repeat, human actions were decidedly required in the political realm. If people applied themselves, God's providence would bless those actions with success. Faced with such a clear formula, Jay offered his readers a choice. The courageous and manly response was to "do your duty." The other option was to accept slavery. To Jay's mind, those who would accept the latter state did not deserve freedom—a point he made repeatedly when he found people or groups failing in their duty.[33]

As the war progressed, Jay continued to urge on American efforts. In his charge to the first grand jury under the New York state constitution, Jay encouraged them to active citizenship by pointing to the divine sanction of the Revolution. He noted "so many marks of the Divine favour and interposition" which has made its success "miraculous." Divine sanction eased the way for Christians to support the government. Americans should ascribe the events to their "*true cause*" and "instead of swelling our breasts, with arrogant ideas of our prowess and importance, kindle in them a flame of gratitude and piety, which may consume all remains of vice and irreligion." Again, Jay was suggesting that America's newly constituted citizens needed to embark on moral and religious reforms. As "the first people whom Heaven has favoured with an opportunity of deliberating upon, and choosing the forms of government under which they should live," Americans had a particularly strong obligation to support their new state constitutions.[34]

With the arrival of peace, Jay asserted his belief that Providence had been active in obtaining it. Writing to his mother-in-law, Jay observed, "I sincerely join with you in ascribing [the peace] and every other of our blessings to the Supreme Author of all the good that ever was and ever will be in the world." Just as Providence had been inspiring the war from the beginning, so it had safely seen the nation to the conclusion of conflict. Jay wanted to make sure adequate recognition was given to God. At the same time, he realized that independence brought even greater responsibility to all Americans. Both divine and human action would have to be combined for the success of the newly recognized republic. Further, since divine help would not fail, only the citizenry could be held responsible for political failure. Such an attitude explains Jay's words to Robert Morris: "The Definitive Treaty is concluded, and we are now thank God in the full Possession of Peace & Independence. If we are not a happy People now it will be our own Fault."[35]

In the years to come, Jay would wonder whether the Americans were proving that their continued unhappiness *was* their own fault. Observing the government's problems at close range, Jay found the nation going astray by failing to practice justice in its conduct. In contrast to the Revolutionary period, Jay observed that "the case is now altered; we are going and doing wrong, and therefore I look forward to evils and calamities." An expectation of punishments following injustice comported well with Jay's providential vision of the nation. Jay believed that part of the reason the national government was doing wrong was because of its weakness, its inability to do right. "When government," Jay wrote, "either from defects in its construction or administration, ceases to assert its rights, or is too feeble to afford security, inspire confidence, and overawe the ambitious and licentious, the best citizens naturally grow uneasy and look to other systems." Not only would the "best citizens" start longing for a secure (even if less free) government, but the "ambitious and licentious" would arise and act as demagogues to lead people astray from their virtue and their liberty.[36]

Once the Philadelphia Convention had produced the Constitution, Jay used his influence to secure ratification in the important state of New York. In several places Jay coupled an argument from Providence with a prudential argument to support ratification. Particularly in *Federalist 2*, Jay employed Providence as an argument for ratification. There Jay began by pointing to the preexisting, divinely ordained unity of the nation. Providence had created a geographic unity, "one fertile, connected, widespreading country," ideal for trade and communication. He further noted America's shared culture, that "Providence has been pleased to give this one connected country to one united people—a people descended from the same ancestors, speaking the same language, professing the same religion, attached to the same principles of government, very similar in their manners and customs." The primary unity lay in a prepolitical condition, defined by religion, culture, and mores—one that had been the will of God. Jay went on to observe that this unity had been forged into political reality through the sacrifice of the War for Independence—a sacrifice that could be secured through the new Constitution. "This country and this people seem to have been made for each other, and it appears as if it was the design of Providence that an inheritance so proper and convenient for a band of brethren, united to each other by the strongest ties, should never be split into a number of unsocial, jealous, and alien sovereignties." For Jay, Providence itself argued for strengthening the Union through adopting the Constitution.[37]

Although a providential sanction of the American nation might have been enough reason to justify the Constitution to some, Jay did not stop there. Instead, he went on to urge practical and prudential reasons for a stronger government. Jay hoped to reinforce the opinion that "the prosperity of America depended on its Union." Thus his conclusion to *Federalist 2* was a lament for the loss of national greatness, if the country failed to adopt the Constitution.[38]

Similarly, in his widely read *Address to the Citizens of New York*, Jay urged practical reasons for ratification, couched in biblical allusions.[39] In this longer pamphlet, Jay used deliberative rhetoric to appeal to his readers and to point to the possibility of positive reform with the adoption of the Constitution. Jay described the Constitution's ability to advance commerce and preserve peace between the states. By showing that republican self-government was possible, Americans could continue to have a worldwide impact on the cause of liberty.[40] Through his activities at New York's ratifying convention, Jay could be satisfied that he had contributed to the creation of a beneficial, just government that could further the aims of Providence.[41]

Jay as Federalist

Jay believed that the Constitution would provide for a stable, orderly government, but his most sanguine hopes were not realized. Instead, during the 1790s political conflict divided the country, as parties developed over the interpretation of the Constitution and the proper response to the French Revolution. Jay himself was at the center of these storms in the mid-1790s. In Jay's analysis, the nation's political differences came from unscrupulous demagogues, immorality on the part of the citizenry, and the influence of infidel (maliciously unorthodox) religious beliefs. Under these pressures, Jay's republican schema for relating religion and politics broke down—forcing Jay to adjust how he dealt with religion's place in politics. As a result, he articulated a federalist perspective, which highlighted religion's place in political and public life. It was much more active, impassioned, and attuned to religious differences than his earlier stance had been. The "moral epidemic" of the 1790s thus allied Jay much more closely with orthodox Federalists such as Jedidiah Morse and Timothy Dwight, who saw orthodox Christianity as the only means of salvaging America's republican experiment.[42]

As tensions with England mounted, Washington asked Jay to act as a minister plenipotentiary to England. Despite his reluctance, Jay accepted. As he remarked to his wife, "I feel the impulse of duty strongly . . . [and] I ought to follow its dictates, and commit myself to the care and kindness of that Providence in which we have both the highest reason to repose the most absolute confidence." Later he opined that he hoped that it would "please God to make me instrumental to the continuance of peace, and in preventing the effusion of blood, and other evils and miseries incident to war." In going, Jay would be doing God's work in the political realm by saving the nation from the hardships and horrors a war would bring. He would be God's providential instrument for helping America. In doing his duty and obeying God, Jay hoped his mission would be a success.[43] In England, Jay avidly worked to defend American interests in the treaty negotiations. He was satisfied with the treaty signed in November 1794, but he feared that it would not receive a positive reception in America.

The conflicts engendered by the treaty crystallized Jay's understanding of the political dynamics in the country. Jay was not inherently opposed to differences in politics, but he feared factions that would use political differences merely to increase their own power, without regard for the public good. Such, he thought, characterized much of the opposition to the treaty. Back in America, confronted by the attacks directed at him, Jay grew increasingly worried about the influence of the Democratic-

Republicans. Concerned with order in society, Jay fretted about the makeup of such groups: "That with these parties would naturally be associated the Jacobin philosophers, the disorganizing politicians, and the malcontents of various descriptions; together with the many who have little to lose and much to covet."[44] Here Jay clearly linked the Republicans with the French—especially the utopian revolutionaries who brought about the Terror. Foreign influence would harm America, as Frenchified idealists would be happy to work with "malcontents" and others who hoped to use the unsettled period for their own gain. They would then take advantage of a mass of men who could easily be led. Once demagogues were allowed to operate, Jay was sure they would do exactly as they had done in France: bloodily destroy all of society. "If . . . the clubs and their associates should acquire a decided ascendancy, there will be reason to apprehend that our country may become the theatre of scenes resembling those which have been exhibited by their brethren in France."[45] Given such dangers, every means of opposition would be justified.

While worried about political dangers, Jay became alerted to an even more insidious one—the danger of religious infidelity, specifically the Bavarian Illuminati. The Illuminati were a shadowy organization supposedly behind the French Revolution and committed to atheism, immorality, and the overthrow of all governments around the world. Jay not only read Jedidiah Morse's fast day sermon that purported to uncover the Illuminati plot, he corresponded with Morse.[46] By the summer of 1798, Jay was convinced of the basic argument Morse had laid out, observing, "It is also remarkable that the most decided and active Enemies are to be found among the admirers & advocates of the new Philosophy, and the abettors of sedition and Licentiousness both in Europe and America." Jay quickly drew out the political implications of Morse's attack. He immediately connected "the new Philosophy"—the dangerous infidelity of which Morse had spoken—with "sedition and Licentiousness"—the Democratic-Republicans.

Jay remained concerned about such connections into 1799, by which time he thought he discerned negative fruit developing. He wrote Morse, "The seeds of trouble are sowing & germinating in our Country, as well as in many others. Infidelity has become a political engine, alarming both by the force & the extent of its operations."[47] Infidelity acting as a political engine gave an even darker color to the actions of his political opponents, the Democratic-Republicans, who were operating in "secret societies." If infidelity was the political engine motivating the Republicans, then they threatened to bring on all the harm that had befallen religion and society in France. For Jay, Morse's concern over the Illuminati and their attendant infidelity had transformed from merely a single event to an ongoing concern that could continuously threaten the public. Its undermining of public morals (immorality) and political sense (its utopian philosophies) remained constant dangers.

Jay showed an increasing tendency to give a religious and moral analysis of current events, believing that the lack of moral character explained a great deal about the political problems of the decade. As early as 1794, he had written Lindley Murray, "I think we are just entering on the age of revolutions, and that the impurities of our moral *atmosphere* (if I may use the expression) are about to be purified by a succession of political storms."[48] The pollution of the moral world produced political upheavals. Jay would only hope that at the conclusion of those upheavals, both morality and politics could be reformed.[49] Along those same lines, Jay grew increasingly convinced that people (such as the Illuminati or infidels) were actively working with his political opponents (the Republicans) to damage the morals of the country, and consequently its political stability.

Given such analysis, Jay came to support several responses, as possible checks to the Democratic-Republican infidel "faction." His first was to resist strenuously any unnecessary reform. He believed that calls for change (in administration, in policy, in form of government) were typical of his opponents. The best strategy was not to give them an inch. "I should not think that man wise," Jay wrote metaphorically, "who should employ his time in endeavouring to contrive a shoe that would fit every foot. . . . I have no objections to men's mending or changing their own shoes, but I object to their insisting on my mending or changing mine." Jay's anti-utopianism had taken on a new stridency. He wanted to defend the constitutional order he and other Federalist cobblers had worked to create. While not denying the possibility of reform, he was denying that the current conditions were right for reform and that those who were calling for reform were the right men to do it. Jay's other response was a renewed appeal to Providence for help in such difficult days.[50] This combination laid the groundwork for Jay's adoption of a federalist outlook on religion and politics.

The clearest expression of his using public religiosity came when, in his first year as governor, Jay took an unprecedented step and issued an official Thanksgiving Day proclamation. Although common in the New England states, such an act was unheard of in New York. Jay's proclamation represented a creative attempt to advance religion's place in New York public life by mirroring New England's godly commonwealths. In the proclamation, Jay stated he was "perfectly convinced that national prosperity depends, and ought to depend, on national gratitude and obedience to the supreme ruler of all nations." This notion that the state's prosperity is tied to its attitude toward God occurred several times in the proclamation. Similarly, he asserted, "The great Creator and Preserver of the Universe is the Supreme Sovereign of Nations, and does . . . reward or punish them by temporal blessings or calamities, according as their national conduct recommends them to his favour and beneficence, or excites his displeasure and indignation." Jay was urging his countrymen to note the significance of his proclamation: divine pleasure or displeasure was hanging in the balance, and the actions of New York's government and citizens mattered desperately.

Jay then asserted that public political actions were necessary to guarantee continued divine favor. The Proclamation insisted on "the public duty of the people of this state collectively considered, to render unto him their sincere and humble thanks for all these his great and unmerited mercies and blessings." Duty was not only a personal category; it could be applied to the citizenry corporately. Jay was thus attempting to obligate the entire community to give thanks and join in prayers. In the Proclamation, Jay mixed religious and political themes. He gave thanks that America had been blessed with "the civilizing light and influence of his holy gospel," with God's leading during the Revolution, and with "wisdom and opportunity to establish governments and institutions auspicious to order, security, and rational liberty." Looking backward, Jay was repeating his belief in the significance of Providence in both the Revolution and the establishment of the Constitution. Looking forward, he encouraged the citizens of the state to pray for God's blessing "to promote the extension of true religion, virtue, and learning—to give us all grace to cultivate national union, concord, and good will; and generally to bless our nation; and all other nations, in the manner and measure most conducive to our and their best interests and welfare."[51] Jay believed that only an acknowledgment of God would produce such benefits.

Jay's desire for a public religiosity also colored several of his other official acts. He introduced into the legislature a measure for Sabbath observation in the state, but he could not get it passed. He also pressed for the abolition of slavery in the state, which he saw as a moral issue. After years of trying, Jay was able to sign a gradual emancipation bill into law in 1799.[52]

Despite such efforts, Jay remained unconvinced that his efforts had produced sufficient results. In his final year as governor, he observed to Rufus King, "The political world appears to be in a strange state every where; nor is the moral world in a much more eligible condition."[53] Unsettled morality and an unsettled political situation went together, and Jay remained concerned. He left office in 1801 without believing that such challenges had been adequately met. His federalist approach to religion's place in defending the nation also appeared insufficient. In his retirement, Jay would seek to influence the nation in realms outside of politics.

Jay as Voluntarist

Jay's growing emphasis on moral and religious concerns explains his adoption of a voluntarist perspective in his final years. Jay supported many explicitly orthodox Christian voluntary societies. For instance, he was a member of the American Board of Commissioners of Foreign Missions, even though he could not attend their meetings. He praised the organization, observing to Jedidiah Morse that "institutions like this are not only to be approved and commended but to be sustained and assisted."[54] Similarly, Jay cheerfully supported the American Society for Educating Pious Youth for the Gospel Ministry.[55] Most important to Jay was the ABS, which he served as president from 1821 to 1825.

In his presidential addresses to the ABS, Jay reiterated his belief in an active Providence and a tie between the nation's spiritual and political health. He asserted the providential origins of Bible societies by arguing, "The mere tendency of these events to promote the coming in of the Gentiles, affords presumptive evidence of their being genuine indications of their approach of the season assigned for it—or, in other words, that they are providential." As his reference to the "coming in of the Gentiles" suggested, Jay believed the societies were being divinely directed to fulfill prophecy. Similarly, Jay continued to see an additional providential purpose of the society in setting up right religion as a bulwark against social and political chaos. The ABS would work against those who "by artfully and diligently encouraging defection from Scripture; and from Scripture doctrines . . . gradually introduced and spread that contempt for both, which in the last century was publicly displayed in impious acts of profaneness, and in dreadful deeds of ferocity."[56] The ABS, by spreading faith in the Scriptures, was thus the nation's best hope to avoid another French Revolution.

At the same time, Jay's addresses pointed to new developments in his thinking about religion and politics, as he emphasized the kingdom of God over the American nation. Jay praised all of the voluntary societies that were being providentially used to advance the kingdom of God, especially missionary societies, missions to the Indians, Bible translation endeavors, and antislavery societies.[57] Together, these societies gave witness to God's providential involvement with America. In considering these manifestations of the kingdom of God, the earthly kingdoms took a much reduced place. Thus in the addresses Jay only mentioned the United States once, and then in regard to the missionary societies. "We have reason to rejoice," Jay observed, "that such institutions have been so greatly multiplied and cherished in the United States; especially as a kind Providence has blessed us, not only with peace and plenty, but also with the full and secure enjoyment of our civil and religious rights and privileges."[58] The value of the United States lay in its ability to nourish societies like the ABS—quite apart from any inherent value. Whereas the public Jay had seen America as a providentially appointed nation, by the end of his life he had recognized that America's value lay in its place in a larger, providential design. Jay's nationalism had been subsumed under a larger, transnational Christian identity.

Jay's development of a voluntarist attitude helps make sense of his final public pronouncement. In honor of the fiftieth anniversary of independence in 1826, New York City invited Jay to attend its celebrations. He declined to come, but he offered very pointed suggestions about the necessity of religion in public life. Jay claimed that it was his "earnest hope that the peace, happiness, and prosperity enjoyed by our beloved country, may induce those who direct her national councils to *recommend* a general and public return of praise and thanksgiving to HIM from whose goodness these blessings descend." Echoing his earlier Thanksgiving Day proclamation, Jay was suggesting that the celebration should not be merely a celebration of the nation, but should instead be forthrightly religious. Jay continued, "The most effectual means of securing the continuance of our civil and religious liberties is, always to remember with gratitude the source from which they flow."[59] Jay's religious commitments had pointed him toward the acknowledgment that religion was at the heart of the American experiment. Such an explicit statement was much sharper than he had made earlier in his public career. It expanded his concern to ensure the continuation of republican government while acknowledging that human action would be powerless without divine aid. Jay's final benediction, then, was a call for greater involvement of religion in the young republic.

Notes

1. John Jay, letter to Jedidiah Morse, Aug. 16, 1809, John Jay Papers, Manuscripts, Rare Books and Manuscripts Library, Columbia University, New York City, Box 25 (hereinafter John Jay Papers, Columbia).

2. Although people with many different beliefs discussed Providence during the Revolutionary era, this chapter argues that Jay used it in a decidedly orthodox fashion—a point enlarged on below.

3. Walter Stahr, *John Jay: Founding Father* (New York: Hambledon and London, 2005), 255–70.

4. For example, John Jay, *The Charge of Chief Justice Jay to the Grand Juries on the Eastern Circuit: At the Circuit Courts held in the Districts of New-York, on the 4th, of

Connecticut on the 22nd days of April; of Massachusetts on the 4th, and of New-Hampshire on the 20th days of May, 1790 (Portsmouth, N.H.: George Jerry Osborne Jr., 1790).

5. Stahr, Jay, 313–30; Stanley Elkins and Eric McKitrick, The Age of Federalism (New York: Oxford University Press, 1993), 406–14.

6. Stahr, Jay, 384.

7. Ibid., xiv, 383.

8. William Jay intentionally portrayed his father as a heroic republican statesman, but in so doing he failed to describe Jay the man. Further, few read the two-volume biography produced years after John Jay's death. William Jay, The Life of John Jay: With Selections from His Correspondence and Miscellaneous Papers (New York: J. & J. Harper, 1833).

9. Frank Monaghan, John Jay: Defender of Liberty, Against Kings & Peoples, Author of the Constitution & Governor of New York, President of the Continental Congress, Co-Author of the Federalist, Negotiator of the Peace of 1783 & the Jay Treaty of 1794, First Chief Justice of the Supreme Court (New York: Bobbs-Merrill, 1935); Stahr, Jay, xiii.

10. Patricia Bonomi, "John Jay, Religion, and the State," New York History 81 (January 2000): 9–18; David L. Holmes, The Faiths of the Founding Fathers (New York: Oxford University Press, 2006), 154–60.

11. William Jay, Life, 1:434–42; Monaghan, Jay, 25; Stahr, Jay, 6–12, 232–36.

12. John Jay, letter to Uzal Ogden, February 14, 1796, John Jay Papers, Columbia, Box 23.

13. John Jay, letter to John Bristed, April 23, 1811, John Jay Papers, Columbia, Box 26.

14. John Jay, letter to Peter Augustus Jay, April 8, 1784, John Jay Papers, Columbia, Box 17; John Jay, letter to Maria and Nancy Jay, June 1, 1792, John Jay Papers, Box 21.

15. William Jay, Life, 1:430–33; John Jay, letter to Rufus King, January 20, 1803, Rufus King Papers, New York Historical Society, New York City, vol. 31, #83; John Jay, letter to Samuel F. Jarvis, May 4, 1818, John Jay Papers, Columbia, Box 28.

16. William Jay, Life, 1:443–44.

17. Alfred H. Partridge, "The Memory of the Just": A Memorial of the Hon. William Jay (New York: Roe, 1860), 13–14.

18. Timothy Dwight, Travels in New England and New York, ed. Barbara Solomon (Cambridge, Mass.: Belknap Press of Harvard University Press, 1969), 148.

19. William Jay, Life, 1:443.

20. John Jay, "Divinity of Christ—from the Revelation of St. John," John Jay Papers, Box 58; John Jay, "Thoughts on Light," John Jay Papers, Columbia, Box 58; John Jay, "Jacob and Esau," May 9, 1814, John Jay Papers, Columbia, Box 58.

21. The passage in question was 1 Corinthians 15:29. John Jay, letter to Jedidiah Morse, October 25, 1813, John Jay Papers, Columbia, Box 27.

22. John Jay, letter to Benjamin Rush, March 22, 1797, John Jay Papers, Columbia, Box 23.

23. Jay's work was apparently known to at least some of the other founders. In a throwaway line about his son John Quincy's role as diplomat at Ghent and the possibility of his forced retirement, John Adams remarked, "I expect, if he makes a peace he will be obliged to retire like a Jay to study Prophecies to the End of his Life." John Adams to Thomas Jefferson, July 16, 1813, in *The Adams-Jefferson Letters*, vol. 2, ed. Lester Cappon (Chapel Hill: University of North Carolina Press for the Institute of Early American History and Culture, 1959), 360.

24. John Jay, Address to the Annual Meeting of the ABS, May 13, 1824, John Jay Papers, ABS, Folder: Correspondence: Addresses, Individuals, 1816–1830.

25. Henry May, *The Enlightenment in America* (New York: Oxford University Press, 1976), 3–101. See also J. David Hoeveler, *Creating the American Mind: Intellect and Politics in the Colonial Colleges* (Lanham, Md.: Rowman & Littlefield, 2002), 129–54.

26. Holmes, *Faiths of the Founding Fathers*, 158.

27. Linda Coley, *Britons: Forging the Nation, 1707–1837* (New Haven, Conn.: Yale University Press, 1992), 11–54; Thomas Kidd, *The Protestant Interest: New England after Puritanism* (New Haven, Conn.: Yale University Press, 2004), 51–73.

28. Monaghan, *Jay*, 59; Stahr, *Jay*, 37.

29. Bonomi, "John Jay," 15–16; Monaghan, *Jay*, 94; Stahr, *Jay*, 78.

30. Monaghan, *Jay*, 95.

31. John Jay, *An Address of the Convention of the Representatives of the State of New-York to Their Constituents* (Fish-kill, N.Y.: S. Loudon, 1776). For a picture of the disheartened American situation at the time, see David Hackett Fisher, *Washington's Crossing* (New York: Oxford University Press, 2004), 81–159. See also Richard Morris, *John Jay: The Making of a Revolutionary* (New York: Harper & Row, 1975), 359–61.

32. Jay, *An Address of the Convention*, 3, 6, 7–9, 13, 18.

33. Ibid., 4–5, 10, 11. For another example of this, see Jay's responses to the faltering Tryon County militia. Morris, *Jay*, 423–24.

34. John Jay, *The Charge Delivered by the Honourable John Jay, Esq. Chief Justice of the State of New-York, to the Grand Jury, at the Supreme Court, Held in Kingston, in Ulster County, September 9, 1777* (Kingston: John Holt, 1777), 6–8.

35. John Jay, letter to Margaret Livingston, Jul. 12, 1783, John Jay Papers, Columbia, Box 17; John Jay, letter to Robert Morris, Sep. 12, 1783, John Jay Papers, Columbia, Box 17.

36. John Jay, letter to George Washington, Jun. 27, 1786, John Jay Papers, Columbia, Box 19; John Jay, letter to John Adams, Nov. 1, 1786, John Jay Papers, Columbia, Box 19.

37. John Jay, *Federalist 2*, in *The Federalist Papers*, ed. Clinton Rossiter (New York: Signet, 1961, 1993), 32–33. Indeed, Jay is the only of the three authors to refer to "Providence." Madison makes a passing reference to "Heaven" in 20,

refers to God in 18 and 43, and speaks of the Almighty and "a finger of that Almighty hand" in 37. Even so, Jay's treatment of the Providential union of America is the longest religious reflection in the *Federalist Papers*. Thomas Engeman, Edward Erler, and Thomas Hofeller, eds., *The Federalist Concordance* (Middletown, Conn.: Wesleyan University Press, 1980), 438, 239, 222.

38. Jay, *Federalist* 2, 35.

39. John Jay, *An Address to the People of the State of New-York, on the Subject of the Constitution, Agreed upon at Philadelphia, The 17th of September, 1787* (New York: Samuel and John Loudon, 1788), 6, 9, 16. Jay, for instance, either directly or indirectly refers to such passages as Mic. 4:4, 1 Kings 12:16, and Prov. 11:14.

40. Ibid., 3, 6, 19.

41. For ratification, see Monaghan, *Jay*, 294–97; Stahr, *Jay*, 255–67; Linda Grant De Pauw, *The Eleventh Pillar: New York State and the Federal Constitution* (Ithaca: Published for the American Historical Association by Cornell University Press, 1966); Stephen L. Schechter, ed., *The Reluctant Pillar: New York and the Adoption of the Federal Constitution* (Troy, N.Y.: Russell Sage College, 1985).

42. John Jay, letter to Jedidiah Morse, Apr. 24, 1800, Jedidiah Morse Papers, New York Public Library, Box 1, Folder: Correspondence, 1800.

43. John Jay, letter to Sarah L. Jay, Apr. 15, 1794, in *Selected Letters of John Jay and Sarah Livingston Jay: Correspondence by or to the First Chief Justice of the United States and His Wife*, ed. Landa Freeman, Louise North, and Janet Wedge (Jefferson, N.C.: McFarland, 2005), 220–21. Also, Jay observed before setting off, "God's will be done; to him I resign; in him I confide. Do the like. Any other Philosophy applicable to this occasion is delusive. Away with it." John Jay, letter to Sarah L. Jay, Apr. 20, 1794, John Jay Papers, Columbia, Box 21.

44. John Jay, letter to James Duane, Sep. 16, 1795, John Jay Papers, Columbia, Box 23.

45. John Jay, letter to Timothy Pickering, Aug. 17, 1795, Timothy Pickering Papers, Massachusetts Historical Society, Boston, Reel 20, #33.

46. Jedidiah Morse, *A Sermon, Delivered at the New North Church in Boston, in the Morning, and in the Afternoon at Charlestown, May 9th, 1798, Being the Day Recommended by John Adams, President of the United States of America, for Solemn Humiliation, Fasting, and Prayer* (Boston: Samuel Hall, 1798). The classic work describing the Illuminati controversy is Vernon Stauffer, *New England and the Bavarian Illuminati* (New York: Columbia University Press, 1918).

47. John Jay, letter to Jedidiah Morse, Sep. 4, 1798, Jedidiah Morse Papers, Box 1, folder: Correspondence: 1798–1799; John Jay, letter to Jedidiah Morse, Jan. 30, 1799, Jedidiah Morse Papers, Box 1, folder: Correspondence: 1798–1799.

48. John Jay, letter to Lindley Murray, Aug. 22, 1794, John Jay Papers, Columbia, Box 22.

49. Ibid.; John Jay, letter to Benjamin Rush, Mar. 22, 1797, John Jay Papers, Columbia, Box 23.

50. John Jay, letter to William Vaughan, May 26, 1796, in William Jay, *Life*, 2:272; John Jay, letter to Timothy Pickering, Aug. 17, 1795, Timothy Pickering Papers, Reel 20, #33.

51. John Jay, "A Proclamation," *American Minerva and the New-York Advertiser*, Nov. 12, 1795.

52. William Jay, *Life*, 1:229–33, 401. See also Daniel Littlefield, "John Jay, the Revolutionary Generation, and Slavery," *New York History* 81 (2000): 131–32.

53. John Jay, letter to Rufus King, Jun. 16, 1800, Rufus King Papers, vol. 31, #12.

54. John Jay, letter to Jedidiah Morse, Jan. 1, 1813, Jedidiah Morse Papers, Box 2, Folder: Correspondence, 1813.

55. Louis Dwight, letter to John Jay, Nov. 21, 1821, John Jay Papers, Columbia, Box 8; Louis Dwight, letter to John Jay, Dec. 21, 1821, John Jay Papers, Columbia, Box 8.

56. John Jay, Address at the Annual Meeting of the ABS, May 9, 1822, in William Jay, *Life*, 1:500, 501; John Jay, Address to the Annual Meeting of the ABS, May 12, 1825, in William Jay, *Life*, 1:513.

57. Address to the Annual Meeting of the ABS, May 9, 1822, in William Jay, *Life*, 1:498–500; Address, May 9, 1823, in William Jay, *Life*, 1:504–6.

58. Address to the Annual Meeting of the ABS, May 13, 1824, John Jay Papers, ABS, Folder: Correspondence: Addresses, Individuals, 1816–1830.

59. John Jay to the Committee of the Corporation of the City of New-York, June 29, 1826 in William Jay, *Life*, 1:456–57.

CHAPTER 8

Thomas Paine's Civil Religion of Reason

DAVID J. VOELKER

Although Thomas Paine (1737–1809) spent only about a quarter of his life in North America, he deserves to be counted among the founders of the United States and as a champion of republican government. *Common Sense*, which Paine published in 1776, just thirteen months after he arrived in Philadelphia, and *Rights of Man* (1791–1792), which he wrote to defend the French Revolution, were two of the most popular and influential political pamphlets of late-eighteenth-century America and Britain. Although Paine sometimes advanced original ideas in these works and others, his distinctive contribution lay more in his style and his intended audience than in his political philosophy. As Harvey Kaye has suggested, by "addressing his arguments to those who had traditionally been excluded from political debate and deliberation, [Paine] helped to transform the very idea of politics and the political nation."[1] This assessment squares with Paine's own description of his aims, which he expressed late in life: "My motive and object in all my political works, beginning with Common Sense, . . . have been to rescue man from tyranny and false systems and false principles of government, and enable him to be free, and establish government for himself."

While Paine's political pamphlets made him famous and even led to his direct, if limited, participation in the revolutionary government of France, his major religious treatise, The Age of Reason (1794–1795), seriously damaged his reputation among Americans. As a deist, Paine expressed belief in a divinely created physical and moral order, but he vehemently rejected the Bible's divine origins, miracles, and the divinity of Christ—mainstays of Christianity. Few Americans could accept his claim that he had a constructive motive for writing The Age of Reason, which Paine said was "to bring man to a right reason that God has given him; to impress on him the great principles of divine morality, justice, mercy, and a benevolent disposition to all men and to all creatures; and to excite in him a spirit of trust, confidence and consolation in his creator, unshackled by the fable and fiction of books, by whatever invented name they may be called."[2] In politics and religion alike, Paine sought to liberate shackled humanity, and he inevitably offended those who cherished the status quo.

For nearly a century after he published The Age of Reason, Paine's reputation suffered on account of his "infidelity." As early as 1807, for instance, a popular Methodist hymn proclaimed:

The WORLD, the DEVIL, and TOM PAINE,
Have try'd their force, but all in vain,
They can't prevail—the reason is,
The Lord defends the Methodist.[3]

Eighty years later, Theodore Roosevelt inaccurately but memorably denounced Paine as a "filthy little atheist."[4] Given the intensity of the invective issued against Paine, it is strange to consider how little his religious views differed from some of his contemporaries whose reputations remained essentially intact. Thomas Jefferson also had deistic inclinations, and he took a pair of scissors to the Bible in order to excise the supernatural elements that he considered dubious. Furthermore, in his Notes on the State of Virginia (first published in English in 1787), he defended the right of conscience with the impious notice: "it does me no injury for my neighbor to say there are twenty gods, or no God. It neither picks my pocket nor breaks my leg."[5] Jefferson's political opponents attempted to capitalize on his glib comment about the harmlessness of atheism, his friendship with Paine, and his refusal as president to call a national day of prayer, but as president he mitigated accusations of political atheism by using religious rhetoric in his public statements, and he easily entered the pantheon of the founders.

Benjamin Franklin, a celebrity in his own time and an American icon, also publicly aired his unorthodox beliefs without sullying his fame. In fact, the simple creed that Franklin published in his widely read *Autobiography* had a great deal in common with Paine's creed from *The Age of Reason*. Franklin professed:

> That there is one God, who made all things.
> That he governs the world by his Providence.—
> That he ought to be worshiped by Adoration, Prayer, and
>   Thanksgiving.
> But that the most acceptable Service of God is doing Good to Man.
> That the Soul is immortal.
> And that God will certainly reward Virtue and punish Vice either
>   here or hereafter.[6]

From a Christian point of view, there are two glaring absences in Franklin's creed, as he mentioned neither Christ nor the Bible. Paine's creed displayed similar lacuna: "I believe in one God, and no more; and I hope for happiness beyond this life. I believe [in] the equality of man, and I believe that religious duties consist in doing justice, loving mercy, and endeavouring to make our fellow creatures happy."[7] The only substantive absence in Paine's creed, compared to Franklin's, is an affirmation of divine providence. It seems clear, however, that Paine and Franklin both rejected special providence, or miraculous intervention, while accepting general providence.[8] Moreover, Paine declared, "My own mind is my own church," and Franklin, who confessed to staying home from Sunday worship in order to study, apparently agreed.[9]

The difference between Franklin and Paine came down largely to their respective styles and their relative confidence in human ability. Franklin famously feigned humility and open-mindedness, and he tempered his confidence in human reason with a sense of humor about the inherent weaknesses of human nature. (Recounting how he had strayed from vegetarianism after being tempted by frying fish that "smelt admirably well," Franklin confessed, "So convenient a thing it is to be a *reasonable Creature*, since it enables one to find or make a Reason for every thing one has a mind to do.")[10] Paine not only lacked a sense of humor about reason and human nature but also tended to conflate his own point of view with universal reason.[11] Furthermore, Franklin's deism was essentially "nonpolitical," and he seemed content to reconcile publicly natural religion and Christianity, because he saw that both could be socially useful. In 1786, Franklin counseled an unidentified acquaintance—perhaps Paine himself—against publishing a deistic treatise, not only because of the enemies that such a work might raise but also because it might do moral damage to society. Paine, however, did not hesitate to launch a vociferous attack on what he deemed to be socially harmful Christian superstition. In some sense, then, Paine became, in Craig Nelson's phrase, "Benjamin Franklin unleashed."[12]

Because of Paine's relative lack of restraint, his reputation also suffered at the hands of various critics and hack biographers who tended to depict him as a godless, penniless drunkard. (One such hostile biographer, George Chalmers, writing as Francis Oldys, was paid by the British government, which had charged Paine with seditious libel for *Rights of Man*.)[13] Despite the many assaults on Paine's reputation, the death of his influence has been greatly exaggerated. As Kaye has argued, "Paine remained a powerful presence in American political and intellectual life," especially for "rebels, reformers, and critics" who "struggled to defend, extend, and deepen freedom, equality, and democracy."[14] Some of Paine's ambivalent admirers since his death have misguidedly attempted to draw a line between his advocacy of democratic republicanism, on the one hand, and his deistic religious views, on the other. But Paine's religious and political views intertwined. Recognizing this fact, Paine's biographers have often used religious language to describe him. Jack Fruchtman, for example, calls Paine an "apostle of freedom," explaining that "beneath [Paine's] criticisms of organized religion lay an abounding faith and belief in the wonders of God's universal creation."[15] Nelson goes so far as to say that the Enlightenment was "a wholly new religion . . . of light," and that Paine became its "greatest missionary."[16]

These biographers make compelling points, but Paine was more than an apostle of an existing ideology. Over the course of his career as a publicist and polemicist, Paine attempted to articulate a universal civil religion of reason that he hoped would promote equality, freedom, and a democratic republican political order.[17] In doing so, he drew more from the Christian tradition than he knew, and he echoed other founders in bestowing upon religion an important civic function—within the context of religious liberty.

The Roots of Paine's Religion

As many biographers have pointed out, the first thirty-seven years of Paine's life were indelibly marked by frustration and failure. He had the good fortune of attending grammar school for several years, but at the age of twelve he became an apprentice staymaker under his father. Paine did not especially enjoy making stays for women's corsets. He abandoned the apprenticeship just before completing his seven-year term, and he ran off to London with plans of going to sea. His father initially prevailed against him, but in 1757, in the midst of the Seven Years War, Paine served briefly as a privateer.[18] Subsequently, he returned to staymaking and married Mary Lambert, who died within a year. In 1762, Paine gained employment as an excise tax officer, but he lost this position because of apparent negligence after about three years.[19] Paine worked again as a staymaker, and in 1765–1767 he served as a teacher in and near London, where he probably began attending scientific lectures. In 1768, Paine was reinstated as an excise officer, and in 1771 he married for a second time. For several years, he lived in Lewes, a stronghold of anti-Catholicism, religious dissent, and republicanism. There he participated in local politics and enjoyed food, drink, and spirited political debate with fellow members of the "Headstrong Club." Neither his job nor his marriage to Elizabeth Ollive lasted for long, however, as Paine shifted his attention to pleading the case of his fellow underpaid excise officers. He prepared a pamphlet on their behalf, and he spent the winter of 1772–1773 in London, campaigning in vain. Subsequently, the excise office dismissed him again, his small business failed, and his marriage disintegrated.

These dismal circumstances led Paine to seek his fortune in America. Luckily, he had associated with several prominent intellectuals in London, including Benjamin Franklin, who was sufficiently impressed to write a letter of introduction, addressed to his son-in-law in Philadelphia. When Paine arrived in America on November 30, 1774, he was seriously ill, but by January of the next year he had recovered his health and secured a position as editor of the *Pennsylvania Magazine.*

Because we know relatively little about Paine's life before he arrived in Philadelphia, he sometimes appears as a propagandist *ex machina*, dropped into the midst of the conflict between Britain and the thirteen colonies to deploy "common sense" to turn the protestors into full-blooded revolutionaries. Recent biographers, especially John Keane, have devoted more extensive study to Paine's life prior to his voyage across the Atlantic, allowing us to see that Paine was very much shaped by his hybrid religious upbringing, his exposure to corrupt and arbitrary political power, and his association with coffeehouse radicals in Lewes and London.[20]

Paine was born on January 29, 1737, in Thetford, England, a modest town about eighty miles northeast of London.[21] He lived in Thetford until his twentieth year, and he came of age in the shadow of "Gallows Hill," where every March criminals faced execution, often for petty crimes against property. As Keane has argued, Paine grew up well aware that the state was the greatest perpetrator of violence in England.[22] He revealed his awareness of this fact, and his sympathy for the impoverished, in his first significant publication, *The Case of the Officers of Excise* (1772). There he argued that "nature never produced a man who would starve in a well-stored larder, because the provisions were not his own." A starving person, facing the question of "to be, or not to be," should not be punished for stealing food, Paine argued, but should be treated with compassion.[23] In addition to observing state violence against the poor, Paine saw political corruption firsthand. Thetford was a pocket borough ruled by a single aristocratic family, the Graftons, who deployed patronage and bribery to control local government and parliamentary elections, in which only thirty men in Thetford could participate (out of a population of about two thousand).[24] Paine thus grew up in the midst of a society of artificial distinctions and arbitrary power—the kind of social order that he would later attack in his republican pamphlets.

Paine's father, Joseph, was a Quaker whose marriage to an Anglican woman had been frowned upon by his fellow dissenters from the established church. While Paine's quasi-Quaker upbringing no doubt influenced him, it is important to note that he grew up in a religiously divided household, which meant that he had to learn to negotiate different values, practices, and points of view. He must have been aware that the state merely tolerated Quakers without fully accepting them.[25] (Later in life, in *Rights of Man*, he called "toleration" a form of despotism.)[26] The young Paine, however, did not suffer much on account of his Quaker father, because his Anglican mother saw that he was baptized and confirmed in the Church of England.[27]

As an adult, Paine held an ambivalent attitude about his Quaker roots. He praised their simple beliefs but criticized their material austerity. He wrote in *The Age of Reason*: "The religion that approaches the nearest of all others to true deism, in the moral and benign part thereof, is that professed by the quakers. . . . Though I reverence their philanthropy, I cannot help smiling at the conceit, that if the taste of a quaker could have been consulted at the creation, what a silent and drab-coloured creation it would have been!"[28] Paine also denied the legitimacy of Quaker pacifism, implying that the American rebellion involved the "unavoidable defence" against "wilful attack."[29]

Despite these complaints, Paine seems to have absorbed many values and principles from his close childhood association with Quakers. The fundamental Quaker principle of the inner or inward light meant that all people had the potential to know God. A divine presence gleaming in the hearts of all humans, the inner light implied human equality and nourished Quaker egalitarianism, a value that Paine certainly shared. (As he wrote when he attacked monarchy in *Common Sense*, "mankind being originally equals in the order of creation, the equality could only be destroyed by some subsequent circumstance.")[30] The inner-light theology also underwrote the Quaker insistence upon the inviolability of the individual conscience, which led them to refuse to pay tithes to the established church and to decline to take oaths to the state. Because of their dual emphasis on equality and conscience, Quakers inherently tended toward antiauthoritarianism, a tendency that Paine also shared.[31]

As important as the Quaker influence was on Paine, it cannot fully explain his mature religious views. He also briefly associated with and preached for Methodists, with whom he shared some common values. With its anti-Calvinist theology and its encouragement of lay activity, Methodism empowered ordinary people.[32] Although Paine later rejected evangelical "enthusiasm" (as opponents of Methodism decried it), his brush with Methodism perhaps helped foster his populist sensibility. In 1758, when he was twenty-one years old, he affiliated himself with a group of Methodists in Dover and even preached to them at their chapel. The next year, Paine relocated to Sandwich in order to establish a stay-making business. Limited evidence suggests that he preached to Methodists there as well, although he probably read aloud sermons by John Wesley rather than delivering sermons of his own conception.[33] Whatever the details regarding Paine's brief stint as a Methodist exhorter (rather than preacher, because he was not ordained), it seems likely that the experience reinforced his own egalitarian tendencies while also giving him some experience as a public speaker. As an active Methodist during 1758 and 1759, Paine also probably augmented his knowledge of the Christian Bible.

Despite his ignorance of (and impatience with) Christian theology, Paine did possess a working familiarity with the Bible, and his contempt for the Bible was less than total. In part one of *The Age of Reason*, he admitted to admiring aspects of both Psalm 19 and the Book of Job. Although Paine could only quote Joseph Addison's paraphrase of the psalm (because he lacked a Bible), the psalm itself complemented Paine's deism with its opening line: "The heavens declare the glory of God; and the firmament sheweth his handywork." He explained away his admiration for the Book of Job by denying that it was a Hebrew text, thus effectively writing it out of the Bible.[34] Still, certain biblical and Judeo-Christian influences are apparent in Paine's thought. The creed that he articulated early in part one of *The Age of Reason* paraphrased the later part of Micah 6:8: "What doth the LORD require of thee, but to do justly, and to love mercy, and to walk humbly with thy God?" Notably, Paine retained "justice" and "loving mercy" but replaced the injunction to "walk humbly with thy God" with "endeavouring to make our fellow creatures happy."[35] Although Paine's God was in some ways a distant designer, the Creator he posited also had personal qualities that derived more from monotheistic traditions than from Newtonianism. In sum, while Paine frequently used the Bible merely as a rhetorical tool to achieve some end—be it attacking monarchy or denouncing Christian superstition—he did not entirely escape its subtle influence. Certain key passages of his pamphlets echo Christian language in unexpected ways, given his arch-infidel status.

One of the difficulties of studying Paine's religious beliefs is that we lack definitive evidence about when he forsook his Christian roots and became an adamant deist. There are hints, to be sure, that as early as 1776 he had become quite impious. (John Adams was taken aback by Paine's "contempt" for the Bible, especially the Old Testament.)[36] Harry Hayden Clark has ably argued that Paine, during his time in London (mainly 1765–1767 and 1772–1773), became enamored with the Newtonian worldview being promoted by Benjamin Martin and James Ferguson.[37] Reviewing the publications of these two Newtonian popularizers, Clark made a convincing case that many of Paine's views regarding both religion and politics derived in part from the Newtonian worldview, which posited an orderly, harmonious universe, governed by the laws laid down by a benevolent divinity. Clark thus aptly labeled Paine a scientific or Newtonian deist. Furthermore, he pointed out that many of Paine's likeminded contemporaries continued to pay some public respect to Christianity.[38] It seems likely, then, that Paine gradually lost the ability to hide his disdain for most Christian beliefs. And the reasons for this change, it would seem, had much to do with his incipient republicanism.

When he journeyed to America in late 1774, Paine took with him broad experiences with established and dissenting Christian traditions, an expansive interest in Newtonian science, and a strong distaste for authority and artificial hierarchies. Doubtless, too, he carried a grudge against the British government that had twice dismissed him from civil service and that he believed perpetuated corruption and poverty. Still, nothing about Paine's life up to 1774 foreshadowed his illustrious future.

Paine's Revolutionary Vision

Between 1776 and 1783, Paine played a crucial role as a promoter of American independence. Indeed, *Common Sense* became perhaps the most influential—and certainly the most widely read—pamphlet of eighteenth-century America. In that work, Paine not only attacked the British constitution and the institution of monarchy, but he also presented a vision of the "promise of America," to borrow Kaye's phrase.[39] He powerfully sketched an image of a democratic republican society, a society where all citizens would be equal, where the law would be king, and where Americans of all origins and faiths could pursue prosperity in peace. In his *American Crisis* series, published between 1776 and 1783, Paine, using the moniker of "Common Sense," continued to support the Revolution and his vision for the future. Paine gave few hints, in these writings, of his true religious views. He frequently cited the Bible to illustrate his arguments, and he often used the language of providence, which he probably imbibed from his former Methodist brethren. *The American Crisis* number 1, for instance, brimmed with providentialism. While professing to have "as little superstition in me as any man living," Paine stated his refusal to believe that God would abandon the Americans, who had so strongly sought to avoid war, to their destruction. Later in the piece, he exclaimed, "I am as confident, as I am that GOD governs the world, that America will never be happy till she gets clear of foreign dominion."[40] Throughout his revolutionary writings, Paine employed a providential language calculated to appeal to American Christians, and there is little reason to doubt his sincerity.

The outlines of Paine's civil religion began to emerge in *Common Sense*. Paine launched the pamphlet with the following epigram: "Man knows no Master save creating Heaven, Or those whom Choice and common Good ordain." This epigram supported republicanism by appealing to a divine order—something that Paine did throughout the work. That divine order was universal in scope, and Paine declared from the opening that "The cause of America is in a great measure the cause of all mankind."[41] Paine conceded that "moral virtue" was inadequate to govern the world, because humans failed to follow their conscience, but he nevertheless expressed confidence in the ability of "the simple voice of nature and of reason" to reveal government's ideal form. In fact, he claimed that he prescribed a republican form of government by drawing on "a principle in nature, which no art can overturn," namely that "the more simple any thing is, the less liable it is to be disordered."[42] Paine relied extensively on the Old Testament to undermine the legitimacy of monarchy, but the more fundamental argument that he made was that human beings were "originally equals in the order of creation"—a premise that he built upon in later works.[43]

Paine's *Rights of Man* (published in two parts in 1791 and 1792, before the French Revolution took an especially bloody turn) in many ways reaffirmed and elaborated upon the political principles that he had first sketched out in *Common Sense*. A response to Edmund Burke's attack on the French Revolution, the pamphlet attracted hundreds of thousands of readers in Britain and America. Because *Rights of Man* posed a threat to monarchical authority, Paine was convicted, in absentia, of seditious libel; his writings were banned in Britain, and he was effectively exiled.[44] In joining the campaign against monarchy and aristocracy, Paine fervently believed that he was supporting the cause of universal peace, freedom, and happiness. Furthermore, *Rights of Man* exuded a Newtonian confidence that "all the great laws of society are laws of nature" and that the human social impulse impelled individuals "into society, as naturally as gravitation acts to a center."[45] Although the *Rights of Man* included little sustained discussion of religion, it nevertheless revealed the religious underpinnings of Paine's political views.

The principle of human equality played as key a role in *Rights of Man* as in *Common Sense*. Paine defended the notion that "that which a whole nation chooses to do, it has a right to do" as a way of denying Burke's assertion that the people of England had forever and irrevocably submitted themselves to the heirs of William and Mary.[46] Paine's diatribe against this sort of "political popery" rested upon clearly stated religious assumptions about "*the unity or equality of man*." What Paine meant by this phrase was that "man is all of *one degree*, and consequently that all men are born equal, and with equal natural rights." (Incidentally, he made qualified citations of both Christian and Hebrew tradition in order to help prove his case.) He concluded that the "divine principle of the equal rights of man . . . has its origin from the Maker of man."[47] Although he was certainly going farther than most Quakers with his social and political egalitarianism, this conclusion shows Quaker influence.

Paine articulated two human moral duties, which he believed originated in creation: "his duty to God, which every man must feel; and with respect to his neighbour, to do as he would be done by."[48] Although Paine elsewhere expressed discomfort with some of Jesus' teachings (such as his commandment to "love your enemies"),[49] he here paraphrased the "great commandment[s]" proffered in the central passage of the Sermon on the Mount: "Thou shalt love the Lord thy God with all thy heart, and with all thy soul, and with all thy mind" and "Thou shalt love thy neighbour as thyself" (Matthew 22:37–39). While Paine saw the second commandment as relatively straightforward, he elaborated upon the duty to God: "The first act of man, when he looked around and saw himself a creature which he did not make, and a world furnished for his reception, must have been devotion; and devotion must ever continue sacred to every individual man, *as it appears right to him*; and governments do mischief by interfering." Paine's most direct statement about religion in *Rights of Man* was his position "*that every religion is good, that teaches man to be good.*" Quite charitably, relative to some of his later comments, Paine observed that "all religions are in their nature mild and benign, and united with principles of morality." State-established religions, however, destroyed these good principles, in favor of enhancing state power. Paine went even further: "Take away the law-establishment, and every religion reassumes its original benignity. In America, a Catholic Priest is a good citizen, a good character, and a good neighbour."[50] Here we can see an implicit argument that established churches spoiled and corrupted the human equality bestowed by the Creator, whom Paine called "the great father of all."[51] Paine's figuring of God as a "father" belied his claim that his religious beliefs derived from nature alone.

Paine drew on his theory of human equality to outline a plan for eliminating poverty in his final revolutionary pamphlet, *Agrarian Justice* (written in 1795–1796 but not published until 1797). Bishop Richard Watson, a foe of Paine's *The Age of Reason*, had published a sermon on God's wisdom in "having made both rich and poor." Paine disagreed and asserted his principle of original equality, that God "made only *Male* and *Female*; and he gave them the earth for their inheritance." Paine proceeded to demonstrate, using American Indians as a point of reference for the "natural state," that poverty arose out of civilization. Poverty and severe inequality, he argued, could be attributed to the cultivation of land and to the erroneous assumption that the land itself—not merely the improvements upon it—became the property of the cultivator. The land, Paine asserted, was properly "the COMMON PROPERTY OF THE HUMAN RACE," and those who monopolized the land owed rent to society. Paine proposed collecting this rent as a sort of inheritance tax, which he defended by denying the natural right of the deceased to control property. The rent would be used to create a national fund, which would provide young people who reached twenty-one years of age with a payment to compensate them for the loss of their "natural inheritance." Paine also proposed annual payments to the elderly, the blind, and the "lame." He especially recommended this plan to France, arguing that "it is a revolution in the state of civilization, that will give perfection to the revolution of France."[52] He was suggesting that basic economic equality, like political equality, derived from the divinely created order.

The Age of Reason

While *Common Sense* and *Rights of Man* revealed that Paine founded his ideal republican order upon his assumptions about divinely instituted human equality, *The Age of Reason* laid out a more fully developed civil religion of reason. Paine had apparently long planned to write a book in order to share his religious views. When he finally took up his pen to compose *The Age of Reason: Being an Investigation of True and of Fabulous Theology*, he did so because of a political emergency—an emergency, indeed, that threatened his own life and liberty. Maximilien Robespierre's Mountain faction had seized control in France, and the moderate Girondins, including Paine, found themselves imprisoned and facing execution. As Paine later explained in an open letter to Samuel Adams, "My friends were falling as fast as the guillotine could cut their heads off," and "the people of France were running headlong into Atheism."[53] The problem, Paine explained at the opening of the second part of *The Age of Reason*, was that "the intolerant spirit of church persecution had transferred itself into politics."[54] (It is revealing of Paine's anticlericalism and anti-Catholicism that he managed to blame the Catholic Church for problems that arose after its official dismantling!) He wrote the first part of *The Age of Reason* in a matter of days, and as he was being escorted to prison, he entrusted the manuscript to American author Joel Barlow. Although *The Age of Reason* has often been remembered primarily as a scurrilous attack on Christianity and revealed religion, Paine also wrote to promote a deistic morality for a revolutionary society that he believed had lost sight of the divinely established moral order. He addressed the work to his fellow American citizens, but he probably wrote with France more than America in mind, and the manuscript was translated into French for publication.

True to its title, *The Age of Reason* repeatedly invoked the power of God-given reason. In his opening note, Paine declared: "The most formidable weapon against errors of every kind is Reason. I have never used any other, and I trust I never shall."[55] Paine thus presented himself as a voice box of universal reason. He supported the right of people to disagree, but he projected great confidence that his fundamental principles and beliefs were universally true. He seemed to believe that if he could speak his thoughts clearly and simply enough, all honest readers would be compelled to believe. God was a reasonable being who had imbued the universe with reasonable principles, and humanity's highest calling was to obey reason, "the choicest gift of God to man."[56]

Paine professed to be writing to save France from atheism and moral degradation, but he devoted most of the work to condemning Christianity. "The Christian theory," he wrote, "is little else than the idolatry of the ancient mythologists, accommodated to the purposes of power and revenue."[57] Paine expressed equally harsh views of the Bible: "When I see throughout the greatest part of this book, scarcely any thing but a history of the grossest vices, and a collection of the most paltry and contemptible tales, I cannot dishonour my Creator by calling it by his name."[58] Paine pointed out that "the bible is filled with murder," and he condemned Moses as a "detestable villain" for giving "an order to butcher the boys, to massacre the mothers, and debauch the daughters" of the enemy.[59] Paine found plenty of objectionable material in the New Testament as well. He recalled being "revolted" as a child by the notion that God had sacrificed his son in order to redeem humanity. As for Jesus, Paine believed that "he was a virtuous and an amiable man" who preached a "benevolent" morality that "has not been exceeded by any." Not surprisingly, however, Paine rejected and condemned the supernatural aura surrounding Jesus, whom he considered to be merely human.[60]

Paine repeatedly implied that the promoters of Christianity had participated in conscious deception and had attacked the "true theology" of natural philosophy. Sciences such as astronomy and mathematics were theological, Paine argued, because their practitioners studied "the works of God."[61] Mincing no words, Paine declared that Christian theology had "abandoned the original and beautiful system of theology, like a beautiful innocent to distress and reproach, to make room for the hag of superstition." Paine accused the Roman Catholic Church of persecuting scientists across the ages in order to protect its lies against true knowledge. He attacked the church's established habit of using "Mystery, Miracle, and Prophecy" to impose ignorance and obscure truth.[62]

Paine fortified his attack on the Christian church and the Bible with a more general assault on written revelation. He insisted that religious claims should be judged by scientific standards of reason and evidence—standards that he deemed the Bible incapable of meeting. Rejecting all religious beliefs that were based on scriptural revelation, he contended that the only divine revelation came from nature. A revelation, he claimed, was "revelation to the first person only, and *hearsay* to every other," and Paine emphatically refused to accept fabulous hearsay as truth.[63] He likewise rejected the miracles reported in the Bible out of hand: "We have never seen, in our time, nature to go out of her course, but we have good reason to believe that millions of lies have been told in the same time; it is therefore at least millions to one, that the reporter of a miracle tells a lie."[64] Given his Newtonian faith in the orderly and stable nature of the universe, Paine simply could not accept the miraculous interruptions described in the Bible.

Neither a materialist nor an atheist, Paine attacked Christianity in order to promote what he called "pure and simple deism."[65] "The true deist," he explained, "has but one Deity; and his religion consists in contemplating the power, wisdom, and benignity of the Deity in his works, and in endeavouring to imitate him in every thing moral, scientifical, and mechanical."[66] He quite firmly believed in a divine creator: "Do we not see a fair creation prepared to receive us the instant we were born—a world furnished to our hands that cost us nothing? Is it we that light up the sun; that pour down the rain; that fill the earth with abundance? Whether we sleep or wake, the vast machinery of the universe still goes on."[67] Although Paine doubted that God had ever communicated directly with humanity, he argued that God revealed his nature and will through creation itself: "THE WORD OF GOD IS THE CREATION WE BEHOLD: And it is in this word, which no human invention can counterfeit or alter, that God speaketh universally to man."[68] (Note the deployment of King James English to increase the rhetorical heft of the statement.) Human language, the language of scriptural revelation, was much too frail and fallible a vessel for God's message to humankind.

Although the message conveyed by creation was spare compared to the Judeo-Christian scriptures, Paine argued that it provided clear moral instruction. Creation revealed much about its maker. He asked: "Do we want to contemplate his power? We see it in the immensity of the creation. Do we want to contemplate his wisdom? We see it in the unchangeable order by which the incomprehensible Whole is governed. Do we want to contemplate his munificence? We see it in the abundance with which he fills the earth. Do we want to contemplate his mercy? We see it in his not withholding that abundance even from the unthankful."[69] Paine suggested that the moral implications of this "book of Creation" were clear: "The Almighty lecturer, by displaying the principles of science in the structure of the universe, has invited man to study and to imitation. It is as if he had said to the inhabitants of this globe that we call ours, 'I have made an earth for man to dwell upon, and I have rendered the starry heavens visible, to teach him science and the arts. He can now provide for his own comfort, AND LEARN FROM MY MUNIFICENCE TO ALL, TO BE KIND TO EACH OTHER.'"[70] Creation, according to Paine, enjoined humanity to follow the golden rule.

Writing as the French Revolution took its turn toward Terror, Paine urged those who loved liberty and equality to accept a simple, rationalistic creed. His prescriptions constituted a civil (or public) religion, because he believed that this creed could provide the moral foundation for a republican civil order. In Paine's eyes, the state could not compel any belief—nor did it have the authority to decide what religious beliefs to tolerate. No external forces should interfere with the rights of conscience. But the republican order that he imagined nevertheless depended upon a consensus about the natural rights granted to humanity by the Creator. Whether naively or not, Paine believed that universal reason could create this consensus, once the ancient tyrannies of church and state had been overthrown.

Given that he not only rejected the basic theological beliefs of Christianity but also insulted them, Paine certainly should have foreseen that his book would cause a negative reaction. But even he must have been surprised by the uproar. The Age of Reason went through an impressive twenty-one American reprints within a decade.[71] But the denunciations came quickly as well. Within fifteen years, the book had been met with almost seventy responses in America and England.[72] In 1796, Harvard University distributed copies of the most comprehensive rebuttal, Bishop Richard Watson's An Apology for the Bible (1796), in hope of steering its students away from infidelity.[73] Several years later, in 1802, after Paine became disillusioned with Napoleon and left France for America, he found that his reputation there had been tarnished. To be sure, some of his old friends welcomed him heartily, as did substantial numbers of Democratic-Republicans. He maintained friendships with Thomas Jefferson (who had helped him return to America), James Monroe (who had helped secure his release from prison in France), and James Madison.

Many of his associates from the Revolutionary period, however, turned their backs on Paine. His old friend Benjamin Rush refused to talk to him. John Adams, who had long disliked and distrusted Paine, no doubt stood firm in his judgment of 1796 that "the Christian religion is, above all the religions that ever prevailed or existed in ancient or modern times, the religion of wisdom, virtue, equity and humanity, let the Blackguard Paine say what he will."[74] Fearful of the influence of Paine and other infidels, Patrick Henry wrote a treatise defending Christianity, but he was substantially dissatisfied with his effort and asked his wife to destroy the manuscript. John Jay read The Age of Reason, too, but he expressed confidence that Christian truth could withstand such attacks.

Elias Boudinot, who had repeatedly served in the Continental Congress (and who had been president of the Congress in 1783 when Paine unsuccessfully requested a pension), wrote a work of over three hundred pages entitled *The Age of Revelation, Or the Age of Reason Shewn to Be the Age of Infidelity* (Philadelphia, 1801). Samuel Adams wrote Paine a letter in which he expressed a profound disappointment in Paine's promulgation of infidelity. "Do you think," Adams wrote, "that *your* pen, or the pen of any other man can unchristianize the mass of our citizens, or have you hopes of converting a few of them to assist you in so bad a cause?"[75]

Unfortunately for Paine, when he returned to America in 1802, he stepped into the middle of a heated political battle between Jefferson's Republicans and the fiercely anti-French and anti-infidel Federalist Party. The Federalist press savaged Paine as a way to strike at President Jefferson.[76] A Boston Federalist paper, for example, responded to Paine's homecoming as follows: "What! Invite to the United States that lying, drunken, brutal infidel, who rejoiced in the opportunity of basking and wallowing in the confusion, devastation, bloodshed, rapine, and murder, in which his soul delights?"[77] Paine continued to write after his return to America, but he never regained his prior prominence, and he suffered the indignity of having his American citizenship denied when he tried to vote. Just before he died in 1809, according to a report by his attending physician, he declined to be visited by Christian ministers, and he refused to accept Christ as his savior.[78] On his deathbed, he remained firm in his deism.

Paine's Legacy

Although Paine did not use the phrase "civil religion" to describe the deistic creed that he outlined, he clearly envisaged that deism could provide a moral and religious foundation for the revolutionized political order that he had helped usher into being. He argued that deism, in contrast to Christianity and other revealed religions, had little susceptibility to corruption. He explained in *The Age of Reason*: "Deism does not answer the purpose of despotic governments. . . . Neither does it answer the avarice of priests."[79] Deism was not, however, impervious to criticism. As responses to *The Age of Reason* pointed out, Paine's natural religion did not account for the reality of moral evil. (It was insufficient to scapegoat the institutions of monarchy and established churches—to do so begged the question about the origins of the institutionalized evil.) Just as glaringly, given Paine's express vision of an orderly and harmonious universe governed by God, was the fact that he utterly ignored the problem of natural evil. Why would a benevolent and omnipotent deity spawn a world so full of suffering? Paine declined to address the question.[80]

Especially in America, however, Paine became an icon of infidelity, both condemned by the faithful and admired and emulated by freethinkers. Throughout the early republican period, religious and political democrats appropriated Paine's ideas and rhetoric to challenge the status quo. Deism itself achieved little popularity, but some defenders of Christianity felt compelled, because of Paine and likeminded critics, to rationalize their beliefs and to seek out new sources of evidence, most notably in the intuition or "heart."[81] Although Paine did not leave behind a religious movement, he inspired generations of freethinkers and religious populists who asserted the primacy of the individual reason and conscience.

The American civil religion that evolved over the century and a half after Paine's death embodied many of the qualities of the civil religion that Paine promoted. From *Common Sense* forward, Paine advocated religious liberty, a value that the founding generation embedded in the Bill of Rights. Paine, alongside such luminaries as George Washington and Benjamin Franklin, argued that religious belief could provide a moral bedrock for a free society. Finally, Paine consistently defended liberty and equality as universal God-given rights. Paine did not invent these values, of course, but he played an important role in the Revolutionary discourse that engendered the Declaration of Independence, which articulated these values in its preamble and later achieved a status of "American Scripture," as Pauline Maier has called it.[82] Paine's negative assessment of Christianity continues to fall outside of the American mainstream, but his positive creed regarding human equality and freedom comports with widely shared assumptions. Despite the vehemence with which many Americans reacted against *The Age of Reason*, American political culture assimilated many of the values that Paine strove to promote.

Notes

The author would like to thank Daniel Dreisbach, Ruth Homrighaus, Brian Steele, and Harvey Kaye for their suggestions on this essay.

1. Harvey J. Kaye, *Thomas Paine and the Promise of America* (New York: Hill and Wang, 2005), 4–5.

2. Both quotations are from an open letter by Paine to John Inskeep, published in the Philadelphia *Commercial Advertiser*, Feb. 10, 1806. Quoted in Moncure Conway, *The Life of Thomas Paine*, 2 vols. (New York: G. P. Putnam's Sons, 1893), 2:374. This letter also appeared in the *Aurora General Advertiser* (Philadelphia) on the same date.

3. This hymn comes from Stith Meade, *A General Selection of the Newest and Most Admired Hymns and Spiritual Songs Now in Use* (Richmond, Va., 1807), 152. See Carlos R. Allen Jr., "Giving the Devil His Due," *William and Mary Quarterly*, 3rd ser., 31 (Jul. 1974): 491–92.

4. Theodore Roosevelt, *Gouverneur Morris* (Boston: Houghton Mifflin, 1888), 289.

5. Thomas Jefferson, *Writings* (New York: Library of America, 1984), 285.

6. Benjamin Franklin, *The Autobiography* (New York: Library of America, 1990), 92. On Franklin's religious views, see Elizabeth E. Dunn, "From a Bold Youth to a Reflective Sage: A Reevaluation of Benjamin Franklin's Religion," *Pennsylvania Magazine of History & Biography* 111 (Oct. 1987): 501–24; Howard L. Lubert, "Benjamin Franklin and the Role of Religion in Governing Democracy," in *The Founders on God and Government*, ed. Daniel L. Dreisbach, Mark D. Hall, and Jeffry H. Morrison (Lanham, Md.: Rowman and Littlefield, 2004), 147–80; and Kerry S. Walters, *Benjamin Franklin and His Gods* (Urbana: University of Illinois Press, 1999), especially 125 ff.

7. Thomas Paine, *The Age of Reason* 1, in *Collected Writings*, ed. Eric Foner (New York: Library of America, 1995), 666.

8. As they both doubted that God made special interventions, they also questioned the efficacy of prayer. Paine, in fact, attacked prayer in an 1803 letter to Samuel Adams (*Collected Writings*, 420). For Franklin's views on prayer, see Lubert, "Benjamin Franklin," 157–58. Walters emphasizes Franklin's ambivalence and suggests that Franklin may have retained some belief in "special providences." See Kerry S. Walters, ed., *The American Deists: Voices of Reason and Dissent in the Early Republic* (Lawrence: University Press of Kansas, 1992), 27, 37, 51.

9. Paine, *Age of Reason* 1, in *Collected Writings*, 666.

10. Franklin, *Autobiography*, 35.

11. Evelyn J. Hinz makes a compelling argument that "Paine's style is better labeled demagogic than democratic" because "his tactic is to invoke reason

rather than to persuade through reason." See "The 'Reasonable' Style of Tom Paine," *Queen's Quarterly* 79 (1972): 240.

12. For the text of Franklin's warning, as well as a discussion of the "non-political" nature of Franklin's deism, see Walters, *American Deists*, 28. On Franklin's belief in the public utility of religion, see Dunn, "From a Bold Youth," 515, as well as numerous statements that Franklin made in his *Autobiography*. The comparison of Franklin and Paine comes from Craig Nelson, *Thomas Paine: Enlightenment, Revolution, and the Birth of Modern Nations* (New York: Viking, 2006), 50. On Franklin's reputation, see Richard D. Miles, "The American Image of Benjamin Franklin," *American Quarterly* 9 (Summer 1957): 117–43.

13. John Keane, *Tom Paine: A Political Life* (New York: Grove Press, 1995), 320, 336.

14. Kaye, *Paine*, 6.

15. Jack Fruchtman Jr., *Thomas Paine: Apostle of Freedom* (New York: Four Walls Eight Windows, 1994), 2.

16. Nelson, *Paine*, 24, 50.

17. On civil religion, see Robert N. Bellah's seminal essay "Civil Religion in America," *Daedalus* 96 (1967): 1–21. Bellah defined American civil religion as a set of publicly shared beliefs and rituals regarding the origins and fundamental principles of the United States. The touchstone document of the American civil religion was the Declaration of Independence, which articulated a set of God-given "inalienable rights" and explained that governments derive their legitimacy from the consent of the governed. The Declaration also expressed a collective reliance on "the protection of divine Providence" (6). Although Paine did not use the phrase "civil religion," the French equivalent of which was coined by Rousseau, his creed was nearly identical to the civil religious creed sketched out by Rousseau in the *Social Contract*. Furthermore, in 1797 Paine briefly participated in the Parisian Society of Theophilanthropy, which was essentially an attempt to found a civil religion. On Rousseau and civil religion, see Fred H. Willhoite Jr., "Rousseau's Political Religion," *The Review of Politics* 27 (Oct. 1965): 501–15. For the lecture that Paine delivered to the Theophilanthropy society in 1797, see Walters, *American Deists*, 232–38.

18. Keane provides the most thorough and accurate account of Paine's early life (see *Paine*, 29–38). See also the entry on Paine by Mark Philip in the *Oxford Dictionary of National Biography*, ed. H. C. G. Matthew and Brian Harrison (Oxford: Oxford University Press, 2004); online ed., ed. Lawrence Goldman, May 2007, http://www.oxforddnb.com/view/article/21133.

19. See Keane, *Paine*, 56–57.

20. Eric Foner's *Tom Paine and Revolutionary America*, updated ed. (New York: Oxford University Press, 2005) made important contributions to the study of Paine's developing political philosophy, and Craig Nelson has also helped to situate Paine within the Enlightenment.

21. Paine did not add the "e" to the end of his name until after his arrival in America.

22. Keane, *Paine*, 3, 8–9.

23. Paine, *The Case of the Officers of Excise*, in *Life and Writings of Thomas Paine*, ed. Daniel Edwin Wheeler, 10 vols. (New York: Vincent Parke, 1908), 10:199. Later, in *Rights of Man*, Paine likewise condemned the "sanguinary punishments" of England and other governments. Paine, *Rights of Man* 1, in *Collected Writings*, 454.

24. Keane, *Paine*, 14; Nelson, *Paine*, 16.

25. Keane, *Paine*, 18–19.

26. Paine, *Rights of Man* 1, in *Collected Writings*, 482.

27. Because of a lapse in record keeping during the months after Paine's birth, his parish records do not show that he was baptized, but his later confirmation, at about the age of twelve, his two marriages in the church, and his two positions as an excise officer all required that he be baptized. Keane, *Paine*, 17.

28. Paine, *Age of Reason* 1, in *Collected Writings*, 703.

29. Paine, *Common Sense*, in *Collected Writings*, 56.

30. Ibid., 12.

31. Keane, *Paine*, 18–23.

32. David Hempton, *Methodism: Empire of the Spirit* (New Haven, Conn.: Yale University Press, 2005), 57–58 and passim.

33. On Paine's association with the Methodists, see Keane, *Paine*, 46–49, and 544n29. Although Keane seems correct in concluding that Paine did informally preach to Methodists in Dover and Sandwich, any conclusions about the impact of this experience on Paine are speculative.

34. Paine, *Age of Reason* 2, in *Collected Writings*, 767.

35. Paine, *Age of Reason* 1, in *Collected Writings*, 666.

36. John Adams recollected his discussion with Paine well after the fact, in a section of his autobiography penned between 1802 and 1807. Adams, who referred to Paine as "a Star of Disaster," had made critical comments to Paine on the section of *Common Sense* that drew on the Old Testament. Adams recalled, "At this he laughed, and said he had taken his Ideas in that part from Milton: and then expressed a Contempt of the Old Testament and indeed of the Bible at large, which surprised me. He saw that I did not relish this, and soon check'd himself, with these Words 'However I have some thoughts of publishing my Thoughts on Religion, but I believe it will be best to postpone it, to the latter part of Life.'" John Adams autobiography, part 1, "John Adams," through 1776, sheet 23 of 53 (electronic edition), *Adams Family Papers: An Electronic Archive*, Massachusetts Historical Society, http://www.masshist.org/digitaladams/.

37. Paine mentioned attending the lectures of Martin and Ferguson in the *Age of Reason* (701), where he also mentioned his acquaintance with astronomer John Bevis.

38. Harry Hayden Clark, "An Historical Interpretation of Thomas Paine's Religion," *University of California Chronicle* 35 (Jan. 1933): 79–81.

39. Kaye, *Paine*.

40. Paine, "The American Crisis," number 1, in *Collected Writings*, 92, 95. Paine mentioned God by name eight times in this brief essay. Stephen Newman has shown that *Common Sense* included a providential framework that echoed Christian millennialism by suggesting that it had been given to Americans to transcend history and start anew. See "A Note on *Common Sense* and Christian Eschatology," *Political Theory* 6 (Feb. 1978): 101–8.

41. Paine, *Common Sense*, 5.

42. Ibid., 8–9.

43. Ibid., 12.

44. On the circulation of *Rights of Man*, see Keane, *Paine*, 331 and 333. On Paine's conviction, see Fruchtman, *Paine*, 288–91.

45. Paine, *Rights of Man* 2, in *Collected Writings*, 553, 551.

46. Paine, *Rights of Man* 1, in *Collected Writings*, 438–39, 437.

47. Paine, *Rights of Man* 2, in *Collected Writings*, 583, and *Rights of Man* 1, in *Collected Writings*, 462–63.

48. Paine, *Rights of Man* 1, in *Collected Writings*, 464.

49. Paine, *Age of Reason* 2, in *Collected Writings*, 823.

50. Paine, *Rights of Man*, 1, in *Collected Writings*, 509n; 2, in *Collected Writings*, 655; 1, in *Collected Writings*, 483–84.

51. Paine, *Rights of Man* 2, in *Collected Writings*, 655.

52. Paine, *Agrarian Justice*, in *Collected Writings*, 396–400, 410.

53. Paine, "To Samuel Adams," January 1, 1803, in *Collected Writings*, 418.

54. Paine, *Age of Reason* 2, in *Collected Writings*, 731.

55. Paine, *Age of Reason* 1, in *Collected Writings*, 665.

56. Ibid., 685.

57. Ibid., 669.

58. Ibid., 680. Paine's attack on the Bible rested upon two arguments, which have been pointed out by Jay E. Smith. The Bible cannot be "the word of God" because it is riddled with contradictions and errors, and, perhaps worse, it depicts God as immoral and unjust. See "Thomas Paine and *The Age of Reason*'s Attack on the Bible," *Historian* 38 (Summer 1996): 753, 756.

59. Paine, *Age of Reason* 2, in *Collected Writings*, 743, 746.

60. Paine, *Age of Reason* 1, in *Collected Writings*, 669–70. It is important to note that for most Christians the rejection of Christ's divinity and saving power was a heresy equivalent to atheism.

61. Paine indicated that his study of science fostered his deism, and he often used Newtonian language to describe creation (*Age of Reason* 1, 703). Additionally, impressed by the unfathomable size of the universe, Paine posited

the "plurality of worlds" (*Age of Reason* 1, 704–10). Paine may have adapted this line of thinking from Voltaire.

62. Paine, *Age of Reason* 1, in *Collected Writings*, 691, 711.

63. Ibid., 668.

64. Ibid., 715.

65. Paine, *Age of Reason* 2, in *Collected Writings*, 825.

66. Paine, *Age of Reason* 1, in *Collected Writings*, 703. Jack Fruchtman, disagreeing with Paine's self-profession of "pure and simple deism," has argued that Paine held incompatible deistic and pantheistic beliefs. Fruchtman suggested that Paine's God was "more than [the] watchmaker" posited by most Newtonian deists. Fruchtman, however, speculated that Paine perhaps borrowed from Benedictus Spinoza (1632–77) a conception of "an immanent divine presence in history." See Jack Fruchtman Jr., *Thomas Paine and the Religion of Nature* (Baltimore: Johns Hopkins University Press, 1993), 3, 53, 58. Although I think that Fruchtman is right that Paine's deism was not purely Newtonian, I am not convinced that Fruchtman's evidence fully warrants his conclusion that Paine had pantheist tendencies. Paine's God ordered the universe and infused humanity with reason, but this does not mean that the creator became immanent, literally, in creation. Paine did often use the language of Providence, which suggested that God imposed his will upon earthly events, but it is unlikely that Paine imagined God directly interfering. Rationalistic Christians and some deists of this time believed that God had essentially designed providential features into creation. In other words, one did not need to accept miraculous interventions to believe in providence.

67. Paine, *Age of Reason* 1, in *Collected Writings*, 674.

68. Ibid., 686.

69. Ibid., 687. Paine repeated this paragraph in his Jan. 1797 address before the first meeting of the Parisian Society of Theophilanthropy on "The Existence of God." See Walters, *American Deists*, 212, 233.

70. Paine, *Age of Reason* 1, in *Collected Writings*, 688, 694. Although Paine clearly believed that his deism implied an ethical system, it is worth noting just how simplistic his views were compared to the moral philosophers of the Scottish Common Sense school, who discussed the role of the conscience or the moral sense and the intuition. Paine seemed to have a more Lockean view of a blank mental slate that could be easily guided to pursue morality. In his speech "On the Existence of God," for instance, he said, "The study of theology in the works of creation produces a direct contrary effect [to the fanaticism and violence inspired by revealed religion]. The mind becomes at once enlightened and serene, a copy of the scene it beholds: information and adoration go hand in hand; and all the social faculties become enlarged." Paine, quoted in Walters, *American Deists*, 233.

71. Peter D. Jauhiainen, "'Reasoning Out of the Scriptures': Samuel Hopkins, the Theological Enterprise, and the Deist Threat," *Journal of Presbyterian History* 79 (Summer 2001): 119–33.

72. Smith, "Thomas Paine," 758. Franklyn K. Prochaska ably analyzed several of the British responses in "Thomas Paine's *Age of Reason* Revisited," *Journal of the History of Ideas* 33, no. 4 (1972): 561–76.

73. Smith, "Thomas Paine," 759. For a discussion of Watson's rebuttal, see Prochaska, "*Age of Reason* Revisited."

74. John Adams, diary entry for Jul. 26, 1796, in John Adams Diary 46, Aug. 6, 1787–Sep. 10, 1796, Jul. 2–Aug. 21, 1804 (electronic edition), *Adams Family Papers: An Electronic Archive.*

75. Samuel Adams, letter to Paine, Nov. 30, 1802, in Paine, *Collected Writings*, 415.

76. Keane, *Paine*, 455–62.

77. *The Mercury and New-England Palladium*, quoted in ibid., 457.

78. Keane, *Paine*, 536.

79. Paine, *Age of Reason 2*, in *Collected Writings*, 825–26.

80. Bishop Richard Watson's *Apology for the Bible*, a 1796 response to *The Age of Reason*, pointed out Paine's failure to address the problem of evil. See also Prochaska, "*Age of Reason* Revisited," 567–68; Hinz, "The 'Reasonable' Style," 237; and James H. Smylie, "Clerical Perspectives on Deism: Paine's *The Age of Reason* in Virginia," *Eighteenth-Century Studies* 6 (Winter 1972–1973): 215–16.

81. On the decline and legacy of deism, in general, see Walters, *American Deists*, 39–46.

82. Pauline Maier, *American Scripture: Making the Declaration of Independence* (New York: Knopf, 1997).

CHAPTER 9

Anglican Moderation

Religion and the Political Thought of Edmund Randolph

KEVIN R. HARDWICK

Edmund Randolph (1753–1813), a central actor in Virginia's revolutionary and constitutional politics from the 1770s to the 1790s, was in many ways a conventional figure. A staunch republican, he celebrated those exemplary Virginians who, he believed, had led Virginia through two foundational, constitutional moments: the first between 1607 and 1624, and the second between 1776 and 1787. For most of his life a devout Episcopalian, Randolph believed there was a direct connection between public virtue and private piety. His appreciation of human character and motivation—indeed, of human psychology—stemmed in logical and unremarkable ways from the theological commitments of the mid-eighteenth-century Church of England. Randolph's theological liberalism, like that of many late-eighteenth-century Virginians, derived organically from the thought of the mid-seventeenth-century Cambridge Platonists, whose positions became Church of England orthodoxy by the late seventeenth century and provided one important source of ethical thought to the eighteenth-century church. Unlike the Reformed tradition of New England, which from the metropolitan vantage of the eighteenth-century British empire was disturbingly heterodox (and which faced the usual pressures of colonial societies to conform to the most traditional forms and values of the metropolitan center), the colonial Church of England consistently viewed itself as an extension of metropolitan values. Even as Randolph decried the injustices of the imperial constitution in the mid-1770s, he, like numerous other Virginians, remained deeply influenced by the understanding of human good inherent in the dominant religion of the empire.[1]

The colonial Church of England of Randolph's youth in many ways represented the fruition of its Elizabethan aspirations. As the church historian David L. Holmes has recently noted, Anglican theologians from the late sixteenth century forward "attempted to make the Church of England a middle way—a *via media*—between Roman Catholicism and Calvinism." Anglicans criticized Catholicism for adding "too much manmade doctrine to Christianity." But equally, they believed that Calvinism "subtracted too much that was important." The result was a conservative and liturgical form of Christian practice that, by the early eighteenth century, easily accommodated the rationalist tendencies of the British Enlightenment. As Holmes correctly emphasizes, the Virginia founders, Randolph among them, remained active members of their parishes, even as some of them followed rationalist critiques of certain church doctrines to become Deists, Socinians, or Unitarians. Most prominent Virginians of Randolph's generation remained formally aligned with the established church of their childhoods. "They married under its auspices," Holmes notes, "consigned their children to its care, and were buried by its clergy." Their religious and ethical sensibilities, then, developed within the embrace of one of England's more conservative institutions, even as their faith encompassed some of the more enlightened elements of metropolitan thought.[2]

Anglican theology diverged most profoundly from that of Calvinism on its assessment of human faculties. Edmund Randolph, like most eighteenth-century thinkers influenced by the Church of England, leaned toward a loosely Pelagian or, perhaps, Arminian understanding of the will. Humanity retained the ability, however imperfect, to make sound moral decisions under the guidance of "right" reason. He was at least implicitly perfectionist in that he believed this crucial human faculty could be improved by self-discipline, sound pedagogy, and emulation of superior role models. Indeed, as we will see, emulation played a critical role in Randolph's appreciation of how a human society achieved refinement and civility. Because the Anglican tradition rejected the stark Calvinist doctrine of total depravity in favor of a more liberal understanding of human will, it could accommodate the rationalism of British natural science far more easily than could its more fully Reformed competitors.[3]

By the early eighteenth century, influential Church of England churchmen and philosophers like John Tillotson and John Locke had articulated a particularly Anglican moral vision that to one degree or another characterized Church of England teaching for the rest of the century. For Locke, the "reasonableness of Christianity" was evident. "Reason is natural revelation," he wrote, "whereby the eternal Father of light, and Fountain of all knowledge, communicates to mankind that portion of the truth which he has laid in reach of their natural faculties." Men could exercise right reason, even in their natural and unregenerate state, to know God's law and act accordingly. John Tillotson, whose sermons remained widely popular throughout the British empire until the end of the century, described Christ's character as that of an ideal gentleman. "The Virtues of his Life are pure, without any Mixture of Infirmity and Imperfection testimonial of good character." The same Anglican moral impulse that informed the early-eighteenth-century Societies for the Reformation of Manners spilled over into the efforts of the Society for the Propagation of Christian Knowledge and the Society for the Propagation of the Gospel in Foreign Parts, which so powerfully shaped the development of the colonial church. Moral and ethical education, perceived as an essential part of the Christian civilizing mission, constituted a fundamental concern of the late colonial Church of England.[4]

The liberal theology of the Church of England, and its attendant moralism, powerfully influenced the public life of eighteenth-century Virginia. Randolph committed himself, in common with many Virginians of his generation, to an ethos of public guardianship by disinterested, leisured gentlemen. The ideal statesman, in this view, was a man who had taken advantage of the opportunities providentially available to him, by his fortunate birth and estate. In his education and breeding he had developed the moral habits to bolster the imperatives of human reason, and thus could moderate his passions and appetites to discern, and then act to achieve, the public good. This is the ethos described by historian Jack P. Greene as "stewardship" and by which, as Greene correctly has emphasized, Virginia's revolutionary leadership was distinguished. Randolph's conventional Episcopalianism, then, makes him a useful figure for historical study, given the importance of the Church of England in Virginia, and given the centrality of Virginia gentlemen to the American founding. This is especially so in light of the continued influence exercised on the thought of political theorists and historians by the penumbra of Perry Miller, and Miller's insistence that it is in Reformed Calvinism that we find the origins of American identity.[5]

Unlike Reformed Calvinist political thought, the Latitudinarian theology to which men like Randolph were heir emphasized a philosophical intellectualism, which accorded to human reason, even in its corrupt natural state, the capacity to motivate the will. "Right reason" presented itself, however dimly, to the perceptions and will of the individual disposed to inculcate it. Young men, especially if they surrounded themselves with good role models, could reasonably aspire to perfect their wills and control and moderate their base, "brutish" desires and appetites. As historian Brooks Holifield makes clear in his recent synthesis of American theology, this was a theological position with a strong future in nineteenth-century America.[6]

In Virginia, this kind of liberal moral thought was tightly integrated into the preaching of the clergy. Thus, for example, William Stith preached an important sermon before the Virginia House of Burgesses in 1753, in which he explicitly denied the fundamental Calvinist doctrines of total depravity, unconditional election, and limited atonement. Christ's sacrifice granted to all men the capacity for salvation, Stith argued. "Faith [is] required on our Part," he preached, "as an indispensable Condition for entering into the Kingdom of Heaven." However, Stith went on to emphasize, this was no easy task. "It requires a steady Course of holy living—Piety and Obedience to GOD, Justice and Charity to Mankind, and a regular Discharge of our Duty to ourselves and families; which, in the present corrupt State of human Nature, cannot be deemed such a trifling and easy Matter." Church of England ministers like Stith emphasized the capacity of men, despite the corruption of original sin, to habituate themselves to virtue. In rejecting the central tenets of Calvinism, mid-eighteenth-century Anglican ministers instead accentuated the human capacity for moral self-improvement, understood and properly guided by right reason. Stith, and ministers like him, preached within the mainstream of the eighteenth-century Church of England. They shared the conviction, as Paul Elmen has put it, "that divine truth was accessible to man not only by revelation, but . . . by the very nature of law," which in turn "could be grasped by natural reason."[7]

A Brief Biography

Edmund Randolph was born into a Virginia family distinguished by its public prominence. His father, John Randolph of Tazewell, served as Virginia's king's attorney, a position held also by his grandfather, Sir John Randolph, and his uncle, Peyton Randolph. Edmund Randolph's maternal grandfather, Edmund Jennings, served as king's attorney for the neighboring colony of Maryland. Edmund Randolph, then, matured in a family long noted for its dedication to public service and to the law. His family took seriously its commitment to the responsibilities that accompanied leisured wealth and education in the colony. Randolph attended the College of William and Mary, like his father before him. Upon graduation he read law in his father's office. Like so many other young men from Virginia's elite families, Edmund Randolph absorbed from a young age the ethic of public service characteristic of Virginia's political class from the middle of the eighteenth century.[8]

Randolph's rise to public prominence, even by the standard of his social station, was rapid. Randolph began his legal practice in 1774, at age twenty-one. Within just a few years, as the Revolutionary crisis intensified, he assumed his expected public duties. In 1775, even as his parents chose to remain loyal to England and left Virginia for the mother country, Randolph joined the Continental Army as an aide to General Washington. A few years later, Randolph served as one of Williamsburg's delegates to the Virginia Convention, where, despite his youth, he helped produce the Virginia Declaration of Rights and the Virginia Constitution.

In 1776 he was selected to be Virginia's first attorney general. In later years he served Virginia as a representative in the Continental Congress, as mayor of Williamsburg, as governor of the State of Virginia, and as a representative to the Annapolis Convention of 1786. By 1787, when at age thirty-four he was appointed to represent his state at the Philadelphia Convention, Randolph was a well-seasoned politician and statesman. Born into one of Virginia's most prominent families, he had successfully fulfilled the high public expectations for which birth, family, education, and inclination had prepared him.

Randolph was a competent statesman, but never a brilliant one. Widely respected for his legal acumen, Randolph ably represented Virginia, and later the United States, as attorney general. As Virginia's attorney, most of his cases pertained to matters of finance or land tenure. Randolph had relatively little to do during his first year as U.S. attorney general, but as the partisan confrontation between Thomas Jefferson and Alexander Hamilton developed in late 1791, President Washington increasingly relied upon Randolph for political advice. True to his moderate sensibilities, Randolph sought the middle ground, as the gulf between Jefferson and Hamilton widened. As his most recent biographer argues, in the early 1790s Randolph "had come to be identified with a kind of pragmatic diplomacy . . . that tested all policy against national interest." When Jefferson resigned as secretary of state on December 31, 1793, Randolph seemed the logical choice to replace him. Randolph's tenure in that office was undistinguished, and he resigned, tainted by scandal, in August 1795.[9]

Randolph had served two consecutive terms as governor of Virginia, from November 30, 1786, to November 12, 1788. As defined by the Virginia constitution of 1776, the office was purposefully weak. Randolph was an energetic executive, given the constraints under which the governor operated, but his role rapidly was overshadowed by the Philadelphia Convention of 1787, and by the subsequent ratification debate. As the chief executive of the wealthiest and most populous state, Randolph was a logical choice to join the Virginia delegation to the Philadelphia Convention. There he introduced the "Virginia Plan" on the convention's second day, and afterwards proved a stalwart proponent of strong national government. Although Randolph ultimately refused to sign the proposed federal constitution, it was not because he feared creation of a forceful national government, but, quite the contrary, because he believed the draft constitution contained too many concessions to the interests of the smaller states. During the Virginia ratifying convention, Randolph's was a powerful voice for ratification, although he continued to view the document as flawed and favored calling a second convention to address what he took to be its flaws.[10]

Randolph's religious convictions changed over the course of his life. His family had an established tradition of religious heterodoxy. Randolph's grandfather, Sir John Randolph, was publicly accused of Socinianism, and likely was Unitarian in his belief. Randolph's father, John Randolph of Tazewell, was infamous in Virginia for his skepticism. Lord Dunmore, Virginia's royal governor, twice nominated John Randolph as a Visitor of the College of William and Mary. Each time, however, more pious and observant Virginia gentlemen successfully opposed his nomination on the grounds that Randolph was not a Christian. As a young man, Edmund Randolph was a deist, as was his uncle Peyton Randolph. He enjoyed the company of freethinkers and religious skeptics, and read widely in the faintly scandalous ruminations of the enlightened British avant-garde.[11]

In 1776, however, Randolph married Elizabeth Nicholas, daughter of Robert Carter Nicholas, and his religion became more orthodox in subsequent years. Robert Carter Nicholas had earned a wide reputation for his probity and public piety, and represented in many ways Randolph's model for the ideal public statesman. By the 1780s Randolph joined and supported the new Protestant Episcopal Church, even as Virginia's established church faced increasing pressures for disestablishment. Late in life, after the death of his wife, Randolph wrote an autobiographical narrative for his children, in which he acknowledged the influence of Elizabeth on shaping his religious beliefs. "When we were united I was a deist," he wrote, "made so by my confidence in some whom I revered, and by the labors of two of my preceptors who, though of the ministry, poisoned me with books of infidelity." During his marriage, however, Randolph recognized his error and converted. "I cannot answer for myself that I should have been brought to examine the genuineness of holy writ if I had not observed the consolatory influence which it brought upon the life of my dearest Betsey."[12]

Religion and Public Life: Randolph's History of Virginia

Randolph left behind few personal papers, and his official correspondence is not especially revealing of the influence of religion on his political thought. However, Randolph was author of a lengthy history of Virginia, in which he narrated the transition of his state through two foundational moments. He devoted almost half of his *History* to the early settlement of Virginia and focused especially on the character of Captain John Smith. The second half of his work tells the story of the Revolution in Virginia and, as in the first half, focuses much of its attention on the character of Virginia's leading statesmen. This major work—some 330 pages in its published form—represents a sustained analysis of the relationship between individual character and public life. In Randolph's analysis of these historical moments, we see most clearly the confluence of his religious beliefs and his understanding of the right ordering of public society.[13]

The Founding of Virginia: Captain John Smith

Captain John Smith figures heroically in Randolph's history of Virginia's early settlement. The moral disposition of the great man influenced subsequent public life in the colony. "With the traits of Smith's character the history of Virginia is decked in various parts," Randolph argued. Character mattered for Randolph because he believed that the men who lead a public society play an especially important role in modeling its values. Smith established the subsequent public order in Virginia and set it on what Randolph took to be a desirable and beneficial course, largely from the force of his example. Those men lower in social standing and with less opportunity to habituate their rational faculties to suppress their appetites could nonetheless learn something of both proper self-government and proper public disposition by imitating their superiors. While Smith led Virginia at an especially important time, when the precedent of his example could establish the essential character of the colony, all public leaders confronted an obligation to model moderate self-government for the people they governed.[14]

Randolph emphasized two aspects of Smith's public temperament that elevated him into a morally exemplary public figure. First, Smith put the public good ahead of his own private interest. When the government of the colony fell to Smith, for example, "as the only remaining efficient member of the Council," Randolph stressed both Smith's disinterestedness and his concern to establish a good model for his inferiors. "He pressed forward the buildings at Jamestown, and by his own example quickly erected lodgings for the accommodation of all but *himself*." Later, the people of the colony repeatedly offered him a public position of power and authority. "With that modesty which almost always mixes with intrinsic worth," Randolph explained, Smith "persisted in refusing it until he saw that it might be rendered particularly subservient to the public good." Similarly, in Randolph's interpretation, Smith from early on could foresee the "new order of power" that would eventually "supersede his entire dominion." While "a man of less patriotism and moderation than his own would sometimes shamefully purchase at any expense of principle" the power of command, Smith instead "labored sincerely and decisively" for the public good. Smith's unwillingness to employ public power for his own private benefit, and indeed his public self-denial, established him as the kind of virtuous man who could be trusted to wield public authority.[15]

Smith was, in Randolph's telling, a thoroughly republican hero. Confronted with a dire conspiracy, he responded by placing his love of country ahead of his own safety. Injured and debilitated by an accident, Smith faced a faction who "conspired to murder him in his bed." His supporters gathered around him and "entreated him only to approve, and they would bring the heads of the boldest of his enemies and lay them before him." Smith, however, virtuously demurred. He "was a genuine patriot, who to the spirit of revenge or personal fears would not sacrifice the welfare of his country." The colony was too weak; it required every able bodied man to sustain it against its Native American enemies.

Moreover, to proceed so vengefully against the conspirators would undermine the very project to which Smith was committed. "There may be perhaps a limit beyond which a patriot cannot be required to forbear," Randolph explained, "but when he causes punishment to be inflicted, let it be done under the sanction of law and in the calmness of inquiry." Even in the most dangerous circumstances, Smith retained his prudential capacity to perceive the long-range effects of his actions. Where a lesser man would have taken the opportunity to seek personal revenge, Smith acted instead to preserve the strength of the colony and its vision of establishing an ordered, English society governed by the rule of law. "The *amor patria* was in him always active, always supported by courage, always guided by prudence," Randolph wrote. "In a word, had it not been for his labors and prowess, Virginia must have been restored to the empire of Powhatan."[16]

Randolph emphasized Smith's exemplary republican character by contrasting him with various anti-heroes. Captain Christopher Newport, for example, was "a frivolous, idle, interested man, timid in difficulties and swollen with conceit," who "thwarted all [Smith's] endeavors." Smith's virtue, however, shined by contrast. "Captain Smith, though vexed with the interruptions which Newport's whims gave to the business of utility and absolute necessity, showed his superiority to the motive of envy by zealously cooperating with him in all the measures which had been adopted by the Council." In other words, Smith had the discipline to suppress his jealous passion by exercising prudential rationality. In contrasting the characters of Smith and Newport, Randolph illustrated the superiority of the self-disciplined, self-governed man. Smith's habituated capacity to exercise reason to control passion is what made him fit to rule.[17]

A second, and more revealing, antagonist in Randolph's narrative is Powhatan, the Native American ruler with whom Smith contested to establish a stable British colony in Virginia. Unlike the moderate, self-controlled Smith, Powhatan "lived in a barbaric state of magnificence and luxury, attended by a large bodyguard, uncontrolled in any gratification of appetite, worshipped by his subjects as a demigod, and generally unrelenting in cruelty, even to torture." Where Smith could set his personal desires for revenge aside in order to pursue the long-term good of his country, Powhatan's actions were dictated by his appetites and passions. Despite his lack of civilization, Randolph emphasized, Powhatan "acted with a savage grandeur and majesty." While there are hints in this depiction of the trope of the "noble savage," Randolph's representation of Powhatan is also an object lesson in the dangers of unrestrained power. Powhatan, whose power within his own society was unrestrained, was a classic tyrant. He was a villain, but his villainy was defined in much the same fashion as British opposition authors in the 1720s and 1730s would define the temptations of power and the dangers of tyranny.[18]

Smith established a model of Virginia statesmanship in a second fashion as well, by his suppression of factionalism. Almost from the beginning, Randolph emphasized, the nascent colony was beset by factions, which the historian described as "a radical evil, and almost natural, since it sprang upon this first settlement of a wilderness." Only strong and exemplary leadership could prevent the disintegration of public order. When a fleet of nine ships carrying some five hundred new colonists set sail from England in May 1609, Smith faced a factional challenge to his authority. "Among them were some who during the voyage infused such jealousies and prejudices against Captain Smith, then president, that a general hatred was implanted against him in the breast of those who were on board before they had seen him." Smith, however, retained the confidence of his men, and "his integrity and prudence soon dissipated the malice of faction." As Randolph later summarized, "in the suppression of faction he was rapid, undaunted, and preemptory." Ultimately, it was not Smith's decisiveness but rather his "stubborn integrity" and moral leadership that contained the ill influence of incipient anarchy. Smith could sustain government in the colony because he had attained inward self-government. Because his psychological faculties were internally well-ordered, Smith could exercise the leadership necessary to sustain external order in the colony. Even though Smith, on the surface, is a thoroughly secular hero, the categories by which Randolph described his character reflect the influence of Latitudinarian theology on Randolph's understanding of the good man and the good society. Smith's enduring influence on the public life of Virginia stemmed from the exemplary model of moderate, temperate leadership that he established.[19]

Virginia's Exemplary Revolutionary Leadership

Edmund Randolph devoted the bulk of his *History* to a second foundational, constitutional moment in Virginia, the Revolution. As in his discussion of Virginia's period of initial settlement, Randolph's method was the same—he interlaced his narrative with character sketches of Virginia's luminous statesmen, counterpoised against antiheroic descriptions of the villains who provided the antagonists in his drama.

Unlike the seventeenth-century founding of Virginia, in which John Smith had figured so prominently, the Revolution was for Randolph distinguished by its republican nature. In Virginia, Randolph implied, a native aristocracy had begun to develop by the middle of the eighteenth century. The patronage positions offered by the royal governor in Virginia traditionally had "conferred a luster upon their incumbents and their connections and placed them in the attitude of expecting from the rest of the community an attention which is the proper tribute of public merit." However, he claimed, during the Revolution these leading public figures had "abolished" the "old standard of distinction." In its place Virginia's public spirited leadership had elevated a new standard, "on the single foundation of fitness for the rising exigency." Thus, "the vanity of pedigree was now justly sunk in the positive force of character." Virginia's traditional elite may have succumbed, in the decades after Captain John Smith, to the inducements of hereditary privilege. Before the Revolution, Virginia's leading families "were from their fortune, birth, and station high on the scale of the aristocracy of the day." But during the Revolution, they cast aristocracy aside. Their underlying commitment to republican ideals, summoned forth during the dispute with Great Britain, was "stripped of every consideration and attachment which virtue, talents, and patriotism did not beget."[20]

Randolph self-consciously introduced his account of the Revolution in Virginia with some fifteen biographical descriptions of Virginia's leading statesmen. He set out in each sketch to capture the character of an imperfect, living individual, and as a consequence, none represented in full his understanding of the ideal Virginia statesmen. Taken together, however, these short biographies (the longest, Randolph's biography of George Washington, spans only four pages in the published version of

the *History*) collectively illuminate the character Randolph thought necessary to sustain a republic. As a rhetorical strategy, Randolph's focus on
biography established the centrality of personal character to his understanding of Virginia's extraordinary success in creating a viable society
based solely on popular sovereignty.

What emerge from these pages are gentlemen whose virtues are overwhelmingly defined by moderation. Thus, for example, Patrick Henry
emulated the zealous oratory of Presbyterian and Baptist ministers in
Virginia, and thereby "unlocked the human heart and transferred into
civil discussions many of the bold licenses which prevailed in the religions." "License" is frequently a pejorative term, implying a will impelled
by passion and not reason. Randolph reinforced this picture of Henry in
his next sentence, suggesting that the source of his oratorical style was
George Whitefield, "that stupendous master of the human passions."
Nonetheless, Randolph carefully qualified an impression that might be
read as suggesting that Henry was nothing more than a demagogue.
Henry's emulation of the oratorical style of mid-eighteenth-century religious dissent was not taken to extremes. "His style of oratory was vehe-
ment, without transporting him beyond the power of self-command or
wounding his opponents by deliberate offense." Thus, Henry's oratory
was efficacious, fit for the times. It did not represent the qualities of his
inward mind, but rather was a stance that Henry could adopt for political
purposes properly guided by right reason. Henry's passions were mod-
erated by his rationality. And while Henry might adopt this stance for
rhetorical purposes, his demeanor was uniformly "inoffensive, concili-
ating, and abounding in good humor." The model he set for the people
around him ultimately was one of studied self-control.[21]

Randolph's character sketches emphasized the example established
by Virginia's leading public figures. Thomas Jefferson, for example, was
"an admirer of elegance and convenience." For those of his "contemporaries who were within the scope of his example, he diffused a style
of living much more refined than that which had been handed down to
them by his and their ancestors." George Washington was "conspicu-
ous for firmness," and for "a prudence which no frivolousness had ever
checkered." As a junior military officer, Washington showed "a pattern
of subordination" to legitimate authority, demonstrating in his obedi-

ence respect for the law, even when the commands he received were wrong-headed. "When orders of the most preposterous and destructive nature were given to him, he remonstrated indeed, but began to execute them as far as it was in his power." In Randolph's descriptions of both men, and of numerous others, he portrayed Virginia's gentlemen as setting the tone for the society over which, by their merits to be sure, they presided. Virginia's gentlemen had the potential to lead for good or ill, but their leadership either way was moral as well as political.[22]

All of these themes came together in Randolph's portrait of his father-in-law, Robert Carter Nicholas. Randolph worried that his effusive praise for Nicholas would be mistaken for partiality. "In speaking of him, I should distrust the warping of personal affection," he wrote, "if all Virginia were not in some measure my witness." Nicholas was widely admired in Virginia for his deep religious convictions and for his successful efforts to pattern his life on that of Christ. "He was bred in the bosom of piety, and his youthful reading impressed upon his mind a predilection for the Established Church, though he selected the law as his profession." As Randolph noted, "I should willingly incur the supposition of a tacit insinuation against the bar in general by laying so great a stress on his virtue, were it not that in the hour of temptation the best men find a refuge and succor in asking themselves how some individual spotless in morality and sincere in Christianity would act on a similar occasion." Nicholas was preeminent because he so powerfully and publicly illustrated throughout his life the statesmanship of the Anglican gentleman. "The propriety and purity of his life were often quoted," Randolph wrote, "to stimulate the old and to invite the young to emulation." Men like Nicholas diffused the habit of virtuous, moderate self-government to the people. By their example, the people as a whole acquired the dispositions to sustain popular government.[23]

As in the first sections of his History, Randolph reinforced his argument by contrasting virtuous heroes with villainous antiheroes. He concluded his lengthy series of biographies of Virginia's Revolutionary protagonists with a short sketch of an antagonist, John Murray, Earl of Dunmore, Virginia's royal governor in the 1770s. Unlike virtuous men like Robert Carter Nicholas, "Dunmore, generally preferring the crooked path, possessed not the genius to conceive, nor the temper to seek, the plain and direct way which nature opens to the human heart." Randolph noted that the Revolutionary situation in Virginia would have tried the character of any royal governor. But Dunmore possessed no exemplary qualifications. "Of those which shed a beam of false luster, and certainly of those of an exalted kind, Dunmore was wholly destitute," Randolph recalled. "To external accomplishments he pretended not, and his manners and sentiments did not surpass substantial barbarism, a barbarism which was not palliated by a particle of native genius nor regulated by one ingredient of religion." How could a man with little refinement, and less piety or self-control, hope to govern Virginia? Dunmore was, in Randolph's telling, in every way the antithesis of Robert Carter Nicholas.[24]

Randolph on Religion and the State

Randolph's History is either partial or incomplete. He published a prospectus of the work in the December 26, 1809, edition of the Richmond Enquirer, in which he divided his narrative into six units. In the published outline, he planned the fifth unit to conclude with the ratification of the Constitution; the sixth, he suggested, would contain "an illustration of the influence of that Constitution upon Virginia, and her general history from the time of its operation in the year 1789." The surviving manuscript, however, concludes in the year 1782. Thus, either the last two units have been lost, or else Randolph never finished them. For our purposes, the missing text is unfortunate, not least because the portion that survives stops tantalizingly short of the debates surrounding Patrick Henry's proposed 1784 law to support "teachers of the Christian Religion" in Virginia that culminated in the repudiation of Henry's bill, and passage instead of Thomas Jefferson's "Bill to Establish Religious Freedom" in 1786. In the extant text, however, there are occasional references to the disestablishment debate that shed some insight onto Randolph's religious and political thought.[25]

Randolph had an ambiguous relationship with Thomas Jefferson, who authored the bill that finally secured passage in 1786. They were close friends and, for much of Randolph's career, political allies. But Randolph did not approve of Jefferson's extreme religious rationalism.

Thus, for example, when Randolph sketched Jefferson's character, he went out of his way to describe his heterodoxy. "When Jefferson first attracted notice, Christianity was denied in Virginia only by a few." As he went on to emphasize, Jefferson "was adept, however, in the ensnaring subtleties of deism and gave it, among the rising generation, a philosophical patronage, which repudiates as falsehoods things unsusceptible of strict demonstration." Given his own commitment to these notions prior to his marriage and religious conversion, Randolph's use of language here was restrained, even as he signaled his censure of extreme rational religion's "ensnaring subtleties."[26]

Randolph explicitly asserted a connection between Jefferson's deism and his ardent support for religious toleration. "It is believed that while such tenets as are in contempt of the Gospel inevitably terminate in espousing the fullest latitude in religious freedom," he wrote, "Mr. Jefferson's love of liberty would itself have produced the same effects." In order to secure passage of Jefferson's bill, Jefferson and Madison needed to rally far more support than existed in Virginia for their brand of religious rationalism, and thus they joined forces with Baptists and Presbyterians hostile to the Episcopal establishment. "His opinions against restraints on conscience ingratiated him with the enemies of the establishment, who did not stop to inquire how far those opinions might border on skepticism or infidelity." As Randolph acidly noted, "parties in religion and politics rarely scan with nicety the peculiar private opinions of their adherents." Randolph's diffident, unenthusiastic description of the political process that led to disestablishment suggests that his support for Jefferson's position stemmed from a different set of convictions. Randolph could agree that disestablishment was desirable, but not for the reasons supplied by deists like Jefferson, nor those of Jefferson's evangelical allies.[27]

For Randolph, a religious establishment of any sort was undesirable because it produced a weak, indolent clergy. Randolph devoted only a few paragraphs to the disestablishment of the Protestant Episcopal Church, an event he surely planned to discuss in one of the missing later sections of his History. Randolph favored religious toleration and regretted that it had not been sooner implemented in Virginia. He attributed this unfortunate neglect to "the established clergy, most of whom delighted rather in the lethargy of fixed salaries than in the trouble of thought, learning, and research, which a vigorous dissenting minister, no longer depressed, might occasion." Disestablishment, then, was for Randolph a salutary development precisely because it invigorated the clergy and penalized the complacency that, in his estimation, a religious establishment cultivated. Whereas Jefferson was a libertarian, and the dissenters remembered with some bitterness their treatment by Church of England clergy and prominent laymen in the 1760s, Randolph favored religious freedom because he believed that in the long run it would best promote commitment to religious devotion in Virginia.[28]

Randolph's discussion of the 1776 Virginia Constitutional Convention and the legislation that stemmed from it similarly made clear his disapproval of any religious establishment. On December 9, 1776, the Virginia legislature passed legislation to relieve religious dissenters from taxation to support the established church, and likewise suspended the law that provided for a fixed salary for ministers. State payment of ministerial salaries, of course, was one of the fundamental props of the religious establishment in Virginia. Passage of these laws was controversial in 1776, which Randolph noted with disapproval. "The first fracture in a chain forged by an unjust principle cannot easily be closed," he wrote. But in the end, "the votaries of that church" were outmaneuvered by the dissenters. Randolph's revolutionary republicanism colored his assessment of this episode. Anglicans "had almost always been on the side of monarchy, while the hearts of the dissenters might truly be said to be in covenant with those who were clamorous against the threats of civil oppression." In the popular imagination, the Church of England was tainted by its association with the British monarchy. "The advocates of the church were apparently unconscious of its imbecility," Randolph explained. "It was enervated by mental activity, and it was palpable that a blow like this must stun it into a lingering, from which it could never wholly recover." Randolph foreshadowed in this description the fuller discussion of disestablishment that is now, unfortunately, missing.[29]

Randolph's discussion of the Church of England in Virginia during the Revolution reveals his commitment to religion, even as he supported religious freedom. He condemned, if only gently, the deism and skepticism of men like Jefferson. Unlike Jefferson, who supported religious freedom for libertarian reasons and who looked to agrarian property ownership to shape the morals of the people, Randolph condemned establishment because he thought it rendered the clergy too sluggishly contented. The passages in which Randolph discussed disestablishment do not suggest any abiding hostility to religion, but quite the contrary a deep concern that it remain a vital force in the lives of the people.

Randolph and Rational Religion

In summary then, Edmund Randolph was a conventional Anglican republican. He worried that the temptations of public power would corrupt the men who exercised it. The best check against this corruption was the virtuous, public-spirited character of the republican statesman who applied power on behalf of the people. Virtuous leaders exercised an important moral role in a republican society, because they diffused good character to the rest of society by the exemplary model they provided. Thus, the long-term health of a republic depended in two ways on the character of the men who governed it: in the short run on their capacity to resist corruption, and in the long run on the example that they established for the people they ruled. Randolph's republicanism, then, had a powerful hierarchical cast to it. For all that he decried aristocracy, he remained deeply committed to aristocratic habits of mind.

Randolph adhered to a simplified variant of standard faculty psychology, derived from English scholasticism, from the pedagogy of Thomas Aquinas, and ultimately from Aristotle. He believed that human faculties consisted of bestial appetites and a higher, more godly rationality. Unlike political thinkers informed by Reformed Calvinism, Randolph believed that natural reason could moderate the passions. In this sense, he was conventionally Anglican. Human reason exercised a weak influence on the will. Because the ability of reason to motivate was weak, Randolph stressed that moderation of the will required the assistance of habit, especially when developed as a young man. Thus, his political philosophy highlighted the importance of good role models in a successful and enduring republic. The people, and especially young people, learned moderation by imitating men they respected. Statesmen of necessity must model virtue for the people subject to their authority.

Randolph believed that rational religion led men to develop the right kind of character. He emphasized the human capacity to make meaningful moral choices. His understanding of "virtue" was Aristotelian. The rightly ordered character could chart a middle path between extremes. This notion was encapsulated within the Anglican ideal of the via media, which not only charted a middle path between the extremes of slavish Catholicism on the one hand and the uncontrolled zealotry of Reformed Christianity on the other, but also provided a metaphor for ordering the internal dispositions of the good man. Thus, the theology of the Church of England supported and reinforced an Aristotelian sense of identity, and linked the success of the good republican society to a particular ideal of classical self-governorship.

Historians and political theorists have tended to minimize the importance of liturgical faiths in early America, and to treat the Reformed Calvinist tradition as American orthodoxy during the colonial period. There can be no question that the Church of England failed to replicate the institutional structure necessary to sustain formal discipline in the colonies and, in that sense, was (as historian Jon Butler terms it) a failure. Too narrow a focus on institutional structure, however, has led some observers to the false inference that we can deduce from institutional weakness the conclusion that Anglican systems of belief lacked theological and intellectual influence in the colonies. The Church of England was the established church of economically important and influential parts of the British empire and the dominant religious influence in metropolitan England. Anglican assumptions permeated British political discourse throughout the eighteenth century and inescapably shaped the intellectual and political world of those eighteenth-century Britons living in the colonies. Even those colonial statesmen who were not explicitly Anglican were nonetheless influenced by the imperial faith, if only to engage with it in order to reject or modify it.

In this sense, Anglicanism in late colonial North America was hegemonic; no colonial thinker could simply ignore it. Scholars who accept the polemical condemnations of the Church of England written by eighteenth-century dissenters as accurate portrayals of Anglican religion in the colonies leave themselves unable to offer much other than a functionalist account of the religious convictions of men like Edmund Randolph or the many Virginia founders like him. This unfortunate historiography has been one reason why until recently it has been easy to portray the American founding as an entirely secular event.[30]

Randolph differed in emphasis from some other American republicans of the founding era primarily because he focused on the moral character of political leaders, not on the citizens as a whole. Where other republican thinkers emphasized the necessity of sustaining a virtuous, vigilant citizenry, Randolph focused primarily on the obligations of republican leadership. In this sense, his political theory was less sophisticated than that of many of his peers. Randolph assumed the existence of properly mannered, moderate gentlemen to set a good example for the people. He never tackled in any thoughtful fashion the circumstances necessary to create such a group of distinguished leaders, nor did he analyze in any detail the process by which democracy can fail in their absence. Randolph analyzed the inward character of the virtuous ruler, which he grounded loosely in piety and religious observance. The schema by which he defined virtue was derived from and affirmed by Anglican theology, but he stopped short of proposing any formal linkage between public society and the teaching of religious values.

As a political thinker, then, Randolph's analysis was incomplete. But he most certainly remains a compelling example of the way in which orthodox religion influenced the political thought of Virginia's ruling elite. In this sense, Randolph remains exemplary today. If we want to understand Virginia's contribution to the founding, we will have to do it by understanding the theology underlying the political thought of men like Edmund Randolph.

Notes

I would like to acknowledge the kindness, wisdom, and generous collegiality of those scholars who read and critiqued earlier drafts of this essay: Jennifer Connerley, Jon Kukla, Gerrald McDermott, Iain MacLean, and Alison Sandman.

1. The standard survey of the Church of England in colonial British America is John Frederick Woolverton, *Colonial Anglicanism in North America* (Detroit: Wayne State University Press, 1984). See also the discussions in Patricia U. Bonomi, *Under the Cope of Heaven: Religion, Society, and Politics in Colonial America*, updated ed. (Oxford: Oxford University Press, 2003); and Jon Butler, *Awash in a Sea of Faith: Christianizing the American People* (Cambridge, Mass.: Harvard University Press, 1990). An excellent brief introduction to the thought of the Cambridge Platonists can be found in J. B. Schneewind, ed., *Moral Philosophy from Montaigne to Kant* (Cambridge: Cambridge University Press, 2003), 275–77.

The standard survey of early American theology is now E. Brooks Holifield, *Theology in America: Christian Thought from the Age of the Puritans to the Civil War* (New Haven, Conn.: Yale University Press, 2003); for Holifield's specific treatment of the Church of England, see 84–92. For placing early American theology in its larger Christian context, I have found especially valuable the superb brief introductory text by Alister E. McGrath, *Reformation Thought: An Introduction*, 3rd ed. (Oxford: Oxford University Press, 1999), and the older, but still quite useful work of John Dillenberger and Claude Welch, *Protestant Christianity: Interpreted through its Development* (New York: Scribner, 1954).

2. David L. Holmes, *The Religion of the Founding Fathers* (Charlottesville, Va.: Ash Lawn-Highland; Ann Arbor: Clements Library, University of Michigan, 2003), 53–56.

3. See William Gibson, *The Church of England, 1688–1832: Unity and Accord* (London: Routledge, 2001), 50–53; Isabel Rivers, *Reason, Grace, and Sentiment: A Study of the Language of Religion and Ethics in England, 1660–1780*, vol. 1: *Whichcote to Wesley* (Cambridge: Cambridge University Press, 1991), 25–88.

4. Locke and Tillotson, as quoted in Roy Porter, *The Creation of the Modern World: The Untold Story of the British Enlightenment* (New York: W. W. Norton, 2000), 100, 103. On the influence of the Society for the Propagation of Christian Knowledge and the Society for the Propagation of the Gospel in Foreign Parts in colonial British America, see Nancy L. Rhoden, *Revolutionary Anglicanism: The Colonial Church of England Clergy during the American Revolution* (New York: New York University Press, 1999), 11–12, 16, 21–24, 29.

5. Jack P. Greene has advanced this argument in a number of essays. See especially "Society, Ideology, and Politics: An Analysis of the Political Culture of Mid-Eighteenth-Century Virginia," in *Negotiated Authorities: Essays in Colonial Political and Constitutional History* (Charlottesville: University Press of Virginia, 1994), 259–318. On the origins of the Virginia ethic of genteel stewardship, see Kevin R. Hardwick, "Narratives of Villainy and Virtue: Governor Francis Nicholson and the Character of the Good Ruler in Early Virginia," *Journal of Southern History* 72, no. 1 (Feb. 2006): 39–74. On the Church of England in colonial Virginia, see Edward L. Bond, *Damned Souls in a Tobacco Colony: Religion in Seventeenth Century Virginia* (Macon, Ga.: Mercer University Press, 2000), esp. 239–86; John K.

Nelson, *A Blessed Company: Parishes, Parsons, and Practitioners in Anglican Virginia, 1690–1776* (Chapel Hill: University of North Carolina Press, 2001); and Edward L. Bond and Joan R. Gundersen, *The Episcopal Church in Virginia, 1607–2007*, published in *Virginia Magazine of History and Biography* 115, no. 2 (2007): 163–344. The best survey of religion in colonial Virginia is Edward L. Bond, "Religion in Colonial Virginia: A Brief Overview," in *Spreading the Gospel in Colonial Virginia: Sermons and Devotional Writings*, ed. Edward L. Bond (Lanham, Md.: Lexington Books, 2004), 1–64. See also Perry Miller, *Errand into the Wilderness* (Cambridge, Mass.: Belknap Press of Harvard University Press, 1956), as illustrative of his work and thesis.

   "Providence" was a term that Randolph used, in common with most of the founders. It took its precise meaning from theology, and thus needs to be placed in the context of the specific theological commitments of the person using it. It did not necessarily signify an actively interventionist divinity. As Calvin made clear in his *Institutes*, even in the sixteenth century variants of the deist "clockmaker" argument existed. The "carnal mind," Calvin suggested, "imagines that all things are sufficiently sustained by the energy divinely infused into them at first." In this sense, Providence was simply the working out in nature of God's will, through normal and natural causes that originated in the Divine. "But faith must penetrate Deeper," Calvin argued. "After learning that there is a Creator, it must forthwith infer that he is also a Governor and Preserver, and that, not by producing a kind of general motion in the machine of the globe as well as in each of its parts, but by a special providence sustaining, cherishing, superintending, all the things which he has made, to the very minutest, even to a sparrow." See John Calvin, *Institutes of the Christian Religion*, book 1, chapter 16, trans. Ford Lewis Battles, ed. John T. McNeill (Philadelphia: Westminster, 1960), 197–98. While Randolph's religious devotion was sincere, his writings do not contain sufficient theological context to allow us to determine just precisely what he intended by the word.

   6. See generally Daniel Walker Howe, *Making the American Self: Jonathan Edwards to Abraham Lincoln* (Cambridge, Mass.: Harvard University Press, 1997); Holifield, *Theology in America*; and Norman Fiering, *Jonathan Edward's Moral Thought and Its British Context* (Chapel Hill: University of North Carolina Press, 1981), esp. 261–321.

   7. William Stith, *The Nature and Extent of Christ's Redemption: A Sermon Preached before the General Assembly, of Virginia, at Williamsburg, November 11th, 1753* (Williamsburg, 1753), reprinted in Bond, ed., *Spreading the Gospel in Colonial Virginia*, 508–22. Compare Stith's understanding of the human condition with that of other ministers whose writings Bond has collected, chapter 9, "The Call to a Moral Life: Occasional Sermons and Other Writings," 469–569. Paul Elmen, "Anglican Morality," in *The Study of Anglicanism*, ed. John Sykes, John Booty, and Jonathan Knight, rev. ed. (London: SPCK; Minneapolis: Fortress, 1998), 368.

8. The standard scholarly biographies are John J. Reardon, *Edmund Randolph: A Biography* (New York: Macmillan, 1974), and Moncure Daniel Conway, *Omitted Chapters of History Disclosed in the Life and Papers of Edmund Randolph* (New York: G. P. Putnam's Sons, 1888).

9. Reardon, *Edmund Randolph*, 66–78, 191–250.

10. Reardon, *Edmund Randolph*, 87–169. The executive papers of Randolph's administration are unpublished; the original manuscripts are held by the Virginia State Library and have recently been cataloged. The catalog contains no mention that Randolph issued proclamations of thanksgiving or other religiously grounded proclamations as governor.

11. Remarkably, the most recent scholarly biography of Randolph devotes no attention whatsoever to his religious convictions. In this paragraph, I follow the account by Conway, *Omitted Chapters*, esp. 11–12, 36–37, 156–57. As noted, Randolph wrote a description of his wife's character, addressed to his children, in which he described his wife's role in his religious conversion. Conway quotes extensively from this essay, 388–90. The original may be found in the manuscript collections of the Alderman Library, University of Virginia, cataloged as "Edmund Randolph's Sketch of His Wife," March 25, 1810.

12. Randolph's "Sketch of his Wife," as quoted in Conway, *Omitted Chapters*, 389.

13. Edmund Randolph, *History of Virginia*, ed. Arthur H. Shaffer (Charlottesville: University Press of Virginia, 1970).

14. Ibid., 42.

15. Ibid., 21, 26, 32.

16. Ibid., 44.

17. Ibid., 26–27.

18. Ibid., 24. On the early-eighteenth-century opposition, the classic interpretation is Bernard Bailyn, *The Origins of American Politics* (New York: Knopf, 1968); subsequent treatments are extensive, but I have found especially useful Shelley Burtt, "The Good Citizen's Psyche: On the Psychology of Civic Virtue," *Polity* 23, no. 1 (Autumn 1990): 23–38, and "The Politics of Virtue Today: A Critique and a Proposal," *American Political Science Review* 87, no. 2 (Jun. 1993): 360–68.

19. Randolph, *History of Virginia*, 36.

20. Ibid., 178–79.

21. Ibid., 179–80.

22. Ibid., 182, 187, 189.

23. Ibid., 184–85.

24. Ibid., 196–97.

25. John Melville Jennings, "The Manuscript," in Randolph, *History of Virginia*, xxxvii–xxxviii.

26. Randolph, *History of Virginia*, 183.

27. Ibid., 183.

28. Ibid., 203. On Anglican repression of dissenters, especially Baptists, in the 1760s, see the various studies by Rhys Isaac, especially "Evangelical Revolt: The Nature of the Baptists' Challenge to the Traditional Order in Virginia, 1765 to 1775," *William and Mary Quarterly*, 3rd Ser., 31, no. 3 (Jul. 1974): 345–68.

29. Randolph, *History of Virginia*, 263–64.

30. Butler, *Awash in a Sea of Faith*, 127; J. C. D. Clark, *The Language of Liberty, 1660–1832: Political Discourse and Social Dynamics in the Anglo-American World* (Cambridge: Cambridge University Press, 1994), 150–51. On the church and British national identity, see Linda Colley, *Britons: Forging the Nation, 1707–1837* (New Haven, Conn.: Yale University Press, 1992).

CHAPTER 10

Benjamin Rush and Revolutionary Christian Reform

ROBERT H. ABZUG

At exactly nine in the morning on July 4, 1788, as a cloudy but rainless sky hung over Philadelphia, the bells of Christ Church joyously announced the beginning of the Grand Federal Procession.[1] Partisans of the recently ratified Constitution had created an unprecedented public extravaganza to celebrate the fulfillment of the Revolution and the future of the new republic. Representative contingents of farmers, manufacturers, civil and military leaders, clergy, professionals, and tradesmen—five thousand in all—paraded placards and floats in a mile-and-a-half-long file. By afternoon the three-mile route had been marched and the orations made, and seventeen thousand citizens gathered to toast Republicanism with glasses of beer and cider.[2]

Dr. Benjamin Rush (1745–1813), signer of the Declaration of Independence and physician to the Continental Army, basked in the warmth of that day. Years of sacrifice during the war, frustrations over the Articles of Confederation, and sober recognition of the many issues that divided the citizens of the land melted away in the fervor of the moment. The procession, he wrote a few days later, had united "the most remarkable transports of the mind which were felt during the war with the great event of the day . . . to produce such a tide of joy as has seldom been felt in any age or country." It had been "the happy means of uniting all our citizens. . . . 'Tis done!" he exclaimed. "We have become a nation."[3]

Rush, in his less enthusiastic moments at least, knew that it would take more than a parade to create a nation. A year before, he had reminded Americans: "There is nothing more common than to confound the terms of *American Revolution* with those of *the late American war*. The American war is over: but this is far from being the case with the American Revolution." Americans had to fashion a united country from thirteen states of varied and often jealously guarded interests, with the knowledge that the greed, factionalism, and corruption of which they accused the British might also be found among themselves. In addition, those who fought as one for independence differed as to how they might fulfill the promise of 1776. From the British surrender at Yorktown through the War of 1812, Americans struggled to define and implement the revolution that "the late American war" had made possible.[4]

In doing so, post-Revolutionary Americans also generated national ideals, conceptions of republicanism, and techniques for solving the problems of society that became for later generations the bases for defining national character. For antebellum reform, and most especially for the abolitionist movement, the Declaration of Independence's bold assertion that all men were created equal overshadowed virtually all other inheritances from the Revolutionary era. Yet in more complex ways, the shape of reform owed much to the Revolutionary period. Nowhere are these contributions more richly represented than in the life and vision of Benjamin Rush.

Rush's own addition to the ferment of thought about the American future, little studied compared to the epochal contributions of Jefferson, Hamilton, Madison, and Adams, addressed problems relatively untouched by the great Constitution makers. Rush emphasized the need not only to create a republic but also "to prepare the principles, morals, and manners of our citizens" so that they would honor and defend it. Only if the very fiber of everyday personal and social life were imbued with a common set of republican values and virtues, he believed, could the great experiment succeed. Toward this end Rush developed a remarkable program for social and personal change: abolition, temperance, elimination of the death penalty, humane treatment of criminals and the insane, educational reform (including provision for female education), and numerous other causes. Unique in their day, the specific concerns and comprehensiveness of his agenda in many ways also prefigured antebellum reform.

Rush's particular approach to nation building drew from three late-eighteenth-century intellectual currents: republicanism, Scottish Enlightenment philosophical and medical thought, and millennial Christianity. Yet his reform vision did not involve the simple merging of abstract ideas. It can only be understood by tracing the ways in which Rush's religious passion shaped an Enlightenment Christian reform vision of individual, society, and cosmos. We see a man deeply concerned with religious issues, but one whose spiritual questioning led him away from the conventional churchly life and toward a vision that drew upon the human body, the social structure, and basic Christianity for its rituals and symbols. In short, he became an idiosyncratic religious virtuoso.

Rush's religious sensibility was molded by men and women whose own intense enthusiasms flourished in the revivals that touched the American colonies from the late 1730s into the 1740s, which scholars have called the Great Awakening. The Awakening defies easy analysis. While the American tour of English evangelist George Whitefield was the catalyst for many of the Awakening revivals, others seemed to have ignited solely from local conditions. Nor were the results consistent. Sometimes revivals led to the crumbling of religious establishments and the founding of new sects, while at other times they aided established churches.

Nonetheless, some dominant themes emerge. Preachers pitted themselves against what they deemed to be cold and rational religion, urging instead a warm piety made possible by conversion. They preached against the corruptions of worldly wealth and emphasized the equality of all men and women before God. Many saw in the heightened emotions of the revival itself a sign that the Second Coming of Christ, which would inaugurate the millennium, was imminent. Whether in packed churches or in vast outdoor meetings, ministers brought together thousands of souls from all sects and walks of life who sometimes shared only spiritual frustration and a thirst for salvation. At the same time, these preachers drew heated opposition from clergy and laymen who found their style ungodly and who saw in their work the destruction of churchly communities. For its adherents, however, amid a cacophony of bitter words between warring factions, the Great Awakening engendered a surge of burning hope for personal conversion and millennial splendor.

Youth and Education

The Awakening had already begun to quiet by the time of Rush's birth on Christmas Eve, 1745, but the boy grew up surrounded by its living legacy. Benjamin, though also descended from Quakers and Presbyterians, was baptized in his father's Anglican faith. However, the death of John Rush five years later left the boy's religious life in the hands of his mother. Susanna Rush, a partisan of the Awakeners in the Presbyterian church, began taking him to Philadelphia's Second Presbyterian Church. Its minister, Gilbert Tennent, had been among the most effective and controversial itinerant preachers during the Awakening. Tennent had calmed down considerably by the 1750s, but his charismatic appeals still deeply impressed the young boy. Rush especially remembered the minister's egalitarianism. "The Rich, and the Poor, Black and White," he wrote on the occasion of Tennent's death in 1764, "had equally free access to his Person."[5]

Rush was exposed more profoundly to Awakening traditions when in 1754, at age eight, he entered Nottingham, the boarding school run by his uncle, the Reverend Samuel Finley. In a famous sermon, Christ Triumphing, and Satan Raging (1741), Finley had argued that the revivals and the opposition they engendered signified nothing less than the prophesied battle between the forces of God and the devil that would precede the millennium. In fact, he proclaimed, "the Kingdom of God is come." Finley's strident millennialism had only slightly faded by the time young Rush came to Nottingham; it infused the boy's education with the mood of cosmic combat and added a piquant edge to a curriculum framed in piety.[6]

In 1759, after six years at Nottingham, Rush entered the College of New Jersey (now Princeton) at the age of fourteen. There he had brief but telling contact with the college's new president, the Reverend Samuel Davies. Davies had been, like Tennent and Finley, in the forefront of the Presbyterian Awakening. In the late 1740s and 1750s, Davies rallied dissenters in the fight for religious toleration. During the French and Indian War he stirred many with patriotic sermons that stressed the unity of the colonies, even as his religious appeals celebrated the unity of the faithful. Rush knew him for only a year, but that was enough time for Davies to make a major impact. He especially took to heart the president's simple command to Rush's graduating class of September 1760: "Bravely live and die, serving your *generation*—your *own* generation."[7]

At graduation, almost fifteen years old and ready to make his mark in the world, Rush found the legacy of his Awakener mentors both rich and troubling. He readily embraced their ideals of piety, religious toleration, millennial hope, and public spirit, as well as their incipient sense of an intercolonial "American" identity. At the same time, this audacious spiritual inheritance posed a difficult question for the young man. Was he worthy of such a trust? An eager student schooled in ideals but too young to understand the limits of human endeavor might find in the challenges of a Tennent, Finley, or Davies a damning indictment of his own shortcomings. This must have been especially true for Rush, who knew little of his own father and was forced to measure himself against distant models rather than the everyday behavior of a father whom he also knew as a real person.

It did not help that Rush the religionist competed with Rush the dashing young gentleman. He might condemn Philadelphia's "vice and profanity" and fear that its young men were "wholly devoted to pleasure and sensuality," but much of that complaint originated in the self-reflection of one whose various transgressions included having illicit relations with a married woman. Perhaps for such secret reasons, his spiritual life ebbed. He worried about his soul but moved only imperfectly toward the change of heart that lay at the center of the Awakening experience. The inheritor of a grand religious vision, he nonetheless could not find his own corner of peace within it.[8]

This sense of being in a spiritual shadow surely informed Rush's choice of career. Though many expected him to become a minister, he himself felt unfit for the task. Late in 1760, after consultation with both

Davies and Finley, he finally chose medicine and began his apprenticeship with Dr. John Redman. "Now how inglorious must this study appear when set in competition with Divinity," Benjamin confessed to a friend in 1761, "—the one employed in advancing temporal happiness, the other eternal—one applying remedies to a fading, mortal Body, the other employed in healing the sickness of a Soul immortal and everlasting."[9]

Rush's apprenticeship and medical study, however, brought him close to contemplation of eternity. As he helped Redman on his rounds during the city's bouts with influenza, yellow fever, and other diseases, it was inevitable that he grapple with issues of the soul in treating and comforting the sick and dying. By the beginning of 1766, Rush began to face his own sinful nature and to thirst for union with God. "The religious impressions that were made upon my mind at this time," he remembered, "were far from issuing in a complete union to God . . . , but they left my mind more tender to sin of every kind, and begat in me constant desires for a new heart."[10]

With this new sensitivity, Rush traveled to Edinburgh in 1766 to continue his medical education. Scotland, home of the most orthodox sort of Presbyterianism, might have provided him a fertile atmosphere for religious fulfillment. He gave his soul every chance, discussing theology with the legendary Whitefield and other ministers. But in these new surroundings his sense of sin abated, and so did his thirsting after God. He became enamored of medical studies and thrilled at the discussion of what for him was a new way of looking at the world: republicanism. Fellow students exposed him to the writings of Algernon Sydney, the seventeenth-century advocate of the ideology, and he came to share his classmates' sense that English history had been the story of corrupt decline since Cromwell.

Republicanism and Antislavery

The alternative that republicanism offered was a country of virtuous individuals who maintained an equally virtuous government through division of authority among various estates and in various governing entities. In the late 1760s, most considered such ideas to be visionary notions.

For Rush, however, as for a small but growing number in England and America, the republican critique was a revelatory set of ideas. Since it challenged the very heart of the monarchical system, it represented at least implicitly a questioning of the bases for all authority. No wonder that Rush later credited the "ferment" in his mind created by discussions of republicanism with unhinging his confidence in every idea he had once taken for granted.[11]

This we know only from Rush's retrospective reflections, and much evidence exists to show that his conversion to republicanism took longer than an instant. Still, his choice of "ferment" seems particularly apt to describe the unsettling mix of excitement and anxiety churning in his mind. In England, through his discovery of republican ideals, Rush had experienced something like a religious change of heart. Even as the future saint might get a glimmer of the wonder of grace but take years to surrender to the fullness of its power, Rush embraced republicanism as an understanding of the world attuned to God but only slowly came to endow it with the specifics of its sacred meaning.

Still, it must have had some immediate impact on Rush's political vision. For one thing, republicanism made sense of events that had already begun to unfold in the American colonies. The year before he came to Scotland, Rush had forthrightly supported protests against the Stamp Act. Then it had been a matter of simple justice and a nascent American pride. The English republicans' theory of decline, however, fit the Stamp Act Crisis into a broader historical struggle against corrupt monarchy. Rush might have gotten a first glimmer that he would be involved in a struggle as heroic and earthshaking as the Great Awakening, the leaders of which had shaped and shadowed his young life.

New signs of crisis met Rush when he returned in 1769 to a Philadelphia alive with political turbulence. No one yet advocated independence, but activists all over the colonies had begun to speak the language of a separate colonial identity. Proclaiming loyalty to the king, at the same time they saw in most demands from the Crown a violation of their rights as English subjects. Like Rush, they had discovered in republicanism the vocabulary with which to express the meaning of their political future. Yet it remained an inchoate vision, governed by an implicit clash of English and American identities that few wished to face.

Though clearly sympathetic to colonial resistance, Rush spent the early 1770s building his medical practice and shunning open participation in politics. Slavery finally sparked him to action. His friend Anthony Benezet, the famous Quaker antislavery activist, asked him to aid efforts to pass a tax bill in the Pennsylvania Assembly that would make importation of slaves highly uneconomical. Rush responded with *An Address to the Inhabitants of the British Settlements in America, upon Slave Keeping*.[12] The pamphlet advocated an end to the slave trade and the gradual emancipation of those already in bondage (Rush himself owned a manservant). It denied that slavery benefited the slave and that Africans were naturally suited for labor in southern climes. It also ridiculed the idea that the existence of slavery among the Hebrews was a legitimate religious defense of the modern institution.

Rush readily admitted that most of his arguments were old. What was new was his presentation of the antislavery case within a framework of American identity and godly judgment, within the millennial/apocalyptic vision so common to colonial religious thought during the Awakening.[13] He asserted that the vaunted English liberties that colonists guarded so jealously could not prosper side by side with slavery, that liberty must be for all or for none. He reminded "ADVOCATES for American Liberty" that the "eyes of all Europe" were upon them, expecting them to preserve "an asylum for freedom in this country" even if it should disappear elsewhere in the world. Furthermore, he argued, slavery was a "Hydra sin," and failure to deal with it would court God's punishment. "Remember that national crimes require national punishments," he warned; ". . . [they] cannot pass with impunity, unless God shall cease to be just or merciful."[14]

Even before the leap to rebellion, then, Rush had fashioned a specific component of America's republican agenda—abolition of slavery and the slave trade—and had linked America's fate in God's universe to that cause. That Rush should also be first stirred to action not by the grievances of his fellow colonists but rather by an evil in which colonists were deeply implicated, underlined a self-scrutiny that became a central feature of his commitment to independence. It was a tone built upon high expectations, for by Rush's light America, if it fulfilled its mission, would lead the world to the Second Coming prophesied by the Great Awakening. While numerous ministers and pamphleteers had begun to envision the colonial struggle as part of a Manichean millennial fray between the forces of God (the colonists) and those of the devil (the king), few as yet had joined Rush and Benezet as critics from within.[15]

There was another significant difference between Rush and most ministers in the construction of the religious meaning of issues abroad in the land. If Rush the religious virtuoso felt obliged to criticize his own society even as he condemned England, he did so outside the domain of theology. He had taken the Awakening spirit of ecumenism one step further in creating sacred issues whose resolution made no reference to sect or particulars of conversion. Rush had forged a vision of a sacred drama in which human actions concerning society sparked God's reward or punishment. In short, he began to display that peculiar sense of piety that would become, a half century later, the hallmark of the antebellum reformer as religious virtuoso.

Concern for Virtue

When the colonists declared independence, Rush devoted himself to the cause with enthusiasm and sacrifice. As a member of Congress and medical advisor to the army, he worked tirelessly to improve the health of the patriot troops. He brought to his labors the same unflinching self-scrutiny that informed his antislavery pamphlet, sometimes appearing to be as hard on his comrades as he was on the British. He sought in the actions of individual Americans a virtue as perfect as his dream of millennial revolution. The corruption of public officials, wavering and often pragmatically changing loyalties, and the exhaustion to be expected in such a struggle: all these mocked Rush's dreams for a republic.

He worried most about military leadership. Perhaps because he imagined the Revolution to be the first battle in a grand millennial fray, Rush described the Continental Army's needs in terms of the Old Testament. "We have only passed the Red Sea," he wrote to Patrick Henry in 1778. "A dreary wilderness is still before us, and unless a Moses or a Joshua are raised up in our behalf, we must perish before we reach the promised land." What he found was something quite different: "4 Major

Generals—Greene, Sullivan, Stirling and Stevens. The 1st a sycophant to the general [Washington], timid, speculative, without enterprise; the 2nd, weak, vain, without dignity, fond of scribbling, in the field a madman. The 3rd, a proud, vain, lazy, ignorant drunkard. The 4th, a sordid, boasting cowardly sot." Rush even questioned Washington's leadership. So insistent were his criticisms that he and a few others were accused of plotting against the Revolutionary leadership.[16]

Military leaders were not the only ones to come under Rush's scrutiny. He and not a few others worried about lack of virtue in common soldiers, especially as symbolized in the practice of growing their hair long. To assertions that this fashion indicated rebellious attitudes and slothfulness, Rush added his scientific argument that long hair caused colds (it stayed wet longer after a rain) and gave lice a convenient nesting ground. He also condemned war profiteering and the generally affluent conditions of the late 1770s as being destructive of the moral fiber needed to win the war. As a result, Rush sometimes expressed satisfaction when conditions took a turn for the worse. For instance, he saw a positive "new era" in American politics caused by the British capture of Charleston, South Carolina, in May 1780. "Our republics cannot long exist in prosperity," he wrote to John Adams on that occasion. "We require adversity and appear to possess most of the republican spirit when most depressed."[17]

Nonetheless, Rush thrilled to final victory over the British in 1783. After all, there remained the challenge of building a republic *despite* success and prosperity. But how would that be done? Most Revolutionary leaders recognized that the translation of revolutionary zeal into a republican reality involved both the creation of new institutions and the preservation of ideals of republican virtue among the populace. Many assumed or hoped that the creation of a republican political system would encourage an enduring sense of public virtue. For most of the Revolutionary leadership, politics and the creation of a new political structure became the field of battle on which various views of human nature and possibility were tested.

Rush approached the problem from a different angle. In the decade after victory at Yorktown, he developed a reform program to remake individuals and institutions into perfect reflections of republican virtue.

He shared the view of many that constitutions and simple freedom would not eradicate the darker side of human nature. Rather, one must start with programs that from birth to death encouraged virtue and built a true republic from the individual outward to society. In this sense Rush was perhaps more sanguine in his revolutionary hopes than most of his fellows, for transforming human nature was no easy task.

Environmentalist Reform

Rush's reform vision covered a great expanse from personal to social activity, but its details can only be understood fully in terms of Rush's underlying assumptions about America, humankind, and cosmic history. As already noted, he shared with many others the belief that the Revolution marked an epochal step toward the millennial day. Some meant by the "millennium" the literal return of Christ, and some meant an age of perfect peace in which Christ's spirit would inform every act and thought. Rush never made his own specific metahistorical vision clear, but he believed that America must lead human efforts to prepare the world for that prophesied era.

Identification of America as the nation to lead the world to millennial splendor was not uncommon and led most often to a simple adoration of the nation in the forms that recent scholars have called "civil religion." Rush the virtuoso, as his earlier pamphlet on slavery indicated, assumed that American leadership in the millennial fray depended upon the nation's ability to maintain its virtue among and above other nations. More specifically, it meant that Americans must fully embrace republicanism, an ideology that he came close to equating with Christianity.

One might properly ask why Rush the religionist felt it necessary to transmute Christianity into republicanism. In an overwhelmingly Christian nation, why not simply promote Christian virtue through revivals of religion? The most obvious answer is that Rush, like so many others of his generation, was swept up in the romance of the Revolution and at first tended to fuse his conceptions of sacred and profane history. The political means of the Revolution became sacralized as the human means for helping to fulfill prophecy.

Equally important, Benjamin Rush had grown to manhood not only influenced by the Great Awakening but also within a society that had grappled with the reality of religious pluralism for some time and had more or less made its peace with toleration. Rush's own background in Presbyterianism, Quakerism, and Anglicanism reflected only part of the spectrum of religions that had learned to live together within Pennsylvania. Finding a ritual life that would bring Christians together meant drawing on a cosmic vision outside of the individual sects, yet celebrating the general human virtues associated with each.

Rush found that vision in the Scottish Enlightenment, and more particularly in the scientific doctrine that lay at the core of his medical system: environmentalism. He summarized his basic views on an environmentalist-based reform program in *The Influence of Physical Causes upon the Moral Faculty* (1786); in it one can see the width and breadth of his vision. He argued that the capacity for choosing between good and evil, although innate, was deeply affected by the climate in which it developed and the condition of the body in which it was housed. Thus clarity of thought and, ultimately, the choice for virtue or vice might be affected by, among other things, climate, diet, choice of drinks, hunger, disease, style of labor, amount of sleep, pain, degree of cleanliness, odors, music, preaching, medicine, forms of punishment, and forms of government.

Rush wished to create a "science of morals" by tracking the environmental origins of virtue and vice. Philosophers, legislators, physicians, parents, schoolmasters, and ministers could consult the findings of such a science and adjust minute environmental influences to produce optimal moral and intellectual performance. In doing so one could eventually "extirpate war, slavery, and capital punishment" from society, make more intelligible the truths of Christianity, and in other ways effect "the reformation and happiness of mankind."[18]

Rush's dynamic sense of environmentalism produced a complex series of rituals and symbols aimed at sustaining a pious Christian republicanism. It distinguished Rush from a number of other important contemporary adherents of environmental doctrine, including Jefferson and his circle, who saw in it a way of explaining the differences exhibited by various races and groups of humankind. Rush, for his part, saw environmentalism as the basis for a careful reshaping of everyday life.

Given the long-term goals as well as the particulars of that reshaping, his reform program amounted to a first step toward perfecting the American republic through the resacralization of everyday life.

Republican Education

The aim of sacralizing the social environment can be seen most comprehensively in Rush's educational ideas, for he viewed the school as the key social instrument for reform and spent much time working out a multifaceted instructional environment. *Of the Mode of Education Proper in a Republic* (1784) set forth his ideas on the schooling of young republicans. Rush argued that education had better be done in America rather than abroad, since the prejudice for patriotism took hold most securely in the first twenty-one years of life. He favored a uniform system of education, one that would "render the mass of the people more homogeneous, and thereby fit them more easily for uniform and peaceable, government." A common education would counterbalance the varieties of American backgrounds.[19]

Rush placed Christianity at the very foundation of a republican education. While "every religion that reveals the attributes of the Deity is worth supporting," and while religious toleration was a cardinal value of republicanism, he nonetheless recommended that the New Testament be a key source of learning. "A Christian cannot fail of being a republican," he noted, and for a variety of reasons. Genesis disproved the divine right of kings; the Gospels inculcated "humility, self-denial, and brotherly kindness" and taught a central republican value, "that no man liveth unto himself." And, of course, the Golden Rule was essential to republican virtue.[20]

He also asserted that the main purpose of education was to train "men, citizens, and Christians" rather than "scholars," that in fact the system should "convert men into republican machines." Unless citizens in a republic "perform[ed] their parts properly, in the great machine of the government of the state," society would soon be spoiled by the reintroduction of monarchy or aristocracy. Each citizen was a part of the republic and "must be fitted to each other by means of education before they can be made to produce regularity and unison in government." Here, though expressed in enlightened republican language, lay the catechistic principles that informed contemporary and later evangelical educational enterprises, from Timothy Dwight's to Horace Bushnell's.[21]

More specific recommendations followed. Anticipating the work of Noah Webster, Rush argued that schools should stress the teaching of the "American language with propriety and grace" so as to create pride in the new country. History, chronology, commerce, and chemistry were all important, as were lessons in "all the means of promoting national prosperity and independence, whether they relate to improvements in manufactures, or inland navigation." All learning in one way or another prepared young citizens for a productive life, useful to self, family, and state.[22]

Rush's environmentalism naturally led him to a companion program of "physical discipline" that would create republican bodies as well as republican minds. Diet should consist of broths, milk, and vegetables. Spirituous liquors should be avoided. The day should proceed in alternating periods of study, manual labor, sleep, and silent solitude; contact with others should be closely watched so that "those great principles in human conduct—sensibility, habit, imitations and association"—could be given "proper direction."[23]

Rush's program had been outlined with men in mind. But he had not forgotten the preparation of women for what he saw as their proper role in a republic. He advocated instruction not only "in the usual branches of female education" but also in "the principles of liberty and government" and the "obligations of patriotism." No champion of equality, Rush nonetheless saw women as crucial to the creation of that environment necessary to promote republican values. After all, women were the silent partners of male endeavor. "The opinions and conduct of men are often regulated by the women in the most arduous enterprises of life," Rush noted, "and their approbation is frequently the principal reward of the hero's dangers, and the patriot's toils." Besides, he observed, "the first impressions upon the minds of children are generally derived from the women. Of how much consequence, therefore, is it in a republic, that they should think justly upon the great subject of liberty and government!"[24]

Having set forth the basic rationale, curriculum, and conditions for a republican education, Rush proceeded in the years that followed to suggest an institutional structure appropriate to his plan. In 1786, he outlined a system of education for Pennsylvania as a model for other states. He advocated a pyramid of institutions: one state university, four colleges located in different regions of the state, and free schools for every township. "By this plan the whole state will be tied together by one system of education," he argued, each institution acting in concert with the others to supply students and teachers with a common culture. "The same systems of grammar, oratory and philosophy, will be taught in every part of the state, and the literary features of Pennsylvania will thus designate one great, and equally enlightened family." Toward this end he helped found Dickinson College and was instrumental in restructuring the curriculum of the University of Pennsylvania. Two years later, Rush broadened this notion of unity through education in his plan for a "Federal University," which would be a source of common culture and concerted republican efforts in a large and diverse country and would spur "a golden age of the United States."[25]

Such grand institutional plans were just one part of Rush's environmental approach to education. At the other end of the spectrum were his tinkerings with every detail of classroom life, a penchant vividly illustrated in another of his major essays, "The Amusements and Punishments Which Are Proper for Schools." He rejected common forms of children's play; they ruined clothing, wasted strength, impaired health, were noisy, excited the passions, and were "calculated to beget vulgar manners." Instead Rush recommended amusements that would be "most subservient to their future employments in life." For instance, he approved of a particular game reportedly played at a Methodist college: "A large lot is divided between the scholars, and premiums are adjudged to those of them who produce the most vegetables from their grounds, or who keep them in the best order." In the winter one might play at mechanical arts. "Where is the boy who does not delight in the use of a hammer—a chisel—a saw?" Rush asked. "And who has not enjoyed a high degree of pleasure in his youth, in constructing a miniature house?" Even if a student were heading for a life in the professions, such exercises in the agricultural and manual arts would be a healthy outlet for creative passions.[26]

Amusements also gave students a break from the classroom. Rush worried about the physical, and therefore moral, injury done young scholars by obliging them "to sit too long in *one place*, or crowding too many of them together in *one room*." Bodies were literally bent out of shape and exposed to fevers and "morbid effluvia, produced by the confined breath and perspiration of too great a number of children." Strength and relief would come from simply getting these bodies outside and moving.[27]

Among amusements to avoid, Rush took special pains to make a case against hunting, or "gunning" as he put it. It hardened the heart, was no longer necessary to provide food, consumed too much time, led boys into "low, and bad company," and exposed the young hunter to accidents, fever, and long abstinence from food that would lead "to intemperance in eating, which naturally leads to intemperance in drinking." But that was not the half of it. To the argument that young men should learn to wield arms for defense of country, Rush countered that such training fostered "hostile ideas towards their fellow creatures." Instead educators should "instill into their minds sentiments of universal benevolence to men of all nations and colours." Since "wars originate[d] in error and vice," they would cease when education had done its job of eradicating war's causes. In case of attack from less virtuous enemies, Rush was sure, God would protect his chosen people. Enemies would turn their ships around because they would "find nothing in us congenial to their malignant dispositions; for the flames of war can be spread from one nation to another, only by the conducting mediums of vice and error." Given the proper chance, the reform of childhood games might lead the world to the abolition of war.[28]

As for punishments, here too Rush advocated replacing "barbarous" practices with those conceived in reason and love. He noted that civilized society had long ago abandoned corporal punishment for adults, and that only in the schools did such practices survive. Abolition of corporal punishment would be a blow against Satan. "I have sometimes suspected that the Devil who knows how great an enemy knowledge is to his kingdom," Rush mused, "has had the address to make the world believe that *feruling, pulling* and *boxing ears, cudgelling, horsing,* &c. and in boarding schools, a *little starving,* are all absolutely necessary for the government of young people, on purpose that he might make both schools, and school-masters odious, and thereby keep our world in ignorance; for ignorance is the best means the Devil ever contrived, to keep up the number of his subjects in our world."²⁹

The alternatives to harsh physical discipline were quiet counseling and admonition, after-school confinement, or silent public disgrace. If none of these worked, the child should be dismissed from school so as to prevent corruption of other children. "It is the business of parents, and not of school masters," Rush maintained, "to use the last means for eradicating idleness and vice from their children." Such a policy would accomplish two things. First, children would be spared the degradation and physical harm attendant to corporal punishment. Second, the schoolmaster, who had previously earned the hatred and ridicule of the community by his association with "despotism and violence," might take his rightful position as, "next to mothers, the most important member of civil society."³⁰

Creating the Christian Republic

Rush saw other important battlefields in addition to education. The foremost enemy was alcohol. As early as 1772, he had advocated moderation in drinking, arguing that spirits stimulated the body and disturbed natural functions. He thus rejected the common medical wisdom, which endorsed the healthful properties of liquor. Undaunted by criticism and only confirmed in his suspicions by observation of Revolutionary soldiers, he reopened his crusade in 1782 with a newspaper piece entitled "Against Spirituous Liquors." It attacked the time-honored custom of supplying farm laborers with rations of liquor. Instead of refreshing the body, he observed, spirits tended to "relax the stomach, quicken the circulation of the blood, and thus dispose it to putrefaction." In addition, spirits were expensive, unloosed quarrels and "indecent language," and inspired other mischief. Rush suggested four substitutes: "bonnie clabber" (sour milk), cider or small beer, Indian corn tea, or, best of all, vinegar and water sweetened with molasses or brown sugar.[31]

Rush published his classic pamphlet on hard drink, *An Enquiry into the Effects of Spirituous Liquors upon the Human Body, and Their Influence upon the Happiness of Society*, in 1784.[32] The *Enquiry* featured an argument similar in its comprehensiveness to his educational theories. Rush began by listing the immediate effects of drinking: talkativeness, good humor expressed in "an insipid simpering," swearing, disclosure of secrets and other forms of immodesty, and combativeness. Some drinkers, he noted, indulged in "singing, hallooing, roaring, imitating the noises of brute animals, jumping, tearing off clothes, dancing naked, breaking glasses and china, and dashing other articles of household furniture upon the ground or floor." The chronic effects were even worse: loss of appetite, "discharge of a frothy and viscid phlegm," obstructions of the liver, jaundice, coughing that often turned into consumption, diabetes, rash like eruptions known as "rum buds," bad breath, belching, epilepsy, gout, and madness.[33]

The social effects of drink mirrored this destruction of the body. Alcohol preyed upon the family, alienating husband from wife and child from parent. The drinking magistrate inspired fears of corruption and "subversion of public order and happiness." Urban drinkers often bankrupted their entire estates to pay "tavern debts"; farmers ruined their land and animals, while their children cavorted "filthy and half clad, without manners, principles and morals." As for the drunkard minister? Here words failed Rush: "If angels weep—it is at such a sight." Rush concluded, "Thus we see poverty and misery, crimes and infamy, diseases and death are all the natural and usual consequences of the intemperate use of ardent spirits."[34]

Later, Rush wrote pamphlets detailing his plans for female education, prison reform and the abolition of capital punishment, peace, humane treatment of the insane, and temperance in the use of tobacco. All expanded on the basic themes of a unity of health between the individual's body and the body politic. All implicitly or explicitly sought to advance the millennial goals of republicanism. All were based on an extremely detailed working out of environmentalist assumptions concerning personal habits and institutional settings, and all assumed that each ill was vulnerable to straightforward, scientific solution. Together these plans constituted a blueprint for the detailed construction of society and the ritual conduct of everyday life, all bent on creating a sacralized Christian republican way of life.

Rush seemed confused on only one issue, the black presence in America. In his *Address to the Inhabitants of the British Settlements . . . on the Slavery of the Negroes* (1773), he had damned slavery and the slave trade. After the Revolution had been won, he continued to campaign against the institution and for the humane treatment of slaves. Not only slavery but also the fate of the free black community in white society vexed Rush's sense of republicanism and Christian benevolence. Most whites, including Rush, did not believe that blacks could be made equal and full partners in the new nation. How could one find a place for them in the republic? Rush had always been able to discover answers to problems in scientific inquiry. He thought he might develop a proper policy toward blacks by joining others who sought to find a reason for their skin color.

In a paper read before the American Philosophical Society in 1797, he speculated that it was caused by "a disease in the skin of the leprous kind." Such a finding dictated that blacks be treated "with humanity and justice" and at the same time justified "keeping up the existing prejudices against matrimonial connections with them." Thus, according to Rush, Republican America could act in humane and Christian fashion and at the same time isolate blacks as one might isolate others with a serious illness. For Rush, this was no thin veil for conscious malevolence. Indeed, within the notion of their maintaining a largely separate community until cured of their leprosy, he championed free blacks in Philadelphia and kept up his campaign against slavery.[35]

Despite his troubled solution to the question of race, Rush's reform program, so careful in its detail and so cosmic in its ultimate goal of a republican road to the millennium, marked a striking break with a pre-Revolutionary world of royal authority and established churches. In place of this crumbling cosmos, Rush envisioned a world in which everyday life would be recast in terms of Christian republican virtue. Not surprisingly, Rush's immersion in reform radically altered his relationship to Presbyterianism. First signs of trouble appeared in 1785, when he accused John Ewing, pastor of the First Presbyterian Church, of "*lying, drunkenness, and unchristian language.*"[36] Political bickering in the churches irked him as well. Most of all, Rush became increasingly convinced that salvation was possible for all humankind, and that the Calvinist doctrine of limited election was antirepublican.

He formally severed his ties with the Presbyterians in 1787.[37] In a letter explaining his move, Rush indicated his new view of the relationship between the churches, religion, and American destiny. "I still wish to maintain a friendly connection with them," he wrote Ashbel Green, "and I heartily forgive them for all the injuries I have received from them, and I pray God to deliver them from the influence of bad men and to spare them to compose a part of the Redeemer's new empire in America." America as a sacred presence had become Rush's new church, beside which all others were minor sects whose truths were to be judged against the imperatives of American millennial mission. His reform program became the standard against which other views were to be judged. Indeed, it might be said that republican reform had become the ritual and symbolic content of this new church.[38]

Having broken with Presbyterianism, Rush felt freer to attack its theological essence. For instance, when in 1788 his tract against capital punishment drew fire from a Boston minister, Rush condemned the minister's response as one based upon "severe Calvinistical principles" and rejected them in no uncertain terms. "It is impossible to advance human happiness," he wrote Jeremy Belknap, "while we believe the Supreme being to possess the passions of weak or wicked men and govern our conduct by such opinions." He then quoted Luke 9:56 to support his reform vision—"The Son of Man came not to destroy men's *lives*, but to *save* them"—and argued that the passage refuted "all the arguments that ever were offered in favor of slavery, war, and capital punishment."[39]

Rush's exasperation with the churches surfaced again in 1791, as he and others helped Philadelphia's blacks to establish their own church. Rush expected little from white congregations. "The clergy and their faithful followers of every denomination," he noted bitterly, "are *too good* to *do good.*" He had already seen Quakers object to blacks making temporary use of a Friends' schoolhouse for worship because part of the service consisted of singing psalms. Rush slyly predicted that most help would "come from the Deists, swearing captains of vessels, and brokers of our city." Over a year later, reporting on the progress of the black church project to Jeremy Belknap, he noted that "the old and established societies look shy at them." Rush drew a succinct lesson from this and similar encounters: "To feel or to exercise the true Spirit of the Gospel nowadays seems to require a total separation from all sects, for they seem more devoted to their forms or opinions than to the doctrines and precepts of Jesus Christ."[40]

His own republican vision had crystallized even as he lost faith in formal churches. "Republicanism is a part of the truth of Christianity," he declared in 1791. "It derives its power from its source. It teaches us to view our rulers in their *true* light." A year later he added that the Bible was against all kinds of monarchy, whether kingly or "whether found in the absurd ideas of apostolic succession or in the aristocracy of Presbyterianism." The republican belief in the universal love of God for all humankind, which Rush saw as prevailing more and more in America, promised both a spiritual and "a temporal kingdom in the Millennium." That hope had become the basis of a "new principle of action prompting a practical godliness." Monarchy, slavery, war, intemperance, ignorance, capital punishment, punishment of any sort the result of which was not reformation: all these would "speedily end" as men and women became instruments for good. "In the meanwhile let us not be idle with such prospects before our eyes," he declared to Jeremy Belknap. "Heaven works by instruments, and even supernatural prophecies are fulfilled by natural means." Millennium was to be made, and neither backward churches nor the devil could deter those, like Rush, who wished to make it. "It is possible we may not live to witness the approaching regeneration of our world," he continued, "but the more active we are in bringing it about, the more fitted we shall be for that world where justice and benevolence eternally prevail."[41]

Retreat from Republican Millennialism

Even as Rush brought together the republican radiant strands of his Christian republican vision, however, darker signs began to appear. Indeed, if the 1780s had been the moment of millennial dreaming, the 1790s became the time of that dream's undoing. On the national scene, controversies over economic policy and the ratification of Jay's Treaty, and heated battles between the political parties, augured badly for Rush's vision of republican government. Violent opposition in the form of the Whisky Rebellion further threw the great experiment in doubt, as did news that the once-admired French Revolution had turned into a bloodbath. In Rush's own Philadelphia, the year 1793 brought a four-month siege of yellow fever, with recurrences in 1794, 1797, and 1798. Rush devoted every waking hour to the treatment of victims and the search for a cure. Controversy over his approach to the fever, in both theory and practice, led to a protracted libel suit. As early as 1793, Rush began to turn to Jeremiah rather than Revelation for inspiration. "The language of heaven in the wars, famine, and pestilence which now prevail more or less all over the world," he wrote to a friend, "seems to be 'Seekest thou great things? Seek them not, for behold, I bring evil on all flesh.'"[42]

By 1798, Rush had begun to separate the religious from the political visions, which he had merged in Christian republicanism, and to move toward religious as opposed to political and social solutions. He said as much to Noah Webster, sympathizing with Webster's bleak Federalist assessment of the world but observing that "it seem[ed] to be reserved to Christianity alone to produce universal, moral, political, and physical happiness." Rush predicted "nothing but suffering to the human race" as long as the world embraced "paganism, deism, and atheism." Eight years later he wrote in despair to John Adams, "All systems of political order and happiness seem of later years to have disappointed their founders and advocates. Civilization, science, and commerce have long ago failed in their attempts to improve the condition of mankind, and even liberty itself, from which more was expected than from all other human means, has lately appeared to be insufficient for that purpose."[43]

Rush was not alone in his retreat from Revolutionary millennialism. The 1790s and early 1800s witnessed a similar move among many ministers who had once preached a millennialism focused on the American Revolution and its role in cosmic history. Now they, like Rush, withdrew from politics and turned to a premillennial vision in which the woeful events of the period—domestic political strife and the violence of France's revolution—became signs of the darkness that would threaten the Earth before the end of days. What mattered now was faith in God, not the futile political ideas of human beings. Yet unlike Rush, the churches and their ministers transformed this retreat into a plan of victory. Rejecting politics as the road to the millennium, they now saw the conversion of the world as the instrument of American destiny and began an earnest campaign of Bible distribution as well as foreign and domestic missions to preach the gospel.[44]

Rush certainly supported the propagation of the faith. In fact, he was instrumental in the founding of Philadelphia's first Sunday school in 1791. In 1808, he helped form a local Bible society.[45] But his heart was not in such efforts, certainly not compared to his zeal for republican reform. A political vision had sparked his life's work and his millennial hopes, and no campaign simply to save souls could possibly compare.

During the War of 1812, Rush found new reasons to condemn the nation. His great hopes for marshalling the resources of American society under the banner of republicanism, with a common language and a common set of values, had disappeared. Party strife, the war itself, and distance from the Revolution had all exacerbated the worst tendencies in the American system. Writing again to Adams, he imagined the nation as a ship "manned by sailors of six different nations. . . . Suppose the ship to be over-taken by a storm," he continued, "and the captain and mates to be able to speak the language of but one class of the sailors. What do you suppose would be the fate of that ship?" His despair drove him back to the Calvinism of his youth, and in particular to Samuel Finley's sermon *On the Madness of Mankind.* "The present times," he lamented, "have added many facts in support of his position."[46]

In March 1813, Rush asked Thomas Jefferson, as a "sincere old friend of 1775," a simple but chastening question: "From the present complexion of affairs in our country, are you not disposed at times to repent of your solicitude and labors and sacrifices during our Revolutionary struggle for liberty and independence?" Five weeks later Rush died. He was buried in the graveyard at Christ Church, whose bells had once proclaimed the Grand Federal Procession but now tolled in mourning for a founder of the republic.[47]

Rush's retreat from reform, his return to the mood if not the theology of Calvinism, and his bitter sense of the nation's future were more the result of crushed hopes than of disastrous realities. Rush had dreamed an implausible dream, the transformation of a diverse and unsettled people into a unified nation whose hallmark would be personal, social, and political virtue. He compounded that folly by seeking such a goal under the banner of republicanism, which in its practical constitutional form insured the kind of individual freedom that made his task well-nigh impossible.

Rush's reform ideas, however, were neither simple folly nor mean-spirited attempts at social control. Rather they echoed an enduring theme in American life, the relation of mission to American identity. As early as the seventeenth century, Puritan ministers had begun preaching jeremiads, warning their flocks that God's wrath would be visited upon them should they forsake what historian Perry Miller highlighted as their "errand into the wilderness." Implicit in the warning was a celebration of chosenness, indeed the creation and reinforcement of a very special relationship to God. By expressing what were ultimately religious concerns in terms of social and medical issues, Rush created a language for the jeremiad suited to a post-Revolutionary America that endorsed pluralism and religious toleration. A new American civil religion had found its critic from within, even if in the 1780s and 1790s few were listening.

In 1798, as Rush reflected upon his growing disillusionment, he could find but one source of hope. "New England may escape the storm which impends our globe," he wrote, "but if she does, it will only be by adhering to the religious principles and moral habits of the first settlers of that country."[48] No doubt he had in mind a holding action conducted by a saving remnant of the republic, yet he had unwittingly identified the region that would give birth to new reform endeavors. Ironies abounded, for New England's nurturing of antebellum reform had much to do with its religious establishment's struggles against pluralism. Reform grew not only from a naive revolutionary zeal but also from the same despair that had poisoned Rush's fondest dreams. Finally, rather than remaining the project of one man, it came to define the work of a significant minority of New Englanders and others who grew up in the forty years prior to the Civil War. Instead of perishing in the anarchy Rush perceived all around him, little more than a decade after his death the dream of a Christian republic reappeared with a holy vengeance.

Notes

1. This chapter was originally published in Robert H. Abzug, *Cosmos Crumbling: American Reform and the Religious Imagination* (New York: Oxford University Press, 1994), 3–29, 233–37, and is reprinted by permission of Oxford University Press, Inc.

2. The most complete account of the parade is in Francis Hopkinson, "An Account of the Grand Federal Process: Performed at Philadelphia on Friday the Fourth of July, 1788," in Hopkinson, *Miscellaneous Essays* (Philadelphia, 1792), 2:349–401.

3. Benjamin Rush, letter to Elias Boudinot (?), Philadelphia, Jul. 9, 1788, in *Letters of Benjamin Rush*, ed. L. H. Butterfield (Princeton, N.J.: Princeton University Press, 1951), 1:470–77 (hereinafter *Letters*). The best biography of Benjamin Rush is David Freeman Hawke, *Benjamin Rush: Revolutionary Gadfly* (Indianapolis: Bobbs-Merrill, 1971).

4. "An Address to the People of the United States . . . on the Defects of the Confederation" (1787), quoted in Donald J. D'Elia, *Benjamin Rush: Philosopher of the American Revolution*, Transactions of the American Philosophical Society, new series, vol. 64, part 5 (Philadelphia: American Philosophical Society, 1974), 5. D'Elia presents a brilliant exposition of Rush's Christian republican vision, one that was extremely helpful in formulating this chapter. John M. Kloos provides an extensive treatment of Rush's religious views and their connection to his political ideas and actions in *A Sense of Deity: The Republican Spirituality of Dr. Benjamin Rush* (New York: Carlson, 1991).

5. D'Elia, *Rush*, 9–10. I wish to emphasize at this point the central significance in the Rush literature of D'Elia's work, which more than any other explores and finds significance in Rush's religious life. For a study that looks at Rush from another angle, see Melvin Yazawa, *From Colonies to Commonwealth: Familial Ideology and the Beginnings of the American Republic* (Baltimore: Johns Hopkins University Press, 1985), especially 137–65. For samples of two sides of Tennent's preaching, see *The Unsearchable Riches of Christ* (1737), in *The Great Awakening: Documents Illustrating the Crisis and Its Consequences*, ed. Alan Heimert and Perry Miller (Indianapolis: Bobbs-Merrill, 1967), 14–19; and *The Danger of an Unconverted Ministry* (1740), in Heimert and Miller, *Great Awakening*, 71–99.

6. Samuel Finley, *Christ Triumphing, and Satan Raging* (1741), in Heimert and Miller, *Great Awakening*, 152–67.

7. Rush, letter to Enoch Green, Philadelphia, 1761, in *Letters*, 1:3; Davies quoted in Hawke, *Rush*, 21.

8. Rush, "Travels through Life," in *The Autobiography of Benjamin Rush: His "Travels Through Life" Together with His Commonplace Book for 1789–1813*, ed. George W. Corner (Princeton, N.J.: Princeton University Press, 1948), 164. Rush, letter to Ebenezer Hazard, Philadelphia, Aug. 2, 1764, in *Letters*, 1:7; Hawke, *Rush*, 41.

9. Rush, letter to Enoch Green, Philadelphia, 1761.

10. Rush, "Travels through Life," 164.

11. George W. Corner, ed., *Autobiography of Benjamin Rush*, 46.

12. A Pennsylvanian [Benjamin Rush], *An Address to the Inhabitants of the British Settlements, on the Slavery of the Negroes in America* (Philadelphia, 1773).

13. Rush's millennial vision, implicit at first, developed quickly during the war and after. Hawke appears to view millennialism at work in Rush's worldview from the beginning. See Hawke, *Rush*, 134.

14. A Pennsylvanian [Benjamin Rush], *An Address to the Inhabitants*, 25–28 and passim. Though one of the earliest and most influential of antislavery tracts of the period, it certainly was not the only one. Quakers, Calvinists, freethinkers such as Jefferson and Paine all campaigned in varying degrees and with various arguments against slavery.

15. See Nathan O. Hatch, *The Sacred Cause of Liberty: Republican Thought and the Millennium in Revolutionary New England* (New Haven, Conn.: Yale University Press, 1977), and Ruth H. Bloch, *Visionary Republic: Millennial Themes in American Thought, 1756–1800* (Cambridge: Cambridge University Press, 1985), esp. 53–115.

16. See Charles Royster, *A Revolutionary People at War: The Continental Army and American Character, 1775–1783* (Chapel Hill: University of North Carolina Press, 1979), 179–85, 146–47; Rush, letter to Patrick Henry, York town, Jan. 12, 1778, in *Letters*, 1:117. Rush's introduction of the parallel with Moses and the Exodus suggests another interesting aspect of his vision of the Revolution, that it was as much a historical as a metahistorical drama. The parallel with historical Israel was much more prevalent in New England preaching and polity, and suggests yet another way in which Rush, though not a New Englander, forged a link between millennium and governance more typical of that region and a key to its leadership in the creation of antebellum reform. See Michael Walzer, *Exodus and Revolution* (New York: Basic Books, 1985), for a fascinating essay that surveys the use of the Exodus archetype in political movements.

17. Royster, *A Revolutionary People*, 236; Rush, letter to Anthony Wayne, Philadelphia, Sep. 29, 1776, in *Letters*, 1:117; Rush, letter to John Adams, Philadelphia, Jul. 13, 1780, in *Letters*, 1:253.

18. Benjamin Rush, "The Influence of Physical Causes upon the Moral Faculty," in *The Selected Writings of Benjamin Rush*, ed. Dagobart D. Runes (New York: Philosophical Library, 1947), 92 (hereinafter *Writings*).

19. "Of the Mode of Education Proper in a Republic," in Writings, 87–89.
20. Ibid., 92.
21. Ibid. For some very interesting discussions of Rush's wonderfully evocative phrase "convert men into republican machines," see Yazawa, From Colonies to Commonwealth, 141–65; Michael Kammen, People of Paradox: An Inquiry Concerning the Origins of American Civilization (New York: Knopf, 1972), 72–75; and David Tyack, "Forming the National Character: Paradox in the Educational Thought of the Revolutionary Generation," Harvard Educational Review 36 (1966): 29–41.
22. "Of the Mode of Education Proper in a Republic," in Writings, 93–95. Especially as regarded language, Rush's advocacy in many ways paralleled that of his friend Noah Webster.
23. Ibid., 91–92.
24. Ibid., 95–96. Thus Rush, along with some others, pioneered the idea of the "moral mother" that became such a key element of antebellum conceptions of gender role. See Ruth H. Bloch, "American Feminine Ideals in Transition: The Rise of the Moral Mother, 1785–1815," Feminist Studies 4 (1978): 101–26.
25. "Education Agreeable to a Republican Form of Government," in Writings, 97–100; "Plan of a Federal University," in Writings, 101–5.
26. "The Amusements and Punishments Which Are Proper for Schools," in Writings, 106–7.
27. Ibid., 107–9.
28. Ibid.
29. Ibid., 109–14.
30. Ibid., 113–14.
31. "To the Editor of the Pennsylvania Journal: Against Spirituous Liquors," in Letters, 1:270–2.
32. Rush limited his assaults to distilled liquor. Wine and beer he categorized as relatively harmless and in fact often of "friendly influence upon health and life." See Rush, "The Effects of Ardent Spirits upon Man," in Writings, 334. This is the most readily available version of the original anti-liquor pamphlet.
33. Ibid., 334–41.
34. Ibid., 339–40.
35. Rush, letter to Thomas Jefferson, Philadelphia, Feb. 4, 1797, in Letters, 2:786 and 786n.
36. Rush, letter to Ashbel Green, Aug. 11, 1787, in Letters, 1:433–34.
37. Ibid.
38. Ibid., 434. In developing this vision of America, Rush had been greatly influenced by the Universalist writer Elhanan Winchester, whose millennial vision extended to all and whose own odyssey from Congregational to Baptist to Universalist beliefs may have helped Rush's own break with Presbyterians. See

Bloch, *Visionary Republic*, 123–31, 209–10; and Stephen A. Marini, *Radical Sects of Revolutionary New England* (Cambridge, Mass.: Harvard University Press, 1982), 69–71.

39. Rush, letter to Jeremy Belknap, Philadelphia, Oct. 7, 1788, in *Letters*, 1:488.

40. Rush, letter to Julia Rush, Philadelphia, Jul. 16, 1791, and Rush, letter to Jeremy Belknap, Philadelphia, Jun. 21, 1792, in *Letters*, 1:600, 620–21.

41. Rush, letter to Jeremy Belknap, Jun. 6, 1791, in *Letters*, 1:584; Rush, letter to Jeremy Belknap, Jun. 21, 1792, in *Letters*, 1:620; Rush, letter to Elhanan Winchester, Philadelphia, May 11, 1791, in *Letters*, 1:582.

42. Rush, letter to James Kidd, Philadelphia, Nov. 25, 1793, in *Letters*, 2:746.

43. Rush, letter to Horatio Gates, Philadelphia, Dec. 26, 1795, in *Letters*, 2:767–68; Rush, letter to John Dickinson, Philadelphia, Oct. 11, 1797, in *Letters*, 2:793; Rush, letter to Noah Webster, Jul. 20, 1798, in *Letters*, 2:799; Rush, letter to John Adams, Philadelphia, Jun. 10, 1806, in *Letters*, 2:799.

44. See Bloch, *Visionary Republic*, 119–231.

45. Charles I. Foster, *An Errand of Mercy: The Evangelical United Front, 1790–1837* (Chapel Hill: University of North Carolina Press, 1960), 158; Clifford S. Griffin, *Their Brothers' Keepers: Moral Stewardship in the United States, 1800–1865* (New Brunswick, N.J.: Rutgers University Press, 1960), 26, 29.

46. Rush, letter to John Adams, Philadelphia, Aug. 21, 1812, in *Letters*, 2:1160–61; Rush, letter to John Adams, Philadelphia, Aug. 8, 1812, in *Letters*, 2:1159.

47. Rush, letter to Thomas Jefferson, Philadelphia, Mar. 15, 1813, in *Letters*, 2:1189.

48. Rush, letter to Noah Webster, Jul. 20, 1798, in *Letters*, 2:799.

CHAPTER 11

Roger Sherman

An Old Puritan in a New Nation

MARK DAVID HALL

By any measure, Roger Sherman is a forgotten founder. He is virtually unknown to the American public, and history and government professors know little about him other than that he helped craft the Connecticut Compromise. Yet as Daniel L. Dreisbach suggests, Sherman deserves to be better known.[1] He served with distinction in a variety of state and national offices, and was the only founder to help draft and sign the Declaration and Resolves (1774), the Articles of Association (1774), the Declaration of Independence (1776), the Articles of Confederation (1777, 1778), and the Constitution (1787). Like Thomas Jefferson, he authored a significant state law concerning religious liberty, and, unlike Jefferson, he participated in debates over the First Amendment. Accordingly, it is striking that when U.S. Supreme Court justices have used history to interpret the First Amendment's religion clauses, they have made 112 distinct references to Jefferson but have mentioned Sherman only 3 times.[2] This invites the questions whether Jefferson merits the attention the justices have lavished upon him and whether Sherman's role (and the roles played by many others) in crafting the constitutional provisions governing church-state relations has been properly acknowledged.

I begin this essay by providing a brief overview of Sherman's life and discussing how he has been treated in the scholarly literature. I then explore his faith and how his theological convictions informed his political ideas and actions. I conclude by focusing on his views of religious liberty and church-state relations. My central argument is that Sherman was a sincere, orthodox Christian in the Reformed theological tradition who embraced religious toleration and thought it appropriate for the state and national governments to promote Christianity.[3] Although his approach to church-state relations may seem parochial or even illiberal today, if the founders' views are relevant for contemporary jurisprudence, then justices should not ignore Sherman.[4] More broadly, scholars who wish to understand the founding era need to consider his contributions to the creation of the American republic.

A Life in Brief

Roger Sherman was born in Massachusetts in 1721 to Mehetabel and William Sherman. William was a farmer and cordwainer, and like many of his fellow citizens he was Congregationalist. William died in 1741, and shortly thereafter Roger moved to New Milford, Connecticut, where he worked as a cordwainer, surveyor, and store owner. He taught himself advanced mathematics, and in 1750 he used his new skills to calculate tables for *Astronomical diary, or, An almanack for the year of our Lord Christ, 1750*. Until 1761, Sherman published annual almanacs containing his tables, moral aphorisms, and other useful information. He also taught himself law, and he was admitted to the Litchfield bar in 1754. Under the guidance of Roger and his older brother, two younger Sherman brothers, Nathaniel and Josiah, attended the College of New Jersey (Princeton), graduating in 1753 and 1754 respectively. They both became Congregational ministers.

As Sherman prospered professionally, he was selected for a variety of local offices and was elected to several six-month terms in the lower house of Connecticut's General Assembly. In 1760, after the death of his first wife (with whom he had seven children), Sherman moved to New Haven. There he opened a store next to Yale College and sold general merchandise, provisions, and books. Sherman married Rebecca Prescott three years later, and the two had eight children. He was again elected to local offices and the lower house of the General Assembly, and in 1766 Connecticut voters chose him to be one of the twelve members of the upper house, or Council of Assistants. Traditionally, four Assistants were selected by the General Assembly to serve with the deputy governor as the judges on Connecticut's Superior Court. Sherman was appointed to this court in 1766, and he held both offices until the legislature separated them in 1785—at which point he chose to remain a Superior Court judge. He retained this position until he became a member of the U.S. House of Representatives in 1789.

Beginning in 1774, Sherman accepted multiple appointments to the Continental Congress. Collectively, he served 1,543 days in that body, more than all but four other men.[5] He was an early advocate of independence because of what he perceived to be Great Britain's move toward tyranny. John Adams wrote that he was "one of the most sensible men in the world. The clearest head and the steadiest heart. . . . one of the soundest and strongest pillars of the revolution."[6] Sherman helped draft and signed Congress's Declaration and Resolves (1774) and Articles of Association (1774), and he was on the five-person committee that drafted the Declaration of Independence (1776). He also served on the committee that drafted the Articles of Confederation, where he famously argued that representation in Congress should be based on both states and population.[7] His suggestion was rejected, although under his leadership it was later incorporated into the U.S. Constitution.

In 1783, Sherman and the aptly named Richard Law accepted the task of revising all of Connecticut's statutes.[8] Four years later, Sherman was appointed to the Federal Constitutional Convention. In spite of his age, he was an active member, speaking more times than all but three delegates and serving as the driving force behind the Connecticut Compromise. Recent studies of the convention suggest that Sherman was among the most effective delegates. Indeed, political scientist David Brian Robertson shows that Sherman often outmaneuvered Madison and concludes that the "political synergy between Madison and Sherman . . . very well may have been necessary for the Constitution's adoption."[9] He was also a leader in Connecticut's ratification convention, and he wrote seven "Letters" for the *New Haven Gazette* responding to Anti-Federalists' objections.[10]

Under the new Constitution, Sherman was first elected to the House of Representatives (1789–1791) and then appointed to the U.S. Senate to fill the unexpired term of William Samuel Johnson (1791–1793). In Congress he played important roles in debates over the Bill of Rights, the assumption of state debts, and the creation of a national bank. Sherman died in Connecticut on July 23, 1793.

A Neglected Founder and a Neglected Faith

Given this impressive résumé, it is surprising that scholars have generally neglected Sherman. Of course he is mentioned in passing in studies on various aspects of the founding era, and American history and government texts often refer to him as author of the Connecticut Compromise. Yet few academics have considered his thoughts and actions in much depth. One exception is Christopher Collier, whose fine biography provides a rich account of Sherman's life in the context of state and national politics. Unfortunately, Collier does not carefully explore Sherman's political theory, and he neglects the significance of his theological convictions.[11] On balance, Scott Gerber's assessment that Sherman "is arguably the most under appreciated, not to mention the most under-studied, political leader of the American Founding" remains correct.[12]

This neglect is particularly interesting in light of the attention scholars have paid in recent years to religion's role in the founding.[13] A few historians have noted in passing that Sherman took his faith very seriously, but none of them has explored its significance in any detail. For instance, Sydney Ahlstrom, in his magisterial *A Religious History of the American People*, points to Sherman as evidence that "theological maturity abounds" in the founding era.[14] Similarly, Mark Noll, Nathan Hatch, and George Marsden refer to him as one of the few founders who "made life-long efforts to base their personal lives on biblical teaching."[15] More recently, James H. Hutson, after noting that "many of the founders were recognized as religious specialists," comments that "no one, perhaps, eclipsed Roger Sherman."[16]

In spite of observations of this nature, historians writing books or articles on Sherman have tended to dismiss the significance of his religious beliefs. James German, for instance, describes Sherman as "ambitious, acquisitive, [and] avaricious" and argues that as a politician he "shifted his own opinions to suit those of his constituents."[17] Similarly, John Rommel proposes that Sherman joined a New Light church for political rather than theological reasons.[18] Collier mentions Sherman's religious views in passing, but he does not consider them in detail until a brief section in the last chapter of his book, where he writes that "one of Roger Sherman's most prominent characteristics was his compromising temper. Indeed, expedience is a hallmark of his political career. His lapses from flexibility were few. Perhaps, however, it is to be expected that a man over seventy would develop some rigidities, especially in religion, and Sherman's part in the New Divinity fracas that rumbled through Connecticut in the late eighties and nineties is most uncharacteristic."[19]

Sherman's Faith

Collier may have arrived at this conclusion because the most extensive documents penned by Sherman concerning theological issues were written after 1789. However, this fact tells scholars little, as relatively few of Sherman's early papers have survived. As Daniel L. Dreisbach points out, this is one reason an important founder like Sherman has been neglected by scholars.[20] In spite of the lack of documents, there are early letters that reveal a serious concern for theology. Moreover, careful consideration of the corpus of his writings, in addition to his life and actions, provides abundant support for the conclusion of Ezra Stiles, president of Yale and Sherman's neighbor, that he was "an exemplary for Piety & serious Religion."[21]

Sherman was raised in a Congregational church in Stoughton, Massachusetts. His modern biographers all mention that he was likely educated, to some extent, by its minister, Samuel Dunbar. However, they do not consider the implications of this possibility or the significance of Dunbar's ministerial influence on Sherman's spiritual and intellectual formation. Dunbar (1704–1783), a protégé of Cotton Mather and a 1723 graduate of Harvard, was fluent in Latin and Greek, and, like many ministers in this era, he likely supplemented his income by teaching. He arrived in Stoughton to pastor the Congregational church in 1727, and he remained there until his death. Because the town's first school was not established until 1735, by which time Sherman was fourteen years old, it is probable that he was educated, at least in part, by Dunbar.[22] This would help explain how a cordwainer had the educational foundation to teach himself surveying, publishing, and law and, eventually, to rise to be one of the founding era's most significant statesmen.

Even if Dunbar did not serve as Sherman's tutor, he was his pastor, and in an eighteenth-century Congregational church this role included a great deal of teaching. George F. Piper notes that a sermon written by Dunbar in the forty-ninth year of his ministry is numbered 8,059, which suggests he composed an average of 164 sermons a year, or more than three a week. If this figure is accurate, before he moved to New Milford, Sherman could have heard as many as 2,460 of Dunbar's sermons.[23]

But what sort of man was Dunbar? According to Jason Haven, who preached his funeral sermon, Dunbar was

> a zealous defender of what he took to be "the faith once delivered to the saints." He treated much on what have been called the peculiar doctrines of grace; these he considered as doctrines according to godliness. . . . He was, on proper occasions, a *Son of Thunder*, endeavoring, by these terrors of the law, to awaken secure and hardened sinners, to point out to them the dreadful danger of a course of sin and impenitency. But he knew how happily to change his voice, and to become a Son of Consolation, and by the soft winning charms of the gospel to lead weary souls to Christ for rest and to comfort those that are cast down.[24]

Dunbar's surviving sermons indicate that he was a conservative Calvinist who emphasized the sovereignty of God and the sinfulness of man. He opposed the revivalism of the Great Awakening because he thought it put too much emphasis on human agency. Like all Calvinists of the era, he believed ministers should provide guidance on political matters.[25]

Dunbar served as chaplain for a regiment in the French and Indian War in 1755, and he quickly joined American opposition to what he deemed tyrannical British actions in the 1770s. When the Suffolk Congress met in Stoughton on August 16, 1774, Dunbar opened the meeting in a prayer that was, according to a contemporary witness, "the most extraordinary liberty-prayer that I ever heard. He appeared to have a most divine, if not prophetical, enthusiasm in favor of our rights."[26]

Dunbar, like many Congregationalist clergy, was serious about his faith, embraced Reformed theology, and was extremely sensitive about the possibility of ungodly rulers infringing upon colonial liberties. Of course one cannot simply impute the views of a pastor/teacher onto a parishioner/student, but at a minimum Dunbar's ministry shines light on the environment in which Sherman was raised. Moreover, in the context of the pattern of evidence described below, it is reasonable to attribute at least part of Sherman's commitment to a Reformed understanding of Christianity and politics to his early minister and teacher.

A few months after joining Dunbar's church, Sherman moved to New Milford, Connecticut, and transferred his church membership to the local Congregational church. Joining a Congregational church in the mid-eighteenth century was not simply a formality, and churches made every effort to elect only pious men to be church leaders (unlike Anglican churches in the South, where local gentry were routinely appointed to be church leaders regardless of their devotion to the faith). Sherman was by all appearances an active member of the church and a godly man. He was appointed deacon "upon trial" in 1755 and an "established deacon" in 1757. He was regularly elected clerk, and he served on a variety of committees, including the school committee.[27]

After moving to New Haven in 1761, Sherman transferred his church membership to White Haven, a New Light Congregational church. A product of the First Great Awakening, New Light churches generally rejected the halfway covenant whereby children of church members were considered to be church members. Instead, New Lights insisted that in order to become a church member, one should be able to articulate his or her own conversion experience. Although "New" implies "progressive," in this case it meant embracing a stricter and more enthusiastic version of Calvinism.

In 1769, Jonathan Edwards Jr. was appointed minister of Sherman's church. Like his more famous father, Edwards's emphasis on theology and concern for piety had a tendency to drive away parishioners. Ezra Stiles estimated that White Haven had 480 members in 1772, but that by 1789 the number had shrunk to "nineteen men and their families."[28] Edwards's biographer contends that "the major reason he was not dismissed in the late 1780's or early 1790's was because he received strong support from Roger Sherman."[29] Among other things, Sherman wrote several letters defending Edwards's theological positions and his conduct.[30]

As in Connecticut's churches, divisions between New and Old Lights were prominent at Yale College in the 1760s. Shortly after President Thomas Clap switched allegiance to the New Lights, he appointed Roger Sherman to be Yale's treasurer. Sherman served in this position from 1765 to 1776. Like other officers of the college, Sherman presumably had to subscribe to the Westminster Catechism, the Saybrook Confession of Faith, and, particularly, "give Satisfaction to them [the trustees] of the Soundness of their Faith in opposition to Armenian and prelaitical Corruptions or any other Dangerous Consequence to the Purity and Peace of our Churches."[31] According to Ezra Stiles, Yale's president from 1778 to 1795, Sherman was "ever a Friend to its [Yale's] Interests, & to its being & continuing in the Hands of the Clergy, whom he judged the most proper to have the Superintendendy of a *religious* as well as a *scientific* College."[32] Sherman's last public act was presiding over laying a foundation stone for a new building at Yale on April 15, 1793.[33]

In addition to his active involvement in churches and Yale, Sherman's writings give no reason to doubt his commitment to orthodox Christianity or, more specifically, Reformed theology. Many of these writings, it is true, are not explicitly religious. For instance, among Sherman's earliest surviving publications are his almanacs.[34] These primarily contain mathematical charts concerning agriculture and the weather, but like other almanacs they also have a healthy dose of proverbs—many with moral and/or religious overtones. Sherman borrowed most of these

proverbs, although he may have composed some himself.[35] Many of them
are generic enough to be acceptable to virtuous men and women everywhere, but some reflect contemporary Reformed notions of the sinfulness of man, national accountability, and the necessity of having godly
men in government. Examples include:

> The Times wherein we live are very bad:
> Let's every one mend our Ways, and we shall soon see
>   better Days. (1751)
> A faithful man in public is a Pillar in a Nation. (1751)
> Self Interest will turn some mens opinions as certainly
>   as the wind will a weather cock. (1753)
> Profaness Intemperance & Injustice presage Calamitious
>   Times. (1753)
> A timely Reformation,
> Wo'd save our Land & Nation. (1758)
> All seek Happiness; but many take wrong Courses to
>   obtain it. (1761)[36]

Sherman's last almanac was published in 1761, and many of his
surviving writings between then and 1789 concern political topics. A
careful reading of these texts reveals the influence of his faith on his
political ideas and actions. This is not to say, however, that all of Sherman's early writings lack an interest in theology proper. For example, in
1772 he wrote a letter to theologian Joseph Bellamy attacking his position that "the covenant between a Minister & People" lasts only at the
"people's pleasure." Instead, Sherman argued on legal, scriptural, and
moral grounds that the covenant between a minister and his congregation cannot be broken except by mutual consent, unless the minister is
unable to fulfill his duties, or for reasons of "Apostacy, Heresy, and Immorality."[37] In spite of letters of this nature, Sherman's later writings are
more explicitly theological than his early ones. Most significant among
the former are his 1789 A Short Sermon on the Duty of Self Examination,
Preparatory to Receiving the Lord's Supper, his 1791 letter to Dr. Nathan Williams on infant baptism and church membership, and his 1790 debate
with Samuel Hopkins.

Sherman's sermon, which according to President Stiles was published but never preached, addressed the question of how a believer should examine himself or herself before receiving the communion.[38] He made five major points, which he summarized in a passage worth quoting at length:

> If upon a careful examination we find, that we have a competent understanding of the gospel way of life by Jesus Christ, and of the nature, use and design of this holy institution of the supper: —If we do heartily repent of all our sins, bewailing them before God, with a deep rooted hatred of, and turning from them to the Lord, and the practice of his commandments: If we sincerely acknowledge Jesus Christ to be our Lord and master, believing him to be an all sufficient and infinitely suitable Saviour, as well as unspeakably willing even for us, and do [constantly?] desire as be interested in, and devoted to him upon the terms of the gospel: with a cheerful confidence in his power and grace for salvation.—If we have reason to think we have that love to God and Christ which is a spring of charity and obedience and at the same time are of [two illegible words] obliging disposition toward our fellow-men and especially our fellow christians; if we are conscious that we use our honest endeavors to live in obedience to all God's commands; and if we have any due sense of our spiritual wants, that we are in ourselves, poor and miserable, wretched and blind and naked. I say, if we can answer such enquiries as these in the affirmative . . . we ought to come and eat of this bread and drink of this wine.[39]

In this brief passage, and throughout the thirteen-page sermon, Sherman's commitment to Reformed Christianity is clear. He leaves no doubt that he believed humans are in "a state of depravity, guilt and misery, exposed to the eternal curse of the law;—dead in trespass and sins;—by nature prone to evil and adverse to good, and unable to deliver ourselves."[40] He contended that the only hope humans have for deliverance is "faith in Jesus," by which he meant that "we receive it for an undoubted truth that Jesus Christ was made an atoning sacrifice for sin."[41] Christians are required to act in a moral manner, but their ability to do so is a result of having been redeemed by Christ's work; it is not a cause of their salvation. Like Jonathan Edwards Sr., he discussed morality in terms of a "love of benevolence" that "is due to all mankind, but in an especial manner" to Christian brothers and sisters.[42]

Sherman attached to his sermon extracts from the *Works* of the English Puritan Richard Baxter (1615–1691). In these excerpts, Baxter argued that infant baptism makes one a member of the church, but that it is necessary for adults to make a profession of faith in order to receive communion.[43] Dr. Nathan Williams wrote a nineteen-page letter to Sherman objecting to a number of elements in these excerpts, especially the necessity for adults to make a profession of faith in order to be admitted to the Lord's Supper and to enjoy other privileges of adult membership in the church.[44] Sherman wrote back, noting that responses from "Dr. Witherspoon, Dr. Stiles, Dr. Wales and several other Ministers" raised no concern about the extracts and that they are in accord with "the general usage of the Congregational Churches in New England." He proceeded to argue that Baxter fleshes out his argument significantly, but stipulated that "I do not think that his, or any other man's opinion is of any authority in the case, unless supported by the word of God." Sherman then offered a lengthy response where he made a variety of scriptural arguments to support Baxter's claims.[45] The details of these arguments need not concern us now; the significant point is that Sherman, like all good Reformed Christians, relied on the Bible, which is, as he noted in an earlier letter, "the only rule of faith in matters of religion."[46]

The most sophisticated theological discussion in which Sherman participated was with Jonathan Edwards's disciple, Samuel Hopkins— founder of the system of theology that bears his name but perhaps better known as the elderly minister in Harriet Beecher Stowe's *The Minister's Wooing* (1859). In 1790, Sherman wrote Hopkins a letter dissenting from two points in his *An Inquiry into the Nature of True Holiness* (1773). Notably, he disagreed with Hopkins's characterization of self-love and his proposition that "it is the duty of a person to be *willing* to give up his eternal interest for the Glory of God."[47] In his criticisms, Sherman demonstrated the ability to engage one of America's most prominent theologians in a sophisticated debate about the nuances of Reformed theology. This assertion is best supported by reading the debate in full, but it is illustrated by the following passage from one of Sherman's letters:

> You do not here distinguish between *occasion and positive cause* though you make a material distinction between them in your sermons on "Sin the *occasion* of great good." President Edwards I think has illustrated this point in his answer to Dr. Taylor on original sin, and in a sermon published with this life, on the enquiry, why natural men are enemies to God. He supposes original righteousness in man was a supernatural principle which was withdrawn on his first transgression, and his natural principles of agency remaining, were exercised wrong, and his affections set on wrong objects in consequence of such withdrawment.[48]

This brief excerpt reveals that Sherman was familiar with key analytical distinctions in Edwards's and Hopkins's works, and that he was interested in theology proper (not just religious ideas or scriptural exegesis— although he was concerned with them as well).[49] His interest in these subjects is illustrated well by the list of books contained in his library at the time of his death, of which about a third (about fifty books) consist of Bibles, concordances, catechisms, confessions of faith, volumes of sermons, and works by prominent Reformed theologians.[50] Although Sherman was not an academic theologian, he clearly demonstrated, in the words of Sydney Ahlstrom, "theological maturity."[51] It seems highly unlikely that Sherman developed this grasp of Scripture and theology merely in his waning days. Moreover, glimpses of his life recorded by others suggest that he made a lifelong effort to live by his convictions.

Sherman's faith affected his political ideas and actions in significant ways, and it influenced his day-to-day life in ways that may seem quaint today. For instance, in 1774 Silas Deane, Sherman's fellow delegate to the Continental Congress, observed, much to his annoyance, that Sherman "is against sending our carriages over the ferry this evening, because it is Sunday; so we shall have a scorching sun to drive forty miles in to-morrow."[52] Similarly, Benjamin Rush recorded that Sherman "once objected to a motion for Congress sitting on a Sunday upon an occasion which he thought did not require it, and gave as a reason for his objection, a regard of the commands of his Maker." Rush also recalled what I take to be an attempt at biblical humor by Sherman: "Upon hearing of the defeat of the American army on Long Island, where they were entrenched and fortified by a chain of hills, he said to me in coming out of Congress 'Truly in vain is salvation hoped for from the hills, and from the multitude of mountains' (Jeremiah xii, 23)."[53]

In summary, Sherman was born into a pious Congregational family in which two of the four sons grew up to be ministers. He came of age under the tutelage of the Reverend Samuel Dunbar, a solid, Old Light Calvinist. He was elected to be an elder in his church and was appointed treasurer of Congregationalist Yale College. He engaged ministers and theologians in sophisticated theological debates, and he remained supportive of Jonathan Edwards Jr. after most of his church abandoned him. Throughout his political career, Sherman's political ideas and actions were significantly influenced by his faith. There is little reason to conclude, as some commentators have suggested, that Sherman simply turned to religion as an old man. Far more accurate is Yale President Timothy Dwight's view, penned in 1811, that "as a man, as a patriot, and as a Christian, Mr. Sherman left behind him an unspotted name. Profoundly versed in Theology, he held firmly to the doctrines of the Reformation. Few men understood them so well; and few were equally able to defend them. What he believed, he practiced. It can excite no wonder, therefore, that he died with bright hopes of a glorious immortality."[54]

Faith and Politics

Sherman's faith influenced his political ideas and actions in a variety of ways. Most obviously, he often appealed directly to Scripture when making political decisions and arguments. When serving in the Continental Congress, for instance, he led opposition to a congressional committee's proposal to increase the maximum number of lashes allowed for military discipline from one hundred to five hundred. John Sullivan reported in a letter to George Washington that "though a Great Majority of Congress were for it, the question was Lost" due to "principles Laid down by Levitical Law Strongly urged by Roger Shearman Esqr and Co."⁵⁵ Although the record does not specify it, Sherman's objection almost certainly stemmed from Deuteronomy 25:3: "Forty stripes he may give him, and not exceed: lest, if he should exceed, and beat him above these with many stripes, then thy brother should seem vile unto thee."

In a similar manner, in *Remarks on a Pamphlet Entitled "A Dissertation on the Political Union and Constitution of the Thirteen United States of North America"* (1784), Sherman paraphrased Acts 17:26, "That God hath made of one blood, all nations of the earth, and hath determined the bounds of their habitation," to defend the right of Native Americans to own the land on which they dwelt prior to the arrival of Europeans.⁵⁶ In this particular case, one can argue that Sherman used Scripture to support Connecticut's claim to lands purchased from the Native Americans.⁵⁷ While this political reality cannot be ignored, it should be noted that Sherman drew from this principle to inform his opposition to slavery—a position difficult to explain in terms of self-interest. Sherman's opposition to slavery was not just theoretical. His 1783 revision of Connecticut's statutes contained a gradual manumission law, which was approved in 1784, while he was still serving as an Assistant.⁵⁸ Similarly, in the Constitutional Convention he called the slave trade "iniquitous" and argued that there should not be a tax on imported slaves as "it implied they were *property.*" However, he was willing to compromise with the slave states in order to keep them in the union because he was convinced that slavery was a dying institution.⁵⁹

Sherman was not averse to appealing directly to Scripture, but he was more likely to rely upon biblical and theological principles when making political decisions. For example, his view of human nature as "vile" helped inform his opposition to concentrated power.⁶⁰ He thought that one important way of avoiding concentrated power is to limit the power of the national government, keep power at the local level, and require it to be exercised in public. He supported this position in his response to Pelatiah Webster by recommending to him

> *once more* to consult his bible, and duly weigh and consider the civil polity of the *Hebrews*, which was planned by Divine Wisdom, for the government of that people although their territory was small; by

preventing an undue monopoly of lands by their reversion to the original proprietors in the lineal descent of the families at the *jubilee*, (which was every half century) it supported vast numbers of inhabitants within very narrow limits—their laws were few and simple—their judges the elders of their cities, well acquainted with the credibility of the parties and their evidence—they held their courts in the places of greatest concourse, the gates of the city, and their processes were neither lengthy nor expensive.[61]

Of particular importance to Sherman was that governments pass laws that promote the common good. As Alan Heimert remarked with respect to evangelical ministers of the era (with whom Sherman had a great deal in common), "in their thought, the purposes of society and of government were one, and their very terms of discussion evinced the urgency with which all their thinking drove to the question of the 'general good.'"[62] Sherman's conviction that the government should promote the common good led him occasionally to reject positions embraced by colleagues more concerned with the protection of private property. For example, at the Constitutional Convention he objected to Rufus King's proposal to prohibit states from interfering with contracts because he "thought the States ought to retain this power in order to prevent suffering & injury to their poor."[63] Likewise, Sherman was one of the few Congressmen to oppose what became the Third Amendment to the Constitution on the grounds that "it was absolutely necessary that marching troops should have quarters, whether in time of peace or war, and that it ought not to be put in the power of an individual to obstruct the public service."[64] Finally, throughout his career he had no objection to sumptuary laws, believing them to encourage the common good. In "Remarks on a Pamphlet," he pointed to luxury as being the chief cause of the downfall of Rome and Great Britain and argued that the Continental Congress should place imposts upon luxuries.[65] Later, as a member of the House of Representatives, he supported an excise tax on distilled spirits because it would contribute to the "general welfare of the community" and "in itself is reasonable and just."[66]

In Sherman's mind, one of the most critical components with respect to the common good is the freedom to worship God in a society that promotes Christian morality. Sherman's willingness to tolerate other Christian traditions is evident as early as the 1750s when, much to the consternation of some of his readers, he inserted observable Days of the Church of England into his almanacs. When several customers complained, Sherman responded that while he felt free to not observe such days, "as I take Liberty in these Matters to judge for myself, so I think it reasonable that Others should have the same Liberty; and since my Design in this Performance is to serve the Publick, and the inserting of those observable Days does not croud out any Thing that might be more serviceable, I hope none of my Readers will be displeased with it for the Future."[67]

Throughout his life Sherman had good relations with his Anglican colleagues—although, as William Casto notes, this was not true with all Connecticut Calvinists.[68] Nevertheless, when Sherman perceived that the Church of England was attempting to impose its understanding of Christianity upon the colonies, he was among the first to raise the alarm. His most specific fear was that a bishop would be appointed for the colonies. As Sherman pointed out in a 1768 letter to William Samuel Johnson, the problem is "not that we are of intolerant principles, nor do we envy the Episcopalian church of the privileges of a Bishop for the purposes of ordination, confirmation, and inspecting the morals of their clergy, provided they have no kind of superiority over, nor power in any way to affect the civil or religious interest of other denominations, or derive any support from them."[69] His key concern was that a bishop would attempt to take over all of the churches within the colonies and set up tyrannical ecclesiastical courts. He went on to point out that "many of the first inhabitants of these Colonies were obliged to seek an asylum among savages in this wilderness in order to escape the tyranny of Archbishop Laud and others of his stamp. . . . We dread the consequences as oft we think of this danger [ecclesiastical tyranny]."[70]

Sherman's fears may seem excessive today, but to an eighteenth-century Calvinist they made perfect sense. Calvinists had often struggled against unfriendly governments, and New England Puritans had come to America precisely because they were unable to reform the Church of England completely. Throughout the eighteenth century some American Anglicans continued to argue that the Congregationalist and Presbyterian churches were not "true" churches because their ministers had not been ordained by bishops. New England Calvinists believed they had to be vigilant lest the Church of England gain control of their churches.[71] That Sherman shared this concern is evidenced by his paying for the publication of a book in 1767 by Noah Welles defending Presbyterian ordination.[72]

Sherman's fears of an Anglican bishop may suggest intolerance for non-Reformed branches of Christianity, but his concerns were always in the context of preventing religious tyranny. In practice, Sherman was remarkably tolerant of other Christians. Ezra Stiles remarked that he had no objection to Yale hiring a professor from France who was Roman Catholic.[73] Moreover, he was on the three-person committee who drew up instructions for commissioners being sent to Canada in hopes of convincing colonists there (particularly French Roman Catholics) to join the fight for independence. Among other things, the commissioners were charged to

> declare, that we hold sacred the rights of conscience, and may promise to the whole people, solemnly in our name, the free and undisturbed exercise of their religion; and, to the clergy, the full, perfect, and peaceable possession and enjoyment of all their estates; that the government of every thing relating to their religion and clergy, shall be left entirely in the hands of the good people of that province, and such legislature as they shall constitute; Provided, however, that all other denominations of Christians be equally entitled to hold offices, and enjoy civil privileges, and the free exercise of their religion, and be totally exempt from the payment of any tythes or taxes for the support of any religion.[74]

These instructions were adopted by Congress on March 20, 1776, and this and other messages were duly relayed to Canada. Unfortunately from the American perspective, they did not have their desired effect. Of course one must be careful not to read too much into this highly political letter, but Sherman's concern for the sacred rights of conscience is reflected as well in his work as a legislator, notably in his "An Act of Securing the

Rights of Conscience in Matters of Religion, to Christians of every Denomination in this State" (1783).

By the 1750s, Connecticut Anglicans, Quakers, Baptists, and Separatists had successfully argued that Parliament's 1689 Act of Toleration required the state to exempt them from compulsory attendance laws and paying taxes to support the established Congregational church. Moreover, they had the right to form societies to tax their own members to support their ministers if they so desired. Sherman's statute continued these exemptions and expanded them to include dissenters from every denomination. As with earlier laws, individuals wanting to take advantage of the act had to provide a certificate from leaders in their church to the clerk of the society with which they were affiliated. The statute is particularly significant as the first Connecticut law protecting religious liberty not required by the Act of Toleration or enacted out of fear that England would interfere with the state's charter.[75]

Sherman composed a preamble for the statute that reflects his view of religious liberty and church-state relations:

As the happiness of a People, and the good Order of Civil Society, essentially depend upon Piety, Religion and Morality, it is the Duty of the Civil Authority to provide for the Support and Encouragement thereof; so as that Christians of every Denomination, demeaning themselves peaceably, and as good Subjects of the State, may be equally under the Protection of the Laws: And as the People of this State have in general, been of one Profession in Matters of Faith, religious Worship, and the mode of settling and supporting the Ministers of the Gospel, they have by Law been formed into Ecclesiastical Societies, for the more convenient Support of their Worship and Ministry: And to the End that other Denominations of Christians who differ from the Worship and Ministry so established and supported, may enjoy free Liberty of Conscience in the Matters aforesaid.[76]

Sherman believed that Christians of every denomination—even Roman Catholics—should be tolerated.[77] He never specified how he thought adherents to non-Christian religions should be treated, but given the principles discussed above, he almost certainly thought they should be tolerated as long as they behaved in an orderly manner. It is worth noting that in the Constitutional Convention Madison recorded Sherman as opposing the constitutional prohibition on religious tests because it is "unnecessary, the prevailing liberality being a sufficient security agst. such tests."[78] However, before one reads too much into this statement, it is important to remember that Sherman was *opposing* adding a constitutional prohibition on religious tests, and that to the extent to which he opposed such a test, he likely had in mind a sectarian test. Because the only Americans of European descent who were not Christians were a few thousand Jews located outside of Connecticut, it may never have occurred to Sherman that Jews, Muslims, Hindus, and other non-Christians would ever run for—much less be elected to—national office.

Sherman was committed to religious toleration, but like many Americans in the late eighteenth century, he believed that Christianity was necessary for political prosperity.[79] Although some Americans were beginning to argue that Christianity flourished best when left alone by the state, in Connecticut there remained a widespread conviction that governments had a duty to encourage Christianity. The religious liberty statute discussed above did not remove the state from the business of funding churches, and it did not explicitly extend to individuals who were not members of a Christian denomination. Moreover, the revised statutes retained laws requiring all citizens "on the Lord's-Day carefully to apply themselves to duties of Religion and Piety, publicly and privately," stipulating that all families must own a Bible, and punishing Sabbath-breakers and blasphemers.[80] However, within the boundaries of Christianity, dissenting Protestant denominations were to be tolerated and even treated with equality.

Sherman thought the state of Connecticut should promote Christianity, but what about the new nation? To address this question appropriately, one must keep in mind that the national government was expected to be one of limited, enumerated powers. Indeed, Sherman opposed the addition of a bill of rights to the Constitution because he believed one to be unnecessary. Like other Federalists, he argued during the ratification debates that the powers of the national government were clearly delineated, and the enumerated powers did not include the power to restrict rights. Although he did not mention religion specifically, he illustrated his point by noting that "liberty of the press can be in no danger, because that is not put under the direction of the new government."[81]

As a representative to the First Congress, Sherman understood that some of his colleagues thought it "their duty" to discuss a bill of rights, but he had "strong objections to being interrupted in completing the more important business."[82] In spite of his initial opposition, he was appointed to the eleven-person House committee that reported constitutional amendments to the House, and the only original draft of the Bill of Rights is in his handwriting.[83] Moreover, he served with Egbert Benson and Theodore Sedgwick on a committee to "prepare an introduction to and arrangement of Articles of Amendment," and with Madison and John Vining on the critical conference committee that reconciled the House and Senate versions of the Bill of Rights.[84] One of his most important contributions was to convince his colleagues to place the amendments after the original text of the Constitution, not within the document as originally proposed by Madison.[85]

On August 15, 1789, the House of Representatives turned to Madison's proposal to insert the phrase "no religion shall be established by law, nor shall the equal rights of conscience be infringed" into Article 1, section 9. Sherman immediately responded that he "thought the amendment altogether unnecessary, insomuch as congress had no authority whatever delegated to them by the constitution, to make religious establishments, he would therefore move to have it struck out." After a short discussion (at least as recorded by *The Congressional Register*, which contains the most extensive account), the House agreed to Livermore's substitution, which read "congress shall make no laws touching religion, or infringing the rights of conscience."[86]

Sherman is not recorded as contributing to the remainder of the brief debates over what became the religion clauses of the First Amendment. However, after Madison proposed adding a provision to what is now the Second Amendment requiring that "no person religiously scrupulous, shall be compelled to bear arms," James Jackson suggested that men exempted from military service should be required to hire a substitute. Sherman responded to Jackson, remarking, "It is well-known that those who are religiously scrupulous of bearing arms, are equally scrupulous of getting substitutes or paying an equivalent; many of them would rather die than do either one or the other—but he did not see an absolute necessity for a clause of this kind. We do not live under an arbitrary government, said he, and the states respectively will have the government of the militia, unless when called into actual service."[87] Sherman was sympathetic to the plight of pacifists, but he preferred to rely upon legislatures—state and federal—to protect them. Madison's proposal was eventually rejected by the Senate, but Sherman's faith in legislatures proved well-founded, as they generally permitted pacifists to either hire a substitute or perform alternative service. At the national level, when Congress debated a militia bill the following year, Sherman seconded Madison's motion to exempt religious pacifists from military service.[88]

Over the past decade, scholars and jurists have debated whether or not the first Congress intended the Free Exercise clause to require exemptions from generally applicable laws that infringe upon religious belief or action.[89] I have found no evidence that Sherman thought it did, but he indisputably believed legislatures could make such exemptions. This position is reflected in his draft statute, "An Act for Enjoyning an Oath of Fidelity to This State," which would have permitted "Quakers, and others who conscientiously scruple the lawfulness of taking an Oath," to "take an affirmation instead."[90] The General Assembly excised Sherman's exemption, although it later passed "An Act Relative to the People Commonly Called Quakers" permitting Quakers, but not others, to affirm rather than swear an oath.[91] Similarly, in the Constitutional Convention, Sherman did not object to allowing state and federal officials to "affirm" rather than "swear" their allegiance to the U.S. Constitution.[92] Finally, as a member of the House of Representatives he supported exempting religious pacifists from military service.

Sherman considered the national government under the Articles of Confederation and the Constitution to have limited power to legislate in matters of religion, but he did think it could encourage religious practices. When serving in the Continental Congress, Sherman helped draft a recommendation that states set aside April 26, 1780, as a day of "fasting, humiliation and prayer." Congress approved his committee's recommendation that the people "implore the sovereign Lord of Heaven and Earth to remember mercy in his judgments; to make us sincerely penitent for our transgressions, . . . to banish vice and irreligion from among us, and establish virtue and piety by his divine grace."[93] Likewise, in the Federal Convention of 1787, Sherman seconded Franklin's motion to ask clergy to begin each day with prayer.[94] More significantly for understanding the First Amendment, on the day after the House approved the final wording of the Bill of Rights, Elias Boudinot proposed that the president recommend a day of public thanksgiving and prayer. In response to objections that such a practice mimicked European customs or should be done by the states, Sherman "justified the practice of thanksgiving, on any signal event, not only as a laudable one in itself, but as warranted by a number of precedents in holy writ: for instance, the solemn thanksgivings and rejoicings which took place in the time of Solomon, after the building of the temple, was a case in point. This example, he thought, worthy of Christian imitation on the present occasion; and he would agree with the gentleman who moved the resolution."[95] The House agreed and appointed Boudinot, Sherman, and Peter Sylvester to a committee to communicate with their counterparts in the Senate. Congress's eventual request resulted in George Washington's famous 1789 Thanksgiving Day Proclamation.[96]

Records of the debates over the Bill of Rights are notoriously incomplete, but in conjunction with Sherman's arguments and actions elsewhere, they illuminate his understanding of the First Amendment's religion clauses. Sherman clearly thought that states had the primary responsibility for promoting religion and morality and protecting religious liberty. Because of its limited powers, Congress could neither create an established church nor restrict religious liberty. However, he believed that the national government could *encourage* religious practices. Although Sherman originally opposed adding a bill of rights, he participated in debates over the religion clauses, served on critical committees that helped craft them, and voted in favor of what became the First Amendment.

Sherman's Significance

In this essay I have attempted to make the case that Sherman should not be a "forgotten founder." Given the important role he played in the founding of the American republic, the general public should at least know his name, and students of the era should study his political ideas and actions. As scholars turn—or return—to Sherman, they should not neglect the influence of Reformed Christianity on his political ideas and actions. With respect to religious liberty and church-state relations, his faith led him to embrace religious toleration *and* state and national support for Christianity.

Sherman's approach to religious liberty and church-state relations may seem parochial today. If, however, the founders' views are relevant for contemporary jurisprudence, then there is no good reason for preferring those of Thomas Jefferson—who was not even in America when the First Amendment was drafted—over Sherman's.[97] Moreover, an excellent argument can be made that Sherman is more representative of the founders with respect to these issues than Jefferson.[98]

In any case, Sherman is worthy of study not only because of his relevance to contemporary jurisprudence, but also because he played an important role in the story of America's founding. This story is worthy of being understood on its own terms, not simply as a stage upon which the actions of a few famous founders may be observed.

Notes

1. See chapter 1 in this volume.

2. Mark David Hall, "Jeffersonian Walls and Madisonian Lines: The Supreme Court's Use of History in Religion Clause Cases," *Oregon Law Review* 85 (2006): 568–69.

3. This is not to deny that Sherman borrowed ideas from a variety of sources and that he was a pragmatic politician. I will provide a more thorough treatment of Sherman's ideas and actions in a book tentatively titled *The Old Puritan in a New Nation: Roger Sherman and the Creation of the American Republic.*

4. The founders had differences with respect to religious liberty and church-state relations, but there were broad areas of agreement. This consensus is often masked by the proclivity of scholars and jurists to give disproportionate weight to unrepresentative founders. One purpose of this volume and its predecessor is to broaden the discussion of "the founders" beyond a narrow focus on a few select founders. See Daniel L. Dreisbach, Mark D. Hall, and

Jeffry H. Morrison, eds., *The Founders on God and Government* (Lanham, Md.: Rowman and Littlefield, 2004); Mark David Hall, "The Sacred Rights of Conscience: America's Founders on Church and State," *Oregon Humanities* (Fall/Winter 2005): 40–46; and Daniel L. Dreisbach and Mark David Hall, eds., *The Sacred Rights of Conscience: Selected Readings on Religious Liberty and Church-State Relations in the American Founding* (Indianapolis: Liberty Fund, 2009).

5. John G. Rommel, *Connecticut's Yankee Patriot: Roger Sherman* (Hartford: American Revolution Bicentennial Commission of Connecticut, 1979), 28.

6. John Adams, letter to John Sanderson, Nov. 19, 1822, in Lewis Boutell, *The Life of Roger Sherman* (Chicago: A. C. McClurg, 1896), 291.

7. Charles Francis Adams, ed., *The Works of John Adams* (Boston: Charles C. Little and James Brown, 1850), 2:499.

8. Sherman and Law had to revise, update, or reject previous statutes, and in some cases they composed entirely new laws. Sherman took statutes beginning with the letters A–L, and Law took the rest, although they consulted together before submitting the final draft to the legislature where the proposed laws were amended and passed or, occasionally, rejected. The draft code is available in the Connecticut State Library (hereinafter Draft Code). The final version of the code was printed in 1784 and reprinted in John D. Cushing, ed., *The First Laws of the State of Connecticut* (Wilmington, Del.: Michael Glazier, 1982).

9. David Brian Robertson, "Madison's Opponents and Constitutional Design," *American Political Science Review* 99 (May 2005): 225–43, 242. See also Robertson, *The Constitution and America's Destiny* (Cambridge: Cambridge University Press, 2005); Jack N. Rakove, *Original Meanings: Politics and Ideas in the Making of the Constitution* (New York: Knopf, 1996). Keith L. Dougherty and Jac C. Heckelman agree with Robertson and Rakove that "Sherman was an effective delegate that historians have traditionally overlooked," but they suggest that his "influence at the Convention was partly the result of the voting scheme and partly his position relative to others." See "A Pivotal Voter from a Pivotal State: Roger Sherman at the Constitutional Convention," *American Political Science Review* 100 (May 2006): 297–302, 302.

10. Sherman's five "Letters of a Countryman" were published between November 14 and December 20, 1787, and his "Letters of a Citizen of New Haven" were published on December 4 and 25, 1788. All seven letters are republished in Paul Leicester Ford, ed., *Essays on the Constitution of the United States* (New York: Burt Franklin, 1970 [1892]), 211–41.

11. Christopher Collier, *Roger Sherman's Connecticut: Yankee Politics and the American Revolution* (Middletown, Conn.: Wesleyan University Press, 1971). Collier's biography surpasses the three other accounts of Sherman's life: Boutell, *Life of Roger Sherman* (1896); Roger Sherman Boardman, *Roger Sherman: Signer and Statesman* (Philadelphia: University of Pennsylvania Press, 1938); and Rommel,

Connecticut's Yankee Patriot. See also Christopher Collier, *All Politics Is Local: Family, Friends, and Provincial Interests in the Creation of the Constitution* (Lebanon, N.H.: University Press of New England, 2003).

12. Scott Gerber, "Roger Sherman and the Bill of Rights," *Polity* 28 (Summer 1996): 531. Sherman was ranked among the most important forgotten founders in a 2008 survey of historians, political scientists, and law professors. Gary L. Gregg and Mark David Hall, eds., *America's Forgotten Founders* (Louisville: Butler Books, 2008), 5.

13. See, for instance, David L. Holmes, *The Faiths of the Founding Fathers* (New York: Oxford University Press, 2006); James Hutson, *Forgotten Features of the Founding: The Recovery of Religious Themes in the Early American Republic* (Lanham, Md.: Lexington Books, 2003); Frank Lambert, *The Founding Fathers and the Place of Religion in America* (Princeton, N.J.: Princeton University Press, 2003); Michael Novak, *On Two Wings: Humble Faith and Common Sense at the American Founding* (San Francisco: Encounter Books, 2002).

14. Sydney E. Ahlstrom, *A Religious History of the American People* (Garden City, N.Y.: Doubleday, 1975), 1:492.

15. Mark A. Noll, Nathan O. Hatch, and George M. Marsden, *The Search for Christian America* (Westchester, Ill.: Crossway Books, 1983), 74.

16. James H. Hutson, ed., *The Founders on Religion: A Book of Quotations* (Princeton, N.J.: Princeton University Press, 2005), xiv.

17. James D. German, "The Social Utility of Wicked Self-Love: Calvinism, Capitalism, and Public Policy in Revolutionary New England," *Journal of American History* 82 (December 1995): 966. German concedes that Sherman took elements of Christianity seriously, but contends that he was able to reconcile his faith with "the frankest pursuit of self interest" (973–74, 970). German may be correct that New Light theology created space in which capitalism could flourish, but his largely unsubstantiated remarks about Sherman are not convincing in light of his life and career.

18. Rommel, *Connecticut's Yankee Patriot*, 12. Similar assertions are made by Richard L. Bushman in *From Puritan to Yankee: Character and Social Order in Connecticut, 1690–1765* (Cambridge, Mass.: Harvard University Press, 1967), 255, and Patricia U. Bonomi in *Under the Cope of Heaven: Religion, Society, and Politics in Colonial America* (New York: Oxford University Press, 1986), 167.

19. Collier, *Roger Sherman's Connecticut*, 323–24.

20. See chapter 1 in this volume.

21. *The Literary Diary of Ezra Stiles*, ed. Franklin Bowditch Dexter (New York: Charles Scribner's Sons, 1901), 3:500.

22. Daniel T. V. Huntoon, *History of the Town of Canton* (Cambridge, Mass.: John Wilson and Son, 1893), 134–35.

23. Ibid., 188–89.

24. Ibid., 192–94.

25. Ellis Sandoz, ed., *Political Sermons of the American Founding Era: 1730–1805*, 2nd ed., 2 vols. (Indianapolis: Liberty Fund, 1998), 1:208–32.

26. Benjamin Kent, letter to Samuel Adams, Aug. 20, 1774, in Richard Frothingham, *Life and Times of Joseph Warren* (Boston: Little, Brown, 1865), 342.

27. Volume one of a typeset copy of the church records, in possession of author, n.p. Although volume one purports to cover 1753–1774, the first entry is for December 18, 1758.

28. Stiles, *Literary Diary*, 3:344.

29. Robert L. Ferm, *Jonathan Edwards the Younger: 1745–1801: Colonial Pastor* (Grand Rapids, Mich.: Eerdmans, 1976), 139.

30. See especially Roger Sherman, letter to David Austin, Mar. 1, 1790, Roger Sherman Collection, Yale University, Box I, folder 12 (hereinafter Sherman Collection).

31. Brooks Mather Kelly, *Yale: A History* (New Haven, Conn.: Yale University Press, 1974), 34, 61. I follow original spelling and punctuation in all eighteenth-century quotations with the exception of replacing the long *s* with the short *s* to conform to modern usage.

32. Stiles, *Literary Diary*, 3:500.

33. Ibid., 3:490–91.

34. Exact titles of each almanac varied, but all concerned "the year of our Lord Christ."

35. Collier, *Roger Sherman's Connecticut*, 11.

36. All aphorisms taken from Victor Hugo Paltsits, *The Almanacs of Roger Sherman: 1750–1761* (Worcester, Mass.: Davis, 1907), 40–48.

37. Roger Sherman, letter to Joseph Bellamy, Jul. 23, 1772, Jonathan Edwards Collection, Beinecke Library, Yale University, Gen. mss. 151, box 28, folder 1538.

38. Stiles, *Literary Diary*, 3:500.

39. Roger Sherman, *A Short Sermon on the Duty of Self Examination, Preparatory to Receiving the Lord's Supper* (New Haven, Conn.: Abel Morse, 1789), 10–11.

40. Ibid., 5.

41. Ibid., 5, 8.

42. Ibid., 8. Cf. Jonathan Edwards, *On the Nature of True Virtue* (1765).

43. Sherman, *A Short Sermon*, 16–17.

44. Dr. Nathan Williams, letter to Roger Sherman, Sep. 23, 1791, Sherman Collection, Box 1, folder 14.

45. Roger Sherman, letter to Dr. Nathan Williams, Dec. 17, 1791. Typed copy in the Broadman Collection of the Connecticut State Library. The original is in the Pennsylvania Historical Society.

46. Roger Sherman, letter to Samuel Hopkins, Jun. 28, 1790, in *Correspondence Between Roger Sherman and Samuel Hopkins*, ed. Andrew P. Peabody (Worcester, Mass.: Press of Charles Hamilton, 1889), 10. Sherman's language here is

similar to that of the answer to Question 3 of the Westminster Larger Catechism, which refers to the Old and New Testaments as "the only rule of faith
and obedience."

47. Roger Sherman, letter to Samuel Hopkins, Jun. 28, 1790, in Peabody,
ed., *Correspondence*, 8.

48. Roger Sherman, letter to Samuel Hopkins, October 1790, in Peabody,
ed., *Correspondence*, 24.

49. For other letters that reveal theological sophistication, see especially
his correspondence with Princeton President Witherspoon on divorce. Roger
Sherman, letter to John Witherspoon, Jul. 10, 1788; John Witherspoon, letter to
Roger Sherman, Jul. 25, 1788, in Boutell, *Life of Roger Sherman*, 277–80.

50. "Division of the Books Belonging to the Estate of Roger Sherman
Esq. Made Nov. 14, 1794." This photostatic copy is in Sherman Collection, Box
I, folder 16.

51. Ahlstrom, *Religious History*, 1:492.

52. Quoted in Collier, *Roger Sherman's Connecticut*, 93.

53. Benjamin Rush, *The Autobiography of Benjamin Rush: His "Travels Through
Life" Together with His Commonplace Book for 1789–1813*, ed. George W. Corner
(Princeton, N.J.: Princeton University Press, 1948), 146. The reference is actually
to Jer. 3:23, not 12:23.

54. Timothy Dwight, *A Statistical Account of the City of New Haven: Part of the
Series: A Statistical Account of the Towns and Parishes in the State of Connecticut* (New
Haven: Connecticut Academy of Arts and Sciences, 1811), vol. 1, number 1, p. 77.

55. John Sullivan, letter to George Washington, Jul. 2, 1781, in *Letters of the
Members of the Continental Congress*, vol. 6, ed. Edmund C. Burnett (Washington,
D.C.: Carnegie Institution, 1933), 133.

56. Connecticut Farmer [Roger Sherman], *Remarks on a Pamphlet Entitled "A
Dissertation on the Political Union and Constitution of the Thirteen United States of North
America by a Citizen of Philadelphia"* (New Haven, Conn.: T. S. Green, 1784), 41.
Sherman was responding to a 1783 pamphlet written by Pelatiah Webster under
the pseudonym of "A Citizen of Philadelphia." No one writing on Sherman has
ever attributed this pamphlet to him, but Joseph Sabin makes a compelling argument for his authorship in *A Dictionary of Books Relating to America* (New York:
Sabin, 1891), 461. Charles Evans also attributes the pamphlet to Sherman in *American Bibliography* (New York: Columbia Press, 1890), 6:326.

57. Sherman, *Remarks on a Pamphlet*, 16–17.

58. Because the slavery statute began with the letter "S," the law was initially revised by Richard Law.

59. Max Farrand, ed., *The Records of the Federal Convention of 1787* (New
Haven, Conn.: Yale University Press, 1911), 2:220, 374; Collier, *Roger Sherman's
Connecticut*, 271–72.

60. Sherman, *Remarks on a Pamphlet*, vi, 14.

61. Ibid., 25–26.

62. Alan Heimert, *Religion and the American Mind: From the Great Awakening to the Revolution* (Cambridge, Mass.: Harvard University Press, 1966), 512.

63. Farrand, *Records*, 2: 439–40.

64. *Documentary History of the First Federal Congress* (Baltimore: Johns Hopkins University Press, 1972–), 11:1289 (hereinafter DHFFC).

65. Sherman, *Remarks on a Pamphlet*, iii, vi–viii.

66. DHFFC, 10:568, 581.

67. Roger Sherman, *Almanack* (1758), as quoted in Paltsits, *The Almanacs of Roger Sherman* (1907), 14–15. Sherman also published the dates of Quaker meetings in his 1750–1755 almanacs. There is no record that anyone complained about this, but he ceased doing so in 1756, when he also stopped publishing dates for other local meetings, such as fairs.

68. See chapter 4 in this volume.

69. Roger Sherman, letter to William Samuel Johnson, 1768, in Boutell, *The Life of Roger Sherman*, 65.

70. Ibid., 66.

71. Bernard Bailyn, *The Ideological Origins of the American Revolution* (Cambridge, Mass.: Harvard University Press, 1967), 95–96; Heimert, *Religion and the American Mind*, 351–52; Bonomi, *Under the Cope of Heaven*, 199–209; Carl Bridenbaugh, *Mitre and Sceptre: Transatlantic Faiths, Ideas, Personalities, and Politics, 1689–1775* (New York: Oxford University Press, 1962); William M. Hogue, "The Religious Conspiracy Theory of the American Revolution: Anglican Motive," *Church History* 45 (1976): 277–92.

72. Noah Welles, *A Vindication of the Validity and Divine Right of Presbyterian Ordination as Set Forth in Dr. Chauncy's Sermon at the Dudleian Lectures; and Mr. Welles Discourse upon the Same Subject in Answer to the Expectations of Mr. Jeremiah Leaming Contained in His Late Defense of the Episcopal Gov't of the Church* (New Haven, Conn.: Samuel Green, 1767). Similarly, Sherman had written to William Samuel Johnson the previous year to suggest that if a "Papist" were to become king, then the colonists would "be at Liberty to joyn with Brittain or not." Quoted in Collier, *Roger Sherman's Connecticut*, 59.

73. Stiles, *Literary Diary*, 2, 297–98.

74. *Journals of the Continental Congress*, ed. Worthington Chauncey Ford (Washington, D.C.: Government Printing Office, 1906), 4:159, 216.

75. Draft Code, 34–35; Cushing, *The First Laws of the State of Connecticut*, 20–21. For further discussion, see M. Louise Greene, *The Development of Religious Liberty in Connecticut* (Boston: Houghton, Mifflin, 1905), esp. 338–41.

76. Draft Code, 34; Cushing, *The First Laws of the State of Connecticut*, 21.

77. On its face, the act protects the religious liberty of all Christians. However, the final paragraph allows only "Protestants" to form societies to tax church members to support ministers. Sherman's draft did not originally contain

the word "Protestant," but it was later inserted into the draft. It is not clear if Sherman added the word or if the legislature did so as the draft was revised. Draft Code, 35; Cushing, *The First Laws of the State of Connecticut*, 22.

78. Farrand, *Records*, 2:468.

79. Hutson, *Forgotten Features*, 1–44, esp. 4–9.

80. Cushing, *The First Laws of the State of Connecticut*, 213–14, 258–59, 67, 43, 87.

81. Roger Sherman, "Letters of a Citizen of New Haven," Dec. 25, 1788, in Ford, ed., *Essays on the Constitution*, 238–39; Farrand, *Records*, 2:587, 617–18.

82. DHFFC, 11:811, 815, 821–27, 836; 4:3–4, 9–12.

83. Ibid., 3:117; Gerber, "Roger Sherman and the Bill of Rights," 521–40.

84. DHFFC, 3:165, 218.

85. Ibid., 11:1208–9.

86. Ibid., 11:1260–62; 3:149–50.

87. Ibid., 11:1285–88.

88. Ibid., 14:162–63. There is no record of Sherman's response to Madison's proposal that "no state shall infringe the equal rights of conscience, nor the freedom of speech, or of the press, nor of the right to trial by jury in criminal cases," but he almost certainly opposed it on the grounds of federalism. The amendment, which Madison considered "to be the most valuable amendment on the whole list," was passed by the House but rejected by the Senate (11:1292; 4:39).

89. See especially the opinions of Justices Antonin Scalia and Sandra Day O'Connor in *City of Boerne v. Flores*, 521 U.S. 507 (1997); Michael W. McConnell, "The Origins and Historical Understanding of Free Exercise of Religion," *Harvard Law Review* 103 (1990): 1409–1517; Ellis M. West, "The Right to Religion-Based Exemptions in Early America: The Case of Conscientious Objectors to Conscription," *Journal of Law and Religion* 10 (1993–1994): 367–401; and Vincent Phillip Muñoz, "The Original Meaning of the Free Exercise Clause: The Evidence from the First Congress," *Harvard Journal of Law & Public Policy* 31 (2008): 1083–120.

90. Draft Code, 112.

91. Cushing, *The First Laws of the State of Connecticut*, 187. Connecticut had offered Quakers this option since the early 1700s so as not to violate the English law.

92. Farrand, *Records*, 2:468.

93. *Journals of Congress*, 16:225, 252–53.

94. Farrand, *Records*, 1:452.

95. DHFFC, 11:1500.

96. George Washington, "Thanksgiving Proclamation," Oct. 3, 1789, in John C. Fitzpatrick, ed., *The Writings of George Washington* (Washington, D.C.: Government Printing Office, 1939), 30:427–38.

97. One reason occasionally asserted for preferring Jefferson over other founders is because of his influence on the framing of the First Amendment. This presumption is effectively challenged in Mark J. Chadsey, "Thomas Jefferson and the Establishment Clause," *Akron Law Review* 40 (2007): 623–46. Jefferson is often cited by advocates of the separation of church and state, but numerous scholars have questioned the extent to which he embraced this position in principle and practice. See, for instance, Daniel L. Dreisbach, *Thomas Jefferson and the Wall of Separation Between Church and State* (New York: New York University Press, 2002).

98. I make this argument in *The Old Puritan in a New Nation*.

CHAPTER 12

Mercy Otis Warren on Church and State

ROSEMARIE ZAGARRI

Among the forgotten founders, Mercy Otis Warren (1728–1814) has been particularly neglected. As a woman she was never eligible to hold elected or appointed office. Yet because of the particular circumstances of her upbringing and her social position as an adult, she was one of the few women who had a public voice. Through her writings, she contributed to the public debate over independence, the controversy over the ratification of the U.S. Constitution, and the discussion of the relationship between church and state in the new nation.

A Brief Biography

Warren was born on September 25, 1728, in Barnstable, Massachusetts, one of thirteen children of Mary Allyne and James Otis Sr. Unlike most girls of her era, she received an extensive and rigorous education at the hands of a private tutor. Along with her brother James Otis Jr., the future patriot, she read history, philosophy, literature, and the classics of ancient Greece and Rome in translation. Yet when her brother went off to college at Harvard, she remained at home, confined, as she once put it, "to the narrow circle of domestic cares." Like most women at the time, she saw her future in terms of her role as a wife and mother.[1]

In 1754, Mercy Otis married James Warren, with whom she had five sons. Even as she became a wife and mother, she remained engaged with the larger world through the men in her life. During the 1760s and 1770s, her household in Plymouth became a center of activity for the growing opposition to Britain. At various times, Warren's father, brother, and husband all held positions of power in the Massachusetts assembly, a body that repeatedly challenged the authority of the Crown's hated representative in the colony, Lieutenant Governor Thomas Hutchinson. Over time, colonial leaders such as Samuel Adams and Johns Adams made a point of stopping at Warren's house to discuss the current political situation and plot the most effective means of resistance. It was said that the idea for creating committees of correspondence, a system for disseminating political news throughout the colony, first emerged there.[2]

Although Warren could not act in any official capacity, by the 1770s she did see a way that she could make her own contributions to the patriot cause. From an early age, she had displayed a gift for writing. At first she wrote poems she shared only with family members and close friends. As the conflict with Britain intensified, John Adams began to encourage her to write propaganda pieces for publication. Her first work, "The Adulateur," which appeared in a Boston newspaper in 1772, was a thinly disguised attack on Thomas Hutchinson and his cronies. Poems celebrating the Boston Tea Party and urging colonists to support the boycott against British goods soon followed. She then published longer satirical pieces in the form of plays, including The Defeat in 1773 and The Group in 1775. Written in blank verse and full of classical allusions, these works lampooned the treachery of British officials and railed against infringements on the colonists' cherished rights and liberties. As war with Britain loomed, she urged her countrymen to reaffirm those virtues that would enable them to triumph over their British foes.[3]

Like most political writers at the time, Warren issued her works anonymously, or under a pseudonym. Nevertheless, among the close-knit circle of political leaders in Massachusetts, she was known, acknowledged, and respected as an author. John Adams praised her work, saying that Warren's "poetical pen" had "no equal that I know of in this country."

After independence she continued to write about political matters. In 1788, she penned a nineteen-page pamphlet, *Observations on the New Constitution, and on the Federal and State Conventions*, which urged citizens to reject the proposed U.S. Constitution. In 1790, she published a volume of her collected poems and plays under her own name. Many fulsome accolades followed.[4]

During the war, Warren began another, even more ambitious project: a full-scale history of the American Revolution. Using her personal knowledge of many of the principals, she collected an impressive archive of private letters and official documents that informed her account and gave it great credibility. She also brought her own extensive reading of political philosophy and English history to bear. Although substantially complete by 1790, the work was not published until 1805. In the interim, she added sections on the ratification of the U.S. Constitution and the presidencies of George Washington and John Adams. Appearing in three volumes, Warren's *History of the Rise, Progress and Termination of the American Revolution Interspersed with Biographical, Political and Moral Observations* was a stunning achievement, a comprehensive history of the new nation from the founding of the colonies until the election of Thomas Jefferson. Not only was it one of the earliest narratives of the War for Independence, it was the first written by a woman.[5]

Yet Warren's *History* did not receive the public acclaim that her Revolutionary-era works had enjoyed. Disaffected from government and alienated from the sources of power, her work was a cautionary tale, warning of the consequences of a decline in public virtue for the future of republican government. Openly critical of former presidents Washington and Adams, and supportive of Thomas Jefferson, Warren's work received a chilly reception in her home state, which remained decidedly Federalist in orientation. Publishing the work under her own name also had consequences. Because many people believed that women should not concern themselves with masculine subjects such as war, politics, and government, she made herself vulnerable to criticism. As one hostile reviewer observed, Warren's *History* was "the product of a mind that had not yet yielded to the assertion that all political attentions lay outside of the road of female life." Although John Adams had originally encouraged Warren to undertake the writing of the history, he later repudiated the work, remarking to his friend Elbridge Gerry, "History is not the Province of the Ladies."[6]

Warren herself, however, had long ago rejected such traditional views of women. Although she continued to believe that women's primary roles were as wives and mothers, she consistently maintained that both sexes shared an equal capacity for mental development and intellectual achievement. Although never an advocate for women's political rights, she believed that women should have as much access to educational opportunities as men. Toward the end of her long life, she found solace in her family and her religious faith. Nonetheless, she knew that she had not only succeeded in fulfilling the traditional feminine role but also overcome its restrictions in a way that few other women of her generation had.[7]

Scholarship on Warren

Although religious faith permeated every aspect of Mercy Otis Warren's life, few scholars have focused specifically on this subject. This is due, in part, to the nature of the scholarly research on Warren. Biographers have long been fascinated with Warren as an example of an exceptional woman who was able to excel in areas that were, for the most part, closed to women of her time. Literary scholars have focused on Warren's role as one of the few published female authors in early America. They have been particularly interested in her plays, which offer insights into the evolution of that genre and into the growth of the theater as an important literary outlet. Historians, in contrast, have tended to focus on Warren's political ideas. Her writings represent important examples of the development of opposition ideology prior to the American Revolution and of the growth of anti-Federalist sentiment against the U.S. Constitution. Women's historians have taken a different route. They have emphasized the ways in which contemporaneous conceptions of womanhood and expectations about gender roles shaped Warren's life, her literary works, and her political ideas.[8]

In the vast majority of these works, Warren's religious beliefs function merely as the backdrop for the exploration of other issues. Two scholars, however, do give the subject more than incidental attention. In an article in *History as Argument: Three Patriot Historians of the American Revolution*, William Raymond Smith portrays Warren as a "latter-day Puritan" whose belief in Providence and in Americans as God's chosen people animated her interpretation of the American Revolution. As a result, Smith says, Warren emerges as an historian who is firmly within an "idealist" tradition of explaining the American past. Another scholar, Lester Cohen, has analyzed Warren's political ideology as it was expressed in her history of the American Revolution. According to Cohen, Warren placed public virtue and private morality at the center of her thought and believed that the fate of the nation depended on the sustained cultivation of these dispositions. Neither Cohen nor Smith, however, attempts any systematic analysis of Warren's understanding of the relationship between church and state, or of the role of religion in public life.[9]

Religious Beliefs

Warren was both a descendant of New England Puritans and a participant in the eighteenth-century Enlightenment. With her husband, she shared a common ancestor in one of the signers of the original *Mayflower* compact, Edward Dotey. As a child, she attended the Second Congregational Church in the East Parish of Barnstable, Massachusetts. As an adult, she and her husband attended services in Plymouth. Jettisoning the fiery Calvinism of her forebears, she favored a more rationalistic and benevolent approach to religion. Her God, she said in her *History*, was "the benevolent Author of nature [who] designed universal happiness as the basis of his works." At the same time, Warren retained a firm belief in many essential Puritan tenets: the sinfulness of human beings, the reality of evil in the world, and the corruptibility of human nature. Although in later years she often found it impossible to attend church because of poor health, her deep faith never wavered.[10]

Warren's religious sentiments frequently found expression in her poems. One early poem expounded on the meaning of the Nineteenth Psalm, with its emphasis on God's glory in all creation and the effulgence of divine light. Throughout her life, whenever she faced suffering or hardship, she expressed her grief in the form of a poem addressing God. Her strong faith allowed her to cope with much grief and many sadnesses, including the insanity of her beloved brother James, professional setbacks for her husband, and the death in early adulthood of three of her five sons.[11]

Although Warren believed in the "God of providence," who intervened in human affairs to mete out rewards and punishments, her reading in Enlightenment philosophy also led her to embrace the "God of nature," who worked through human institutions in an orderly and rational manner. On numerous occasions, she referred to God as the "Divine oeconomist," suggesting the orderliness and predictability of the natural world.[12] As she saw it, God had created the world to conform to certain existing rules and patterns. By applying their intellectual faculties, people could come to understand the operation of the divine order in nature. Although in certain extraordinary circumstances God might choose to contravene the natural order, for the most part the world proceeded in accordance with the laws inscribed in nature

Warren's poem "On a Survey of the Heavens" reflects her embrace of both faith and reason. She begins by asking whether any "infidel" can look up to the heavens and not see "proofs of Deity":

> And there surveys the spangled skies;
> The glitt'ring stars, the worlds that shine,
> And speak their origin divine,
> Bid him adore, and prostrate fall,
> And own one Lord, supreme o'er all.

She then goes on to suggest that although science might explain the wonders of the universe, the ultimate explanation lay with God:

> Not even Newton's godlike mind,
> Nor all the sages of mankind,
> Could e'er assign another cause,
> Though much they talk of nature's laws;
> Of gravity's attractive force,

They own the grave, eternal source,
Who, from the depths of chaos' womb,
Prepar'd the vaulted, spacious dome;
He spake—a vast foundation' laid,
And countless globes thereon display'd.[13]

For Warren, there was no conflict between reason and faith, science and religion, Enlightenment rationalism and Calvinist awe. All were comprehended in God's plan.

Political Philosophy

Historians have frequently characterized Warren's political philosophy as the reflection of a classical republican notion of politics that can be traced back to ancient Greece and Rome.[14] Actually, her vision encompassed both classical republican notions and quintessentially Christian views. She integrated her Puritan faith with a civic republican ideal that came by way of her reading of classical republican theorists, such as Machiavelli, Milton, Algernon Sydney, James Harrington, and Edward Gibbon. Especially in her History, she echoed their deep-seated concern about the fragility of republican government. According to these theorists, republics, among all forms of government, were particularly susceptible to corruption and decay. Over time, they tended to deteriorate into oligopolies or despotisms, thus putting the people's liberties at risk. A republican form of government also demanded more from its citizens than other forms of government. Inhabitants of republics must participate actively in governing themselves, remain vigilant against corruption in their leaders, and be ready to take action to prevent the usurpation of their rights and privileges.[15]

In Warren's understanding, the notion of virtue, as both a private attribute and a public commodity, was the pivot on which all else turned. Before the Revolution, Warren had written poems and plays in order to encourage colonists to make sacrifices for the sake of the common good. Valuable as civic virtue was in and of itself, this trait would also strengthen the colonists' resolve and enable them to assert their moral superiority over their British foes. In a poem written in the 1770s, Warren, for example, encouraged women to boycott a huge array of British goods, including imported cloth, china, tea, and other luxury items. "[By] quit-[ting] the useless vanities of life," she proclaimed, women would make it possible "at once to end the great politic strife." In another poem, she contrasted the dissipation and corruption of the British, whose "Virtue turn'd pale, and freedom left the isle," with the industry and uprightness of the colonists: "They quitted plenty, luxury, and ease, / Tempted the dangers of the frozen seas." Such virtues would, if necessary, enable Americans to make the ultimate sacrifices: to give up their fortunes, or even their lives, for their country. To do less might allow the British to undermine their liberties and reduce the colonists to the condition of slaves.[16]

Although intimations of Warren's political philosophy appeared in her pre-Revolutionary poems and plays, she expressed her ideas most fully in her multivolume *History of the Rise, Progress and Termination of the American Revolution*, published in 1805. In this work, Warren argued that Americans had enjoyed other special circumstances that cultivated the people's commitment to liberty and freedom. Having been "born under no feudal tenure, nurtured in the bosom of mediocrity [equality of condition], and educated in the schools of freedom," Americans had learned, Warren said, "to vie with their European ancestors in arts [and] in arms, . . . in the same space of time that most other colonies have required to pare off the ruggedness of their native ferocity, establish the rudiments of civil society, and begin the fabric of government and jurisprudence."[17] In her view, the particular convergence of geography and tradition had contributed to the growth of freedom in the British colonies.

Warren also maintained that God had played a special role in enabling Americans to secure their freedom and establish the United States as a beacon of liberty to other nations in the world. Americans, she noted, "seemed to have been remarkably directed by the finger of Divine Providence, and led on from step to step beyond their own expectations, to exhibit to the view of distant nations, millions freed from the bondage of a foreign yoke, by that spirit of freedom, virtue, and perseverance, which they had generally displayed from their first emigrations to the wilderness, to the present day." Yet Warren did not believe that American success was inevitable or permanent. Americans, she insisted, must continue to practice the virtues that supported republican government.[18]

Even during the War for Independence, Warren had begun to express concern that her countrymen were falling away from their historical commitment to frugality, simplicity, and equality as a way of life. All around her people were making fortunes by profiting from the war, seeking their own advancement at the expense of the common good, or indulging in consumer goods at a time when the need for self-sacrifice was paramount. In 1778, she wrote to John Adams, "A state of war has ever been deemed unfavourable to virtue. But such a total change of manners in so short a period, I believe was never known in the history of man. Rapacity and profusion, pride and servility, and almost every vice is contrasted in the same heart." This tendency, she noted, continued after the war, leading to "avarice without frugality, and profusion without taste." Although Warren hoped that Americans might return to simpler values, she feared for the country's future. By the late 1780s, when the Confederation government was in crisis, she wondered whether Americans would ever be able to support a political system in which they governed themselves. "We are," she wrote in 1789 to her friend, the historian Catharine Macaulay, "too poor for Monarchy—too wise for Despotism, and too dissipated, selfish, and extravagant for Republicanism."[19]

After the ratification of the new Constitution, her fears persisted. In her view, the new government concentrated political power in the hands of a few, strengthened the leverage of merchants and men of capital, and created a powerful engine of oppression by sanctioning the existence of a standing army. Perhaps even more alarming was the extent to which the American people themselves had fallen away from their pre-Revolutionary commitment to public virtue and private morality. For Warren, the diminution of popular willingness to sacrifice for the public good represented a serious threat to the republican experiment, a change that might "weaken the sinews of state." The people, she wrote in her *History*, had "in a great measure lost [their] simplicity of manners, and those ideas of mediocrity [equality] which are generally the parent of content; the Americans are already in too many instances hankering after the sudden accumulation of wealth and the proud distinctions of fortune and title. They have too far lost that general sense of moral obligation, formerly felt by all classes in America." Moral regeneration, she believed, went hand-in-hand with political freedom.[20]

In contrast to the works of most modern historians, Warren's analysis of the American Revolution possessed a normative dimension that reflected her belief in the centrality of virtue and morality in public life. Warren did not want her *History* simply to describe the ideas and events related to the American Revolution; she wanted to galvanize Americans into action, to make them behave in a way that was conducive to the success of the republican experiment. Her prescriptions flowed as much from her own belief in divine Providence as from her acceptance of classical republican political philosophy. Despite her trust in God, she knew that the country's ultimate success or failure depended on the people themselves. Her tone of moral indignation resembled nothing so much as the jeremiads issued by the Puritan ministers of old. Like her forefathers, she hoped that by rebuking the people she would lead them back to the path of moral righteousness.

Thoughts on Religious Freedom

As much as Warren believed in the importance of virtue and morality to republican government, she was equally committed to the cause of religious freedom. For Warren, one of the most important benefits of the American Revolution was to secure the blessings of religious liberty for inhabitants of the new nation. In fact, one of her objections to the proposed U.S. Constitution was its failure to provide sufficient safeguards "for the rights of conscience." She firmly believed that government must play a role in preserving individual religious liberty.[21]

In her *History*, Warren condemned religious intolerance and persecution whenever she observed it. Although a descendant of the Puritans, she vehemently objected to the Puritans' treatment of religious dissenters. In the first chapter, Warren provided a brief overview of the founding and settlement of the North American British colonies in which she criticized the New England Puritans for their lack of religious toleration. Their governments, she believed, reflected the "corrupt principles of the Stuarts" and were "a mixture of Jewish theocracy, monarchic government, and the growing principles of republicanism."[22] Although the Puritans themselves were fleeing from religious persecution, their governments in the New World, she pointed out, persecuted individuals and groups on the basis of their religious preferences. Instead of bringing an enlightened view of religious toleration to the New World, Puritans perpetuated much of what was bad about the Old World.

Warren was particularly critical of the Puritans' treatment of the Quakers. On numerous occasions, their magistrates had ostracized, banished, or, even executed those who supported the Society of Friends. "It is natural," Warren commented, "to suppose a society of men who had suffered so much from a spirit of religious bigotry would have stretched a lenient hand towards any who might differ from themselves, either in mode or opinion, with regard to the worship of the Deity. But from a strange propensity in human nature to reduce every thing within the vortex of their own ideas, the same intolerant and persecuting spirit, from which they had so recently fled, discovered itself in those bold adventurers, who had braved the dangers of the ocean and planted themselves in a wilderness for the enjoyment of civil and religious liberty." Much to Warren's dismay, instead of granting to other groups the dispensations they would have liked to have received, Puritans perpetuated the same patterns of religious harassment that they had experienced.[23]

Warren also believed that government efforts to impose religious uniformity on its inhabitants inevitably led to conflict, violence, and bloodshed. Reflecting on European history since the Reformation, she noted that the "same spirit of superstition and bigotry has been the pretext for establishing inquisitions, for Smithfield fires, for massacres, wars, and rivers of human blood poured out on the earth, which groans beneath the complicated crimes of man." Warren concluded that the only rational solution was for the state to grant religious freedom to all groups and to tolerate all varieties of religious belief. Through toleration, she hoped, "nations [that] had long been immersed in errors, might be led to embrace a religion admirably adapted to the promotion of the happiness of mankind on earth, and to prepare a rational agent for some higher stage of existence."[24]

In this regard, her views resembled those of the political leader she admired most, Thomas Jefferson. In his Statute for Religious Freedom, passed in Virginia in 1786, Jefferson promoted the position that government should disentangle itself from religious matters and allow individuals complete freedom of conscience in matters involving the belief in God or a supreme deity. Yet Warren did not go as far as Jefferson in advocating a complete separation of church and state. She did not trust that people would remain virtuous without the external constraints imposed by organized religion. "There may be a danger," she warned, "that in the enthusiasm for *toleration*, indifference to all religion may take place." In the absence of state support for religion, she feared that people might lose their commitment to religious institutions and fall into a state of unbelief and immorality that would make them unfit for the purposes of self-government. Republican governments, she insisted, benefited from having a religious population. In modern republics, Warren said, "religion has been the grand palladium of their institutions." Religion forged bonds between and among citizens, and by encouraging morality, strengthened the government. "Perhaps," she admitted, "few will deny that religion, viewed merely in a political light, is after all the best cement of society, the great barrier of just government, and the only certain restraint of the passions, those dangerous inlets to licentiousness and anarchy."[25] Without the restraints imposed by religious obligations, freedom might degenerate into anarchy.

Particularly in Warren's home state of Massachusetts, early Americans struggled to find an equitable balance between the desire to provide limited government support for religion while at the same time acknowledging a belief in individual freedom of conscience. Unlike Virginians, many citizens of Massachusetts balked at the prospect of a complete separation of church and state. They wanted to create a framework that would allow the government to provide tax monies to support religious institutions and pay a salary to Christian ministers, particularly those associated with the Congregational church. The Massachusetts constitution of 1780, written in large part by John Adams, provided a compromise. Article 2 of the Massachusetts Declaration of Rights affirmed religious toleration, stating that "no subject shall be hurt, molested, or restrained, in his person, liberty, or estate, for worshipping God in the manner and season most agreeable to the dictates of his own conscience." Article 3, however, authorized the legislature to collect taxes "for the institution of public worship and for the support and maintenance of public Protestant teachers of piety, religion, and morality in all cases where such provisions shall not be made voluntarily." However much in tension, these clauses represented a good-faith effort to reconcile deeply felt imperatives that were often in conflict with one another.[26]

Warren herself never commented publicly on the issue of the establishment of religion. Her private views, however, seem to have accorded with those of the Congregational majority in Massachusetts. As she observed in a 1780 letter to John Adams, "Baptists, Deists, Quakers, Priests, and Politicians have laboured assiduously to expunge all religious establishments in the new Constitution of Government. But I believe in spite of the whole group the form of Godliness, will yet be kept up among us." She was presumably relieved when the state continued to provide for the public support of religion and extended its protection only to those who were Protestant Christians. Members of dissenting sects, however, objected to the compromise. Baptist minister Isaac Backus, for example, argued that the provision requiring citizens to pay taxes for the support of religious ministers favored Congregationalists. In fact, Massachusetts retained its system of state-sanctioned support for religion until 1833. Over time, however, it became increasingly clear that religious toleration differed fundamentally from freedom of conscience, and that anything less than the latter failed to guarantee the rights of all individuals.[27]

By the 1790s, Warren's views on religious freedom faced a different kind of challenge. As she was composing the closing chapters of her *History*, the full horrors of the French Revolution had become apparent. The Terror ravaged French society, destroyed the Catholic Church, and produced social chaos. Just as troubling to Warren was the fact that French revolutionaries had sought "the annihilation of all religion." Religious skepticism and atheism were rampant. As a supporter of Jefferson and of France, Warren found herself in a difficult position. Although an advocate of liberty, equality, and fraternity, she could not and did not sanction such violent excesses. At the same time, American critics of France warned that the country provided a cautionary tale about the pitfalls of republican government. They warned that these same vices might come to afflict the United States as well.[28]

Holding fast to her faith in republican government, Warren sought to prove that republicanism did not inevitably produce a decay of religious belief. According to Warren, its insufficiencies did not arise from the theory of republicanism itself but from the particular conditions under which republican government arose in France. The French people had not been prepared for self-government in the same way as Americans had. In fact, they had suffered under particularly difficult forms of oppression, having been duped and misled by their leaders. The French monarch had taxed people to the point of penury; the French aristocracy had engaged in luxury, effeminacy, and other forms of self-indulgence; and the Catholic Church had persecuted dissenters while enriching itself at the people's expense. These circumstances left the French people unable to cope with freedom.

Having been "degraded by oppression," the French people could not, once the bonds of oppression were loosened, handle the responsibilities of freedom. Liberty quickly became licentiousness. "All religious opinions," Warren said, "were set afloat, the passions set loose, and distinctions leveled. Thus was republicanism disgraced by the demoralization of the people, and a cloud of infidelity darkened the hemisphere of France." Despite what happened in France, then, neither social chaos nor religious indifference was an inevitable consequence of the republican form of government.[29]

If republicanism did not necessarily lead to a decline in religious belief and public virtue, Warren nonetheless felt compelled to rally her countrymen in order to prevent the United States from ever sharing the fate of France. Toward the end of her *History*, she urged Americans to recommit themselves to the values of the revolutionary generation and live up to the standards set by their predecessors. Americans, she said, must "hold up the contrast between a simple, virtuous, and free people, and a degenerate, service race of beings, corrupted by wealth, effeminated by luxury, impoverished by licentiousness." Only by continuing to nurture the connection between religion and morality would the experiment in liberty survive. Her country, she insisted, must "preserve a national character of her own, free from any symptoms of pernicious deviation from the purest principles on morality, religion, and civil liberty." Religious freedom must not be allowed to degenerate into religious indifference, skepticism, or atheism.[30]

Thus despite her immense admiration for Thomas Jefferson and the values of his political party, Warren nurtured a much darker vision of human nature than Jefferson. In advocating the disestablishment of the state church, Jefferson promoted an ideal in which free discussion and debate, without interference from the state, would allow religious truth to emerge. He rejected the connection between private morality and public order and insisted that state coercion led only to hypocrisy and resentment. His was ultimately an optimistic view of human potentiality.

In contrast to Jefferson, Warren chose to enhance the power of the state, even at the expense of individual freedom. Although a supporter of religious toleration, she believed that the human tendency toward sin and corruption would continually threaten Americans' commitment to independence, frugality, and virtue. State support for religion would promote civic virtue and encourage citizens to make the sacrifices that would allow the republic to survive and thrive. For Warren, any other alternative might risk all the freedoms that had been won through the brutal war against British tyranny. Unlike Jefferson, she did not care to put the proposition to the test.

Notes

1. Mercy Otis Warren, letter to Abigail Adams, Feb. 1774, in Mercy Otis Warren Papers, Letterbook, Massachusetts Historical Society, Boston, 1:145. For biographical information, see Rosemarie Zagarri, A Woman's Dilemma: Mercy Otis Warren and the American Revolution (Wheeling, Ill.: Harlan Davidson, 1995), 1–21.
2. Zagarri, A Woman's Dilemma, 22–47.
3. Ibid., 48–77.
4. John Adams, letter to James Warren, Dec. 22, 1773, in Works of John Adams, ed. Charles Francis Adams (Boston: Little, Brown, 1854), 9:335; Mrs. M. Warren, Poems, Dramatic and Miscellaneous (Boston: I. Thomas and E. T. Andrews, 1790); [A Columbian Patriot], "Observations on the New Constitution, and on the Federal and State Conventions" (Boston, 1788), in The Complete Anti-Federalist, ed. Herbert J. Storing (Chicago: University of Chicago Press, 1981), 4:270–87; Zagarri, A Woman's Dilemma, 119–23.

5. Mercy Otis Warren, *History of the Rise, Progress and Termination of the American Revolution Interspersed with Biographical, Political and Moral Observations*, ed. Lester H. Cohen (Indianapolis: Liberty Classics, 1988 [1805]).

6. *The Panoplist; or The Christian's Armory* 2 (Boston), Jan. 1807, 380; John Adams, letter to Elbridge Gerry, Apr. 17, 1813, in *Warren-Adams Letters, Being Chiefly a Correspondence among John Adams, Samuel Adams, and James Warren* (Boston: Massachusetts Historical Society, 1917), 2:380.

7. For Warren's view on women's role, see Zagarri, *A Woman's Dilemma*, 78–95.

8. For examples, see Alice Brown, *Mercy Warren* (New York: Charles Scribner's Sons, 1968 [1896]); Katharine S. Anthony, *First Lady of the Revolution: The Life of Mercy Otis Warren* (New York: Doubleday, 1959); Jean Fritz, *Cast for a Revolution: Some American Friends and Enemies, 1728–1814* (Boston: Houghton Mifflin, 1972); Jeffrey H. Richards, *Mercy Otis Warren* (New York: Twayne, 1995); Theresa Freda Nicolay, *Gender Roles, Literary Authority and Three American Women Writers: Anne Dudley Bradstreet, Mercy Otis Warren, Margaret Fuller Ossoli* (New York: Peter Lang, 1995); Pauline E. Schloesser, *The Fair Sex: White Women and Racial Patriarchy in the Early American Republic* (New York: New York University Press, 2002); Kate Davies, *Catharine Macaulay and Mercy Otis Warren: The Revolutionary Atlantic and the Politics of Gender* (Oxford: Oxford University Press, 2005).

9. William Raymond Smith, *History as Argument: Three Patriot Historians of the American Revolution* (The Hague: Mouton, 1966), 73–119; Lester H. Cohen, "Mercy Otis Warren: The Politics of Language and the Aesthetics of Self," *American Quarterly* 35 (1983): 481–98, and "Explaining the Revolution: Ideology and Ethics in Mercy Otis Warren's Historical Theory," *William and Mary Quarterly*, 3rd ser., 37 (Apr. 1980): 200–18.

10. Warren, *History*, 1:11; Zagarri, *A Woman's Dilemma*, 1–21.

11. See, for example, "The Nineteenth Psalm," "A Thought on the Inestimable Blessing of Reason, Occasioned by Its Privation to a Friend of Very Superior Talents and Virtues[,] 1770," and "An Address to the Supreme Being," in Edmund M. Hayes, ed., "The Private Poems of Mercy Otis Warren," *New England Quarterly* 59 (Jun. 1981): 207, 213, 223.

12. Warren, *History*, 2:684, 698; Mercy Otis Warren, letter to John Adams, Mar. 15, 1779, in Warren Papers, 1:175.

13. Mercy Otis Warren, "On a Survey of the Heavens," in *The Plays and Poems of Mercy Otis Warren*, ed. Benjamin Franklin V (Delmar, N.Y.: Scholars' Facsimiles and Reprints, 1980 [1790]), 198–99.

14. See Cohen, "Explaining the Revolution," 200–18; Paul A. Rahe, *Republics Ancient and Modern: Classical Republicanism and the American Revolution* (Chapel Hill: University of North Carolina Press, 1992), 351; Linda K. Kerber, "The Republican Ideology of the Revolutionary Generation," *American Quarterly* 37 (Fall 1985): 483.

15. Ruth H. Bloch, "The Gendered Meanings of Virtue in Post-Revolutionary America," *Signs: Journal of Women in Culture and Society* 13 (1987): 37–58.

16. Warren, "To the Hon. J. Winthrop, Esq.," "A Political Reverie," in *Plays and Poems*, 191–92, 211–12.

17. Warren, *History*, 1:14.

18. Ibid., 2:641.

19. Mercy Otis Warren, letter to John Adams, May 8, 1780, in Warren Papers, 1:179–80; Warren, *History*, 2:390; Mercy Otis Warren, letter to Catharine Macaulay, Jul. 1789, in Warren Papers, 1:28.

20. Warren, *History*, 2:644.

21. [A Columbian Patriot], "Observations on the New Constitution," 4:276.

22. Warren, *History*, 1:9.

23. Ibid.

24. Ibid., 1:337, 339; Frank Lambert, *The Founding Fathers and the Place of Religion in America* (Princeton, N.J.: Princeton University Press, 2003), 225–35.

25. Ibid., 2:680; 1:12.

26. Lambert, *Founding Fathers*, 222–23. See also John Witte Jr., "One Public Religion, Many Private Religions: John Adams and the 1780 Massachusetts Constitution," in *The Founders on God and Government*, ed. Daniel L. Dreisbach, Mark D. Hall, and Jeffry H. Morrison (Lanham, Md.: Rowman and Littlefield, 2004), 23–52.

27. Mercy Otis Warren, letter to John Adams, May 8, 1780, in Warren Papers, 1:179; Lambert, *Founding Fathers*, 223–25.

28. Warren, *History*, 1:12n.

29. Ibid., 2:646, 680.

30. Ibid., 1:10–11.

For Further Reading

Abzug, Robert H. *Cosmos Crumbling: American Reform and the Religious Imagination.* New York: Oxford University Press, 1994.

Adair, Douglass, and Marvin Harvey. "Was Alexander Hamilton a Christian Statesman?" *William and Mary Quarterly,* 3rd ser., 12 (Apr. 1955): 308–29.

Adams, Arlin M., and Charles J. Emmerich. *A Nation Dedicated to Religious Liberty: The Constitutional Heritage of the Religion Clauses.* Philadelphia: University of Pennsylvania Press, 1990.

Albanese, Catherine L. *Sons of the Fathers: The Civil Religion of the American Founding.* Philadelphia: Temple University Press, 1976.

Aldridge, Alfred Owen. *Benjamin Franklin and Nature's God.* Durham, N.C.: Duke University Press, 1967.

Allen, Brooke. *Moral Minority: Our Skeptical Founding Fathers.* Chicago: Ivan R. Dee, 2006.

Alley, Robert S., ed. *James Madison on Religious Liberty.* Buffalo, N.Y.: Prometheus Books, 1985.

Baird, Robert. *Religion in America; or, an Account of the Origin, Progress, Relation to the State, and Present Condition of the Evangelical Churches in the United States. With Notices of the Unevangelical Denominations.* New York: Harper and Brothers, 1844.

Baldwin, Alice M. *The New England Clergy and the American Revolution.* Durham, N.C.: Duke University Press, 1928.

Baron, Hans. "Calvinist Republicanism and its Historical Roots." *Church History* 8 (1939): 30–42.

Beneke, Chris. *Beyond Toleration: The Religious Origins of American Pluralism.* New York: Oxford University Press, 2006.

Bercovitch, Sacvan. *The American Jeremiad.* Madison: University of Wisconsin Press, 1978.

Boller, Paul F., Jr. *George Washington and Religion.* Dallas: Southern Methodist University Press, 1963.

———. "George Washington and Religious Liberty." *William and Mary Quarterly,* 3rd ser., 17 (1960): 486–506.

Bond, Edward L., ed. *Spreading the Gospel in Colonial Virginia: Preaching Religion and Community: with Selected Sermons and Other Primary Documents.* Lanham, Md.: Lexington Books; Colonial Williamsburg Foundation, 2005.

Bonomi, Patricia U. "John Jay, Religion, and the State." *New York History* 81 (Jan. 2000): 8–18.

———. *Under the Cope of Heaven: Religion, Society, and Politics in Colonial America.* New York: Oxford University Press, 1986.

Botein, Stephen. "Religious Dimensions of the Early American State." In *Beyond Confederation: Origins of the Constitution and American National Identity,* edited by Richard Beeman, Stephen Botein, and Edward C. Carter II. Chapel Hill: University of North Carolina Press, 1987.

Bradford, M. E. *Founding Fathers: Brief Lives of the Framers of the United States Constitution.* 2nd ed., rev. Lawrence: University Press of Kansas, 1994.

———. "Religion and the Framers: The Biographical Evidence." *Benchmark* 4, no. 4 (1990): 349–58.

Bradley, Gerard V. *Church-State Relationships in America.* Westport, Conn.: Greenwood Press, 1987.

Brauer, Jerald C., ed. *Religion and the American Revolution.* Philadelphia: Fortress, 1976.

Bridenbaugh, Carl. *Mitre and Sceptre: Transatlantic Faiths, Ideas, Personalities, and Politics, 1689–1775.* New York: Oxford University Press, 1962.

Brown, Richard D. "The Founding Fathers of 1776 and 1787: A Collective View." *William and Mary Quarterly,* 3rd ser., 33 (Jul. 1976): 465–80.

Buckley, Thomas E., S.J. *Church and State in Revolutionary Virginia, 1776–1787.* Charlottesville: University Press of Virginia, 1977.

———. "The Political Theology of Thomas Jefferson." In *The Virginia Statute for Religious Freedom: Its Evolution and Consequences in American History,* edited by Merrill D. Peterson and Robert C. Vaughan. New York: Cambridge University Press, 1988.

Butler, Jon. *Awash in a Sea of Faith: Christianizing the American People.* Cambridge, Mass.: Harvard University Press, 1990.

Casto, William R. *Oliver Ellsworth and the Creation of the Federal Republic.* New York: Second Circuit Committee on History and Commemorative Events, 1997.

———. "Oliver Ellsworth's Calvinism: A Biographical Essay on Religion and Political Psychology in the Early Republic." *Journal of Church and State* 36 (1994): 507–26.

————. *The Supreme Court in the Early Republic: The Chief Justiceships of John Jay and Oliver Ellsworth*. Columbia: University of South Carolina Press, 1995.

Cherry, Conrad, ed. *God's New Israel: Religious Interpretations of American Destiny*. Englewood Cliffs, N.J.: Prentice-Hall, 1971.

Clark, Harry Hayden. "An Historical Interpretation of Thomas Paine's Religion." *University of California Chronicle* 35 (Jan. 1933): 56–87.

Clebsch, William A. *From Sacred to Profane America: The Role of Religion in American History*. New York: Harper and Row, 1968.

Conkin, Paul K. "The Religious Pilgrimage of Thomas Jefferson." In *Jeffersonian Legacies*, edited by Peter S. Onuf. Charlottesville: University Press of Virginia, 1993.

Cord, Robert L. *Separation of Church and State: Historical Fact and Current Fiction*. New York: Lambeth Press, 1982.

Cornelison, Isaac A. *The Relation of Religion to Civil Government in the United States of America: A State Without a Church, but Not Without a Religion*. New York: G. P. Putnam's Sons, 1895.

Cousins, Norman, ed. *"In God We Trust": The Religious Beliefs and Ideas of the American Founding Fathers*. New York: Harper and Brothers, 1958.

Curry, Thomas J. *The First Freedoms: Church and State in America to the Passage of the First Amendment*. New York: Oxford University Press, 1986.

Davis, Derek H. *Religion and the Continental Congress, 1774–1789: Contributions to Original Intent*. New York: Oxford University Press, 2000.

Dreisbach, Daniel L. *Thomas Jefferson and the Wall of Separation Between Church and State*. New York: New York University Press, 2002.

————, ed. *Religion and Politics in the Early Republic: Jasper Adams and the Church-State Debate*. Lexington: University Press of Kentucky, 1996.

Dreisbach, Daniel L., and Mark David Hall, eds. *The Sacred Rights of Conscience: Selected Readings on Religious Liberty and Church-State Relations in the American Founding*. Indianapolis: Liberty Fund, 2009.

Dreisbach, Daniel L., Mark D. Hall, and Jeffry H. Morrison, eds. *The Founders on God and Government*. Lanham, Md.: Rowman and Littlefield, 2004.

Dunn, Charles W., ed. *American Political Theology: Historical Perspective and Theoretical Analysis*. New York: Praeger, 1984.

Eidsmoe, John. *Christianity and the Founding Fathers: The Faith of Our Founding Fathers*. Grand Rapids, Mich.: Baker Book House, 1987.

Espinosa, Gastón, ed. *Religion and the American Presidency*. New York: Columbia University Press, 2009.

Evans, M. Stanton. *The Theme Is Freedom: Religion, Politics, and the American Tradition.* Washington, D.C.: Regnery, 1994.

Foote, Henry Wilder. *The Religion of Thomas Jefferson.* Boston: Beacon Press, 1947.

Fruchtman, Jack, Jr. *Thomas Paine and the Religion of Nature.* Baltimore, Md.: Johns Hopkins University Press, 1993.

Gaustad, Edwin S. *Faith of Our Fathers: Religion and the New Nation.* San Francisco: Harper and Row, 1987.

———. *Sworn on the Altar of God: A Religious Biography of Thomas Jefferson.* Grand Rapids, Mich.: William B. Eerdmans, 1996.

Gelles, Edith B. *Abigail Adams: A Writing Life.* New York: Routledge, 2002.

———. *Portia: The World of Abigail Adams.* Bloomington: Indiana University Press, 1992.

Greene, Evarts B. *Religion and the State: The Making and Testing of an American Tradition.* New York: New York University Press, 1941.

Griffin, Keith L. *Revolution and Religion: American Revolutionary War and the Reformed Clergy.* New York: Paragon House, 1994.

Hall, David W. *The Genevan Reformation and the American Founding.* Lanham, Md.: Lexington Books, 2003.

Hall, Mark David. "Jeffersonian Walls and Madisonian Lines: The Supreme Court's Use of History in Religion Clause Cases." *Oregon Law Review* 85 (2006): 563–614.

———. *The Political and Legal Philosophy of James Wilson, 1742–1798.* Columbia: University of Missouri Press, 1997.

———. "Religion and the American Founding." In *The U.S. Political System: An Interdisciplinary Encyclopedia of American Political Development,* vol. 2, edited by Daniel J. Tichenor and Richard A. Harris. Santa Barbara: ABC-CLIO, 2009.

———. "The Sacred Rights of Conscience: America's Founders on Church and State." *Oregon Humanities* (Fall/Winter 2005): 40–46.

Hall, Timothy L. *Separating Church and State: Roger Williams and Religious Liberty.* Urbana: University of Illinois Press, 1998.

Hamburger, Philip. *Separation of Church and State.* Cambridge, Mass.: Harvard University Press, 2002.

Hardwick, Kevin R., and Warren R. Hofstra, eds. *Virginia Reconsidered: New Histories of the Old Dominion.* Charlottesville: University of Virginia Press, 2003.

Hart, Benjamin. *Faith and Freedom: The Christian Roots of American Liberty.* Dallas: Lewis and Stanley, 1988.

Hartnett, Robert C. "The Religion of the Founding Fathers." In *Wellsprings of the American Spirit*, edited by F. Ernest Johnson. New York: Cooper Square, 1964.

Hatch, Nathan O. *The Sacred Cause of Liberty: Republican Thought and the Millennium in Revolutionary New England*. New Haven, Conn.: Yale University Press, 1977.

Healey, Robert M. *Jefferson on Religion in Public Education*. New Haven, Conn.: Yale University Press, 1962.

Heimert, Alan. *Religion and the American Mind: From the Great Awakening to the Revolution*. Cambridge, Mass.: Harvard University Press, 1966.

Hoffman, Ronald, and Peter J. Albert, eds. *Religion in a Revolutionary Age*. Charlottesville: University Press of Virginia, 1994.

Holmes, David L. *The Faiths of the Founding Fathers*. New York: Oxford University Press, 2006.

———. *The Religion of the Founding Fathers*. Charlottesville, Va.: Ash Lawn-Highland; Ann Arbor, Mich.: Clements Library, 2003.

Hood, Fred J. *Reformed America: The Middle and Southern States, 1783–1837*. Tuscaloosa: University of Alabama Press, 1980.

Humphrey, Edward Frank. *Nationalism and Religion in America, 1774–1789*. Boston: Chipman Law Publishing, 1924.

Huntley, William B. "Jefferson's Public and Private Religion." *South Atlantic Quarterly* 79 (1980): 286–301.

Hutson, James H. *Church and State in America: The First Two Centuries*. New York: Cambridge University Press, 2008.

———. *Forgotten Features of the Founding: The Recovery of Religious Themes in the Early American Republic*. Lanham, Md.: Lexington Books, 2003.

———, ed. *The Founders on Religion: A Book of Quotations*. Princeton, N.J.: Princeton University Press, 2005.

———. *Religion and the Founding of the American Republic*. Washington, D.C.: Library of Congress, 1998.

———, ed. *Religion and the New Republic: Faith in the Founding of America*. Lanham, Md.: Rowman and Littlefield, 2000.

Hyneman, Charles S., and Donald S. Lutz, eds. *American Political Writing during the Founding Era: 1760–1805*. 2 vols. Indianapolis, Ind.: Liberty, 1983.

Ives, J. Moss. *The Ark and the Dove: The Beginning of Civil and Religious Liberties in America*. New York: Longmans, Green, 1936.

Jacoby, Susan. *Freethinkers: A History of American Secularism*. New York: Metropolitan Books, 2004.

Ketcham, Ralph L. "James Madison and Religion—A New Hypothesis." *Journal of the Presbyterian Historical Society* 38 (Jun. 1960): 65–90.

Kloos, John M. *A Sense of Deity: The Republican Spirituality of Dr. Benjamin Rush.* New York: Carlson, 1991.

Kramnick, Isaac, and R. Laurence Moore. *The Godless Constitution: The Case Against Religious Correctness.* New York: W. W. Norton, 1996.

Lambert, Frank. *The Founding Fathers and the Place of Religion in America.* Princeton, N.J.: Princeton University Press, 2003.

———. *Religion in American Politics: A Short History.* Princeton, N.J.: Princeton University Press, 2008.

Levy, Leonard W. *The Establishment Clause: Religion and the First Amendment.* 2nd ed. Chapel Hill: University of North Carolina Press, 1994.

Lillback, Peter A., with Jerry Newcombe. *George Washington's Sacred Fire.* Bryn Mawr, Pa.: Providence Forum, 2006.

Lindsay, Thomas. "James Madison on Religion and Politics: Rhetoric and Reality." *American Political Science Review* 85 (1991): 1321–37.

Littell, Franklin Hamlin. *From State Church to Pluralism: A Protestant Interpretation of Religion in American History.* Garden City, N.Y.: Anchor Books, 1962.

Lutz, Donald S. *The Origins of American Constitutionalism.* Baton Rouge: Louisiana State University Press, 1988.

———. "The Relative Influence of European Writers on Late Eighteenth-Century American Political Thought." *American Political Science Review* 78 (1984): 189–97.

Mapp, Alf J., Jr. *The Faiths of Our Fathers: What America's Founders Really Believed.* Lanham, Md.: Rowman and Littlefield, 2003.

McKenna, George. *The Puritan Origins of American Patriotism.* New Haven, Conn.: Yale University Press, 2007.

McLoughlin, William G. *New England Dissent, 1630–1833: The Baptists and the Separation of Church and State.* 2 vols. Cambridge, Mass.: Harvard University Press, 1971.

Meacham, Jon. *American Gospel: God, the Founding Fathers, and the Making of a Nation.* New York: Random House, 2006.

Meade, William. *Old Churches, Ministers, and Families of Virginia.* 2 vols. Philadelphia: J. B. Lippincott, 1857.

Meyer, Donald H. "Franklin's Religion." In *Critical Essays on Benjamin Franklin,* edited by Melvin H. Buxbaum. Boston: G. K. Hall, 1987.

Miller, Howard. "The Grammar of Liberty: Presbyterians and the First American Constitutions." *Journal of Presbyterian History* 54 (1976): 142–64.

Miller, Perry. "The Contribution of the Protestant Churches to Religious Liberty in Colonial America." *Church History* 4 (1935): 57–66.

———. *Errand Into the Wilderness.* Cambridge, Mass.: Belknap Press of Harvard University Press, 1956.

Miller, William Lee. *The First Liberty: Religion and the American Republic.* New York: Alfred A. Knopf, 1986.

Moore, Frank, ed. *The Patriot Preachers of the American Revolution, 1766–1783.* New York, 1860.

Morris, B. F. *Christian Life and Character of the Civil Institutions of the United States, Developed in the Official and Historical Annals of the Republic.* Philadelphia: George W. Childs, 1864.

Morrison, Jeffry H. *John Witherspoon and the Founding of the American Republic.* Notre Dame, Ind.: University of Notre Dame Press, 2005.

———. "John Witherspoon and 'The Public Interest of Religion.'" *Journal of Church and State* 41 (Summer 1999): 551–73.

———. *The Political Philosophy of George Washington.* Baltimore: Johns Hopkins University Press, 2009.

Muñoz, Vincent Phillip. "George Washington on Religious Liberty." *The Review of Politics* 65 (Winter 2003): 11–33.

———. *God and the Founders: Madison, Washington, and Jefferson.* Cambridge: Cambridge University Press, 2009.

———. "James Madison's Principle of Religious Liberty." *American Political Science Review* 97 (Feb. 2003): 17–32.

Noll, Mark A. *America's God: From Jonathan Edwards to Abraham Lincoln.* New York: Oxford University Press, 2002.

Noll, Mark A., Nathan O. Hatch, and George M. Marsden. *The Search for Christian America.* Westchester, Ill.: Crossway Books, 1983.

Noonan, John T., Jr. *The Believer and the Powers that Are: Cases, History, and Other Data Bearing on the Relation of Religion and Government.* New York: Macmillan, 1987.

———. *The Lustre of Our Country: The American Experience of Religious Freedom.* Berkeley: University of California Press, 1998.

Novak, Michael. *On Two Wings: Humble Faith and Common Sense at the American Founding.* San Francisco: Encounter Books, 2002.

Novak, Michael, and Jana Novak. *Washington's God: Religion, Liberty, and the Father of Our Country.* New York: Basic Books, 2006.

Oberg, Barbara B., and Harry S. Stout, eds. *Benjamin Franklin, Jonathan Edwards, and the Representation of American Culture.* New York: Oxford University Press, 1993.

Olasky, Marvin. *Fighting for Liberty and Virtue: Political and Cultural Wars in Eighteenth-Century America*. Wheaton, Ill.: Crossway, 1995.

Perry, William Stevens. *The Faith of the Signers of the Declaration of Independence*. Tarrytown, N.Y.: William Abbatt, 1926.

Peterson, Merrill D., and Robert C. Vaughan, eds. *The Virginia Statute for Religious Freedom: Its Evolution and Consequences in American History*. New York: Cambridge University Press, 1988.

Plumstead, A. W., ed. *The Wall and the Garden: Selected Massachusetts Election Sermons, 1670–1775*. Minneapolis: University of Minnesota Press, 1968.

Sandoz, Ellis. *A Government of Laws: Political Theory, Religion and the American Founding*. Baton Rouge: Louisiana State University Press, 1990.

———, ed. *Political Sermons of the American Founding Era: 1730–1805*. Indianapolis, Ind.: Liberty Press, 1991.

———. "Religious Liberty and Religion in the American Founding Revisited." In *Religious Liberty in Western Thought*, edited by Noel B. Reynolds and W. Cole Durham Jr. Atlanta: Scholars, 1996.

———. *Republicanism, Religion, and the Soul of America*. Columbia: University of Missouri Press, 2006.

Sanford, Charles B. *The Religious Life of Thomas Jefferson*. Charlottesville: University Press of Virginia, 1984.

Schaff, Philip. *Church and State in the United States; or, The American Idea of Religious Liberty and Its Practical Effects*. New York: G. P. Putnam's Sons; American Historical Society, 1888.

Shain, Barry Alan. *The Myth of American Individualism: The Protestant Origins of American Political Thought*. Princeton, N.J.: Princeton University Press, 1994.

Sheldon, Garrett Ward, and Daniel L. Dreisbach, eds. *Religion and Political Culture in Jefferson's Virginia*. Lanham, Md.: Rowman and Littlefield, 2000.

Sheridan, Eugene R. "Liberty and Virtue: Religion and Republicanism in Jeffersonian Thought." In *Thomas Jefferson and the Education of a Citizen*, edited by James Gilreath. Washington, D.C.: Library of Congress, 1999.

Singer, C. Gregg. *A Theological Interpretation of American History*, rev. ed. Phillipsburg, N.J.: Presbyterian and Reformed Publishing, 1981.

Smith, Gary Scott. *Faith and the Presidency: From George Washington to George W. Bush*. New York: Oxford University Press, 2006.

Smith, Jay E. "Thomas Paine and *The Age of Reason*'s Attack on the Bible." *The Historian* 58 (Summer 1996): 745–61.

Smylie, James H. "Clerical Perspectives on Deism: Paine's *The Age of Reason* in Virginia." *Eighteenth-Century Studies* 6 (Winter 1972–73): 203–20.

———. "Madison and Witherspoon: Theological Roots of American Political Thought." *Princeton University Library Chronicle* 22 (Spring 1961): 118–132.

———. "Protestant Clergy, the First Amendment, and Beginnings of a Constitutional Debate, 1781–1791." In *The Religion of the Republic*, edited by Elwyn A. Smith. Philadelphia: Fortress, 1971.

Spalding, Matthew. "Faith of Our Fathers." *Crisis* (May 1996): 30–34.

Stokes, Anson Phelps. *Church and State in the United States.* 3 vols. New York: Harper and Brothers, 1950.

Stout, Harry S. *The New England Soul: Preaching and Religious Culture in Colonial New England.* New York: Oxford University Press, 1986.

Thornton, John Wingate, ed. *The Pulpit of the American Revolution; or, The Political Sermons of the Period of 1776.* Boston: Gould and Lincoln, 1860.

Turner, James. *Without God, Without Creed: The Origins of Unbelief in America.* Baltimore, Md.: Johns Hopkins University Press, 1985.

Waldman, Steven. *Founding Faith: Providence, Politics, and the Birth of Religious Freedom in America.* New York: Random House, 2008.

West, John G., Jr. *The Politics of Revelation and Reason: Religion and Civic Life in the New Nation.* Lawrence: University Press of Kansas, 1996.

Witte, John, Jr. *Religion and the American Constitutional Experiment: Essential Rights and Liberties.* Boulder, Colo.: Westview, 2000.

Zagarri, Rosemarie. *A Woman's Dilemma: Mercy Otis Warren and the American Revolution.* Wheeling, Ill.: Harlan Davidson, 1995.

Contributors

ROBERT H. ABZUG is Oliver H. Radkey Regents Professor of History at the University of Texas at Austin and author of *Cosmos Crumbling: American Reform and the Religious Imagination* (Oxford University Press, 1994).

THOMAS E. BUCKLEY, S.J., is professor of American religious history at the Jesuit School of Theology at Berkeley and author of *Church and State in Revolutionary Virginia, 1776–1787* (University Press of Virginia, 1977).

WILLIAM R. CASTO is Paul Whitfield Horn University Professor at Texas Tech University and author of *The Supreme Court in the Early Republic: The Chief Justiceships of John Jay and Oliver Ellsworth* (University of South Carolina Press, 1995).

JONATHAN DEN HARTOG is assistant professor of history at Northwestern College, St. Paul, Minnesota.

DANIEL L. DREISBACH is professor of justice, law, and society at American University and author of *Thomas Jefferson and the Wall of Separation between Church and State* (New York University Press, 2002).

GREGG L. FRAZER is professor of political studies at The Master's College, Santa Clarita, California.

EDITH B. GELLES is senior scholar at the Michelle R. Clayman Institute for Gender Research, Stanford University, and author of *Portia: The World of Abigail Adams* (Indiana University Press, 1992).

MARK DAVID HALL is Herbert Hoover Distinguished Professor of Political Science at George Fox University and author of *The Political and Legal Philosophy of James Wilson, 1742–1798* (University of Missouri Press, 1997).

KEVIN R. HARDWICK is associate professor of history at James Madison University and editor of *Virginia Reconsidered: New Histories of the Old Dominion* (University of Virginia Press, 2003).

JEFFRY H. MORRISON is associate professor of government at Regent University and author of *John Witherspoon and the Founding of the American Republic* (University of Notre Dame Press, 2005).

MARK A. NOLL is Francis A. McAnaney Professor of History at the University of Notre Dame and author of *America's God: From Jonathan Edwards to Abraham Lincoln* (Oxford University Press, 2002).

GARY SCOTT SMITH is professor of history at Grove City College, Grove City, Pennsylvania, and author of *Faith and the Presidency: From George Washington to George Bush* (Oxford University Press, 2006).

DAVID J. VOELKER is associate professor of humanistic studies and history at the University of Wisconsin at Green Bay.

ROSEMARIE ZAGARRI is professor of history at George Mason University and author of *Revolutionary Backlash: Women and Politics in the Early American Republic* (University of Pennsylvania Press, 2007).

Index

Warren, Mercy Otis, xi, xvii, 14,
20, 29; as anti-Federalist, 280;
biography, 278–81; classical
republicanism of, 284;
education of, 278–79, 284;
family, 279; as forgotten
founder, 278; on French
Revolution, 290–91;
historiography, 281–82;
*History of the Rise, Progress
and Termination of the American
Revolution*, 280–82, 284–87,
290–91; on human nature,
292; political philosophy,
284–87; political writings,
279–81; on providence,
282–83, 285, 287; on public
virtue, 284–87; on Puritans,
287–88; religious beliefs of,
282–84, 287; on religious
establishments, 290; on
religious liberty, 287–91
Washington, George, ix, xiii–xiv,
xv, 5, 148, 208; Edmund Randolph on, 208–9; as famous
founder, 2, 4–6, 9, 40, 127;
Farewell Address of, ix, xiv, 8,
103, 110, 113; presidency, 280;
on providence, 46; on religion
as support of society, 189;
Thanksgiving Day Procla-
mation of 1789, 269
Watson, Bishop Richard: *An Apology
for the Bible*, 187
Webster, Noah, 75, 233, 241
Webster, Pelatiah, 261
Wells, William V., 44
Westminster Catechism, 255
Westminster Confession of Faith, 68
Whitefield, George, 222, 225;
influence on Patrick Henry, 208
Wigglesworth, Edward, 45
Wilberforce, William, 148
William and Mary, College of, 130
Williams, Nathan, 256, 258
Williams, William Appleman, 44
Wilson, James, xvi, 2, 7, 16
Winthrop, John, 53
Wirt, William, 127
Witherspoon, John, xvi, 2, 9, 258;
as forgotten founder, 12–13,
17–18
Wolcott, Oliver, 117
Wood, Gordon S., 11

Yates, Robert, 10

DANIEL L. DREISBACH

is professor in the School of Public Affairs at American University. He is the author of *The Founders on God and Government*.

MARK DAVID HALL

is the Herbert Hoover Distinguished Professor of Political Science at George Fox University. He is the author of *The Political and Legal Philosophy of James Wilson, 1742–1798*.

JEFFRY H. MORRISON

is associate professor of government at Regent University. He is the author of *John Witherspoon and the Founding of the American Republic* (Notre Dame Press, 2005).